D0548720

The Taste of Home entertaining COOKBOOK

REIMAN MEDIA GROUP, INC. • GREENDALE, WISCONSIN

Taste of Home Reader's Digest

A Taste of Home/Reader's Digest Book

Editor: Heidi Reuter Lloyd
Associate Project Editor: Julie Schnittka
Content Production Supervisor: Julie Wagner
Cover Design: Ardyth Cope
Proofreaders: Jean Steiner, Linne Bruskewitz
Editorial Assistant: Barb Czysz
Recipe Testing and Editing: Taste of Home Test Kitchen
Food Photography: Reiman Photo Studio

Senior Editor, Retail Books: Jennifer Olski
Creative Director: Ardyth Cope
Vice President, Executive Editor/Books: Heidi Reuter Lloyd
Senior Vice President, Editor in Chief: Catherine Cassidy
Chief Marketing Officer: Lisa Karpinski
President, Consumer Marketing: Dawn Zier
President, Food & Entertaining: Suzanne M. Grimes
President and Chief Executive Officer: Mary G. Berner

PICTURED ON THE COVER:
Toasted Butter Pecan Cake (p. 245), Grits 'n' Shrimp Tarts (p. 223), Apple and Goat Cheese Salad (p. 405) and Honey Garlic Ribs (p. 221).

International Standard Book Number (10): 0-89821-698-2
International Standard Book Number (13): 978-0-89821-698-1
Library of Congress Control Number: 2007943842

For other Taste of Home books and products, visit www.tasteofhome.com.
For more Reader's Digest products and information, visit
www.rd.com (in the United States)
www.rd.ca (in Canada)

Printed in China. 1 3 5 7 9 10 8 6 4 2

SPRING

SUMMER

FALL

WINTER

YEAR-ROUND

SPRING

SUMMER

FALL

WINTER

YEAR-ROUND

Celebrate Good Times with Great Food and Party Tips!

IF YOU'VE EVER offered to host a special holiday dinner with family or a more casual get-together with friends, you might have become panic-stricken when it actually came down to planning the menu. But those dread-filled days are over!

That's because *The Taste of Home Entertaining Cookbook* is packed with 434 recipes to make celebrations throughout the year easy on the hostess. We provide menu options, timetables and tried-and-true recipes...so entertaining is simple!

- SPRING. Among the springtime celebrations sprouting up in this cookbook are Easter, Passover, Kentucky Derby, Graduation and Mother's Day.
- SUMMER. From a Memorial Day backyard party or July 4th ice cream social to a casual beach picnic or ladies' luncheon in the garden, warm-weather fare is at your fingertips.
- FALL. You'll have a ball planning a tailgate party for the gang or a Halloween bash for little goblins. Hesitant to host the Thanksgiving gala? Turn over a new leaf with our two terrific Thanksgiving dinner ideas!
- WINTER. From Christmas and New Year's to Mardi Gras and Valentine's Day, wintertime is a flurry of activity. But hosting an event doesn't have to be a slippery slope.
- YEAR-ROUND. Occasions throughout the year also call for special celebrations, like a child's birthday, a girl's Sweet 16 or an elegant afternoon tea with friends.

To make every gathering even more special, we've included a host of ideas for creating timeless table toppers, easy yet impressive napkin folds, fantastic party favors and more.

With an assortment of appetizers, side dishes, entrees, desserts, party ideas and menus, *The Taste of Home Entertaining Cookbook* makes entertaining enjoyable for you...and memorable for your friends and family!

Spring Entertaining

Rise-and-Shine Easter Brunch

SPRING has sprung. So set aside the heavy fare you've served all winter and bring out a sunnier selection suited for warmer weather.

Hop to it this Easter and have your family over for an inviting mid-morning brunch.

Even cooks who are green in the kitchen can prepare the "eggs-cellent" foods featured here with confidence.

Asparagus Strudel is an elegant entree that starts with convenient frozen phyllo dough.

Cool, creamy Mock Devonshire Cream pairs well with both tender Citrus Scones and assorted fresh fruit. (All recipes are shown at right.)

Round out your delicious brunch buffet with a selection of this chapter's enticing egg dishes, French toast and crepes.

Early Day Dining

(Clockwise from bottom)

Asparagus Strudel (p. 10)

Mock Devonshire Cream (p. 10)

Citrus Scones (p. 12)

Mock Devonshire Cream

(Pictured on page 9)

I always serve this tasty, no-fuss cream with fresh fruit to usher in a new season. Prepare it the day before for added convenience.
—Lillian Julow, Gainesville, Florida

- **1 package (3 ounces) cream cheese, softened**
- **1 cup (8 ounces) sour cream**
- **3 tablespoons confectioners' sugar**
- **1 cup heavy whipping cream**

In a small mixing bowl, beat cream cheese until fluffy. Beat in sour cream and confectioners' sugar until smooth. Add whipping cream. Beat on medium speed until combined; beat on high speed until stiff peaks form. Refrigerate until serving. **Yield:** 3-1/4 cups.

Asparagus Strudel

(Pictured on page 8)

Celebrate the arrival of spring by serving this delightful strudel for Easter brunch. Watch the savory slices disappear from the table!
—Dona Erhart, Stockbridge, Michigan

- **2 cups water**
- **3/4 pound fresh asparagus, trimmed and cut into 1-inch pieces**
- **2 medium leeks (white portion only), thinly sliced**
- **1-1/4 cups butter, *divided***
- **2 cups (8 ounces) shredded Gruyere *or* Swiss cheese**
- **3 eggs, lightly beaten**
- **2 tablespoons lemon juice**
- **2 tablespoons minced fresh parsley**
- **1 tablespoon minced fresh mint**
- **1 tablespoon minced fresh dill**
- **1/3 cup sliced almonds, toasted**
- **Dash cayenne pepper**
- **32 sheets phyllo dough (14 inches x 9 inches)**

In a large skillet, bring water to a boil. Add the asparagus; cover and boil for 3 minutes. Drain and immediately place the asparagus in ice water. Drain and pat dry. In the same skillet, saute the leeks in 1/4 cup butter for 5 minutes or until tender.

In a large bowl, combine the asparagus, leeks, cheese, eggs, lemon juice, parsley, mint, dill, almonds and cayenne.

Melt remaining butter. Place one sheet of phyllo dough on a work surface (keep remaining dough covered with plastic wrap and a damp towel to avoid drying out). Brush with butter. Repeat layers seven times. Spoon a fourth of the vegetable mixture along the short end of dough to within 1 in. of edges. Fold long sides 1 in. over filling. Roll up jelly-roll style, starting with a short side. Place seam side down on a greased baking sheet.

Repeat, making three more strudels. Brush tops with remaining butter. Bake at 350° for 40-45 minutes or until golden brown. Cool for 10 minutes before slicing. **Yield:** 16 servings.

Blueberry-Stuffed French Toast

(Pictured at right)

I came across this recipe in a local newspaper several years ago. The fruity French toast is truly company fare.
—Myrna Koldenhoven, Sanborn, Iowa

1-1/2 cups fresh *or* frozen blueberries
3 tablespoons sugar, *divided*
8 slices Italian bread (1-1/4 inches thick)
4 eggs
1/2 cup orange juice
1 teaspoon grated orange peel
Dash salt
BLUEBERRY ORANGE SAUCE:
3 tablespoons sugar
1 tablespoon cornstarch
1/8 teaspoon salt
1/4 cup orange juice
1/4 cup water
1-1/2 cups orange segments
1 cup fresh *or* frozen blueberries
1/3 cup sliced almonds

In a small bowl, combine blueberries and 2 tablespoons sugar. Cut a pocket in the side of each slice of bread. Fill each pocket with about 3 tablespoons berry mixture.

In a shallow bowl, whisk the eggs, orange juice, orange peel, salt and remaining sugar. Carefully dip both sides of bread in egg mixture (do not squeeze out filling). Place in a greased 15-in. x 10-in. x 1-in. baking pan. Bake at 400° for 15 minutes, gently turning once.

Meanwhile, in a small saucepan, combine the sugar, cornstarch and salt. Gently whisk in orange juice and water until smooth. Bring to a boil; cook and stir for 1-2 minutes or until thickened. Reduce heat; stir in oranges and blueberries. Cook for 5 minutes or until heated through. Serve over French toast; sprinkle with almonds. **Yield:** 8 servings.

Family Traditions

EACH YEAR, Easter dinner at my house concludes with an assortment of my homemade pies—coconut cream, banana cream, lemon meringue and butterscotch. The pie crust recipe was passed on to me from my mother, and it has received uncountable compliments over the years.

—Janis Engle, San Jose, California

Citrus Scones

(Pictured on page 9)

My family enjoys these tender scones fresh from the oven with cream cheese. The recipe makes enough to include the scones on a brunch buffet.
—Debra Savory, Simcoe, Ontario

- **4 cups all-purpose flour**
- **1 cup sugar**
- **2-1/2 teaspoons baking powder**
- **1 teaspoon salt**
- **1/2 teaspoon baking soda**
- **1 cup cold butter, cubed**
- **1/2 cup buttermilk**
- **1/3 cup orange juice**
- **1 egg**
- **2 tablespoons lemon juice**
- **1 tablespoon grated orange peel**
- **2 teaspoons grated lemon peel**
- **1 teaspoon lemon extract**

In a large bowl, combine the flour, sugar, baking powder, salt and baking soda. Cut in butter until mixture is crumbly. Combine the remaining ingredients; stir into crumb mixture just until moistened.

Turn dough onto a floured surface; knead gently 5-6 times. Gently pat into two 8-in. circles; transfer to two greased 9-in. round baking pans. Cut each circle into eight wedges but do not separate. Bake at 350° for 20-25 minutes or until lightly browned. Remove from pans to wire racks. **Yield:** 16 scones.

Sausage and Cheese Souffle

I created this souffle based on a recipe from my great aunt. I even make it for Sunday dinner with applesauce, bread and a tossed salad.
—Linda Paxton, Halethorpe, Maryland

- **1/2 pound bulk pork sausage**
- **1/4 cup butter**
- **1/4 cup all-purpose flour**
- **1/4 teaspoon salt**
- **1-1/4 cups milk**
- **1 cup (4 ounces) shredded cheddar cheese**
- **4 eggs, *separated***

In a small skillet, cook sausage over medium heat until no longer pink; drain and set aside. In a large saucepan, melt butter over medium heat. Stir in flour and salt; gradually stir in milk. Bring to a boil; cook and stir for 2 minutes or until thickened. Reduce heat; stir in cheese until melted.

Remove from the heat. Stir a small amount of hot mixture into the egg yolks; return all to the pan, stirring constantly. Stir in the sausage. In a small mixing bowl, beat egg whites on high speed until stiff peaks form. Fold into sausage-cheese mixture.

Transfer to an ungreased 2-qt. baking dish. Place in a large baking pan. Add 1 in. of hot water to larger pan. Bake, uncovered, at 325° for 45-50 minutes or until a knife inserted near the center comes out clean. **Yield:** 4-6 servings.

Ham and Apricot Crepes

(Pictured at right)

A sweet apricot sauce nicely complements these savory ham crepes.
—Candy Evavold
Sammamish, Washington

1-1/2 cups milk
2 eggs, lightly beaten
1 tablespoon butter, melted
1 cup all-purpose flour
20 thin slices deli ham
SAUCE:
1 can (15-1/4 ounces) apricot halves
2/3 cup sugar
2 tablespoons cornstarch
1/8 teaspoon salt
2 cans (5-1/2 ounces *each*) apricot nectar
2 tablespoons butter
2 teaspoons lemon juice

In a large mixing bowl, combine the milk, eggs and butter. Add flour and mix well. Cover and chill for 1 hour.

Heat a lightly greased 8-in. nonstick skillet; pour 2 tablespoons batter into the center of skillet. Lift and tilt pan to evenly coat bottom. Cook until top appears dry; turn and cook 15-20 seconds longer. Remove to a wire rack. Repeat with remaining batter, greasing skillet as needed. When cool, stack crepes with waxed paper or paper towels in between.

Place a slice of ham on each crepe; roll up. Place in two greased 13-in. x 9-in. x 2-in. baking dishes. Bake, uncovered, at 350° for 20 minutes.

Meanwhile, drain apricots, reserving syrup. Cut apricots into 1/4-in. slices; set aside. In a large saucepan, combine the sugar, cornstarch and salt. Add apricot nectar and reserved syrup; stir until smooth. Bring to a boil; cook and stir for 1-2 minutes or until thickened. Remove from the heat; stir in the butter, lemon juice and apricot slices. Serve with crepes. **Yield:** 10 servings.

Crepe-Making Pointers

- Let the batter sit at least 1 hour before using to reduce any air bubbles.
- Lightly coat the pan with nonstick cooking spray, butter or oil; heat over medium-high.
- Add a small amount of batter to the hot pan. Tilt the pan to evenly coat the bottom.
- When the edges are dry and pull away from pan, gently turn; cook the other side.
- To prevent crepes from sticking before filling, let them cool on a wire rack or waxed paper. Then stack crepes with waxed paper or paper towel in between.

Potato Sausage Frittata

With sausage, bacon, eggs and potatoes, this frittata is a meal in one. I usually double the recipe and rarely have leftovers.
—Patricia Lee, Eatonton, Georgia

- **1/2 pound bulk pork sausage**
- **6 bacon strips, diced**
- **1-1/2 cups finely chopped red potatoes**
- **1 medium onion, finely chopped**
- **8 eggs**
- **2 teaspoons dried parsley flakes**
- **3/4 teaspoon salt**
- **1/8 teaspoon pepper**

In a large ovenproof skillet, cook sausage over medium heat until no longer pink. Remove and set aside. In the same skillet, cook bacon over medium heat until crisp. Using a slotted spoon, remove to paper towels; drain, reserving 2 tablespoons drippings.

In the drippings, saute potatoes and onion until tender. In a large bowl, whisk the eggs, parsley, salt and pepper. Return sausage and bacon to the skillet; top with egg mixture.

Cover and cook over low heat for 8-10 minutes or until eggs are almost set. Uncover; broil 6 in. from the heat for 2 minutes or until eggs are set. Cut into wedges. **Yield:** 4 servings.

Curried Eggs in Shrimp Sauce

I like to dress up ordinary hard-cooked eggs with a special shrimp sauce. You can assemble this casserole the day before and bake it the next morning.
—M. Beatrice Mann, Vernon, Vermont

- **3 tablespoons butter, *divided***
- **2 tablespoons all-purpose flour**
- **1 can (10-3/4 ounces) condensed cream of shrimp soup, undiluted**
- **1 cup milk**
- **1/2 cup shredded cheddar cheese**
- **1/2 pound frozen cooked small shrimp, thawed and chopped**
- **12 hard-cooked eggs**
- **1/2 cup mayonnaise**
- **1/4 teaspoon curry powder**
- **1/4 teaspoon ground mustard**
- **1/4 teaspoon paprika**
- **1/8 teaspoon salt**
- **1 cup soft bread crumbs**

In a large saucepan, melt 2 tablespoons butter; whisk in flour until smooth. Gradually add soup and milk. Bring to a boil; cook and stir over medium heat for 2 minutes or until thickened. Remove from the heat; stir in cheese until melted. Stir in shrimp.

Pour 2 cups of sauce into a greased 13-in. x 9-in. x 2-in. baking dish; set remaining sauce aside. Cut the eggs in half lengthwise; arrange whites over sauce. In a bowl, mash the yolks. Stir in the mayonnaise, curry powder, mustard, paprika and salt. Spoon into egg whites. Top with the reserved sauce.

Melt the remaining butter; toss with bread crumbs. Sprinkle over the top. Bake, uncovered, at 350° for 15-20 minutes or until heated through. **Yield:** 12 servings.

Bunny Napkin Fold

(Pictured at right)

FOR a "hare-raising" reaction at your Easter brunch, fashion these festive napkin folds in the shape of bunnies!

All you need are well-starched square napkins in the color of your choice. (In keeping with our green theme, we used green polka dot napkins.) Then just follow the folding instructions below.

For a brunch buffet, you may want to create a "warren" of rabbits by placing the folded napkins on a nest of shredded scrapbook papers. We selected a variety of papers, then shredded them with a paper cutter. But a 1/4-inch straight-edge paper shredder could also be used.

Bunny Napkin Fold

TO MAKE these festive napkin folds, start with well-starched square napkins. Fold the bottom third of the napkin up and the top third down, making a rectangle.

1. Find the center along the top fold and fold the top corners down, making sure the bottom ends are even.

2. Fold up the outside bottom corners.

3. Fold left and right sides so that they meet in the center.

4. Turn the napkin over and flip the top to bottom. Fold bottom point up.

5. Fold the left and right corners to the back and tuck one corner into the other to hold.

6. Hold the tucked corners securely and pull out the bunny ears on the other end.

Inviting Easter Dinner

WHY PREPARE a traditional ham dinner at Easter when you can enjoy the warm weather as you barbecue in the backyard?

Lamb with Spinach and Onions stars moist and tender lamb chops, which are marinated, then grilled alongside onion wedges. This innovative entree also features a bed of sauteed spinach and a savory onion sauce.

(For folks who expect to see ham on the table, you'll find an on-the-grill version on page 21.)

Every "bunny" will love simply seasoned Chive Buttered Carrots.

For a light yet luscious ending to this special spring meal, serve slices of Lemon Ricotta Cheesecake. (All recipes shown at right.)

A SUPPER FOR SPRING

(Clockwise from top)

Lemon Ricotta Cheesecake (p. 19)

Lamb with Spinach And Onions (p. 20)

Chive Buttered Carrots (p. 18)

Easter Day Dinner Agenda

A Few Weeks Before:

- Prepare two grocery lists—one for nonperishable items to purchase now and one for perishable items to purchase a few days before Easter.

Two to Three Days Before:

- Buy remaining grocery items.

The Day Before:

- Set the table.
- Buy daffodils and assemble the Daffodil Topiary (see page 22).
- For Lamb with Spinach and Onions, marinate the lamb chops. Make the onion sauce; cover and chill.
- Wash and slice carrots for Chive Buttered Carrots. Refrigerate in a resealable plastic bag.
- Make the Savory Leek Soup up to the point of adding the cream, salt and pepper. Cover and refrigerate.
- Bake Whole Wheat Swirl Bread. Cool and store in an airtight container.
- Prepare the Lemon Ricotta Cheesecake; chill.

Easter Day:

- For Lamb with Spinach and Onions, grill the lamb and onion wedges. Saute the spinach. Reheat the onion sauce and serve with lamb, onions and spinach.
- Reheat the Savory Leek Soup; add the cream, salt and pepper until heated through.
- Prepare the Chive Buttered Carrots.
- Slice the Whole Wheat Swirl Bread and serve with butter.
- Serve Lemon Ricotta Cheesecake for dessert.

Chive Buttered Carrots

(Pictured on page 16)

It's nice to have a reliable side dish like this that pairs well with any entree. A friend shared the recipe with me several years ago, and I use it often.
—Opal Snell, Jamestown, Ohio

2-1/2 pounds carrots, diagonally sliced 1/2 inch thick
6 tablespoons butter *or* margarine
1/4 to 1/2 teaspoon seasoned salt
1/4 teaspoon pepper
4-1/2 teaspoons minced chives

Place 1 in. of water and carrots in a large saucepan. Bring to a boil. Reduce heat; cover and simmer for 4-5 minutes or until crisp-tender. Drain well. In a large skillet, melt butter. Add seasoned salt, pepper and carrots; cook and stir for 1-2 minutes or until carrots are tender. Sprinkle with chives. **Yield:** 6 servings.

Lemon Ricotta Cheesecake

(Pictured at right and on page 17)

I'm an avid recipe collector and can't recall where I found this one. I do know its delicate flavor is well received whenever I make it for a special occasion.
—Julie Nitschke, Stowe, Vermont

1-1/2 cups vanilla wafer crumbs (about 45 wafers)
1/4 cup butter *or* margarine, melted
1 teaspoon grated lemon peel
FILLING:
2 packages (8 ounces *each*) cream cheese, softened
1 carton (15 ounces) ricotta cheese
1-1/4 cups sugar
1/4 cup cornstarch
4 eggs
2 cups half-and-half cream
1/3 cup lemon juice
3 teaspoons grated lemon peel
2 teaspoons vanilla extract
Fresh mint and lemon slices, optional

In a bowl, combine wafer crumbs, butter and lemon peel. Press onto the bottom of a greased 9-in. springform pan. Bake at 325° for 12-14 minutes or until lightly browned. Cool.

In a large mixing bowl, beat cream cheese and ricotta until smooth. Combine sugar and cornstarch; add to cheese mixture and beat well. Add eggs and cream, beating on low speed just until combined. Beat in lemon juice, peel and vanilla just until blended. Pour into crust. Place pan on a baking sheet.

Bake at 325° for 70-80 minutes or until center is almost set. Cool on a wire rack for 10 minutes. Carefully run a knife around edge of pan to loosen; cool 1 hour longer. Refrigerate overnight. Remove sides of pan. Garnish with mint and lemon if desired. **Yield:** 12-14 servings.

Lamb with Spinach and Onions

(Pictured on page 16)

Grilling is a wonderful way to prepare lamb. The marinade and on-the-side onion sauce enhance the meat's naturally terrific taste.
—Sarah Vasques, Milford, New Hampshire

1/2 cup lime juice
1/4 cup dry red wine *or* 1 tablespoon red wine vinegar
1 small onion, chopped
2 tablespoons minced fresh rosemary *or* 2 teaspoons dried rosemary, crushed
2 tablespoons olive *or* vegetable oil
2 tablespoons Worcestershire sauce
3 garlic cloves, minced
1 tablespoon minced fresh thyme *or* 1 teaspoon dried thyme
1/4 teaspoon pepper
Dash liquid smoke, optional
12 rib lamb chops (1 inch thick)

ONION SAUCE:
2 tablespoons finely chopped green onions
1 teaspoon butter *or* margarine
1 cup balsamic vinegar
1 cup dry red wine *or* 1/2 cup beef broth and 1/2 cup grape juice
1/2 cup loosely packed fresh mint leaves, chopped
1 tablespoon sugar
1 large sweet onion, cut into quarters
Olive *or* vegetable oil
Salt and pepper to taste

SPINACH:
1/4 cup finely chopped green onions
3 garlic cloves, minced
3 tablespoons olive *or* vegetable oil
3 tablespoons butter *or* margarine
12 cups fresh baby spinach
Salt and pepper to taste

In a large resealable plastic bag, combine the first 10 ingredients; add lamb chops. Seal bag and turn to coat; refrigerate for 8 hours or overnight.

In a saucepan, saute green onions in butter until tender. Add vinegar and wine or broth and grape juice; bring to a boil. Add mint and sugar. Reduce heat; simmer, uncovered, for 30 minutes or until sauce is reduced to 3/4 cup. Strain; discard mint. Set sauce aside.

Thread onion wedges onto metal or soaked wooden skewers. Brush with oil; sprinkle with salt and pepper. Discard marinade from lamb. Grill chops, covered, over medium-hot heat for 5-6 minutes on each side or until meat reaches desired doneness (for medium, a meat thermometer should read 160°; well-done, 170°). Grill onion skewers for 2-3 minutes or until tender.

In a large skillet, saute green onions and garlic in oil and butter until tender. Add the spinach, salt and pepper; saute for 2-3 minutes or until spinach just begins to wilt and is heated through. Place on a serving platter. Remove onion from skewers; place onion and lamb chops over spinach. **Yield:** 6 servings.

Savory Leek Soup

(Pictured at right)

There's no mistaking that savory is the main herb seasoning this rich and creamy soup.
—Eleanor Davis
Pittsburgh, Pennsylvania

4 medium leeks (white portion only), chopped
1/2 cup minced chives
1/2 cup butter *or* margarine
4 cups chicken broth
2 cups mashed potatoes (prepared with milk and butter)
2 tablespoons minced fresh savory *or* 2 teaspoons dried savory
3 cups half-and-half cream
Salt and pepper to taste

In a large saucepan, saute leeks and chives in butter until tender. Add the broth, potatoes and savory; bring to a boil. Reduce heat; simmer, uncovered, for 8-10 minutes. Cool slightly. Process in batches in a blender or food processor until smooth; return to pan. Stir in the cream, salt and pepper; heat through. **Yield:** 8-10 servings.

Orange Barbecued Ham

This recipe decreases the amount of time I spend in the kitchen... because my husband does the grilling!
—Lucy Kampstra, Bradenton, Florida

1/2 cup ketchup
1/3 cup orange marmalade
2 tablespoons finely chopped onion
2 tablespoons vegetable oil
1 tablespoon lemon juice
1 to 1-1/2 teaspoons ground mustard
3 to 5 drops hot pepper sauce
1 boneless fully cooked ham slice (1-1/2 pounds and 3/4 inch thick)

In a bowl, combine the first seven ingredients. Pour half of the sauce into a microwave-safe bowl; set aside. Grill ham, covered, over indirect low heat for 3 minutes on each side. Baste with the remaining sauce. Grill 6-8 minutes longer or until heated through, turning and basting occasionally. Cover and microwave reserved sauce on high for 30 seconds or until heated through. Serve with ham. **Yield:** 6 servings.

Daffodil Topiary

(Pictured at right and on page 17)

The sight of daffodils is one of the surest ways to know that spring is finally in full bloom. So make this topiary featuring those lovely yellow flowers and bring a ray of sunshine to your Easter table.

Floral foam
Small white ceramic flowerpot with saucer
About 1/2 cup marbles *or* floral stones
Straight-sided glass to fit inside flowerpot
About 36 daffodils
Wide rubber band
Natural raffia
Natural wood excelsior

Cut a piece of floral foam to fit into bottom of flowerpot. Place marbles or floral stones inside glass. Push glass into floral foam to secure and place inside the flowerpot.

Arrange the daffodils, keeping flower heads compact and uniform all around. Wrap a wide rubber band around the ends of the stems to secure. Trim stem ends so they are even. Wrap raffia around stems and tie ends in a large bow.

Place the assembled arrangement into the glass, making sure stems are straight. Carefully add water. Arrange excelsior around the base of the topiary to cover the glass and inside of the flowerpot.

Making a Daffodil Topiary

1. Cut floral foam to fit bottom of flowerpot. Place marbles or stones inside glass. Push glass into foam and set inside pot.

2. Make a bouquet of daffodils; secure with a rubber band and raffia. Place bouquet in the glass; add water.

3. Arrange excelsior around the base of the topiary to cover the glass.

Whole Wheat Swirl Bread

I developed this pretty swirl bread by combining two different recipes.
—Estelle Hardin, Washington, Utah

2 packages (1/4 ounce *each*) active dry yeast
1 teaspoon sugar
3 cups warm water (110° to 115°), *divided*
1 cup nonfat dry milk powder
1/3 cup vegetable oil
1/3 cup honey
3 teaspoons salt
7-1/2 to 8-1/2 cups all-purpose flour
WHOLE WHEAT DOUGH:
2 packages (1/4 ounce *each*) active dry yeast
1 teaspoon sugar
3 cups warm water (110° to 115°), *divided*
1 cup nonfat dry milk powder
1/3 cup vegetable oil
1/3 cup honey
3 teaspoons salt
5 cups whole wheat flour
2-1/2 to 3-1/2 cups all-purpose flour

In a large mixing bowl, dissolve yeast and sugar in 1/2 cup warm water; let stand for 5 minutes. Add the milk powder, oil, honey, salt and remaining water. Beat for 1 minute. Add 4 cups flour; beat on medium for 3 minutes. Stir in enough remaining flour to form a soft dough. Turn onto a floured surface; knead until smooth and elastic, about 6 minutes. Place in a greased bowl, turning once to grease top. Cover and let rise in a warm place until doubled, about 1 hour.

Meanwhile, in a large mixing bowl, dissolve yeast and sugar in 1/2 cup warm water. Add the milk powder, oil, honey, salt and remaining water. Beat for 1 minute. Add whole wheat flour. Beat on medium for 3 minutes. Stir in enough all-purpose flour to form a soft dough. Turn onto a floured surface; knead until smooth and elastic, about 6 minutes. Place in a greased bowl, turning once to grease top. Cover and rise in a warm place until doubled, about 1 hour.

Punch each dough down; divide into fourths. Roll one white portion and one whole wheat portion into 14-in. x 10-in. rectangles. Place whole wheat dough on top of white dough; roll up jelly-roll style. Pinch ends to seal and tuck under. Repeat with remaining dough. Place in four greased 9-in. x 5-in. x 3-in. loaf pans. Cover and let rise until doubled, about 40 minutes. Bake at 350° for 40-45 minutes or until golden brown. Remove from pans to wire racks to cool. **Yield:** 4 loaves.

Seasonal Breads Rise to the Occasion

THROUGH HISTORY, people have baked rich, elaborate breads to announce the arrival of spring and to celebrate the end of sparse meals associated with religious fasting.

Why not bake up a delicious Easter morning tradition of your own and prepare one of the specialty breads featured here?

Italian Easter Bread is a sweet yeast bread dotted with colorful nesting eggs.

For fruit-filled favorites, try Strawberry Braid and Crumb-Topped Blueberry Muffins. (All recipes shown at right.)

If you're looking to complement your Easter dinner, this chapter also offers a savory selection of oven-fresh breads.

Festively Fresh

(Clockwise from top)

Crumb-Topped Blueberry Muffins (p. 28)

Strawberry Braid (p. 27)

Italian Easter Bread (p. 26)

Italian Easter Bread

(Pictured on page 24)

This traditional Easter bread is topped with colored raw eggs, which cook as the bread bakes. It makes for a pretty centerpiece.
—June Formanek, Belle Plaine, Iowa

2-3/4 to 3-1/4 cups all-purpose flour
1/4 cup sugar
1 package (1/4 ounce) active dry yeast
1 teaspoon salt
2/3 cup milk
3 tablespoons butter, *divided*
2 eggs
1/2 cup chopped mixed candied fruit
1/4 cup chopped blanched almonds
1/2 teaspoon aniseed
5 uncooked eggs, dyed
GLAZE:
1 cup confectioners' sugar
1/4 teaspoon vanilla extract
1 to 2 tablespoons milk
Decorator candies, optional

In a large mixing bowl, combine 1 cup flour, sugar, yeast and salt. In a saucepan, heat milk and 2 tablespoons butter to 120°-130°. Add to dry ingredients; beat on medium speed for 2 minutes. Add eggs; mix well. Stir in enough remaining flour to form a soft dough. Turn onto a lightly floured surface; knead until smooth and elastic, about 6-8 minutes. Place in a greased bowl, turning once to grease top. Cover and let rise in a warm place until doubled, about 1 hour.

Punch dough down; turn onto a lightly floured surface. Knead in fruit, almonds and aniseed until blended. Let rest for 10 minutes. Divide dough in half. Shape each portion into a 24-in. rope. Loosely twist ropes together; place on a greased baking sheet and form into a ring. Pinch ends together. Melt remaining butter; brush over dough. Gently separate ropes and tuck dyed eggs into openings. Cover and let rise until doubled, about 40 minutes.

Bake at 350° for 30-35 minutes or until golden brown. Cool on a wire rack. For glaze, in a bowl, combine the confectioners' sugar, vanilla and enough milk to achieve desired consistency; drizzle over bread. Sprinkle with candies if desired. **Yield:** 1 loaf.

Making Italian Easter Bread

WITH your hands, gently separate ropes of dough. Tuck dyed raw eggs into the openings. Cover and let rise until doubled, about 40 minutes. Bake as directed.

Strawberry Braid

(Pictured at right and on page 24)

Before moving to Oklahoma, I owned a catering business in Tennessee. This recipe was a favorite with my clients. I appreciate that the dough starts with a convenient hot roll mix.

—Elizabeth Area, Stillwater, Oklahoma

1 package (16 ounces) hot roll mix
1 cup strawberry jam
1/2 cup finely chopped dried apricots
1/4 cup chopped walnuts
1 tablespoon butter, melted
2 teaspoons sugar

Prepare hot roll mix according to package directions. While dough is resting, combine the jam, apricots and walnuts in a bowl. Turn dough onto a lightly floured surface; roll into a 14-in. x 9-in. rectangle. Place on a greased foil-lined baking sheet.

Spread filling down center third of rectangle. On each long side, cut 1-in.-wide strips about 2-1/2 in. into center. Starting at one end, fold alternating strips at an angle across filling. Pinch ends to seal. Cover and let rise until doubled, about 30 minutes. Brush braid with butter and sprinkle with sugar. Bake at 350° for 25-30 minutes or until golden brown. Cool on a wire rack. **Yield:** 10-12 servings.

Crumb-Topped Blueberry Muffins

(Pictured on page 25)

For years I've searched for the perfect blueberry muffins without success. Then I came up with this winning recipe.
—Helen Woronik, Salem, Connecticut

4 cups all-purpose flour
1 cup sugar
6 teaspoons baking powder
1/2 teaspoon salt
1 cup cold butter
2 eggs, lightly beaten
1-1/3 cups milk
2 teaspoons grated orange peel
2 teaspoons almond extract
1 teaspoon vanilla extract
2 cups fresh blueberries
TOPPING:
1/4 cup sugar
3 tablespoons all-purpose flour
1/4 teaspoon ground cinnamon
2 tablespoons cold butter

In a bowl, combine the flour, sugar, baking powder and salt. Cut in butter until mixture resembles coarse crumbs. Combine the eggs, milk, orange peel and extracts; stir into crumb mixture just until moistened. Gently fold in blueberries (batter will be stiff). Fill paper-lined or greased muffin cups two-thirds full.

In a bowl, combine the sugar, flour and cinnamon. Cut in butter until mixture resembles coarse crumbs. Sprinkle about 1 teaspoonful over each muffin. Bake at 375° for 20-25 minutes or until a toothpick comes out clean. Cool for 5 minutes before removing from pans to wire racks. **Yield:** 2 dozen.

Bake Bigger Blueberry Muffins

CRUMB-TOPPED Blueberry Muffins can also be baked in one dozen jumbo-size muffin cups. Bake at 375° for 25-30 minutes or until a toothpick comes out clean.

Sweet Cream Biscuits

People are surprised that these three-ingredient biscuits have such wonderful homemade flavor.
—Dee Saron, Spring Valley, California

2 cups biscuit/baking mix
2/3 cup heavy whipping cream
2 tablespoons sugar

In a bowl, combine the biscuit mix, cream and sugar; stir just until moistened. Turn onto a lightly floured surface; knead 8-10 times. Pat or roll out to 1/2-in. thickness; cut with a floured 2-1/2-in. biscuit cutter. Place 2 in. apart on a lightly greased baking sheet. Bake at 450° for 10-12 minutes or until golden brown. Remove to a wire rack. Serve warm. **Yield:** 1 dozen.

Paska Easter Bread

(Pictured at right)

Paska is a traditional Easter bread prepared with lots of eggs, making it much richer than ordinary sweet breads. The beautifully braided top will earn you many compliments.
—Millie Cherniwchan
Smoky Lake, Alberta

2 packages (1/4 ounce *each*) active dry yeast
1 teaspoon plus 1/3 cup sugar, *divided*
4 cups warm water (110° to 115°), *divided*
1 cup nonfat dry milk powder
13-1/2 to 14-1/2 cups all-purpose flour, *divided*
6 eggs, beaten
1/2 cup butter, melted
1 tablespoon salt
EGG GLAZE:
1 egg
2 tablespoons water

In a large mixing bowl, dissolve yeast and 1 teaspoon sugar in 1 cup warm water. Let stand for 5 minutes. Add remaining water. Beat in the milk powder and 5 cups flour until smooth. Cover and let rise in a warm place until bubbly, about 20 minutes. Add eggs, butter, salt and remaining sugar; mix well. Stir in enough remaining flour to form a soft dough. Turn onto a floured surface; knead until smooth and elastic, about 8-10 minutes. Place in a greased bowl, turning once to grease top. Cover and let rise in a warm place until doubled, about 1 hour.

Punch dough down. Turn onto a lightly floured surface; divide in half and set one portion aside. Divide remaining portion in half; press each portion into a well-greased 10-in. springform pan. Divide reserved dough into six balls. Shape each ball into a 30-in. rope; make two braids of three ropes each. Place a braid around the edge of each pan, forming a circle. Trim ends of braids, reserving dough scraps. Pinch ends of braids to seal. Shape scraps into two long thin ropes; form into rosettes or crosses. Place one decoration in the center of each loaf. Cover and let rise until doubled, about 1 hour.

In a small bowl, beat egg and water; brush over dough. Bake at 350° for 50-60 minutes or until golden brown. Remove from pans to wire racks to cool. **Yield:** 2 loaves.

Cream Cheese Bundles

A cream cheese center provides a pleasant surprise when folks bite into these rich rolls.
—Maxine Cenker, Weirton, West Virginia

5-1/2 cups all-purpose flour
1/2 cup sugar
2 packages (1/4 ounce *each*) quick-rise yeast
1/2 teaspoon salt
1 cup water
1/2 cup butter
3 eggs
FILLING:
1 package (8 ounces) cream cheese, softened
1 egg
1/4 cup sugar
1/2 teaspoon vanilla extract
TOPPING:
2 tablespoons butter, melted
1-1/2 cups confectioners' sugar
2 to 3 tablespoons milk
1/2 teaspoon vanilla extract
1/3 cup finely chopped pecans, toasted

In a large mixing bowl, combine 3 cups flour, sugar, yeast and salt. In a saucepan, heat water and butter to 120°-130°; stir into dry ingredients. Beat in eggs until smooth. Stir in enough remaining flour to form a soft dough. Turn onto a floured surface; knead until smooth and elastic, about 6-8 minutes. Cover and let rest for 10 minutes.

Meanwhile, in a small mixing bowl, combine the filling ingredients; beat until smooth. Roll out dough to a 21-in. x 14-in. rectangle, about 1/4 in. thick. Let rest for 5 minutes. Cut into 3-1/2-in. squares. Spoon 1 tablespoon of filling onto each square. Bring corners together over filling; pinch seams to seal. Place seam side down in greased muffin cups. Cover and let rise until doubled, about 1-1/2 hours.

Bake at 375° for 15-20 minutes or until golden brown. Remove from pans to wire racks to cool. Brush with butter. In a small bowl, combine the confectioners' sugar, milk and vanilla until smooth; drizzle over bundles. Sprinkle with pecans. Refrigerate leftovers. **Yield:** 2 dozen.

Dilly Cheese Ring

As a stay-at-home mom with three children, I don't have time for a lot of involved cooking. This delicious bread goes together in a flash thanks to a biscuit mix.
—Peggy-Jo Thompson, Lebanon, Tennessee

3 cups biscuit/baking mix
1-1/2 cups (6 ounces) shredded cheddar cheese
1 tablespoon sugar
1/2 to 1 teaspoon dill weed
1/2 teaspoon ground mustard
1 egg, lightly beaten
1-1/4 cups milk
1 tablespoon vegetable oil

In a large bowl, combine the first five ingredients. In a small bowl, combine the egg, milk and oil. Stir into dry ingredients just until moistened. Pour into a greased 10-in. fluted tube pan. Bake at 350° for 35-40 minutes or until a toothpick inserted near the center comes out clean. Cool for 10 minutes before removing from pan to a wire rack. **Yield:** 1 loaf.

Chocolate-Hazelnut Swirl Bread

(Pictured at right)

Homemade breads are my favorite goodies to give. After delivering these lovley loaves to friends and family one Christmas, people kept asking me for the recipe. I was happy to share it!
—Nancy Tafoya, Fort Collins, Colorado

1/2 cup butter, softened
1 cup sugar
2 eggs
1 teaspoon almond extract
1 teaspoon vanilla extract
2 cups all-purpose flour
1 teaspoon baking powder
1 teaspoon baking soda
1/4 teaspoon salt
1 cup (8 ounces) sour cream

TOPPING:

1/3 cup finely chopped hazelnuts
1/3 cup miniature semisweet chocolate chips
3 tablespoons sugar
3/4 teaspoon ground cinnamon

In a mixing bowl, cream butter and sugar. Add eggs, one at a time, beating well after each addition. Beat in extracts. Combine the flour, baking powder, baking soda and salt; add to the creamed mixture alternately with sour cream.

Pour half of the batter into a greased 9-in. x 5-in. x 3-in. loaf pan. Combine topping ingredients; sprinkle two-thirds over the batter. Top with the remaining batter. Sprinkle with remaining topping; press down lightly. Bake at 350° for 60-70 minutes or until a toothpick inserted near the center comes out clean. Cool for 10 minutes before removing from pan to a wire rack. **Yield:** 1 loaf.

History of Hot Cross Buns

IF YOU PASS a pan of hot cross buns around your dinner table at Easter, enlighten guests with this bit of history.

English immigrants brought to America the recipe for these traditional Easter buns dotted with raisins and currants. A cross is cut into the top before baking, then piped with frosting when baked and cooled.

Apricot Pecan Bread

Enjoy slices of this fruit and nut quick bread alongside breakfast or as a snack any time of day. One loaf won't last long!
—Beatrice Pratten, Canton, Illinois

2 cups all-purpose flour
3/4 cup sugar
1/2 teaspoon baking soda
1/2 teaspoon salt
1/4 teaspoon baking powder
1 egg, lightly beaten
1 cup orange juice
3 tablespoons butter, melted
1 cup chopped pecans
1/2 cup finely chopped dried apricots

In a large bowl, combine the flour, sugar, baking soda, salt, and baking powder. In another bowl, combine the egg, orange juice and butter. Stir into the dry ingredients just until moistened. Fold in the pecans and apricots.

Pour into a greased 9-in. x 5-in. x 3-in. loaf pan. Bake at 325° for 50-60 minutes or until a toothpick inserted near the center comes out clean. Cool for 10 minutes before removing from pan to a wire rack. **Yield:** 1 loaf.

Caraway Rye Rolls

These mild-flavored rolls appeal to folks of every age and pair well with a variety of menus. I sometimes shape the dough into loaves for sandwiches.
—Sue Stitzel, Craig, Colorado

2 cups rye flour
1/4 cup sugar
2 packages (1/4 ounce *each*) active dry yeast
1 tablespoon salt
2 to 3 teaspoons fennel seed
2 teaspoons caraway seeds
3-1/2 to 4-1/2 cups all-purpose flour
2-1/2 cups water
3 tablespoons shortening

In a large mixing bowl, combine the rye flour, sugar, yeast, salt, fennel seed, caraway seeds and 2 cups all-purpose flour. In a saucepan, heat water and shortening to 120°-130°. Add to the dry ingredients; beat just until moistened. Beat on medium speed for 3 minutes. Stir in enough remaining flour to form a firm dough. Turn onto a floured surface; knead until smooth and elastic, about 6-8 minutes. Place in a greased bowl, turning once to grease top. Cover and let rise in a warm place until doubled, about 1 hour.

Punch dough down. Turn onto a lightly floured surface; divide into six portions. Divide each portion into 10 pieces; shape each piece into a ball. Place three balls in each greased muffin cup. Cover and let rise until doubled, about 30 minutes. Bake at 375° for 15-20 minutes or until golden brown. Cool for 5 minutes before removing from pans to wire racks. **Yield:** 20 rolls.

Herbed Onion Focaccia

(Pictured at right)

This recipe makes three savory flat breads, but don't be surprised to see them all disappear from your dinner table!
—Melanie Eddy, Manhattan, Kansas

1 tablespoon active dry yeast
1-1/2 cups warm water (110° to 115°), *divided*
1 teaspoon sugar
6 tablespoons olive oil, *divided*
2 teaspoons salt
4 to 4-1/2 cups all-purpose flour
3 tablespoons finely chopped green onions
1-1/2 teaspoons minced fresh rosemary *or* 1/2 teaspoon dried rosemary, crushed
1-1/2 teaspoons small fresh sage leaves *or* 1/2 teaspoon rubbed sage
1-1/2 teaspoons minced fresh oregano *or* 1/2 teaspoon dried oregano
Seasoned olive oil *or* additional olive oil, optional

In a large mixing bowl, dissolve yeast in 1/2 cup warm water. Add sugar; let stand for 5 minutes. Add 4 tablespoons oil, salt, 2 cups flour and remaining water. Beat until smooth. Stir in enough remaining flour to form a soft dough. Turn onto a floured surface; knead until smooth and elastic, about 6-8 minutes. Place in a greased bowl, turning once to grease top. Cover and let rise in a warm place until doubled, about 1 hour.

Punch dough down. Divide into three portions. Cover and let rest for 10 minutes. Shape each portion into an 8-in. circle; place on greased baking sheets. Cover and let rise until doubled, about 30 minutes. Using the end of a wooden spoon handle, make several 1/4-in. indentations in each loaf. Brush with remaining oil. Sprinkle with green onions, rosemary, sage and oregano. Bake at 400° for 20-25 minutes or until golden brown. Remove to wire racks. Serve with olive oil for dipping if desired. **Yield:** 3 loaves.

Passover Celebration

PASSOVER is an 8-day Jewish holiday marking the physical freedom of the Hebrews (under the leadership of Moses) from the Egyptian Pharaoh.

On the first 2 nights, friends and family share a festive meal called Seder, meaning "order."

Here we offer one idea for a mouth-watering meal to serve during Passover.

Veal Breast with Farfel Stuffing bakes for a few hours, resulting in a tender, tasty entree.

The pleasant flavor of rich Onion Kugel appeals to all... even folks who don't care for onions.

Refreshing Cucumber Salad is a cool and crisp complement to the oven-fresh dishes. (All recipes shown at right.)

Seder Supper

(Top to bottom)

Onion Kugel (p. 37)

Veal Breast with Farfel Stuffing (p. 38)

Refreshing Cucumber Salad (p. 36)

Passover Dinner Plan

A Few Weeks Before:

- Prepare two grocery lists—one for nonperishable items to purchase now and one for perishable items to purchase a few days before your dinner.
- Order a veal breast from your butcher.
- Bake Passover Bagels; cool. Freeze in a heavy-duty resealable plastic bag.

Two Days Before:

- Set the table.
- Buy remaining grocery items, including the veal breast you ordered.
- Prepare the Refreshing Cucumber Salad; cover and chill.

The Day Before:

- Assemble the stuffing for Veal Breast with Farfel Stuffing. Cover and refrigerate. (Do not stuff into the veal breast until ready to bake.)
- Finely chop the onions for Onion Kugel. Refrigerate in an airtight container.
- Make Matzo Ball Soup. Let cool; cover and chill.
- Prepare Chicken Liver Pate; cover and refrigerate.
- Bake the Flourless Apricot Pecan Tart but don't add the garnish. Cover with foil; store at room temperature overnight.

The Day of Your Passover Dinner:

- In the morning, thaw Passover Bagels at room temperature.
- Garnish the tart and recover.
- Stuff the veal breast and bake as directed.
- As guests arrive, set out Chicken Liver Pate and assorted crackers.
- Assemble the Onion Kugel and bake.
- If desired, wrap the bagels in foil and reheat in a 350° oven for 15 to 20 minutes.
- Reheat Matzo Ball Soup and offer it as a first course.
- Serve Refreshing Cucumber Salad with a slotted spoon.
- For dessert, cut the Flourless Apricot Pecan Tart.

Refreshing Cucumber Salad

(Pictured on page 34)

This refreshing salad from our home economists can be prepared days in advance.

3 medium cucumbers, thinly sliced
1 medium onion, thinly sliced
1/3 cup lemon juice
3/4 teaspoon salt

In a large bowl, combine the cucumbers and onion. Stir in lemon juice and salt. Cover and refrigerate for 1-2 days, stirring occasionally. Serve with a slotted spoon. **Yield:** 6-8 servings.

Onion Kugel

(Pictured at right and on page 35)

This traditional dish from our Test Kitchen resembles a delicious souffle. Sliced eggplant, sliced green peppers or shredded cabbage can be used in place of the onions.

6 eggs, *separated*
2 cups finely chopped onions
1/3 cup matzo meal
1/3 cup vegetable oil
3/4 teaspoon salt
1/4 teaspoon pepper

In a large mixing bowl, beat the egg yolks on high speed for 2 minutes or until thick and lemon-colored. Add the onions, matzo meal, oil, salt and pepper; mix well. In another mixing bowl, beat egg whites on high until stiff peaks form; fold into onion mixture.

Pour into an ungreased round 2-qt. baking dish. Bake, uncovered, at 350° for 35-40 minutes or until a knife inserted near the center comes out clean. Serve immediately. **Yield:** 8 servings.

The Meaning of Matzah

IT'S SAID that when Moses led the Jews to freedom, they left so quickly they didn't wait for their bread to rise. That's why the crunchy, flat bread called Matzah is eaten during Passover.

Matzo meal is finely ground from matzah. It's used as the main ingredient in matzo balls, as a breading for fried foods and as a thickening agent. It's also used in baked goods.

Veal Breast with Farfel Stuffing

(Pictured on page 35)

I prepare this entree often for Passover Seder. It bakes up golden brown and tastes terrific.
—Sala Simonds, Lancaster, California

1 cup chopped celery
1/4 cup chopped onion
1/4 cup rendered chicken fat *or* vegetable oil
4 cups matzo farfel
1/4 cup minced fresh parsley
1 egg, lightly beaten
1 cup chicken broth
1 teaspoon salt
1 teaspoon rubbed sage
1 teaspoon paprika
1/4 teaspoon pepper
1 bone-in veal breast with pocket (7 to 8 pounds)
Olive oil

In a large skillet, saute celery and onion in chicken fat until tender. Add farfel; cook and stir over medium heat until lightly browned. Stir in the parsley. Combine the egg, broth, salt, sage, paprika and pepper; add to farfel mixture. Cook over low heat until liquid is absorbed, stirring occasionally.

Just before baking, evenly fill the veal breast pocket with stuffing; close and tie several times with kitchen string. Place in a shallow greased roasting pan. Brush veal with olive oil. Bake, uncovered, at 350° for 1-3/4 to 2 hours or until a meat thermometer reads 160° for veal and 165° for stuffing, basting occasionally. Let stand for 10 minutes before slicing. **Yield:** 8-10 servings.

Story of the Seder Plate

DURING the Seder, the story of the Exodus is reenacted using a special Seder Plate (like the one shown on page 34). It contains the following key elements of Passover:

- Betzah (a roasted or boiled egg), commemorating the destruction of the Temple in Jerusalem.
- Charoset (a fruit and nut mixture), symbolizing the mortar used by Jews to build Egyptian structures.
- Karpas (spring greens such as radishes, onions, parsley or celery). The Karpas is dipped in salted water, which symbolizes the tears shed by the Jewish people. The spring greens and the salted water together symbolize life.
- Marror (bitter herbs), usually horseradish or romaine lettuce, commemorating the harsh conditions of slavery in ancient Egypt.
- Zeroa (roasted or boiled meat or poultry), recalling the Pascal sacrifice of the original Exodus.

In addition, red wine is consumed during the course of the Seder to commemorate the redemption of the Jewish people.

Matzo Ball Soup

(Pictured at right)

Our Test Kitchen shares the recipe for this traditional soup. You can make the soup a day ahead and reheat it just before serving.

10 cups water
12 garlic cloves, peeled
3 medium carrots, cut into chunks
3 small turnips, peeled and cut into chunks
2 medium onions, cut into wedges
2 medium parsnips, peeled and cut into chunks
1 medium leek (white portion only), sliced
1/4 cup minced fresh parsley
2 tablespoons snipped fresh dill
1 teaspoon salt
1 teaspoon pepper
3/4 teaspoon ground turmeric

MATZO BALLS:

3 eggs, *separated*
3 tablespoons water *or* chicken broth
3 tablespoons rendered chicken fat
1-1/2 teaspoons salt, *divided*
3/4 cup matzo meal
8 cups water

For broth, combine the first 12 ingredients in a large soup kettle or stockpot. Bring to a boil. Reduce heat; cover and simmer for 2 hours.

Meanwhile, in a mixing bowl, beat the egg yolks on high speed for 2 minutes or until thick and lemon-colored. Add the water, chicken fat and 1/2 teaspoon salt. In another mixing bowl, beat egg whites on high until stiff peaks form; fold into yolk mixture. Fold in matzo meal. Cover and refrigerate for at least 1 hour or until thickened.

In another large stockpot, bring water to a boil; add remaining salt. Drop eight rounded tablespoonfuls of matzo ball dough into boiling water. Reduce heat; cover and simmer for 20-25 minutes or until a toothpick inserted into a matzo ball comes out clean (do not lift cover while simmering).

Strain broth, discarding vegetables and seasonings. Carefully remove matzo balls from water with a slotted spoon; place one matzo ball in each soup bowl. Add broth. **Yield:** 8 servings.

Passover Bagels

We use these traditional bagels to make sandwiches throughout Passover. But they can also be served as rolls with dinner.
—Myrna Lief, Burlington, Massachusetts

1 cup water
1/2 cup vegetable oil
1 tablespoon sugar
1/4 teaspoon salt
1 cup matzo meal
4 eggs

In a large saucepan, bring the water, oil, sugar and salt to a boil. Add matzo meal all at once and stir until a smooth ball forms. Remove from the heat; let stand for 5 minutes. Add eggs, one at a time, beating well after each addition. Continue beating until mixture is smooth and shiny.

Drop dough into 12 mounds 3 in. apart on two greased baking sheets. Bake at 450° for 10 minutes. Reduce heat to 350°; bake 12-15 minutes longer or until golden brown. Remove to wire racks. Immediately cut a slit in each to allow steam to escape; cool. **Yield:** 1 dozen.

Chicken Liver Pate

My family loves this spread with crackers. But I've also put it to use as a sandwich filling with lettuce and tomato.
—Roberta Wolff, Waltham, Massachusetts

1 pound chicken livers
1 small onion, chopped
1/3 cup rendered chicken fat *or* margarine
1/2 pound fresh mushrooms, quartered
2 hard-cooked eggs, quartered
1 to 2 tablespoons sherry *or* chicken broth
3/4 teaspoon salt
1/4 teaspoon pepper
Melba toast *or* assorted crackers

In a skillet, saute chicken livers and onion in chicken fat for 10 minutes or until livers are no longer pink. Transfer to a food processor; cover and process until chicken livers are coarsely chopped.

Add the mushrooms, eggs, 1 tablespoon sherry or broth, salt and pepper. Cover and process until smooth, adding more sherry or broth if needed for pate to reach desired consistency. Transfer to a bowl. Cover and refrigerate for at least 3 hours. Serve with melba toast or crackers. **Yield:** 12 servings.

Flourless Apricot Pecan Tart

(Pictured at right)

Apricot and chocolate are pleasing partners in this elegant dessert created in our Test Kitchen. It doesn't contain flour, so it's appropriate for people with gluten allergies.

12 ounces dried apricots, chopped
1 cup water
6 tablespoons sugar
1 tablespoon minced fresh gingerroot
1 tablespoon lemon juice
1 teaspoon grated lemon peel

CRUST:
1 tablespoon matzo meal
4 cups pecan halves, toasted
1-1/2 cups sugar
1/2 teaspoon ground ginger
1/4 teaspoon salt
2 eggs
4 squares (1 ounce *each*) semisweet chocolate

GARNISH:
2 squares (1 ounce *each*) semisweet chocolate
1/2 cup pecan halves
Dried apricots

In a heavy saucepan, combine the apricots, water, sugar, gingerroot, lemon juice and peel; bring to a boil. Reduce heat; cover and simmer for 30-35 minutes or until apricots are tender. Uncover; simmer 5-10 minutes longer or until thickened and liquid is absorbed. Transfer to a food processor; cover and pulse five times or until mixture is smooth and thickened. Pour into a bowl; cool.

Trace the removable bottom of an 11-in. tart pan on waxed paper; set aside. Grease tart pan; dust with matzo meal and set aside.

In a food processor, combine the pecans, sugar, ginger and salt; cover and process until pecans are finely ground. Add eggs; cover and process until mixture forms a moist ball. Place half of the dough in a bowl; cover and refrigerate. Press remaining dough over the bottom and up the sides of prepared pan.

Bake at 350° for 12-15 minutes or until crust is puffed and lightly browned. Press bottom of crust lightly to flatten if necessary. Cool on a wire rack.

In a microwave, melt chocolate; stir until smooth. Spread over crust. Chill for 10 minutes or until set. Spread apricot filling over chocolate. Press remaining dough over waxed paper circle. Invert dough over filling; carefully peel off waxed paper and discard. Press edges of dough to edge of tart pan to seal.

Bake at 350° for 35-40 minutes or until lightly browned and dry to the touch. Cool completely in pan on a wire rack. Cover with foil and let stand overnight.

For garnish, melt chocolate; stir until smooth. Drizzle 2 tablespoons over tart. Dip pecans halfway in remaining chocolate. Garnish tart with dipped pecans and dried apricots. **Yield:** 12-14 servings.

Kentucky Derby Gala

AND THEY'RE OFF! Those three simple words signal the start of the most famous two-minute horse race in history.

The first Kentucky Derby race took place in 1875 and has been held on the first Saturday in May ever since, making it one of America's oldest sporting events.

If you can't get to Churchill Downs to see the Derby in person, host a winning TV-viewing party at home!

Guests will be jockeying for a position at the buffet table to sample born-and-bred dishes such as Mint Juleps, Benedictine Spread and Kentucky Chocolate Pecan Pie.

Finish the meal in fine fashion with other classics like Southern Fried Chicken and Cheese 'n' Grits Casserole. (All recipes are shown at right.)

Southern Comfort Food

(Clockwise from top right)

Cheese 'n' Grits Casserole (p. 49)

Benedictine Spread (p. 48)

Southern Fried Chicken (p. 44)

Mint Juleps (p. 47)

Kentucky Chocolate Pecan Pie (p. 45)

Special Kentucky Derby Table Setting

THE "run for the roses" conjures up images of well-to-do gentlemen in suits and Southern belles in flowing dresses and wide-brimmed hats. Pair this chapter's casual food with an elegant table for a lovely look. Here's how:

- As the "mane" attraction on your buffet table, look for an inexpensive horse sculpture. We purchased the one pictured on page 43 at a local gardening and gift store. Or have a field day and set out a collection of horse figurines.
- Remember the red roses! Place stems in one or several silver vases or scatter rose petals on the table.
- Top tables with linen cloths and coordinating napkins.
- This is the perfect occasion for displaying sterling silver platters and bowls. Present silverware in the Cloth Silverware Holder shown on page 49.
- Put aside the paper plates and bring out your everyday dishes or china.
- Consider holding the event outside. If your budget allows, rent a tent and chairs.
- Greet guests with Mint Juleps (see recipe on page 47) served in traditional cups. You can find both silver plated and plastic mint julep cups on-line and at party stores.

Southern Fried Chicken

(Pictured on page 43)

In the South, fried chicken is served with creamy, seasoned gravy. Our Test Kitchen home economists share their recipe here.

1 cup all-purpose flour
1 teaspoon onion powder
1 teaspoon paprika
3/4 teaspoon salt
1/2 teaspoon rubbed sage
1/2 teaspoon pepper
1/4 teaspoon dried thyme
1 egg
1/2 cup milk
1 broiler/fryer chicken (3 to 3-1/2 pounds), cut up
Oil for frying
CREAMY GRAVY:
1/3 cup all-purpose flour
1/4 teaspoon salt
1/4 teaspoon dried thyme
1/4 to 1/2 teaspoon pepper
2-1/2 cups milk
1/2 cup heavy whipping cream

In a large resealable plastic bag, combine the first seven ingredients. In a shallow bowl, beat egg and milk. Dip chicken pieces into egg mixture, then add to flour mixture, a few pieces at a time, and shake to coat.

In a large skillet, heat 1/4 in. of oil; fry chicken until browned on all sides. Cover and simmer for 35-40 minutes or until juices run clear and chicken is tender, turning occasionally. Uncover and cook 5 minutes longer. Drain on paper towels and keep warm.

Drain skillet, reserving 3 tablespoons drippings. For gravy, in a small bowl, combine the flour, salt, thyme and pepper. Gradually whisk in milk and cream until smooth; add to skillet. Bring to a boil over medium heat; cook and stir for 2 minutes or until thickened. Serve with chicken. **Yield:** 6 servings.

Kentucky Chocolate Pecan Pie

(Pictured at right and on page 42)

This is our Test Kitchen's version of the regional classic. The chocolate pecan pie is infused with Kentucky bourbon.

3 eggs
2 egg yolks
3/4 cup packed brown sugar
2/3 cup light corn syrup
1/3 cup butter, melted
2 tablespoons Kentucky bourbon, optional
1 teaspoon vanilla extract
Dash salt
1 cup coarsely chopped pecans
1 unbaked pastry shell (9 inches)
1 egg white, lightly beaten
3/4 cup semisweet chocolate chips
1 cup heavy whipping cream
2 tablespoons confectioners' sugar

In a large bowl, whisk the eggs, yolks, brown sugar, corn syrup, butter, bourbon if desired, vanilla and salt. Stir in pecans.

Brush pastry shell with egg white. Sprinkle with chocolate chips. Pour filling over chips. Bake at 350° for 40-45 minutes or until set. Cool on a wire rack.

In a small chilled mixing bowl, beat cream until it begins to thicken. Add confectioners' sugar; beat until stiff peaks form. Dollop on pie just before serving. Refrigerate leftovers. **Yield:** 6-8 servings.

Victory Corn Salad

This crisp vegetable salad from our Test Kitchen adds color and unique freshness to your table.

3 cans (11 ounces *each*) white *or* shoepeg corn, drained
3 plum tomatoes, seeded and chopped
3/4 cup chopped celery
1/2 cup chopped sweet red pepper
1/3 cup thinly sliced green onions
2 tablespoons minced fresh parsley
3 tablespoons cider vinegar
3 tablespoons vegetable oil
1 teaspoon sugar
1/2 teaspoon salt
1/4 teaspoon pepper

In a large bowl, combine the corn, tomatoes, celery, red pepper, onions and parsley. In a small bowl, whisk the vinegar, oil, sugar, salt and pepper. Pour over vegetables and toss to coat. Cover and refrigerate for at least 1 hour or until chilled. **Yield:** 8 servings.

Peach Rice Pudding

This old-fashioned rice pudding is layered with sliced peaches, then topped with a sweet raspberry sauce. It makes for a pretty presentation in parfait glasses.
—Lorraine Wisvader, Millbrook, Illinois

6 cups milk
1 cup uncooked long grain rice
1/2 teaspoon salt
1/4 cup sugar
2 tablespoons butter
1/2 teaspoon vanilla extract

RUBY PORT WINE SAUCE:

1 cup sugar
1 cup fresh *or* frozen raspberries
1 cup red currant jelly
4 teaspoons cornstarch
1/4 cup port wine *or* red grape juice
4 cups sliced peeled fresh *or* frozen peaches, thawed

In a large saucepan, bring milk, rice and salt just to a boil. Reduce heat; cover and simmer for 25-30 minutes or until rice is tender and most of the liquid is absorbed, stirring occasionally. Remove from the heat. Stir in the sugar, butter and vanilla; cool.

In a small saucepan, combine the sugar, raspberries and jelly. Bring to a boil, stirring constantly. Cook and stir over medium heat for 5 minutes. Press mixture through a fine strainer or sieve; discard seeds. Return raspberry sauce to pan. Combine cornstarch and wine or grape juice until smooth; stir into sauce. Bring to a boil; cook and stir for 1-2 minutes or until thickened. Remove from the heat; cool.

In individual dessert dishes or in a 2-1/2-qt. trifle bowl, layer the rice pudding and peaches. Serve with sauce. **Yield:** 12 servings.

Mint Juleps

(Pictured at right and on page 42)

Our home economists know it wouldn't be Kentucky Derby Day without Mint Juleps! They even offer a nonalcoholic version that tastes just as great.

MINT SYRUP:
2 cups sugar
2 cups water
2 cups coarsely chopped loosely packed fresh mint
BEVERAGE:
2/3 to 1-1/4 cups bourbon
Cracked ice
10 mint sprigs

For syrup, combine the sugar, water and mint in a saucepan. Bring to a boil over medium heat; cook until sugar is dissolved, stirring occasionally. Remove from the heat; cool to room temperature.

Line a mesh strainer with a double layer of cheesecloth or a coffee filter. Strain syrup; discard mint. Cover and refrigerate syrup for at least 2 hours or until chilled.

For each serving, combine 1/4 cup mint syrup and 1-2 tablespoons bourbon. Pour into a glass over cracked ice. Garnish with a mint sprig. **Yield:** 10 servings.

Mock Mint Julep: Prepare mint syrup as directed; after straining, add 1/2 cup lemon juice. Cover and refrigerate for at least 2 hours or until chilled. For each serving, combine 1/2 cup club soda and 1/4 cup mint syrup. Pour into a glass over cracked ice. Garnish with a mint sprig.

Family Traditions

HERE in Louisville, the Kentucky Derby is preceded by 3 weeks of festivities. Practically everyone hosts or attends a Derby party. A popular hot dish to serve is Burgoo, a savory stew made of different cooked meats and vegetables. Folks begin preparing Burgoo days in advance.

—*Sherry Hulsman, Louisville, Kentucky*

Corn Pillows

We live quite far north and nothing warms us up on cold days like warm breads and rolls. This wonderful recipe comes from a dear friend.
—Martha Nunn, Vanderhoof, British Columbia

1 tablespoon active dry yeast
1/4 cup warm water (110° to 115°)
1-3/4 cups milk
1/2 cup cornmeal
1/3 cup vegetable oil
1/3 cup sugar
2 teaspoons salt
1 can (18-1/2 ounces) cream-style corn
2 eggs, beaten
6 to 7 cups all-purpose flour
Oil for deep-fat frying
Confectioners' sugar

In a large mixing bowl, dissolve yeast in warm water. In a large saucepan, heat the milk, cornmeal, oil, sugar and salt to 110°-115°, add to yeast mixture. Add corn, eggs and 6 cups flour; beat until smooth. Stir in enough remaining flour to form a soft dough.

Turn onto a lightly floured surface; knead until smooth and elastic, about 6-8 minutes. Place in a greased bowl, turning once to grease top. Cover and let rise until doubled, about 1 hour.

Punch dough down. Turn onto a lightly floured surface; divide in half. Roll each portion into a 15-in. x 12-in. rectangle. Cut into 3-in. x 1-1/2-in. strips.

In a deep-fat fryer, heat oil to 375°. Drop dough strips in batches into oil; fry for 45-75 seconds or until golden brown. Drain on paper towels. Dust with confectioners' sugar. **Yield:** about 6-1/2 dozen.

Benedictine Spread

(Pictured on page 43)

This variation of a traditional, Kentucky cucumber spread comes from our Test Kitchen. Serve it as an appetizer dip or sandwich filling.

1 package (8 ounces) cream cheese, softened
1 tablespoon mayonnaise
1/4 teaspoon salt
1/8 teaspoon white pepper
1/8 teaspoon dill weed
1 drop green food coloring, optional
3/4 cup finely chopped peeled cucumber, patted dry
1/4 cup finely chopped onion
Pita bread wedges *or* snack rye bread

In a small mixing bowl, combine the cream cheese, mayonnaise, salt, white pepper, dill and food coloring if desired; beat until smooth. Stir in cucumber and onion. Cover and refrigerate until serving. Serve with pita or snack rye bread. **Yield:** 1-3/4 cups.

Cloth Silverware Holder

(Pictured at right)

ADD a bit of pizzazz to your Kentucky Derby buffet by displaying cutlery in a unique way.

Place a large, starched cloth napkin wrong side up on a flat surface. (Our napkin measured 22 inches.) Fold up the bottom third of napkin, forming a rectangle.

Carefully turn the napkin over. Fold bottom folded edge halfway up.

On each short end, tuck about 1-1/2 inches of the napkin under to form a long pocket. Insert silverware into the pocket.

Cheese 'n' Grits Casserole

(Pictured on page 43)

Grits are a staple in Southern cooking. Serve this as a brunch item with bacon or as a side dish for dinner.
—Jennifer Wallis, Goldsboro, North Carolina

- **4 cups water**
- **1 cup uncooked old-fashioned grits**
- **1/2 teaspoon salt**
- **1/2 cup milk**
- **1/4 cup butter, melted**
- **2 eggs, beaten**
- **1 cup (4 ounces) shredded cheddar cheese**
- **1 tablespoon Worcestershire sauce**
- **1/8 teaspoon cayenne pepper**
- **1/8 teaspoon paprika**

In a large saucepan, bring water to a boil. Stir in grits and salt. Reduce heat; cover and simmer for 5-7 minutes or until thickened. Cool slightly. Gradually whisk in the milk, butter and eggs. Stir in the cheese, Worcestershire sauce and cayenne.

Transfer to a greased 2-qt. baking dish. Sprinkle with the paprika. Bake, uncovered, at 350° for 30-35 minutes or until bubbly. Let stand 10 minutes before serving. **Yield:** 8 servings.

Make Mother's Day Special

ONE WAY to make Mom feel like a million on Mother's Day is by having Dad rouse the kids and whisk them to the kitchen to prepare breakfast in bed for her!

Golden Oat Pancakes and Green Onion Scrambled Eggs deliciously prove that great-tasting foods don't require complicated recipes. (Dishes shown at right.)

Do you prefer not to disturb Mom on her special morning? Skip the breakfast and serve up a soup and sandwich lunch at the kitchen table. Or dish out a hearty helping of pasta salad.

We even offer timetables that make menu planning extra easy!

Rise-and-Shine Surprise

Golden Oat Pancakes (p. 53)

Green Onion Scrambled Eggs (p. 53)

Mother's Day Breakfast Plan

One Week Before:

- Come up with the menu and make a grocery list.
- Have the kids make a card or draw a picture for Mom. (If desired, pick up an inexpensive photo frame for the drawing. See page 59 for one idea.)
- Look at home for a breakfast tray or pick one up from the store. You don't have to use a tray with legs...any tray (even a plastic one for outdoor entertaining) will do.

Two Days Before:

- Stop at the grocery store for any needed items.
- Put marbles in a drinking glass. Surround with a ponytail holder and crayons if desired. (See page 59 for directions.) Hide the glass from Mom!

The Day Before:

- Make Lemon-Blueberry Tea Bread and cool completely. Store in a resealable plastic bag on the counter overnight.
- Combine the flour, baking powder, brown sugar and salt for Golden Oat Pancakes. Place in an airtight container; store at room temperature.

Mother's Day Morning:

- Get up early with the kids and let Mom sleep in!
- Have older kids add water and fresh-cut flowers from your yard to the marble-filled drinking glass; set on the breakfast tray along with the kid-crafted greeting card or framed drawing.
- Slice Lemon-Blueberry Tea Bread.
- Make Fruit Smoothies or pour Mom a cup of coffee, orange juice or her favorite morning beverage.
- While the Golden Oat Pancakes are cooking on the griddle, prepare Green Onion Scrambled Eggs in a skillet.
- Top the pancakes with fresh fruit or syrup.
- Serve Mom breakfast in bed!

Golden Oat Pancakes

(Pictured at right and on page 51)

My husband's face lights up when I serve these country-style flapjacks. Serve them with fresh fruit or syrup.
—Raymonde Bourgeois, Swastika, Ontario

1-1/3 cups milk
1 cup old-fashioned oats
2 eggs, lightly beaten
3 tablespoons vegetable oil
2/3 cup all-purpose flour
4 teaspoons baking powder
4 teaspoons brown sugar
1/4 teaspoon salt

In a bowl, combine the milk and oats; let stand for 5 minutes. Stir in eggs and oil. Combine the flour, baking powder, brown sugar and salt; stir into oat mixture just until moistened. Pour batter by 1/4 cupfuls onto a greased hot griddle; turn when bubbles form on top of pancakes. Cook until second side is lightly browned. **Yield:** 10 pancakes.

Green Onion Scrambled Eggs

(Pictured above and on page 51)

Our Test Kitchen home economists added cream cheese and green onions to create these deliciously different scrambled eggs.

4 green onions, chopped
2 tablespoons butter
8 eggs
1 package (3 ounces) cream cheese, cubed
1/2 teaspoon seasoned salt

In a large skillet, saute onions in butter for 2 minutes. In a bowl, beat the eggs; add cream cheese and seasoned salt. Pour into the skillet. As eggs set, gently move a spatula across bottom and sides of pan, letting uncooked portion flow underneath. Continue cooking and stirring until the eggs are completely set. **Yield:** 4 servings.

Lemon-Blueberry Tea Bread

Moist slices of this cake-like bread are bursting with blueberries and lots of lemon flavor.
—Wendy Masters, Grand Valley, Ontario

1/2 cup butter, softened
1 cup sugar
2 eggs
1 teaspoon grated lemon peel
1-1/2 cups all-purpose flour
1 teaspoon baking powder
1/4 teaspoon salt
1/2 cup milk
1 cup fresh *or* frozen blueberries
1/4 cup confectioners' sugar
1 tablespoon lemon juice

In a small mixing bowl, cream the butter and sugar. Add the eggs, one at a time, beating well after each addition. Beat in lemon peel. Combine the flour, baking powder and salt; add to creamed mixture alternately with milk. Fold in blueberries.

Pour into a greased 8-in. x 4-in. x 2-in. loaf pan. Bake at 350° for 65-70 minutes or until a toothpick inserted near the center comes out clean. Cool for 10 minutes before removing from pan to a wire rack. In a small bowl, combine confectioners' sugar and lemon juice until smooth; drizzle over warm bread. **Yield:** 1 loaf.

Editor's Note: If using frozen blueberries, do not thaw before adding to batter.

Fruit Smoothies

Instead of pouring a glass of ordinary orange juice, our Test Kitchen suggests making Mom this refreshing smoothie that's quickly prepared in a blender.

2 cups milk
1 cup frozen unsweetened peach slices
1 cup frozen unsweetened strawberries
1/4 cup orange juice
2 tablespoons honey

In a blender, combine all ingredients. Cover and blend until smooth. Pour into chilled glasses; serve immediately. **Yield:** 4 servings.

Strawberry Swirl Mousse Tarts

(Pictured above)

Our Test Kitchen created a delicious dessert that requires only six ingredients.

1-1/2 cups cold milk
1 package (3.3 ounces) instant white chocolate pudding mix
1 cup whipped topping
1 package (6 count) individual graham cracker tart shells
1/4 cup strawberry ice cream topping
6 fresh strawberries

In a small bowl, gradually whisk milk and pudding for 2 minutes. Let stand for 2 minutes or until soft-set. Gently fold in whipped topping. Spoon into tart shells. Drizzle with strawberry topping. Refrigerate for at least 30 minutes. Garnish with strawberries. **Yield:** 6 servings.

Plate of Distinction

IN THE PHOTO above, we used the well-known "You Are Special Today" plate by Waechtersbach.

This stunning, signature red plate is a fun, family heirloom that's wonderful to have on hand to celebrate many occasions throughout the year.

Pineapple Chicken Salad Sandwiches

(Pictured on page 55)

These sandwiches are always welcome at lunchtime around our home. Sweet pineapple and crunchy pecans are nice additions to ordinary chicken salad.
—Carol Alexander, Midland, Michigan

2 cups cubed cooked chicken breast
1/2 cup crushed pineapple, drained
1/4 cup chopped pecans
1/4 cup chopped celery
2 tablespoons finely chopped onion
2 tablespoons sweet pickle relish
1/2 cup mayonnaise
1/4 teaspoon onion salt
1/4 teaspoon garlic salt
1/4 teaspoon paprika
6 lettuce leaves
6 sandwich rolls, split

In a small bowl, combine the first six ingredients. Combine the mayonnaise, onion salt, garlic salt and paprika; add to chicken mixture and mix well. Serve on lettuce-lined rolls. **Yield:** 6 servings.

Getting Cooked Chicken

WHEN recipes like Pineapple Chicken Salad Sandwiches call for cubed cooked chicken, stop by the deli counter and have them cut a thick slice of cooked chicken breast sandwich meat for you to cut up at home.

Speedy Spud Soup

(Pictured on page 55)

I'm a busy wife and mother with not a lot of time to spend in the kitchen. This time-saving soup recipe relies on frozen potatoes and canned soup.
—Stacy Barron, Bentonville, Arkansas

1 package (24 ounces) frozen shredded hash brown potatoes, thawed
1/2 cup chopped onion
1/2 cup butter, cubed
4 cups milk
1 can (10-3/4 ounces) condensed cream of chicken soup, undiluted
1 cup (4 ounces) shredded cheddar cheese
1/2 teaspoon garlic salt
Cooked crumbled bacon

In a large saucepan, cook and stir the potatoes and onion in butter over medium-low heat for 10 minutes. Stir in the milk, soup, cheese and garlic salt. Cook, uncovered, for 20 minutes or until potatoes are tender. Garnish with bacon. **Yield:** 8 servings (2 quarts).

Crab Pasta Salad

(Pictured at right)

The medley of crab, pasta and vegetables in a creamy dressing make this a special salad for company as well as everyday.
—Estelle Hardin, Kanab, Utah

2 cups uncooked tricolor spiral pasta
2 cups imitation crabmeat, chopped
1 cup (8 ounces) sour cream
1/2 cup mayonnaise
3/4 teaspoon celery seed
3/4 teaspoon garlic powder
1/4 teaspoon salt
Pepper to taste
1 cup fresh broccoli florets
1 cup fresh caulifllowerets

Cook pasta according to package directions; drain and rinse in cold water. In a bowl, combine the crab, sour cream, mayonnaise, celery seed, garlic powder, salt and pepper. Stir in the pasta, broccoli and cauliflower. Cover and refrigerate for at least 2 hours before serving. **Yield:** 6-8 servings.

Cinnamon Dip

This creamy dip can be prepared the night before and chilled. Serve with apple wedges or an assortment of cookies for a sweet anytime snack.
—Jessica Flory, Queen Creek, Arizona

1 package (8 ounces) cream cheese, softened
3 tablespoons milk
2 tablespoons brown sugar
1 teaspoon vanilla extract
1 teaspoon ground cinnamon
1/4 teaspoon ground nutmeg
Apple wedges

In a small mixing bowl, combine the cream cheese, milk, brown sugar, vanilla, cinnamon and nutmeg; beat until smooth. Transfer to a serving bowl. Refrigerate until serving. Serve with apple wedges. **Yield:** 1 cup.

Mother's Day Lunch Plan

One Week Before:

- Decide if you want to serve Crab Pasta Salad as the only main course or the Pineapple Chicken Salad Sandwiches with Speedy Spud Soup.
- Prepare a grocery list.
- Have the kids make a card or draw a picture for Mom. (If desired, pick up an inexpensive photo frame for the drawing. See opposite page for one idea.)

Two Days Before:

- Stop at the grocery store for any needed items.
- Put marbles in a drinking glass. Surround with a ponytail holder and crayons if desired. (See opposite page for directions.) Hide the glass from Mom!

The Day Before:

- Make the Crab Pasta Salad or the filling for Pineapple Chicken Salad Sandwiches; refrigerate in an airtight container.
- Prepare Cinnamon Dip; cover and chill.

Mother's Day:

- As a mid-morning snack, serve Mom the Cinnamon Dip with apple wedges.
- Enlist the kids to set a special seat at the table for Mom.
- Have older kids add water and fresh-cut flowers from your yard to the marble-filled drinking glass; set on the table along with the kid-crafted greeting card or framed drawing.
- About 45 minutes before lunchtime, assemble Strawberry Swirl Mousse Tarts; place on a baking sheet and refrigerate until ready to serve.
- If serving Speedy Spud Soup, make it about 30 minutes before lunch. While the soup is simmering, assemble Pineapple Chicken Salad Sandwiches.
- Make Mom a plate of Crab Pasta Salad. Or serve her the soup and sandwich combination. Don't forget to pour Mom a beverage!
- For dessert, offer Mom the Strawberry Swirl Mousse Tarts.

Mementos for Mom

(Pictured above)

THE GIFTS that Mom cherishes most are the ones hand-crafted by her own kids. When you present Mom with a mouth-watering breakfast in bed or a lovely lunch at the kitchen table, have the kids make their mark with a one-of-a-kind tray or table topper.

Instead of buying a greeting card, enlist the little ones to make a card at home. Or have them draw a pretty picture and place it in a frame. (Inexpensive canvas or paper-covered photo frames are available at craft stores.)

Fresh-picked daisies bring a touch of spring inside...and a kid-crafted vase is the perfect way to display the bright bouquet!

While you start making the meal, have the kids hunt down some of their marbles and place them in a regular drinking glass. Tuck daisy stems into the marbles, then fill with water.

For an even more colorful arrangement, place a decorative ponytail holder around the marble-filled glass. Slide crayons between the glass and holder until the entire glass is covered.

Graduation Get-Together

WHEN you have a child graduating, your days leading up to the big event are packed with endless extra-curricular activities.

Address your dilemma of what to serve on commencement day by preparing the pleasing picnic meal shown at right.

With hot pork sausage and a special sauce, Sweet 'n' Spicy Meatballs make the grade for all of your hungry guests.

You'll earn top honors when you serve Crowd-Pleasin' Muffuletta as your main course.

For a stellar side that never fails to satisfy, dish out Marinated Vegetable Salad.

A purchased sheet cake from a local bakery concludes the memorable feast.

Cuisine With Class

(Clockwise from top right)

Sweet 'n' Spicy Meatballs (p. 65)

Marinated Vegetable Salad (p. 62)

Crowd-Pleasin' Muffuletta (p. 63)

Marinated Vegetable Salad

(Pictured on page 61)

I was known only as an average cook before I first made this lip-smacking salad!
—Mrs. Earl Anderson Jr., Stockton, California

4 cups fresh broccoli florets
4 cups fresh cauliflowerets
5 medium carrots, cut into 2-inch thin strips
2 cups grape tomatoes
1 can (15 ounces) whole baby corn, drained and cut widthwise into quarters
1 can (6 ounces) pitted ripe olives, drained and halved
1 cup olive oil
2/3 cup white wine vinegar
1/3 cup sherry *or* chicken broth
4 teaspoons Dijon mustard
3 garlic cloves, minced
2 teaspoons salt
1/2 teaspoon pepper

Place the broccoli, cauliflower and carrots in a large steamer basket; place in a large saucepan over 1 in. of water. Bring to a boil; cover and steam for 4-6 minutes or until crisp-tender. Place basket in ice water for 1-2 minutes or until vegetables are cooled; drain well.

Transfer the cooled vegetables to a large resealable plastic bag. Add the tomatoes, corn and olives. In a bowl, whisk the oil, vinegar, sherry or broth, mustard, garlic, salt and pepper. Pour over vegetables. Seal bag and turn to coat; refrigerate for at least 8 hours or overnight.

Remove from the refrigerator 30 minutes before serving. Turn bag to coat; pour salad into a serving bowl. Serve with a slotted spoon. **Yield:** 15 servings.

Sweet Heat Drumettes

Sweet maple syrup plays down the heat from the cayenne pepper in these finger-lickin'-good drumettes. Use a chafing dish to keep them warm at a party.
—Deb Zurawski, Jamesport, New York

1 cup maple syrup
1 cup chili sauce
1/2 cup minced chives
1/4 cup soy sauce
2 teaspoons ground mustard
1/2 to 1 teaspoon cayenne pepper
4 pounds frozen chicken drumettes *or* wingettes, thawed

In a bowl, combine the syrup, chili sauce, chives, soy sauce, mustard and cayenne. Set aside 2/3 cup for basting. Divide remaining marinade between two large resealable plastic bags; add chicken. Seal bags and turn to coat. Cover and refrigerate for 1 hour.

Drain and discard marinade. Place chicken in two greased 15-in. x 10-in. x 1-in. baking pans. Bake, uncovered, at 375° for 30 minutes; drain. Turn chicken over; baste with some of the reserved marinade. Bake for 10 minutes; turn and baste again. Bake 10-15 minutes longer or until juices run clear and sauce is thickened. **Yield:** about 4 dozen.

Crowd-Pleasin' Muffuletta

(Pictured at right and on page 60)

A garlic-olive paste is the delicious difference in this hearty make-ahead sandwich.
—Jeannie Yee, Fremont, California

1 cup stuffed olives, finely chopped
1 cup pitted ripe olives, finely chopped
2/3 cup olive oil
1/2 cup chopped roasted sweet red peppers
3 tablespoons minced fresh parsley
2 tablespoons red wine vinegar
3 garlic cloves, minced
1 round loaf (2 pounds) unsliced Italian bread
1 pound thinly sliced deli turkey
12 ounces thinly sliced mozzarella cheese (about 16 slices)
1 pound thinly sliced hard salami
1 pound thinly sliced deli ham

In a large bowl, combine the first seven ingredients; set aside. Cut bread in half horizontally. Carefully hollow out top and bottom, leaving a 1-in. shell (save removed bread for another use).

Spread 1-1/2 cups olive mixture over bottom of bread shell. Spread remaining olive mixture over top of bread shell. In bottom of bread, layer the turkey, half of the cheese, salami, remaining cheese and ham. Replace bread top. Wrap tightly in plastic wrap. Refrigerate for 4 hours or overnight. Cut into wedges to serve. **Yield:** 12-14 servings.

Meatless Muffuletta

IF YOU PREFER, make Crowd-Pleasin' Muffuletta without meat. Replace the turkey, salami and ham with grilled portobello mushroom caps, fresh tomato slices and spinach leaves. You could also sprinkle some drained and rinsed cannellini beans on top.

Old-Fashioned Potato Salad

I've been making this comforting salad since I was old enough to help Mom in the kitchen.
—Karen Taylor-Guthrie, Cedar Point, North Carolina

3 tablespoons sugar
4-1/2 teaspoons all-purpose flour
3 teaspoons salt, *divided*
3/4 cup milk
1 egg, lightly beaten
1/4 cup cider vinegar
1 tablespoon prepared mustard
5 pounds red potatoes
12 hard-cooked eggs
3 cups finely chopped celery
1 medium sweet onion, finely chopped
2 cups mayonnaise
3/4 teaspoon pepper

In a small saucepan, combine the sugar, flour and 1 teaspoon salt. Stir in milk until smooth. Cook and stir over medium-high heat until thickened and bubbly. Reduce heat; cook and stir 2 minutes longer.

Remove from the heat. Stir a small amount of hot mixture into egg; return all to the pan, stirring constantly. Bring to a gentle boil; cook and stir 2 minutes longer. Remove from the heat. Gently stir in vinegar and mustard. Cool without stirring to room temperature.

Cut potatoes into 1/2-in. cubes; place in a large kettle and cover with water. Bring to a boil. Reduce heat; cover and simmer for 8-10 minutes or until tender. Drain; rinse in cold water and drain again.

Set aside one hard-cooked egg for garnish; chop the remaining eggs. In a large bowl, combine the potatoes, chopped eggs, celery and onion. Whisk the mayonnaise, pepper and remaining salt into cooled milk mixture. Pour over potato mixture; toss gently to coat. Cover and refrigerate for at least 2 hours. Garnish with reserved egg. **Yield:** 22 servings.

Southern Barbecued Pork

My dear friend Ruby gave me this authentic recipe when my family lived in North Carolina. Ruby has since passed away and we've moved North, but these zesty sandwiches bring back memories!
—Sue Alleva, Lake Elmo, Minnesota

1 boneless pork shoulder roast (3 to 4 pounds), trimmed
1 large onion, chopped
1 cup white vinegar
1/2 cup Worcestershire sauce
1/2 cup ketchup
3 tablespoons brown sugar
3 tablespoons ground mustard
1 teaspoon salt
1/2 teaspoon cayenne pepper
12 kaiser rolls, split
3 cups deli coleslaw, optional

Place the pork roast and onion in a Dutch oven. In a small bowl, whisk the vinegar, Worcestershire sauce, ketchup, brown sugar, mustard, salt and cayenne; pour over roast. Cover and bake at 325° for 3-4 hours or until meat is very tender.

Remove roast; shred meat with two forks. Skim fat from pan juices. Return meat to the pan. Use a slotted spoon to serve on rolls. Top with coleslaw if desired. **Yield:** 12 servings.

Cherry Cream Trifle

(Pictured at right)

Not only is this dessert cool and creamy, it's a conversation piece when presented in a punch bowl!
—Juanita Davis, Martin, Tennessee

1 package (18-1/4 ounces) yellow cake mix
2 packages (3.4 ounces *each*) instant vanilla pudding mix
2 cans (21 ounces *each*) cherry pie filling
2 cans (20 ounces *each*) crushed pineapple, drained
2 cartons (16 ounces *each*) frozen whipped topping, thawed
2 cups chopped pecans

Prepare and bake cake according to package directions for a 13-in. x 9-in. x 2-in. pan. Cool on a wire rack. Prepare pudding according to package directions.

Cut cake into 1-1/2-in. cubes; place a third of the cubes in an 8-qt. punch bowl. Top with a third of the pie filling, pineapple, pudding, whipped topping and pecans; repeat layers twice. Cover and refrigerate until serving. **Yield:** 25-30 servings.

Sweet 'n' Spicy Meatballs

(Pictured on page 61)

You'll usually find a batch of these meatballs in my freezer. The slightly sweet sauce nicely complements the spicy pork sausage.
—Genie Brown, Roanoke, Virginia

2 pounds bulk hot pork sausage
1 egg, lightly beaten
1 cup packed brown sugar
1 cup red wine vinegar
1 cup ketchup
1 tablespoon soy sauce
1 teaspoon ground ginger

In a large bowl, combine the sausage and egg. Shape into 1-in. balls. Place on a greased rack in a shallow baking pan. Bake at 400° for 15-20 minutes or until meat is no longer pink; drain. Meanwhile, in a saucepan, combine the brown sugar, vinegar, ketchup, soy sauce and ginger. Bring to a boil. Reduce heat; simmer, uncovered, until sugar is dissolved.

Transfer meatballs to a 3-qt. slow cooker. Add the sauce and stir gently to coat. Cover and keep warm on low until serving. **Yield:** about 4 dozen.

Cream-Filled Cake Bars

This recipe has been circulated around our church for years. Keep a batch in the freezer for a cool summer snack at the ready.
—Pearl Stuenkel, Spokane Valley, Washington

1 package (18-1/4 ounces) chocolate cake mix
1-1/3 cups water
1/2 cup vegetable oil
3 eggs
FILLING:
5 tablespoons all-purpose flour
1-1/2 cups milk
1 cup shortening
1/2 cup butter, softened
1 cup sugar
1 teaspoon vanilla extract
FROSTING:
1 cup sugar
1 cup packed brown sugar
1/2 cup butter, cubed
1/2 cup milk
1 cup (6 ounces) semisweet chocolate chips
1 teaspoon vanilla extract

In a large mixing bowl, combine the cake mix, water, oil and eggs. Pour into two greased 13-in. x 9-in. x 2-in. baking pans. Bake at 350° for 18-20 minutes or until a toothpick inserted near the center comes out clean. Cool on wire racks.

For filling, in a small saucepan, combine flour and milk until smooth. Bring to a boil; cook and stir for 2 minutes or until thickened. Cool. In another mixing bowl, cream the shortening, butter and sugar. Add the cooled milk mixture and vanilla; beat until smooth and fluffy, about 5 minutes. Spread evenly over cakes. Cover and refrigerate for 1 hour.

For frosting, in a large saucepan, combine the sugars, butter and milk. Bring to a boil; cook and stir for 2 minutes or until sugar is dissolved. Remove from the heat. Add chocolate chips and vanilla; stir until chips are melted. Transfer to a large mixing bowl; cool to room temperature. Beat on medium speed until light and fluffy. Spread over filling. Cut into bars. **Yield:** about 3 dozen.

Praline Cereal Crunch

A sweet and salty snack like this is hard to resist. The recipe makes 10 cups, so it's great to make when hosting a party.
—Gelene Bolin, Paradise, California

8 cups Crispix cereal
2 cups pecan halves
1/2 cup packed brown sugar
1/2 cup light corn syrup
1/2 cup butter, cubed
1 teaspoon vanilla extract
1/2 teaspoon baking soda

In a 13-in. x 9-in. x 2-in. baking pan, combine cereal and pecans; set aside. In a microwave-safe bowl, combine the brown sugar, corn syrup and butter. Microwave, uncovered, on high for 2 to 2-1/2 minutes or until mixture comes to a boil, stirring occasionally. Stir in vanilla and baking soda.

Pour over cereal mixture; stir to coat evenly. Bake at 250° for 1 hour, stirring every 20 minutes. Turn onto waxed paper to cool. Break into bite-size pieces. **Yield:** 10 cups.

Artichoke Veggie Pizza

(Pictured at right)

Our Test Kitchen home economists used sun-dried tomato spread as the base for this vegetable-laden appetizer.

1 tube (13.8 ounces) refrigerated pizza crust
1 package (8 ounces) cream cheese, softened
1/2 cup sun-dried tomato spread
1 can (14 ounces) water-packed artichoke hearts, rinsed, drained and finely chopped
1/2 cup chopped sweet onion
1 can (4-1/4 ounces) chopped ripe olives, drained
3/4 cup sliced carrots
3/4 cup chopped green pepper
1-1/2 cups fresh broccoli florets, chopped
1 cup (4 ounces) shredded Italian-blend cheese

Press pizza dough into a greased 15-in. x 10-in. x 1-in. baking pan. Prick dough thoroughly with a fork. Bake at 400° for 13-15 minutes or until golden brown. Cool.

In a small mixing bowl, beat cream cheese and tomato spread until blended. Stir in the artichokes. Spread over crust. Sprinkle with onion, olives, carrots, green pepper, broccoli and cheese; press down lightly. Chill for 1 hour. Cut into squares. Refrigerate leftovers. **Yield:** 3 dozen.

Saucy Baked Beans

My family enjoys these baked beans with corn bread, but they also round out any cookout. Canned pork and beans make preparation easy.
—Phyllis Schmalz, Kansas City, Kansas

2 cans (31 ounces *each*) pork and beans
1-1/2 cups packed brown sugar
1/2 pound sliced bacon, cooked and crumbled
1 cup finely chopped onion
1 cup ketchup
1 cup cola
2 tablespoons ground mustard

In a large bowl, combine all ingredients. Pour into a greased 3-qt. baking dish. Bake, uncovered, at 325° for 1-1/4 hours or until bubbly. **Yield:** 12-15 servings.

Greek Tortellini Salad

A bold homemade dressing gives this pasta salad a burst of flavor. Watch it disappear from your buffet table!
—Sue Braunschweig, Delafield, Wisconsin

16 to 18 ounces refrigerated *or* frozen cheese tortellini
1 medium sweet red pepper, julienned
1 medium green pepper, julienned
3/4 cup sliced red onion
1/4 cup sliced ripe olives
1/2 cup olive oil
1/2 cup white wine vinegar
3 tablespoons minced fresh mint *or* 1 tablespoon dried mint flakes
3 tablespoons lemon juice
1-1/2 teaspoons seasoned salt
1 teaspoon garlic powder
1/2 teaspoon pepper
1/8 to 1/4 teaspoon crushed red pepper flakes
1/2 cup crumbled feta cheese

Cook tortellini according to package directions; drain and rinse in cold water. In a large bowl, combine the tortellini, peppers, onion and olives.

In a jar with a tight-fitting lid, combine the oil, vinegar, mint, lemon juice, seasoned salt, garlic powder, pepper and pepper flakes; shake well. Pour over salad and toss to coat. Cover and refrigerate for at least 4 hours. Just before serving, sprinkle with feta cheese. **Yield:** 10 servings.

Grade-A Graduation Party!

Get the Grad's Input. Ask the graduate if he or she would like a big bash with lots of relatives and friends or a more intimate gathering with immediate family.

Pick a Date. With last-minute school events, work schedules and other graduation parties to attend, choosing a date may be your biggest challenge. Consider hosting the party later in the summer when you're less harried and when most other parties have already taken place.

Chose a Setting. Backyards and parks are great places to host a casual graduation party. Make sure to offer enough seating and some shelter from bad weather. (Consider renting tables, chairs and even a tent.) If you'll be going to a restaurant, call for reservations well in advance.

Pick a Theme. Although school colors are a natural choice when decorating for a graduation party, the sky's the limit so get as creative as you desire!

Spotlight the grad with a table filled with memorabilia...awards and honors, prom photos, senior pictures, diploma, mortarboard, pompons, yearbooks, pennants, etc.

Address and Mail Invitations. Most schools offer graduation announcements and invitations, which gives you one less thing to think about. (But again, feel free to be creative!) Send out the invitations about 4 weeks before the party. Include directions or small maps if you're expecting out-of-town guests.

Plan the Menu. When hosting a party for a large group, buffets are the way to go. There's no serving involved, which allows you to mingle while keeping an eye on the table for refills. Look for recipes that can be prepared ahead. Save foods with lots of last-minute preparation for smaller, intimate gatherings.

Graduation Caps

(Pictured at right)

I made these cute treats for my daughter's graduation. They really topped off the party fun!
—Margy Stief, Essington, Pennsylvania

24 miniature peanut butter cups
1 tube (6 ounces) decorating frosting in color of your choice
24 After Eight thin mints
24 milk chocolate M&M's in color of your choice *or* 24 semisweet chocolate chips

Remove paper liners from peanut butter cups; place upside down on waxed paper. Place a small amount of frosting on each peanut butter cup; center a mint on each. Using frosting, make a loop for the cap's tassel. Place an M&M on top of loop. **Yield:** 2 dozen.

Summer Entertaining

Memorial Day Get-Together

IT'S TEMPTING to treat Memorial Day simply as the unofficial start of summer.

But when you gather with family and friends over this long weekend, take time to remember those who lost their lives defending our country.

One way to pay tribute is by planning a picnic with an all-American meal.

Topped with Sweet Brown Mustard and Pepper Onion Saute, Grilled Seasoned Bratwurst will shine in this stars-and-stripes menu.

Instead of making an ordinary green salad, display Tomato Zucchini Salad on a pretty platter.

Guests will be in their glory when you tap into Lemon Chiffon Blueberry Dessert. (All recipes shown at right.)

Patriotic Picnic

(Clockwise from bottom)

Tomato Zucchini Salad (p. 76)

Grilled Seasoned Bratwurst with Sweet Brown Mustard (p. 74)

Pepper Onion Saute (p. 74)

Lemon Chiffon Blueberry Dessert (p. 75)

Grilled Seasoned Bratwurst

(Pictured on page 72)

Whether you're hosting a picnic at home or at a park, our Test Kitchen home economists suggest cooking the bratwurst on the stovetop first. Then you can quickly brown them on the grill.

- **8 uncooked bratwurst links**
- **3 cans (12 ounces *each*) beer *or* nonalcoholic beer**
- **1 large onion, halved and sliced**
- **2 tablespoons fennel seed**
- **8 bratwurst sandwich buns, split**

Place the bratwurst in a large saucepan or Dutch oven; add the beer, onion and fennel. Bring to a boil. Reduce heat; cover and simmer for 8-10 minutes or until meat is no longer pink. Drain and discard beer mixture.

Grill bratwurst, covered, over indirect medium heat for 7-8 minutes or until browned. Serve on buns. **Yield:** 8 servings.

Sweet Brown Mustard

(Pictured on page 73)

This versatile sweet and slightly spicy mustard goes well with a variety of meats.
—Rhonda Holloway, Port Richey, Florida

- **1 can (14 ounces) sweetened condensed milk**
- **1 cup spicy brown mustard**
- **2 tablespoons prepared horseradish**
- **2 tablespoons Worcestershire sauce**

In a small bowl, combine all of the ingredients until smooth. Cover and store in the refrigerator for up to 2 weeks. **Yield:** 2-1/3 cups.

Pepper Onion Saute

(Pictured on page 73)

Dress up brats and burgers with this colorful condiment that combines sweet onions and red peppers.
—Pati Fried, Oakland, California

- **2 large onions, sliced**
- **1/2 teaspoon Italian seasoning**
- **2 tablespoons olive oil**
- **2 large sweet red peppers, julienned**

In a large skillet, saute onions and Italian seasoning in oil until tender. Add peppers. Saute until onions begin to brown. **Yield:** 8-10 servings.

Lemon Chiffon Blueberry Dessert

(Pictured at right and on page 73)

This cool and creamy no-bake dessert is perfect for hot summer days. I sometimes replace raspberries for half of the blueberries to make it look more patriotic.
—Jodie Cederquist, Muskegon, Michigan

1-1/2 cups graham cracker crumbs (about 24 squares)
1-1/3 cups sugar, *divided*
1/2 cup butter, melted
1-1/2 cups fresh blueberries, *divided*
1 package (3 ounces) lemon gelatin
1 cup boiling water
2 packages (one 8 ounces, one 3 ounces) cream cheese, softened
1 teaspoon vanilla extract
1 carton (16 ounces) frozen whipped topping, thawed

In a small bowl, combine the cracker crumbs, 1/3 cup sugar and butter. Set aside 2 tablespoons for topping. Press the remaining crumb mixture into a 13-in. x 9-in. x 2-in. dish. Sprinkle with 1 cup blueberries.

In a small bowl, dissolve gelatin in boiling water; cool. In a large mixing bowl, beat cream cheese and remaining sugar. Add vanilla; mix well. Slowly add dissolved gelatin. Fold in whipped topping. Spread over blueberries. Sprinkle with reserved crumb mixture and remaining blueberries. Cover and refrigerate for 3 hours or until set. Refrigerate leftovers. **Yield:** 12-15 servings.

Tomato Zucchini Salad

(Pictured on page 73)

If making this pretty vegetable salad for a potluck, make sure you use a platter with raised sides to prevent it from spilling when transporting it.
—Charlotte Bryont, Greensburg, Kentucky

4 medium zucchini, cut into 1/4-inch slices
3 medium tomatoes, cut into 1/4-inch slices
1/3 cup vegetable oil
3 tablespoons white vinegar
1-1/2 teaspoons lemon juice
1 teaspoon sugar
1/2 teaspoon salt
1/2 teaspoon ground mustard
1/2 teaspoon dried oregano
1/4 teaspoon coarsely ground pepper
Pitted ripe olives

Place 1 in. of water and zucchini in a skillet; bring to a boil. Reduce heat; cover and simmer for 2-3 minutes or until crisp-tender. Drain and pat dry. Arrange zucchini and tomatoes in alternating circles on a serving platter.

In a jar with a tight-fitting lid, combine the oil, vinegar, lemon juice, sugar, salt, mustard, oregano and pepper; shake well. Drizzle over zucchini and tomatoes. Cover and refrigerate for at least 2 hours. Place olives in center of vegetables. **Yield:** 6 servings.

Summer Squash Secrets

SUMMER SQUASH have edible thin skins and soft seeds. Zucchini, pattypan and crookneck are the most common varieties.

Choose firm summer squash with brightly colored skin that's free from spots and bruises. Generally, the smaller the squash, the more tender it will be. Refrigerate summer squash in a plastic bag for up to 5 days.

Before using, wash squash and trim both ends. If using sliced summer squash in salads or stir-fries, blot dry with a paper towel.

One pound summer squash equals about 3 medium or 2-1/2 cups chopped.

Memorable Dill Dip

It's nice to rely on a classic recipe like this when hosting a get-together.
—Bonnie Davis, Easton, Pennsylvania

1 cup (8 ounces) sour cream
1 cup mayonnaise
1 tablespoon dried minced onion
1 tablespoon dried parsley flakes
1 tablespoon dill weed
1/4 teaspoon celery salt
1/4 teaspoon garlic powder
1/4 teaspoon coarsely ground pepper
1/8 teaspoon sugar
Assorted fresh vegetables

In a bowl, combine the first nine ingredients. Cover and refrigerate overnight. Serve with vegetables. **Yield:** 2 cups.

Vegetable Shrimp Salad

(Pictured at right)

With shrimp, asparagus and a blend of peppers, this refreshing salad is not only delicious but pleasing to the eye as well!
—Elizabeth Rivera Ortiz
Jayuya, Puerto Rico

1 cup uncooked long grain rice
1/4 pound fresh asparagus, cut into 1-inch pieces
3/4 pound cooked medium shrimp, peeled and deveined
2 jars (7-1/2 ounces *each*) marinated artichoke hearts, drained
1/4 pound fresh snow peas, cut into 1-inch pieces
1/2 cup *each* julienned sweet red, yellow and green pepper
4 green onions, thinly sliced
1 celery rib, sliced
1/4 cup olive oil
3 tablespoons lemon juice
1 tablespoon minced fresh parsley
1 tablespoon soy sauce
1/2 teaspoon lemon-pepper seasoning
Salt and pepper to taste

Cook rice according to package directions; drain and rinse with cold water. Place in a large serving bowl; cool. Place the asparagus in a small saucepan; add a small amount of water. Bring to a boil; cook for 3 minutes. Drain and rinse with cold water.

Add the asparagus, shrimp, artichokes, snow peas, peppers, onions and celery to the rice. In a small bowl, whisk the oil, lemon juice, parsley, soy sauce, lemon-pepper, salt and pepper. Pour over shrimp mixture and toss gently. Chill until serving. **Yield:** 6 servings.

Confetti Guacamole

Whenever I make this colorful guacamole for summer get-togethers, I'm sure to double the recipe because one batch just isn't enough!
—Cindy Colley, Othello, Washington

2 medium ripe avocados, peeled
1 cup frozen corn, thawed
1 cup canned black beans, rinsed and drained
1 medium tomato, peeled, seeded and diced
1/4 cup lemon juice
1 tablespoon chopped green onion
1 jalapeno pepper, seeded and chopped*
1/2 to 1 teaspoon minced garlic
1/2 teaspoon salt
Corn *or* tortilla chips

In a bowl, mash the avocados. Gently stir in the corn, beans, tomato, lemon juice, onion, jalapeno, garlic and salt. Serve immediately with chips. **Yield:** 3-1/2 cups.

***Editor's Note:** When cutting or seeding hot peppers, use rubber or plastic gloves to protect your hands. Avoid touching your face.

Seeding a Jalapeno Pepper

TO REDUCE the heat of jalapenos and other hot peppers, cut the peppers in half; remove and discard the seeds and membranes. If you like very spicy foods, add the seeds to the dish you're making instead of discarding them.

Ham 'n' Swiss Potato Salad

With red potatoes, ham, Swiss cheese and olives, this potato salad stands out from any others. I submitted the recipe to our kitchen at work, and now it's on the cafeteria menu!
—Jauneen Hosking, Greenfield, Wisconsin

3 pounds unpeeled small red potatoes, cooked and sliced
1/2 pound Swiss cheese, cut into 1/2-inch cubes
1-1/2 cups mayonnaise
1 teaspoon salt
1 teaspoon minced chives
1/4 teaspoon white pepper
1/4 teaspoon cayenne pepper
1/2 cup cubed fully cooked ham
1 can (2-1/4 ounces) sliced ripe olives, drained

In a large bowl, combine the potatoes and cheese. In a small bowl, combine the mayonnaise, salt, chives, white pepper and cayenne; pour over potato mixture and toss gently to coat. Gently fold in the ham and olives. Cover and chill for 4 hours or until serving. **Yield:** 12 servings.

Antipasto-Stuffed Baguettes

(Pictured at right)

These Italian-style sandwiches can be served as an appetizer or as a light lunch. A homemade olive paste makes every bite delicious.
—Dianne Holmgren, Prescott, Arizona

1 can (2-1/4 ounces) sliced ripe olives, drained
2 tablespoons olive oil
1 teaspoon lemon juice
1 garlic clove, minced
1/8 teaspoon *each* dried basil, thyme, marjoram and rosemary, crushed
2 French bread baguettes (8 ounces *each*)
1 package (4 ounces) crumbled feta cheese
1/4 pound thinly sliced Genoa salami
1 cup packed fresh baby spinach
1 jar (7-1/4 ounces) roasted red peppers, drained and chopped
1 can (14 ounces) water-packed artichoke hearts, drained and chopped

In a blender or food processor, combine the olives, oil, lemon juice, garlic and herbs; cover and process until olives are chopped. Set aside 1/3 cup olive mixture (refrigerate remaining mixture for another use).

Cut the top third off each baguette; carefully hollow out bottoms, leaving a 1/4-in. shell (discard removed bread or save for another use). Spread olive mixture in the bottom of each loaf. Sprinkle with feta cheese. Fold salami slices in half and place over cheese. Top with the spinach, red peppers and artichokes, pressing down as necessary. Replace bread tops. Wrap loaves tightly in foil. Refrigerate for at least 3 hours or overnight.

Serve cold, or place foil-wrapped loaves on a baking sheet and bake at 350° for 20-25 minutes or until heated through. Cut into slices; secure with a toothpick. **Yield:** 3 dozen.

Editor's Note: 1/3 cup purchased tapenade (olive paste) may be substituted for the olive mixture.

Peanut Butter Oatmeal Cookies

These soft cookies are a favorite of relatives and friends. When I double the recipe and take them to work, they always disappear.
—Kristi Christianson, East Grand Forks, Minnesota

1 jar (12 ounces) peanut butter
1/2 cup butter, softened
1 cup plus 2 tablespoons packed brown sugar
1 cup sugar
3 eggs
2 teaspoons baking soda
3/4 teaspoon vanilla extract
3/4 teaspoon corn syrup
4-1/2 cups quick-cooking oats
1 cup (6 ounces) miniature semisweet chocolate chips
1/2 cup English toffee bits *or* almond brickle chips

In a large mixing bowl, cream the peanut butter, butter and sugars. Add eggs, one at a time, beating well after each addition. Beat in baking soda, vanilla and corn syrup. Stir in the oats, chips and toffee bits.

Drop by rounded tablespoonfuls 2 in. apart onto greased baking sheets. Bake at 350° for 10-12 minutes or until lightly browned. Cool for 1 minute before removing to wire racks. **Yield:** about 6-1/2 dozen.

Editor's Note: Reduced-fat or generic brands of peanut butter are not recommended for this recipe. This recipe does not use flour.

Bacon-Wrapped Beef Patties

My family loves these spruced-up hamburgers all year long. Bacon flavors the meat and adds a tasty twist.
—Jody Bahler, Wolcott, Indiana

1 cup (4 ounces) shredded cheddar cheese
2/3 cup chopped onion
1/4 cup ketchup
2 eggs, lightly beaten
3 tablespoons Worcestershire sauce
2 tablespoons grated Parmesan cheese
1 teaspoon seasoned salt
1/4 teaspoon pepper
2 pounds ground beef
10 bacon strips
10 hamburger buns, split, optional

In a bowl, combine the first eight ingredients. Crumble beef over mixture and mix well. Shape into ten 3/4-in.-thick patties. Wrap each patty with a bacon strip; secure with toothpicks.

Grill patties, uncovered, over medium heat for 5-6 minutes on each side or until juices run clear and a meat thermometer reads 160°. Serve on buns if desired. **Yield:** 10 servings.

Banana Split Ice Cream

(Pictured at right)

Summer celebrations with my family aren't complete until I dish out tasty homemade ice cream. This recipe from my mom is a favorite.
—Kara Cook, Elk Ridge, Utah

3/4 cup plus 2 tablespoons sugar
1 cup water
1 cup milk
2 cups miniature marshmallows
4 teaspoons lemon juice
1 can (8 ounces) crushed pineapple, undrained
2 medium ripe bananas, finely chopped
1/2 cup chopped maraschino cherries, drained and patted dry
1 cup heavy whipping cream, whipped
Chocolate syrup

In a heavy saucepan, bring the sugar, water and milk to a boil. Reduce heat; cook until sugar is dissolved. Add marshmallows and stir until melted. Remove from the heat; cool for 15 minutes. Stir in lemon juice. Cover and refrigerate for 8 hours or overnight.

Stir in the pineapple, bananas and cherries. Fold in whipped cream. Fill cylinder of ice cream freezer two-thirds full; freeze according to manufacturer's directions. Refrigerate remaining mixture until ready to freeze. Allow to ripen in ice cream freezer or firm up in the refrigerator freezer for 2-4 hours before serving. Serve with chocolate syrup. **Yield:** 1-1/2 quarts.

Remembering the Meaning of Memorial Day

ALTHOUGH Memorial Day has simply come to symbolize the start of summer for many people, its true purpose is to honor the men and women who lost their lives while serving our country.

Here are a few ways you can observe the real meaning of Memorial Day with your family:

- Take time to explain the meaning of Memorial Day to children or grandchildren.
- Proudly fly the American flag.
- Take your family to a Memorial Day parade in your community.
- Place a donation in an American Legion kettle and get a red poppy for your lapel.
- Make a point of attending a ceremony at the local war memorial.
- Stop by a local cemetery and place flags on the graves of fallen soldiers.

Backyard Hawaiian Luau

IF YOU'RE not planning a trip to Hawaii any time soon, bring the flavors of the Pacific Rim to your own backyard!

It's easy to re-create the lavish luaus in Hawaii with the luscious on-the-deck dinner shown here.

Say "Aloha" to guests as they arrive out back by offering them a tall glass of Luau Refresher.

Grilled Mahi Mahi showcases a fabulous fruit salsa, which is a pleasing complement to the mild fish flavor.

Macadamia Citrus Couscous is a special side dish that can either be served warm or chilled.

A breathtaking bounty of fresh fruit rounds out the delightful dinner.

A Taste of the Tropics

(Top to bottom)

Luau Refresher (p. 85)

Macadamia Citrus Couscous (p. 86)

Grilled Mahi Mahi (p. 84)

Grilled Mahi Mahi

(Pictured on page 82)

Instead of grilling out the usual hamburgers or chicken breasts, prepare this mahi mahi from our Test Kitchen and reel in raves!

- **3/4 cup reduced-sodium teriyaki sauce**
- **2 tablespoons sherry *or* pineapple juice**
- **2 garlic cloves, minced**
- **8 mahi mahi fillets (6 ounces *each*)**

TROPICAL FRUIT SALSA:

- **1 medium mango, peeled and diced**
- **1 cup diced seeded peeled papaya**
- **3/4 cup chopped green pepper**
- **1/2 cup cubed fresh pineapple**
- **1/2 medium red onion, chopped**
- **1/4 cup minced fresh cilantro**
- **1/4 cup minced fresh mint**
- **1 tablespoon chopped seeded jalapeno pepper**
- **1 tablespoon lime juice**
- **1 tablespoon lemon juice**
- **1/2 teaspoon crushed red pepper flakes**

In a large resealable plastic bag, combine the teriyaki sauce, sherry or pineapple juice and garlic; add mahi mahi. Seal bag and turn to coat; refrigerate for 30 minutes. In a bowl, combine the salsa ingredients. Cover and refrigerate until serving.

Coat grill rack with nonstick cooking spray before starting the grill. Drain and discard marinade. Grill mahi mahi, covered, over medium heat for 4-5 minutes on each side or until fish flakes easily with a fork. Serve with salsa. **Yield:** 8 servings.

Editor's Note: When cutting or seeding hot peppers, use rubber or plastic gloves to protect your hands. Avoid touching your face.

Frozen Coconut Dessert

A crunchy coconut and macadamia nut garnish pairs well with this cool and creamy dessert.
—Charlotte Mallet-Prevost, Frederick, Maryland

- **1-1/3 cups water**
- **2/3 cup sugar**
- **2-1/3 cups flaked coconut, *divided***
- **2 teaspoons vanilla extract**
- **1 pint heavy whipping cream**
- **1/3 cup coarsely chopped macadamia nuts**

In a large saucepan, bring water and sugar to a boil. Cook, uncovered, for 5 minutes. Cool. Stir in 2 cups coconut and vanilla. In a small mixing bowl, beat cream until soft peaks form; fold into coconut mixture. Pour into serving dishes. Cover and freeze overnight.

Remove from the freezer 45 minutes before serving. Toast the remaining coconut; sprinkle over dessert. Top with macadamia nuts. **Yield:** 8 servings.

Luau Refresher

(Pictured at right and on page 82)

To tie into our tropical feast, our home economists created this recipe featuring passion fruit juice. For the most fizz, stir in the soda just before serving.

4-1/2 cups sweet white wine, chilled
3 cups passion fruit juice blend, chilled
3 tablespoons lemon juice
3 tablespoons lime juice
1-1/2 cups grapefruit soda *or* citrus soda, chilled
Ice cubes

In a 3-qt. pitcher or punch bowl, combine the wine and juices. Stir in soda. Serve over ice. **Yield:** 9 servings.

Cucumber Whimsies

During the heat of summer, it's nice to offer lighter fare. These cold snacks are a great addition to a picnic buffet.
—Cheryl Stevens, Carrollton, Texas

2 cans (6 ounces *each*) crabmeat, drained, flaked and cartilage removed
1/4 cup mayonnaise
1 small tomato, chopped
2 tablespoons snipped fresh dill
1 green onion, chopped
1 teaspoon grated lemon peel
1/8 teaspoon cayenne pepper
Dash salt
3 medium cucumbers, cut into 1/4-inch slices
Lemon-pepper seasoning
Dill sprigs

In a bowl, combine the first eight ingredients. Cover and refrigerate for 1 hour. Sprinkle cucumber slices with lemon-pepper. Top each with about 1-1/2 teaspoons crab mixture; garnish with a dill sprig. Refrigerate until serving. **Yield:** 5 dozen.

Macadamia Citrus Couscous

(Pictured on page 82)

Our Test Kitchen provides this tasty twist on couscous salad. It pairs well with many entrees. Or toss in some cooked shrimp for a meal on the lighter side.

1/4 cup chopped sweet onion
1 garlic clove, minced
1 teaspoon olive oil
1 cup chicken broth
1 cup passion fruit juice blend
1/2 cup orange marmalade
1 tablespoon Worcestershire sauce
1 tablespoon minced fresh gingerroot
Dash cayenne pepper
1 package (10 ounces) couscous
1 teaspoon grated orange peel
1/2 cup chopped macadamia nuts
1/2 cup orange-flavored dried cranberries
3 tablespoons minced fresh cilantro
3 green onions, sliced

In a large saucepan, saute onion and garlic in oil for 2 minutes or until tender. Add the broth, fruit juice, marmalade, Worcestershire sauce, ginger and cayenne. Bring to a boil; stir in couscous and orange peel. Cover and remove from the heat; let stand for 10 minutes. Stir in the macadamia nuts, cranberries, cilantro and green onions. Serve warm or chilled. **Yield:** 8 servings.

Papaya-Avocado Tossed Salad

Fruit is a terrific addition to green salads in summer. Here our home economists tossed in papaya and avocado.

4 cups torn red leaf lettuce
4 cups torn green leaf lettuce
1 medium papaya, peeled, seeded and sliced
1 large ripe avocado, peeled and sliced
1/2 cup sliced red onion
DRESSING:
1/4 cup olive oil
3 tablespoons lemon juice
1 tablespoon grated lemon peel
2 teaspoons white wine vinegar
1 teaspoon sugar
1/8 teaspoon salt

In a large salad bowl, gently toss the lettuce, papaya, avocado and onion. In a jar with a tight-fitting lid, combine the dressing ingredients; shake well. Drizzle over salad and toss to coat. **Yield:** 8 servings.

Shrimp on Rosemary Skewers

(Pictured at right)

Fresh sprigs of rosemary are the clever skewers for these shrimp kabobs. You can serve this as an appetizer or as a main course.

—Amber Joy Newport
Hampton, Virginia

8 fresh rosemary sprigs, about 6 inches long
1/2 cup orange marmalade
1/2 cup flaked coconut, chopped
1/4 teaspoon crushed red pepper flakes
1/4 teaspoon minced fresh rosemary
1-1/2 pounds uncooked large shrimp, peeled and deveined

Soak rosemary sprigs in water for 30 minutes. In a small bowl, combine the marmalade, coconut, pepper flakes and minced rosemary; set aside 1/4 cup for serving.

Coat grill rack with nonstick cooking spray before starting the grill. Thread shrimp onto rosemary sprigs. Grill for 4 minutes. Turn; baste with some of the remaining marmalade mixture. Grill 3-4 minutes longer or until shrimp turn pink; baste again. Serve with reserved marmalade mixture. **Yield:** 8 servings.

History of the Luau

BEFORE 1819, it was a traditional Hawaiian practice for men and women to dine apart from each other. A feast where King Kamahameha II ate with women was the symbolic act ending this custom... and the luau was born.

A favorite dish at these royal feasts was called luau (a combination of leaves of the taro plant and chicken baked in coconut milk).

Mats were rolled out for people to sit on and the food was eaten with the fingers. Breathtaking centerpieces were made with ferns and native flowers.

Dicing a Mango

MANGOES have a large flat seed that doesn't easily separate from the flesh. So the flesh needs to be cut away from the seed.

1. Slice off one of the wide sides of the mango, cutting as close as possible to the seed. Repeat on the other wide side, then slice off the other two ends.

2. Being careful not to cut through the skin, score the flesh in one direction. Then make perpendicular scores in the opposite direction.

3. With your fingers, push up on the skin so that the mango turns inside out. Slice the diced flesh off of the skin. (A small spoon can also be used to remove the flesh.)

Cutting Up a Fresh Pineapple

IF YOU FAVOR the flavor of fresh pineapple but aren't sure how to cut one up, follow these easy steps!

1. Cut off the top; trim the bottom so the pineapple stands upright. Starting at the top and working down, cut off wide strips of peel all the way around the fruit.

2. Lay the pineapple on its side. Remove the eyes by cutting narrow wedge-shaped grooves diagonally around the fruit, following the pattern of the eyes.

3. Stand the pineapple upright. Starting at the top and working down, slice off one side of the pineapple, cutting as close to the core as possible. Repeat on the remaining three sides. Cut flesh into slices or chunks.

Fruit Platter Centerpiece

(Pictured at right)

FOR A NATURAL centerpiece at your Hawaiian luau, set out a tray topped with a bounty of fresh fruits!

For the photo at right, we included family favorites such as apples, oranges, kiwi, star fruit and cantaloupe. Don't forget tropical favorites like mango, passion fruit and pineapple. (See the hints at left for cutting up mango and pineapple.) You may also want to tuck in bunches of red grapes for a burst of contrasting color.

Instead of tossing out the top of the pineapple, we placed it in the center of our platter, then tucked in fresh edible orchids. (You can also use the orchids to make a lei. See page 88 for instructions.)

Rosemary Pineapple Chicken

I brought this recipe with me from Germany. It's my family's favorite way to eat chicken.
—Christl Haymond, Duvall, Washington

- **4 bone-in chicken breast halves (8 ounces *each*)**
- **1 tablespoon butter**
- **1 teaspoon salt**
- **1/2 teaspoon minced fresh rosemary**
- **1/2 teaspoon ground ginger**
- **1/2 teaspoon paprika**
- **1/4 teaspoon pepper**
- **1 medium onion, thinly sliced and separated into rings**
- **2 cans (6 ounces *each*) unsweetened pineapple juice**

In a large skillet, brown chicken in butter on both sides. Sprinkle with salt, rosemary, ginger, paprika and pepper. Transfer to a greased 13-in. x 9-in. x 2-in. baking dish. Place onion rings over chicken; pour pineapple juice over chicken. Bake, uncovered, at 350° for 45-55 minutes or until chicken juices run clear. **Yield:** 4 servings.

SUMMER *Entertaining*

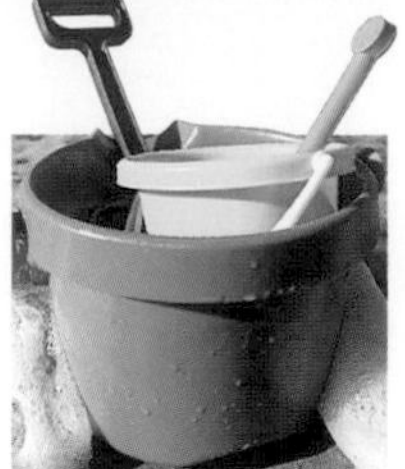

July 4th Ice Cream Social

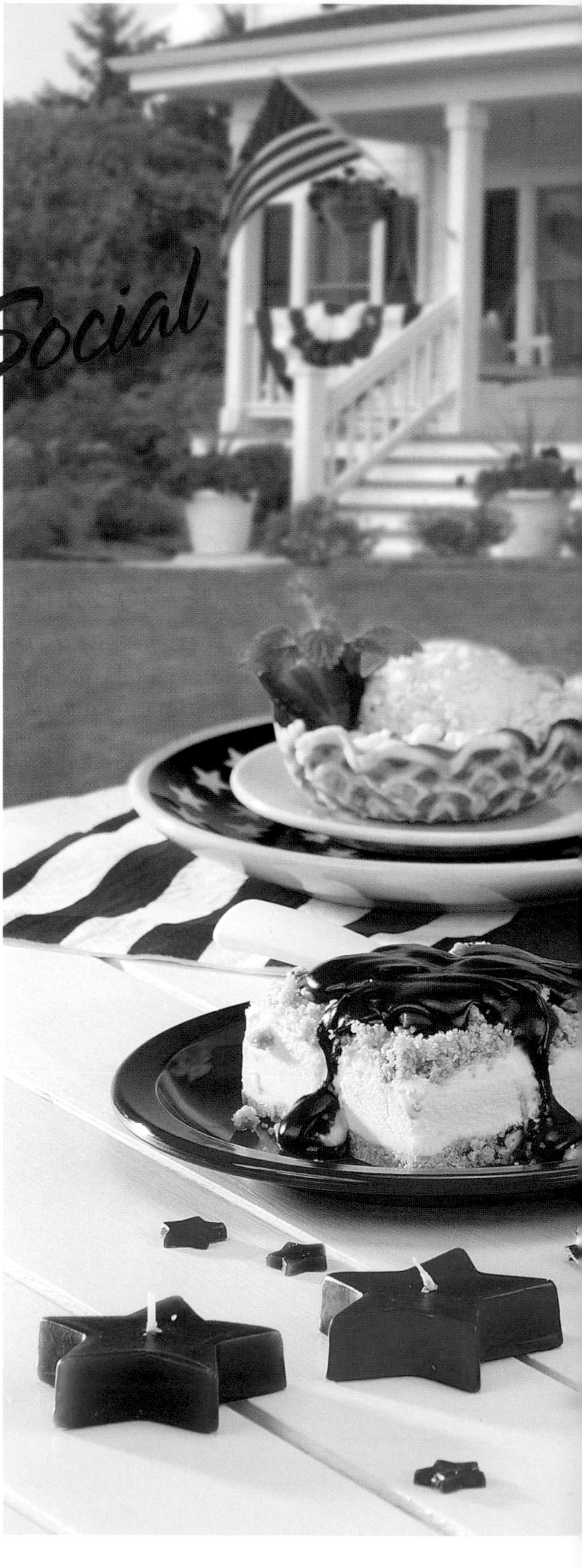

IT SEEMS like the heat of summer has a habit of hitting on Independence Day.

So as you celebrate our country's birthday with family and friends, cool things off with a tried-and-true ice cream social.

Why settle for store-bought when you can serve scoops of tasty Strawberry Ice Cream in homemade Ice Cream Bowls?

Kids will create lasting memories when they sip Old-Fashioned Ice Cream Sodas. (And older "kids" will fondly recall days gone by!)

For a terrific do-ahead treat that can be kept in the freezer for a week, rely on Delicious Ice Cream Dessert. (All recipes shown at right.)

Ice Cream, You Scream!

(Clockwise from top right)

Old-Fashioned Ice Cream Sodas (p. 96)

Strawberry Ice Cream (p. 98) in Ice Cream Bowls (p. 96)

Delicious Ice Cream Dessert (p. 94)

Delicious Ice Cream Dessert

(Pictured on page 92)

We appreciate a cool and creamy dessert like this in summer. It stays fresh in the freezer for one week. Top with the fudgy sauce before serving.
—Mrs. Earl Brewer, Jackson, Mississippi

1 package (12 ounces) vanilla wafers, crushed
1/2 cup chopped pecans
3/4 cup butter, melted
1/2 gallon vanilla ice cream (in rectangular package)
FUDGE TOPPING:
1 cup sugar
5 tablespoons baking cocoa
3 tablespoons all-purpose flour
1 cup milk
2 tablespoons butter, softened

In a bowl, combine the wafer crumbs, pecans and butter. Press half of the mixture into a 13-in. x 9-in. x 2-in. dish. Freeze for 30 minutes. Remove ice cream from package; cut into slices and place over crust. Sprinkle with remaining crumb mixture. Cover and freeze for at least 4 hours.

For topping, combine the sugar, cocoa and flour in a small saucepan; stir in milk until smooth. Bring to a boil, stirring constantly; cook and stir for 2 minutes. Stir in butter. Serve over dessert. **Yield:** 12-16 servings.

Hot Fudge Topping

(Pictured at far right)

I've been making this thick and tasty hot fudge sauce for years. Use it to top ice cream, cake or any other dessert!
—Judy Carl, Duluth, Minnesota

1 package (11-1/2 ounces) milk chocolate chips
4 squares (1 ounce *each*) unsweetened chocolate
1 cup butter, cubed
2 cans (14 ounces *each*) sweetened condensed milk
1/3 cup evaporated milk

In a large saucepan over low heat, combine the chocolate chips, chocolate squares and butter; heat until melted, stirring occasionally. Gradually stir in condensed milk and evaporated milk; heat through. Store leftovers in the refrigerator. **Yield:** 5-1/2 cups.

Mint Chocolate Chip Ice Cream

(Pictured at right)

Our sons enjoy helping me make this rich and creamy ice cream. It's better than any store-bought variety.
—Marcia Peters, Baldwin City, Kansas

2 quarts half-and-half cream
2 cups sugar
1 can (14 ounces) sweetened condensed milk
1 pint heavy whipping cream
1 package (3.4 ounces) instant vanilla pudding mix
3 tablespoons vanilla extract
1 teaspoon peppermint extract
1-1/2 cups miniature semisweet chocolate chips
Green food coloring
Hot Fudge Topping (recipe at left), optional

In a large saucepan, heat half-and-half to 175°. Add sugar and milk; stir until sugar is dissolved. Remove from the heat; cool completely.

In a bowl, whisk whipping cream and pudding mix until smooth (mixture will be thick). Add extracts. Stir into cooled cream mixture. Stir in chocolate chips and enough food coloring to tint mixture light green. Cover and refrigerate for at least 30 minutes.

Fill cylinder of ice cream freezer two-thirds full; freeze according to manufacturer's directions. Refrigerate remaining mixture until ready to freeze, stirring before freezing each batch. Allow to ripen in ice cream freezer or firm up in the refrigerator freezer for 2-4 hours before serving. Serve with Hot Fudge Topping if desired. **Yield:** 3 quarts.

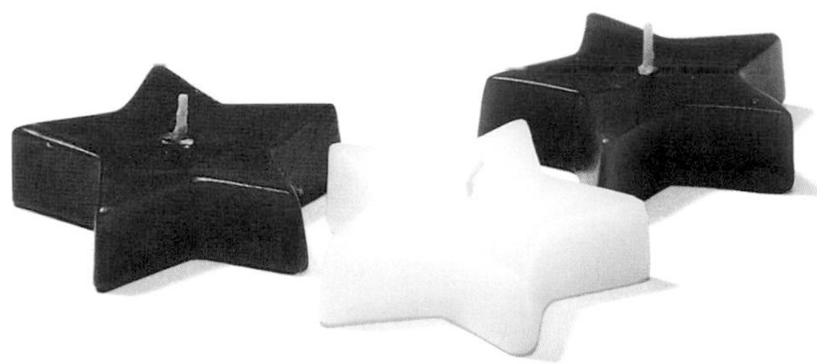

Old-Fashioned Ice Cream Sodas

(Pictured on page 93)

I keep the ingredients for these ice cream sodas on hand so I can enjoy a treat any time I want. You can easily make more when feeding a crowd.
—Anna Erickson, Terrebonne, Oregon

3/4 cup chocolate syrup
1 cup milk
4 cups carbonated water, chilled
8 scoops chocolate *or* vanilla ice cream
Whipped cream in a can, optional

Place 3 tablespoons chocolate syrup in each of four 16-oz. glasses. Add 1/4 cup milk and 1 cup carbonated water to each; stir until foamy. Add two scoops of ice cream to each glass. Top with whipped cream if desired. **Yield:** 4 servings.

Ice Cream Bowls

(Pictured on page 93)

Once you sample these homemade waffle ice cream bowls from our Test Kitchen, you'll want to serve them time and again! You can either prepare them with pretty designs in a special pizzelle cookie maker or without designs in the oven.

3 eggs
3/4 cup sugar
1/2 cup butter, melted
2 teaspoons vanilla extract
1-1/2 cups all-purpose flour
2 teaspoons baking powder

In a small mixing bowl, beat eggs on medium speed until blended. Gradually beat in sugar. Add butter and vanilla. Combine flour and baking powder; gradually add to egg mixture. Invert two 6-oz. custard cups on paper towels; coat with nonstick cooking spray.

Prepare cookies in a preheated pizzelle maker according to manufacturer's directions, using 2 tablespoons batter for each cookie. Immediately remove pizzelles and drape over inverted custard cups. To shape into bowls, place another custard cup coated with nonstick cooking spray over each pizzelle. Let stand until set. Remove from custard cups and set aside.

To make ice cream bowls in the oven, line a baking sheet with parchment paper. Draw two 7-in. circles on paper. Spread 2 tablespoons batter over each circle. Bake at 400° for 4-5 minutes or until edges are golden brown. Immediately remove cookies and drape over inverted custard cups. Shape into bowls as directed above. Store in an airtight container. **Yield:** 16 servings.

Making Ice Cream Bowls

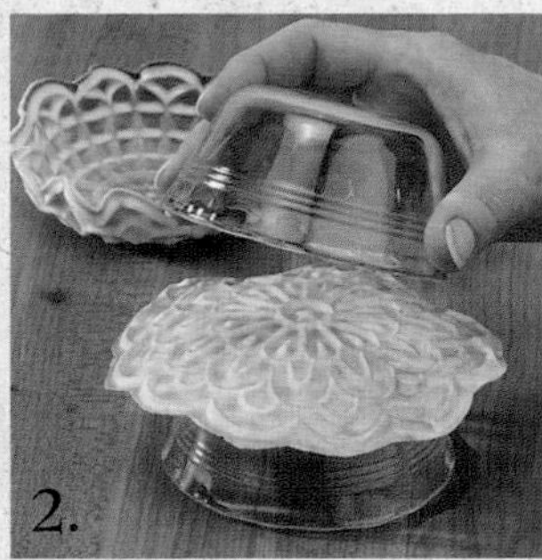

1. Drop 2 tablespoons batter into a hot pizzelle maker; cook until both sides are golden brown. (Follow manufacturer's directions for more details.)

2. Drape hot pizzelle over inverted custard cup; top with another inverted custard cup to form the bowl.

Strawberry Banana Ice Pops

(Pictured at right)

My brothers and sisters (as well as my Dad!) are thrilled when they see me making these ice pops. They can hardly wait for them to set up in the freezer.
—Valerie Belley, St Louis, Missouri

- **1 package (3 ounces) strawberry gelatin**
- **1/2 cup boiling water**
- **1 package (10 ounces) frozen sweetened sliced strawberries, thawed**
- **1 can (8 ounces) crushed pineapple, undrained**
- **1/2 cup mashed ripe banana**
- **1/4 to 1/2 cup chopped walnuts**
- **1 cup (8 ounces) sour cream**
- **1 teaspoon sugar**
- **1/4 teaspoon vanilla extract**
- **12 Popsicle molds *or* plastic cups (3 ounces) and Popsicle sticks**

In a large bowl, dissolve gelatin in boiling water. Stir in the strawberries, pineapple, banana and nuts. Pour 2 cups into a 13-in. x 9-in. x 2-in. dish coated with nonstick cooking spray. Refrigerate until set, about 1 hour. Set remaining gelatin mixture aside.

In a small bowl, combine the sour cream, sugar and vanilla. Spread over gelatin. Top with reserved gelatin mixture. Chill for 1 hour. Spoon 1/3 cup into each mold. Freeze until firm, about 5 hours. **Yield:** 1 dozen.

Strawberry Ice Cream

(Pictured on page 93)

Nothing says "Welcome Home" to out-of-town relatives as well as homemade ice cream. I make this for every family reunion.
—Barbara Sue Jones, Cedar City, Utah

- **2 cups fresh strawberries, crushed**
- **3 cups sugar, *divided***
- **3 tablespoons all-purpose flour**
- **3 cups half-and-half cream**
- **2 eggs, beaten**
- **3 cups heavy whipping cream**
- **1-1/3 cups orange juice**
- **1/2 cup lemon juice**
- **1 teaspoon vanilla extract**

In a small bowl, combine strawberries and 3/4 cup sugar; set aside. In a heavy saucepan, heat the half-and-half to 175°. In a large saucepan, combine the flour and remaining sugar; stir in the half-and-half until smooth.

Whisk a small amount of the hot mixture into eggs. Return all to the pan, whisking constantly. Cook and stir over low heat until mixture reaches at least 160° and coats the back of a metal spoon. Remove from the heat. Cool quickly by placing pan in a bowl of ice water; stir for 2 minutes.

Stir in whipping cream, orange juice, lemon juice, vanilla and reserved strawberry mixture. Press plastic wrap onto surface of custard. Refrigerate for several hours or overnight.

Fill cylinder of ice cream freezer two-thirds full; freeze according to manufacturer's directions. Refrigerate remaining mixture until ready to freeze. Allow to ripen in ice cream freezer or firm up in refrigerator freezer for 2-4 hours before serving. **Yield:** 4-1/2 quarts.

Tropical Sorbet

Every summer when I was young, Mother would serve her special sorbet. The recipe has been in the family for generations.
—Charlene Jackson, Jackson, Mississippi

- **1 cup sugar**
- **1 cup boiling water**
- **1-1/2 cups orange juice**
- **1-1/2 cups mashed ripe bananas (about 3 medium)**
- **2/3 cup lemon juice**
- **1 can (8 ounces) crushed pineapple, undrained**

In a heat-proof bowl, dissolve sugar in boiling water; cool completely. Stir in the remaining ingredients. Chill for several hours. Fill cylinder of ice cream freezer; freeze according to manufacturer's directions. Transfer sorbet to a freezer container; cover and freeze for 4 hours or until firm. Remove from the freezer 10 minutes before serving. **Yield:** about 1-1/2 quarts.

Lemon Ice Cream

(Pictured at right)

Just five ingredients (and no ice cream maker!) are all you need to make this refreshing ice cream. We enjoy generous scoops of it in summer.
—Janet Eisner, Portland, Oregon

1 cup milk
1 cup sugar
1/3 cup lemon juice
1 cup heavy whipping cream
1/2 teaspoon vanilla extract

In a small saucepan, heat milk to 175°; stir in sugar until dissolved. Cool completely. Stir in lemon juice. In a large mixing bowl, beat cream until stiff; fold in vanilla and cooled milk mixture. Pour into a 9-in. square dish. Freeze for 4 hours or until firm, stirring at least once. Remove from the freezer 10 minutes before serving. **Yield:** 1 quart.

Very Berry Topping

Frozen berries allow me to prepare this colorful ice cream sauce all year-round. You can also stir in one 20-ounce can of drained pineapple tidbits.
—Sheri Rarick, Galloway, Ohio

1 package (16 ounces) frozen unsweetened blueberries, thawed
1 package (16 ounces) frozen unsweetened strawberries, thawed
1 package (12 ounces) frozen unsweetened raspberries, thawed
2 cups frozen unsweetened blackberries, thawed
3/4 to 1 cup sugar
3 tablespoons cornstarch

In a large bowl, combine the berries; stir in desired amount of sugar. Let stand for 1 hour. Drain and reserve the juice. Return berries to the bowl; cover and refrigerate.

In a saucepan, combine cornstarch and 1/4 cup reserved juice until smooth. Stir in the remaining juice. Bring to a boil; cook and stir for 2 minutes or until thickened. Remove from the heat. Cool to room temperature, stirring several times. Pour over berries and stir gently. **Yield:** about 6 cups.

Chocolate Fudge Bombe

Four convenience items come together in this easy yet eye-catching dessert. It's a great way to wow guests with little effort.
—Margaret Wilson, Hemet, California

- **1 package fudge brownie mix (13-inch x 9-inch pan size)**
- **1/2 gallon fudge ripple *or* caramel swirl ice cream, softened**
- **3/4 cup chocolate frosting**
- **1 jar (12 ounces) seedless raspberry jam**

Prepare brownie mix for cake-like brownies and bake according to package directions in a greased 13-in. x 9-in. x 2-in. baking pan. Cool completely on a wire rack.

Cut brownies into squares; place on the bottom and up the sides of a 2-1/2-qt. bowl lined with plastic wrap. Spoon ice cream into brownie bowl; cover and freeze for 8 hours or until firm.

Place frosting in a small microwave-safe bowl; cover and microwave on high for 45 seconds or until soft. Invert brownie bombe onto a large plate; spread with frosting. Cut into wedges. Warm the jam; drizzle over dessert plates. Top with a wedge. Serve immediately. **Yield:** 12 servings.

Coffee Ice Cream

My husband doesn't drink coffee, but he can't get enough of this coffee ice cream!
—Esther Bergen, Clarendon Hills, Illinois

- **4 cups milk**
- **2 cups sugar**
- **3 cups cold strong brewed coffee**
- **1 pint heavy whipping cream**
- **2 teaspoons vanilla extract**

In a Dutch oven, heat milk to 175°. Stir in sugar until dissolved; cool. Transfer to a 3-qt. freezer container. Stir in the coffee, cream and vanilla. Cover and freeze for 4-5 hours or until mixture is slushy. Beat with an electric mixer until smooth. Freeze until firm. Remove from the freezer 30 minutes before serving. **Yield:** 12 servings.

Sandwich Your Ice Cream

HOMEMADE ice cream sandwiches are another fun idea for an ice cream social.

Place 1/2 cup of any flavor ice cream on the flat side of a 3-in. cookie of your choice. Place another cookie, bottom side down, on top of the ice cream. Gently press cookies together until ice cream is even with the edges.

If desired, roll edges of the sandwich in toppings (like miniature chocolate chips, chopped nuts and chocolate jimmies) until covered.

Serve immediately or wrap in plastic wrap and freeze.

Creative Ice Cream Cones

(Pictured above)

EVEN an ice cream social can be made special with just a little extra effort. Your guests will be in their glory when they catch sight of assorted decorated ice cream cones at your July Fourth festivities.

Start by purchasing a variety of waffle, cake and sugar cones. Place toppings in separate small bowls. (We used flaked coconut, chopped nuts, colored sprinkles and chocolate jimmies.)

Melt white and/or milk chocolate candy coating; dip the tops of the cones into the melted chocolate. Roll the chocolate-covered top of each cone into toppings of your choice. Set decorated cones in ice cream cone holders until chocolate is set. (If making these cute cones a few days in advance, store in airtight containers at room temperature, using waxed paper to separate layers.)

Peachy Berry Shakes

I love making smoothies on summer afternoons. This fruity shake is refreshingly cool on sweltering days!
—Adrienne Hollister, Sultan, Washington

1/2 cup milk
3 cups vanilla ice cream
1-1/2 cups fresh *or* frozen sliced peeled peaches
1 cup fresh *or* frozen unsweetened strawberries
3/4 cup vanilla, peach *or* strawberry yogurt
Whipped cream, slivered almonds and whole fresh strawberries

In a blender, combine the milk, ice cream, peaches, strawberries and yogurt; cover and process until smooth. Pour into glasses. Garnish with whipped cream, almonds and strawberries. **Yield:** 4 servings.

Pecan Praline Sauce

As a working mother, I need fast recipes that are guaranteed to satisfy my family. This nutty ice cream topping is a hit.
—Evelyn Logan, Fresno, California

1/2 cup sugar
1/2 cup packed brown sugar
2 tablespoons all-purpose flour
Dash salt
1 cup water
1/4 cup orange juice
1/2 cup miniature marshmallows
2 tablespoons butter
1 cup chopped pecans, toasted
1 teaspoon vanilla extract

In a large saucepan, combine the sugars, flour, salt, water and orange juice until smooth. Bring to a boil; cook and stir for 2 minutes or until thickened. Stir in the marshmallows and butter; cook and stir until blended. Remove from the heat; stir in pecans and vanilla. Serve warm. **Yield:** 2 cups.

Family Traditions

ON JULY FOURTH, my husband and I invite our four boys and their families home for a big barbecue featuring grilled chicken, fresh watermelon and a variety of picnic foods. After a day of yard games and fun, we scoop out heaping bowls of ice cream. There's nothing better than a relaxing day with good food and family. *—Bertha Johnson, Indianapolis, Indiana*

Patriotic Sundae Bar

(Pictured above)

SUNDAE BAR fixings make a fun and festive centerpiece on the Fourth of July! For the patriotic presentation shown above, we set red, white and blue bowls on and around an attractive tiered plant stand.

Guests will forever remember this stars-and-stripes celebration when you feature color coordinated items like maraschino cherries, raspberries, blueberries, strawberries and candy-coated chocolate candies.

Don't forget to include such standbys as bananas, nuts, canned whipped cream and hot fudge. If you like, finish off the dynamic display with a daisy-filled vase.

Bursting with Berries!

WHETHER you pick your own, grow them in a garden or buy them at the grocery store, a bounty of fresh berries is the highlight of summer.

But the season often seems to come and go too quickly. So why not plan a party centered around these mouth-watering morsels today?

Sweet and savory slices of deliciously different Raspberry Pork Roast will bring rave reviews to the table.

Surprise relatives and friends with a fun, fruity side dish such as Blueberry Tossed Salad.

Genoise with Fruit 'n' Cream Filling features assorted fresh berries, tender cake layers and an irresistible sweet filling. (All recipes are shown at right.)

Fresh 'n' Fruity

(Clockwise from the top)

Blueberry Tossed Salad (p. 106)

Genoise with Fruit 'n' Cream Filling (p. 107)

Raspberry Roast Pork (p. 108)

Blueberry Tossed Salad

(Pictured on page 105)

My friends look forward to having this salad at picnics throughout summer. It's deliciously different.
—Joan Solberg, Ashland, Wisconsin

8 cups torn mixed salad greens
2 cups fresh blueberries
1 cup (4 ounces) shredded Monterey Jack cheese
1/2 cup sliced almonds, toasted
1/2 cup sunflower kernels
DRESSING:
1/2 cup vegetable oil
1/3 cup sugar
1/4 cup chopped onion
3 tablespoons red wine vinegar
1-1/2 teaspoons ground mustard
1-1/2 teaspoons poppy seeds

In a large bowl, combine the greens, blueberries, cheese, almonds and sunflower kernels. In a blender, combine the oil, sugar, onion, vinegar and mustard; cover and process until blended. Stir in poppy seeds. Drizzle over salad and toss to coat. **Yield:** 10 servings.

Lemon Torte with Fresh Berries

I appreciate recipes like this that can be made ahead and that are guaranteed to be great. A cool slice is so refreshing on warm days.
—Edith Lyon, Martinsburg, West Virginia

1 package (3 ounces) lemon gelatin
1/2 cup boiling water
1/3 cup lemonade concentrate
1 can (12 ounces) evaporated milk
3 cups angel food cake cubes
3 cups fresh raspberries *or* sliced strawberries
1 tablespoon sugar

In a large mixing bowl, dissolve gelatin in boiling water. Stir in lemonade concentrate and milk. Cover and refrigerate for 1-2 hours.

Place the cake cubes in a 9-in. springform pan coated with nonstick cooking spray. Beat gelatin mixture on medium speed for 5 minutes or until fluffy; pour over cake cubes. Cover and chill for 4 hours or until firm. In a small bowl, combine the berries and sugar; chill for 2 hours.

Just before serving, carefully run a knife around edge of pan to loosen; remove sides of pan. Spoon berry mixture over torte. Refrigerate leftovers. **Yield:** 12 servings.

Genoise with Fruit 'n' Cream Filling

(Pictured at right and on page 105)

Sweet syrup soaks into the tender layers of this sponge cake from our Test Kitchen. Complete the presentation with sweetened whipped cream and assorted fresh berries.

6 eggs, lightly beaten
1 cup sugar
1 teaspoon grated lemon peel
1 teaspoon lemon extract
1 cup all-purpose flour
1/2 cup butter, melted and cooled
SUGAR SYRUP:
3 tablespoons boiling water
2 tablespoons sugar
1/4 cup cold water
1-1/2 teaspoons lemon extract
FILLING:
1 cup heavy whipping cream
1/2 cup confectioners' sugar
1 teaspoon vanilla extract, optional
3 cups mixed fresh berries

Cake Capers

Genoise (pronounced zhayn-WAHZ) is a rich, delicate sponge cake that contains lots of eggs and sugar but little or no fat. It was created in Genoa, Italy and adapted by the French.

Line two greased 9-in. round baking pans with waxed paper and grease the paper; set aside. In a large heatproof mixing bowl, combine eggs and sugar; place over a large saucepan filled with 1-2 in. of simmering water. Heat over low heat, stirring occasionally, until mixture reaches 110°, about 8-10 minutes.

Remove from the heat; add lemon peel and extract. Beat on high speed until mixture is lemon-colored and more than doubles in volume. Fold in flour, 1/4 cup at a time. Gently fold in butter. Spread into prepared pans.

Bake at 350° for 25-30 minutes or until a toothpick inserted near the center comes out clean. Cool for 10 minutes before removing from the pans to wire racks to cool completely.

In a bowl, combine boiling water and sugar; stir until sugar is dissolved. Stir in cold water and extract. Using a fork, evenly poke 1/2-in.-deep holes in each cake. Spoon sugar syrup over cake surface. In a small mixing bowl, beat cream until it begins to thicken. Add sugar and vanilla if desired; beat until soft peaks form.

Place one cake on a serving platter; spread with half of the whipped cream and top with half of the berries. Repeat layers. Store in the refrigerator. **Yield:** 10-12 servings.

Raspberry Roast Pork

(Pictured on page 104)

Our home economists pair a sage- and pepper-seasoned pork roast with raspberry sauce for an easy, yet elegant entree.

- **4-1/2 cups fresh *or* frozen raspberries**
- **3 tablespoons sugar**
- **1/2 cup unsweetened apple juice**
- **1/4 cup red wine vinegar**
- **2 garlic cloves, minced**
- **3/4 teaspoon rubbed sage, *divided***
- **1 tablespoon cornstarch**
- **1 tablespoon water**
- **1/2 teaspoon salt**
- **1/2 teaspoon pepper**
- **1 boneless whole pork loin roast (3-1/2 to 4 pounds)**

Place raspberries in a bowl; sprinkle with sugar and mash. Let stand for 15 minutes; mash again. Strain, reserving juice; discard pulp and seeds.

In a small saucepan, combine the raspberry juice, apple juice, vinegar, garlic and 1/4 teaspoon sage. Simmer, uncovered, for 5 minutes. In a small bowl, combine cornstarch and water until smooth; stir into raspberry juice mixture until smooth. Bring to a boil; cook and stir for 1 minute or until thickened.

Combine the salt, pepper and remaining sage; rub over roast. Place fat side up on a rack in a shallow roasting pan. Spread with 1/2 cup raspberry sauce. Bake, uncovered, at 350° for 1-3/4 to 2 hours or until a meat thermometer reads 160°. Let stand for 10-15 minutes before slicing. Meanwhile, reheat the remaining raspberry sauce; serve with pork. **Yield:** 8-10 servings.

Berry Basics

FOR maximum freshness and flavor, follow these tips for buying and storing berries.

- Purchase berries that are brightly colored and plump. Blueberries should have a silver frosted appearance. While raspberries and blackberries should not have their hulls attached, strawberries should.
- At home, remove any berries that are soft, shriveled or moldy. Place in a single layer on a paper towel-lined plate, cover loosely and refrigerate. Don't wash berries until ready to use.
- Berries are very perishable. Blackberries, raspberries and strawberries stay fresh for up to 2 days. Blueberries should be used within 5 days.
- Whole berries can also be frozen for up to 1 year. Wash, blot dry and arrange in a single layer on a jelly-roll pan. Freeze until firm, then transfer to a heavy-duty resealable plastic bag. You can also freeze sliced or halved strawberries. Place in a heavy-duty resealable plastic bag and sprinkle with sugar if desired; seal bag.
- One pint of blackberries yields 1-1/2 to 2 cups; one pint of blueberries or raspberries equals 2 cups; one pint of strawberries yields 1-1/2 to 2 cups, sliced.

Berry Bruschetta

(Pictured at right)

Our Test Kitchen is the source of this fantastic fruit bruschetta. It's a tasty twist from the traditional tomato variety and can be served as an appetizer or a dessert.

1 French bread baguette (1 pound)
2 tablespoons olive oil
1-1/2 cups chopped fresh strawberries
3/4 cup chopped peeled fresh peaches
1-1/2 teaspoons minced fresh mint
1/2 cup Mascarpone cheese

Cut baguette into 32 slices, about 1/2 in. thick; place on ungreased baking sheets. Brush with oil. Broil 6-8 in. from the heat for 1-2 minutes or until lightly toasted.

In a small bowl, combine the strawberries, peaches and mint. Spread each slice of bread with cheese; top with fruit mixture. Broil for 1-2 minutes or until cheese is slightly melted. Serve immediately. **Yield:** 32 appetizers.

Strawberry Ice

I came across this delightful dessert while looking for a simple recipe to get my daughter some experience in the kitchen. She loves this treat and asks to make it often.
—KeriAnne Zimmerman, Glen Burnie, Maryland

1-1/2 cups water
1/2 cup honey
2 tablespoons lemon juice
3 cups fresh strawberries, hulled

In a blender, combine all ingredients; cover and process until smooth. Pour into an 8-in. square dish; cover and freeze for 2-1/2 hours or until almost frozen.

Spoon mixture into a blender; cover and process until smooth. Return to the dish; cover and freeze until firm, about 2 hours. About 15 minutes before serving, place dessert in the refrigerator to soften. **Yield:** 1 quart.

Raspberry Mousse

This creamy, smooth mousse from our Test Kitchen is a refreshing finale to any summer meal.

- **2 cups fresh raspberries**
- **1/2 cup sugar**
- **1 tablespoon lemon juice**
- **1-1/2 teaspoons unflavored gelatin**
- **1/4 cup cold water**
- **1 cup heavy whipping cream**

Place the raspberries in a food processor; cover and puree. Strain and discard seeds. Place puree in a bowl. Stir in sugar and lemon juice; set aside.

In a small saucepan, sprinkle gelatin over cold water; let stand for 1 minute. Stir over low heat until gelatin is completely dissolved. Stir into raspberry mixture. Refrigerate until slightly thickened, about 1 hour.

Transfer to a mixing bowl. Beat on high speed until foamy. Gradually add cream; beat until thickened, about 2 minutes. Spoon into dessert dishes. Cover and refrigerate for 1-2 hours or until set. **Yield:** 8 servings.

Blueberry Cheese Torte

Blueberries are plentiful here in the Northwest.
I keep my freezer stocked so I can make this torte any time of year.
—John Eilman, Sequim, Washington

- **1-1/2 cups finely chopped macadamia nuts**
- **3/4 cup all-purpose flour**
- **1/2 cup packed brown sugar**
- **6 tablespoons butter, melted**
- **3 packages (8 ounces *each*) cream cheese, softened**
- **1 can (14 ounces) sweetened condensed milk**
- **3 eggs, lightly beaten**
- **1/4 cup lemon juice**
- **3 cups fresh *or* frozen blueberries**
- **1-1/2 teaspoons cornstarch**
- **1 tablespoon cold water**

In a bowl, combine the nuts, flour and brown sugar; stir in butter. Set aside 1/3 cup for the filling. Press remaining nut mixture onto the bottom and 2 in. up the sides of a greased 9-in. springform pan. Place pan on a baking sheet. Bake at 350° for 10 minutes. Cool on a wire rack.

In a large mixing bowl, beat cream cheese and milk until smooth. Add eggs; beat on low speed just until combined. Add lemon juice; beat just until blended. Stir in reserved nut mixture. Pour into crust.

Return pan to baking sheet. Bake at 350° for 40-45 minutes or until center is almost set. Cool on a wire rack for 10 minutes. Carefully run a knife around edge of pan to loosen; cool 1 hour longer. Refrigerate overnight.

In a large saucepan, cook blueberries over medium heat until heated through. Combine cornstarch and water until smooth; stir into blueberries. Bring to a boil; cook and stir for 2 minutes or until thickened. Cool; cover and refrigerate until serving. Remove sides of springform pan. Spoon blueberry topping over cheesecake. Refrigerate leftovers. **Yield:** 12 servings.

Chilled Mixed Berry Soup

(Pictured at right)

As a lovely addition to a luncheon menu, our home economists recommend this cool, fruity soup featuring three kinds of berries.

1 cup sliced fresh strawberries
1/2 cup fresh raspberries
1/2 cup fresh blackberries
1 cup unsweetened apple juice
1/2 cup water
1/4 cup sugar
2 tablespoons lemon juice
Dash ground nutmeg
2 cartons (6 ounces *each*) raspberry yogurt

In a heavy saucepan, combine the berries, apple juice, water, sugar, lemon juice and nutmeg. Cook, uncovered, over low heat for 20 minutes or until berries are softened. Strain, reserving juice. Press berry mixture through a fine meshed sieve; discard seeds. Add pulp to reserved juice; cover and refrigerate until chilled.

Place berry mixture in a food processor or blender; add yogurt. Cover and process until smooth. Pour into bowls. **Yield:** 4 servings.

A "Souper" Serving Suggestion

SKIP ordinary soup mugs or bowls and serve Chilled Mixed Berry Soup in special stemmed glasses. And for a lovely color contrast, top each serving with a blackberry and fresh mint leaves.

Plan a Picnic at the Beach

WHEN YOU pack your picnic basket and head to the beach this summer, skip the standard sandwiches and whet your appetite with some seaside sensations!

Because it can be served cold as well as warm, Oven-Fried Picnic Chicken is a hearty take-along entree that's great for get-togethers all season long.

Beat the summer heat with a cold soup such as Shrimp Gazpacho, featuring the fresh flavors of shrimp, tomatoes, cucumbers and more.

When having fun in the sun, it's best to skip chocolate desserts that can melt. Instead, make a batch of crowd-pleasing Almond-Coconut Lemon Bars. (All recipes shown at right.)

Waterfront Fare

(Clockwise from top right)

Almond-Coconut Lemon Bars (p. 114)

Shrimp Gazpacho (p. 115)

Oven-Fried Picnic Chicken (p. 114)

Almond-Coconut Lemon Bars

(Pictured on page 113)

Our Test Kitchen home economists give traditional lemon bars a tasty twist with the addition of almonds and coconut.

1-1/2 cups all-purpose flour
1/2 cup confectioners' sugar
1/3 cup blanched almonds, toasted
1 teaspoon grated lemon peel
3/4 cup cold butter, cubed
FILLING:
3 eggs
1-1/2 cups sugar
1/2 cup flaked coconut, chopped
1/4 cup lemon juice
3 tablespoons all-purpose flour
1 teaspoon grated lemon peel
1/2 teaspoon baking powder
Confectioners' sugar

In a food processor, combine the flour, confectioners' sugar, almonds and lemon peel; cover and process until nuts are finely chopped. Add butter; pulse just until mixture is crumbly. Press into a greased 13-in. x 9-in. x 2-in. baking dish. Bake at 350° for 20 minutes.

Meanwhile, in a bowl, whisk eggs, sugar, coconut, lemon juice, flour, lemon peel and baking powder; pour over the hot crust. Bake for 20-25 minutes or until light golden brown. Cool on a wire rack. Dust with confectioners' sugar. Cut into squares. **Yield:** 3-4 dozen.

Oven-Fried Picnic Chicken

(Pictured on page 112)

My great-grandson Austin eats only chicken, so it appears on the menu at every family gathering. This version, which marinates chicken in lemonade, is among his favorites.
—Anneliese Deising, Plymouth, Michigan

1 can (12 ounces) frozen lemonade concentrate, thawed
1 broiler/fryer chicken (3 to 4 pounds), cut up
1/2 cup plus 2 tablespoons all-purpose flour
1-1/2 teaspoons salt
1/2 teaspoon pepper
1 cup vegetable oil
2 tablespoons butter, melted

Refrigerate 1/4 cup lemonade concentrate for basting. Pour remaining concentrate into a large resealable plastic bag; add chicken. Seal bag and turn to coat; refrigerate for 4 hours, turning occasionally.

Drain and discard marinade from chicken. In a large resealable plastic bag, combine the flour, salt and pepper. Add chicken, a few pieces at a time, and shake to coat. In a large skillet, brown chicken in oil for 1-1/2 to 2 minutes on each side or until golden brown.

Place chicken on a rack in a shallow roasting pan. Brush with butter. Bake, uncovered, at 350° for 50-55 minutes or until juices run clear, basting with reserved lemonade concentrate every 15 minutes. Serve warm or cold. **Yield:** 4-6 servings.

Shrimp Gazpacho

(Pictured at right and on page 113)

This refreshing tomato-based soup from our Test Kitchen features shrimp, cucumber and avocados.

6 cups spicy V8 juice
2 cups cold water
1 pound cooked medium shrimp, peeled and deveined
2 medium tomatoes, seeded and diced
1 medium cucumber, seeded and diced
2 medium ripe avocados, diced
1/2 cup lime juice
1/2 cup minced fresh cilantro
1/2 teaspoon salt
1/4 to 1/2 teaspoon hot pepper sauce

In a large bowl, combine all ingredients. Cover and refrigerate for 1 hour. Serve cold. **Yield:** 12 servings (about 3 quarts).

Editor's Note: This recipe is best served the same day it's made.

Plastic Cups Serve as Soup Bowls!

WHEN hosting an informal gathering like a beach picnic, keep the dinnerware casual as well. For example, serve Shrimp Gazpacho in disposable plastic drinking cups along with plastic spoons, as shown in the photo above.

Disposable plastic serving dishes are easy to transport and can be tossed away when finished, leaving you with fewer things to pack up at the end of the day.

Simple Citrus Punch

There's no doubt this refreshing beverage will quench your summertime thirst!
—Irene Kusler, Eureka, South Dakota

1 can (12 ounces) frozen limeade concentrate, thawed
3/4 cup lemonade concentrate
2 cups water
1/4 cup sugar, optional
2 liters ginger ale, chilled
Ice cubes

In a large punch bowl, combine the limeade and lemonade concentrates. Stir in water and sugar if desired. Stir in the ginger ale. Serve immediately over ice. **Yield:** about 3 quarts.

Peppery Grilled Steaks

Coarsely ground pepper adds the perfect amount of spice to flank steaks. We enjoy this grilled entree year-round.
—Lynn McAllister, Mt. Ulla, North Carolina

1/4 cup red wine vinegar
1/4 cup olive oil
1/4 cup Dijon mustard
4 garlic cloves, minced
2 green onions, chopped
4 teaspoons coarsely ground pepper
1 teaspoon dried thyme
1 teaspoon dried rosemary, crushed
1/2 teaspoon salt
3 beef flank steaks (about 1 pound *each*)

In a large resealable plastic bag, combine the vinegar, oil, mustard, garlic, onions, pepper, thyme, rosemary and salt; add steaks. Seal bag and turn to coat; refrigerate for 8 hours or overnight.

Drain and discard marinade. Grill steaks, covered, over medium heat for 6-10 minutes on each side or until meat reaches desired doneness (for rare, a meat thermometer should read 145°; medium, 160°; well-done, 170°). **Yield:** 10-12 servings.

Vegetable Barley Salad

I often serve this salad as an entree on summer nights when it's too hot to eat a heavy meal. The recipe makes a big batch, which is terrific for taking to potlucks.
—Patricia Lewandowski, Warwick, Massachusetts

4 cups water
2 cups uncooked medium pearl barley
2 cups fresh broccoli florets
2 cups diced carrots
1 cup halved cherry *or* grape tomatoes
1/2 cup chopped green onions
1/2 cup julienned sweet red *or* green pepper
1/4 cup sunflower kernels
1/2 cup lemon juice
1/2 cup olive oil
1/4 cup white wine vinegar
2 teaspoons grated lemon peel
2 garlic cloves, peeled
1/2 teaspoon salt
1/4 to 1/2 teaspoon pepper
1 tablespoon grated Parmesan cheese

In a large saucepan, bring water to a boil. Add the barley. Reduce heat; cover and cook for 30-35 minutes or until tender. Rinse with cold water; drain well.

Place broccoli and carrots in a steamer basket. Place in a saucepan over 1 in. of water; bring to a boil. Cover and steam for 3-4 minutes or until crisp-tender. Rinse with cold water; drain.

In a large salad bowl, combine the barley, broccoli and carrots, tomatoes, onions, red pepper and sunflower kernels. In a blender, combine the lemon juice, oil, vinegar, lemon peel, garlic, salt and pepper; cover and process until combined. Pour over barley mixture and stir to coat. Refrigerate for at least 1 hour. Just before serving, sprinkle with Parmesan cheese. **Yield:** 14 servings.

Crab-Salad Jumbo Shells

(Pictured at right)

I received this recipe from a friend and adjusted the ingredients to suit my family's tastes. It's a fun and flavorful way to serve crab salad.
—JoAnne Anderson, Knoxville, Iowa

30 jumbo pasta shells
1 cup finely chopped fresh broccoli florets
1 garlic clove, minced
2 packages (8 ounces *each*) imitation crabmeat, chopped
1 cup (8 ounces) sour cream
1/2 cup mayonnaise
1/4 cup finely shredded carrot
1/4 cup diced seeded peeled cucumber
1 tablespoon chopped green onion
1 teaspoon dill weed

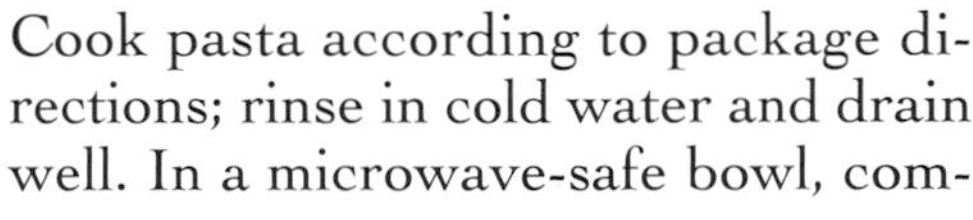

Cook pasta according to package directions; rinse in cold water and drain well. In a microwave-safe bowl, combine the broccoli and garlic. Cover and microwave on high for 1 minute or until crisp-tender. Transfer to a large bowl; stir in the remaining ingredients. Stuff into pasta shells. Cover and refrigerate overnight. **Yield:** 30 stuffed shells.

Family Traditions

Every summer we head to North Carolina's Outer Banks for a week-long vacation with my husband's family. To prevent chaos in the kitchen of our rented beach house, we've developed a schedule where each family cooks dinner one night, while another family cleans up. We've had fun sampling a variety of foods!
—Diana Leskauskas
Chatham, New Jersey

Chicken-Spinach Pasta Salad

Hot summer nights call for cool salads such as this. I created the recipe by accident one day when tossing together whatever ingredients I had on hand.
—Diane Weiss, Royal Oak, Michigan

1-3/4 cups uncooked small pasta shells
4 cups baby spinach
2-1/2 cups julienned cooked chicken
1/2 cup crumbled blue cheese
1/4 cup pine nuts
DRESSING:
1 tablespoon water
1 tablespoon lemon juice
1 tablespoon white balsamic vinegar
1 tablespoon vegetable oil
1 tablespoon minced chives
1/2 teaspoon Dijon mustard
1/4 teaspoon dried basil
Dash *each* garlic powder and cayenne pepper

Cook pasta according to package directions; rinse in cold water and drain well. In a large bowl, gently toss the pasta, spinach, chicken, blue cheese and pine nuts. In a small bowl, whisk the dressing ingredients. Drizzle over salad and toss to coat. Serve immediately. **Yield:** 6-8 servings.

Al Fresco Watermelon Salad

This unique onion and watermelon salad makes appearances at many family gatherings in summer. The savory seasonings complement every bite of sweet melon.
—Lorraine Wilson, Woodsfield, Ohio

4 cups cubed seeded watermelon
1 medium sweet onion, quartered and thinly sliced
2 tablespoons minced fresh basil
1/4 cup balsamic vinegar
Salt and pepper to taste

In a large bowl, combine the watermelon, onion and basil. Drizzle with vinegar; toss gently. Add salt and pepper. Refrigerate for up to 1 hour. Serve with a slotted spoon. **Yield:** 4-6 servings.

Are You Sweet on Onions?

FOR the best flavor, make Al Fresco Watermelon Salad (above) with sweet onions, such as Vidalia, Walla Walla or Bermuda.

Hazelnut Madeleine Cookies

(Pictured at right)

As an appropriate dessert for a beach picnic, our home economists came up with these cookies, which bake in a shell-shaped Madeleine pan.

1/2 cup whole hazelnuts, toasted
1 tablespoon confectioners' sugar
1 tablespoon plus 1/2 cup butter, *divided*
2 tablespoons plus 1 cup all-purpose flour, *divided*
2 eggs, *separated*
2/3 cup sugar
1/4 teaspoon vanilla extract
1 teaspoon baking powder
1/8 teaspoon salt
Additional confectioners' sugar, optional

In a food processor, combine the hazelnuts and confectioners' sugar; cover and process until nuts are finely chopped. Set aside. Melt 1 tablespoon butter. Brush two Madeleine pans with butter. Dust with 2 tablespoons flour; tap pans to remove excess flour and set aside. Place remaining butter in a saucepan. Melt over low heat for 4-5 minutes or until a light amber color; set aside to cool.

In a large mixing bowl, beat egg yolks and sugar until thick and a pale lemon color. Stir in melted butter and vanilla. Combine the baking powder, salt and remaining flour; stir into butter mixture just until combined. In a small mixing bowl, beat egg whites on high speed until stiff peaks form; fold into batter. Gently fold in reserved nut mixture.

With a tablespoon, fill prepared pans two-thirds full. Bake at 325° for 18-20 minutes or until golden brown. Cool for 2 minutes before inverting pans onto wire racks to remove cookies. Cool completely. Lightly dust with additional confectioners' sugar if desired. **Yield:** 2 dozen.

Editor's Note: Madeleine pans can be ordered from Sweet Celebrations. Call 1-800/328-6722 or visit their Web site, *www.sweetc.com*. They are also available from Williams-Sonoma. Call 1-877/812-6235 or visit their Web site, *www.williams-sonoma.com*.

Making Madeleine Cookies

BRUSH Madeleine pans with melted butter. Dust with flour; tap pans to remove excess. Fill pans two-thirds full with batter; bake as directed.

Pineapple Mango Salsa

This fruit salsa served with tortilla chips is great for summer barbecues. It also can be served alongside fish and chicken entrees.
—Mary Gloede, Lakewood, Wisconsin

1 cup chopped peeled mango
1 cup pineapple tidbits
1/2 cup diced sweet red pepper
1 plum tomato, seeded and chopped
3 tablespoons minced fresh cilantro
2 green onions, sliced
2 tablespoons lime juice
1 tablespoon lemon juice
1 jalapeno pepper, finely chopped*
Tortilla chips

In a bowl, combine the first nine ingredients. Cover and refrigerate for 1 hour or until chilled. Serve with tortilla chips. **Yield:** 2-2/3 cups.

***Editor's Note:** When cutting or seeding hot peppers, use rubber or plastic gloves to protect your hands. Avoid touching your face.

Nifty Natural Paper Weight

SPEND any time at the beach and you know it can get pretty breezy! To stop a gust of wind from blowing away paper plates and napkins, create a paper weight from an ordinary rock, as shown in the photo at right and on page 112.

Chicken Salad Croissants

Fresh dill is the secret to the success of these cold sandwiches. I like to use miniature croissants when serving them as an appetizer.
—Jessie Yates, Monette, Arkansas

3 cups diced grilled chicken
1 can (11 ounces) mandarin oranges, drained and halved
1 cup halved seedless red grapes
2 celery ribs, finely chopped
1/2 cup mayonnaise
1/4 cup sunflower kernels
2 tablespoons minced fresh dill *or* 2 teaspoons dill weed
7 croissants *or* 21 miniature croissants, split

In a bowl, combine the first seven ingredients. Spoon onto croissants; replace tops. If using large croissants, cut into thirds. Serve immediately. **Yield:** 21 servings.

Homemade Sand Castles

(Pictured above)

These cute sand castles remain intact indefinitely. You can use them as a table topper at home or take them to the beach for a picnic table centerpiece.

1/3 cup all-purpose flour
2 tablespoons sugar
1 cup cold water
6 cups moist sand
Sand castle molds of various shapes and sizes
Nautical rope, rocks and seashells

In a saucepan, combine flour and sugar. Gradually add cold water; mix well. Cook and stir over low heat until mixture thickens to pudding consistency.

Place sand in a large pail; stir in flour mixture. When cool to the touch, mix together with your hands, adding more water if needed so that sand holds its shape. Firmly pack into molds. Invert on a flat surface; remove molds.

Let dry completely before handling. Depending on the humidity, this may take a few days.

To create a centerpiece, weave rope between the sand castles; fill in with sand, rocks and seashells.

Editor's Note: The sand mixture will keep for weeks when stored in an airtight container.

Making Homemade Sand Castles

1. Stir the warm flour mixture into the sand. When cool to the touch, mix together with your hands.

2. Firmly pack sand mixture into sand castle molds.

3. Unmold onto a flat surface. Let stand until completely dry.

Ladies' Luncheon in the Garden

AT THE HEIGHT of summer, it's fun to incorporate fresh herbs and edible flowers into every aspect of your cooking.

Celebrate the fabulous flavors of this all-too-short season by hosting a glorious garden party for a few friends.

Start by setting up a table in the backyard to catch a cool breeze through the trees.

As guests arrive, welcome them around back for a refreshing beverage like Peachy Lemonade.

Soak up every second of summer as you nibble on Herbed Shrimp Appetizer and a selection of fresh breads topped with Garlic Basil Butter. (All recipes shown at right.)

This chapter also features a selection of entrees, side dishes and desserts that showcase the summer's freshest flavors.

Garden Party

Peachy Lemonade (p. 127)

Herbed Shrimp Appetizer (p. 125)

Garlic Basil Butter (p. 129)

Thyme 'n' Thyme Again Salad Dressing

You just can't beat the flavor of fresh herbs. For a little extra zest, I sometimes use lemon or caraway thyme.
—Barbara Balazs, Huntington Beach, California

1/3 cup olive oil
1/4 cup red wine vinegar
1/4 cup crumbled feta cheese
2 tablespoons minced fresh thyme
1 tablespoon minced fresh oregano
1 tablespoon minced fresh marjoram
1 tablespoon Dijon mustard
1 garlic clove, minced
1-1/2 to 2 teaspoons sugar
1/4 teaspoon white pepper
1/8 teaspoon salt
Mixed salad greens

In a jar with a tight-fitting lid, combine the first 11 ingredients. Shake well just before serving over salad greens. Store in the refrigerator. **Yield:** 1 cup.

Lemon Balm Bread

This moist quick bread tastes best the day after it's made. Lemon balm is a lovely addition to both the batter and glaze.
—Connie Yeagley, Cleona, Pennsylvania

1/2 cup butter, softened
1 cup sugar
1/4 cup finely chopped lemon balm leaves
2 eggs
1-1/2 cups all-purpose flour
1-1/2 teaspoons baking powder
1/4 teaspoon salt
1/2 cup milk
1/4 cup chopped walnuts, optional
1 tablespoon grated lemon peel

GLAZE:
1/3 cup sugar
2 tablespoons water
1 tablespoon lemon juice
2 tablespoons finely chopped lemon balm leaves

In a large mixing bowl, cream the butter, sugar and lemon balm. Add eggs, one at a time, beating well after each addition. Combine the flour, baking powder and salt; add to creamed mixture alternately with milk. Stir in walnuts if desired and lemon peel. Pour into a greased 8-in. x 4-in. x 2-in. loaf pan. Bake at 350° for 50-60 minutes or until a toothpick comes out clean.

In a small bowl, whisk the sugar, water and lemon juice; stir in lemon balm. Spoon over warm bread while still in pan. Cool for 10 minutes before removing from pan to a wire rack to cool completely. **Yield:** 1 loaf.

Herbed Shrimp Appetizer

(Pictured at right and on page 123)

As guests arrive at your garden party, encourage them to sample these marinated shrimp from our Test Kitchen. Herbs, lime juice and red peppers give them great flavor.

3/4 cup olive oil
1/3 cup lime juice
1/3 cup diced sweet red pepper
1/3 cup diced sweet onion
3 garlic cloves, minced
4 teaspoons minced chives
2 teaspoons minced fresh tarragon
2 teaspoons snipped fresh dill
1-1/2 pounds cooked large shrimp, peeled and deveined
Nasturtiums, calendula, rosemary, dill sprigs and flat leaf parsley

In a bowl, combine the first eight ingredients. Place the shrimp in a large resealable plastic bag; add herb mixture. Seal bag and toss to coat. Refrigerate for at least 4 hours. With a slotted spoon, transfer shrimp to a serving bowl. Garnish with flowers and herbs. **Yield:** about 4 dozen.

How to Cook Raw Shrimp

TO COOK raw shrimp in water, add 1 pound shrimp (with or without shells) and 1 teaspoon salt to 3 quarts boiling water. Reduce heat and simmer, uncovered, for 1 to 3 minutes or until the shrimp turns pink.

Watch closely to avoid overcooking. The meat of uncooked shrimp will turn from translucent when raw to pink and opaque when cooked. Drain immediately.

Pesto Chicken

These pesto-filled chicken rolls-ups from our Test Kitchen can be served warm as an entree or cooled and sliced for an elegant appetizer.

1 cup loosely packed fresh basil leaves
1/4 cup minced fresh parsley
1/4 cup grated Parmesan cheese
1/4 cup olive oil
1 tablespoon pine nuts
1 to 2 garlic cloves
4 boneless skinless chicken breast halves
1/2 teaspoon salt
1/4 teaspoon pepper
2 tablespoons butter, melted

For pesto, combine the first six ingredients in a blender; cover and process until blended. Flatten chicken to 1/4-in. thickness; sprinkle with salt and pepper. Spread each with 2 tablespoons pesto to within 1/2 in. of the edges. Roll up jelly-roll style, starting with a short side; secure with a toothpick or small metal skewer.

Place chicken in a greased 11-in. x 7-in. x 2-in. baking dish; brush with butter. Bake, uncovered, at 375° for 30 to 35 minutes or until chicken juices run clear. Remove toothpicks or skewers. Serve warm as a main course.

For an appetizer, cool for 15 minutes, then refrigerate until chilled. Cut cold chicken into 1/2-in. slices. **Yield:** 4 main course or 12-16 appetizer servings.

Dandelion Potato Salad

Friends and family will love the crunchy produce in this tasty potato salad. Dandelion leaves are a deliciously different addition in spring.
—Florence Tice, Rushville, Indiana

4 hard-cooked eggs
1-1/3 cups water
1-1/2 teaspoons salt, *divided*
4 cups cubed peeled potatoes
1/2 cup sugar
4 teaspoons all-purpose flour
1/2 cup white vinegar
1 teaspoon prepared mustard
1-1/2 cups diced onions
1/4 cup mayonnaise
3/4 teaspoon celery salt
1/4 teaspoon garlic powder
1/4 teaspoon pepper
1/2 cup chopped green pepper
1/2 cup chopped sweet red pepper
1/2 cup sweet pickle relish
1 to 1-1/2 cups snipped dandelion *or* spinach leaves
Paprika

Peel eggs. Chop three eggs and slice one for garnish; set aside. In a saucepan, bring water and 1 teaspoon salt to a boil over medium heat. Add potatoes. Cook until tender. Meanwhile, in another saucepan, combine sugar, flour, vinegar and mustard until smooth. Bring to a boil; cook and stir for 2 minutes or until thickened. Add onions; cook 2 minutes longer. Drain potatoes; add onion mixture.

In a small bowl, combine the mayonnaise, celery salt, garlic powder, pepper and remaining salt. Add to the potato mixture; toss to coat. Stir in the chopped eggs, green and red peppers, pickle relish and dandelion leaves. Cover and refrigerate until serving. Garnish with sliced egg; sprinkle with paprika. **Yield:** 10-12 servings.

Peachy Lemonade

(Pictured at right and on page 123)

Our home economists perk up plain lemonade with peach nectar. Frozen peach slices serve as clever ice cubes that keep this beverage cool without diluting the flavor.

2 quarts lemonade
2 cans (5-1/2 ounces *each*) peach *or* apricot nectar
1 cup frozen peach slices
Fresh mint sprigs, snapdragons and lemon balm

In a 3-qt. glass pitcher, combine the lemonade and nectar; refrigerate until chilled. Just before serving, stir the lemonade mixture; add frozen peach slices. Place mint sprigs along the sides of the pitcher and float the flowers on top of the lemonade. **Yield:** about 2-1/2 quarts.

Beaded Beverage Covers

ALONG with summer's beautiful weather come pesky bugs and bees! Discourage these uninvited guests from sampling your Peachy Lemonade by making Beaded Beverage Covers (as shown above).

Purchase small square cloth doilies. To create weights, string beads onto a threaded needle and sew them onto each corner of the doily.

Have these beaded doilies on the table so that guests can keep their beverages covered.

Marigold Cheese Dip

Have a backyard bed of marigolds? Share some with guests the next time you entertain by adding them to a cream cheese dip. It's a surprisingly delicious appetizer.
—Dixie Terry, Marion, Illinois

1 package (8 ounces) cream cheese, softened
1 cup (8 ounces) sour cream
1/4 teaspoon vanilla extract
1/4 to 1/2 teaspoon salt
1/4 teaspoon coarsely ground pepper
1 teaspoon minced chives
1 teaspoon minced fresh savory
1 teaspoon minced fresh marigold petals
Assorted crackers

In a small mixing bowl, beat the cream cheese, sour cream, vanilla, salt and pepper until smooth. Stir in the chives, savory and marigold petals. Cover and refrigerate for at least 1 hour. Serve with crackers. **Yield:** 2 cups.

Asparagus Soup with Herbs

The fresh flavor of herbs shines through in this special soup. Because it calls for frozen asparagus, you can make it any time of year.
—Bev Smith, Ferndale, Washington

1 large onion, chopped
2 garlic cloves, minced
2 tablespoons olive oil
2 cans (14-1/2 ounces *each*) chicken broth
1 cup minced fresh parsley
1 large carrot, cut into 1-inch pieces
5 fresh basil leaves, minced
1 to 2 teaspoons minced fresh tarragon
1/2 teaspoon salt
1/4 teaspoon pepper
Dash cayenne pepper
1 package (10 ounces) frozen asparagus spears, thawed
Sour cream and chopped tomatoes, optional

In a large saucepan, saute onion and garlic in oil until tender. Stir in the broth, parsley, carrot, basil, tarragon, salt, pepper and cayenne. Cut asparagus into 1-in. pieces; set tips aside. Add asparagus pieces to saucepan. Bring to a boil. Reduce heat; cover and simmer for 20 minutes or until vegetables are tender. Cool slightly.

Puree soup in batches in a blender. Return to the saucepan. Stir in asparagus tips; cook for 5 minutes or until crisp-tender. Garnish with sour cream and tomatoes if desired. **Yield:** 4 servings.

Garlic Basil Butter

(Pictured at right and on page 123)

Instead of serving plain butter alongside an assortment of fresh breads, prepare this herb-laden whipped butter from our home economists.

1/2 cup butter, softened
4 teaspoons minced fresh basil
1-1/2 teaspoons minced fresh parsley
1/2 teaspoon garlic powder
Fresh sage and thyme

In a small mixing bowl, combine the butter, basil, parsley and garlic powder. Beat on medium-low speed until mixture is combined. Garnish with sage and thyme. **Yield:** 1/2 cup.

Mint Salad Dressing

Fresh mint is a popular perennial herb that will grow in almost any soil. Here it stars in a special salad dressing.
—Suzanne McKinley, Lyons, Georgia

1/2 cup sugar
1/4 cup water
1 tablespoon minced fresh mint leaves
1/2 cup olive oil
4 teaspoons lemon juice
1 teaspoon salt
1/2 teaspoon paprika
Mixed salad greens

In a saucepan, combine the sugar, water and mint. Simmer for 1-2 minutes or until sugar is dissolved. Remove from the heat; cover and let stand for 1 hour. Strain and discard mint.

Place olive oil in a small bowl; whisk in mint syrup. Whisk in lemon juice, salt and paprika. Drizzle over salad greens. **Yield:** 3/4 cup.

Rose Petal Sorbet

(Pictured at right)

Hot summer days call for a refreshing sorbet.
This recipe from our Test Kitchen combines pleasing citrus and floral flavors.

2 cups red *or* pink rose petals
2-1/4 cups sugar, *divided*
4 cups water
6 medium juice oranges
6 to 14 drops red food coloring, optional

With kitchen scissors, cut off the white portion at the stem end of each rose petal. With a mortar and pestle or in a food processor, mash or process petals into a paste, gradually adding 1/4 cup sugar. In a saucepan, bring water to a boil. Stir in remaining sugar until dissolved. Stir in the rose paste. Boil, without stirring, for 10 minutes. Remove from the heat; cool for at least 1 hour.

Strain, reserving rose syrup. Discard rose pulp. Squeeze the juice from the oranges and strain; discard pulp and seeds. Add 2-2/3 cups orange juice and food coloring if desired to the rose syrup. Transfer to a freezer container; cover and freeze for at least 8 hours or until firm. **Yield:** 10 servings.

Parmesan Salmon Fillets

Our home economists top pan-fried salmon with a salsa-like compote for a colorful summer entree.
If you can't find lovage leaves, use celery leaves instead.

TOMATO LOVAGE COMPOTE:
2 large tomatoes, seeded and chopped
1/2 cup finely chopped red onion
1/3 cup minced lovage *or* celery leaves
1/4 cup lemon juice
1/4 cup olive oil
1 tablespoon grated lemon peel
1/2 teaspoon salt
1/2 teaspoon hot pepper sauce
SALMON:
1 egg
2 tablespoons milk
1 cup dry bread crumbs
1/2 cup grated Parmesan cheese
4 salmon fillets (6 ounces *each*)
3 tablespoons vegetable oil

In a large bowl, gently toss the compote ingredients. Cover and let stand at room temperature for 1 hour.

In a shallow bowl, whisk the egg and milk. In another shallow bowl, combine bread crumbs and Parmesan cheese. Pat salmon dry with paper towels. Dip in milk mixture, then coat with crumb mixture. In a large nonstick skillet, cook the salmon in oil over medium-high heat until fish flakes easily with a fork, turning once. Serve with compote. **Yield:** 4 servings.

Citrus-Scented Geranium Cookies

(Pictured at right)

Geraniums are one of my favorite flowers. Not only are they beautiful garden accents, but they can enhance any culinary dish. Any scented geranium leaf can be used in this cookie recipe.
—Emma Marshall, Savannah, Georgia

1 cup butter, softened
1-1/2 cups confectioners' sugar
1 egg
2 tablespoons finely chopped lemon-, lime- *or* orange-scented geranium leaves
1 tablespoon lemon juice
1 teaspoon vanilla extract
1/8 teaspoon almond extract
2-1/2 cups all-purpose flour
1 teaspoon baking soda
1 teaspoon cream of tartar
LEMON GLAZE:
1 cup confectioners' sugar
2 teaspoons lemon juice
2 to 3 teaspoons water
1/4 teaspoon vanilla extract

In a large mixing bowl, cream butter and confectioners' sugar. Beat in the egg, geranium leaves, lemon juice and extracts. Combine the flour, baking soda and cream of tartar; gradually add to creamed mixture. Cover and refrigerate for 2 hours or until easy to handle.

Divide dough in half. On a lightly floured surface, roll out each portion to 1/4-in. thickness. Cut with a 2-in. cookie cutter dipped in sugar. Place 2 in. apart on greased baking sheets. Bake at 375° for 9-10 minutes or until edges are lightly browned. Remove to wire racks to cool. In a small bowl, combine glaze ingredients. Brush over cooled cookies. **Yield:** 3 dozen.

Avocado Pineapple Salsa

This colorful salsa developed by our home economists features the leaves of lovage, which is an aromatic perennial herb. Sweet pineapple balances perfectly with tart lime.

1 fresh pineapple, peeled and diced
1 medium ripe avocado, peeled and diced
1/3 cup finely chopped red onion
5 lovage *or* celery leaves, finely chopped
1 jalapeno pepper, seeded and chopped*
3 tablespoons lime juice
1 teaspoon grated lime peel
1/4 teaspoon salt
Tortilla chips

In a bowl, combine the first eight ingredients. Cover and refrigerate for at least 30 minutes before serving. Serve with tortilla chips. **Yield:** 5 cups.

***Editor's Note:** When cutting or seeding hot peppers, use rubber or plastic gloves to protect your hands. Avoid touching your face.

Strawberry Vinegar

If you're looking for a fun and flavorful way to enjoy juicy strawberries, try this vinegar from our Test Kitchen. Use it to make the Creamy Strawberry Salad Dressing on the opposite page.

2 pints fresh strawberries, halved
2 cups cider vinegar
2 tablespoons sugar

In a large saucepan, combine strawberries and vinegar; let stand for 1 hour. Add sugar; bring to a boil. Reduce heat; cover and simmer for 10 minutes. Cool. Strain through a double layer of cheesecloth; do not press fruit. Let stand for 1 hour. Store in a sterilized jar in a cool dark place. **Yield:** 2-1/2 cups.

Fresh Strawberry Facts

LOOK for brightly colored, plump and fragrant strawberries with the green hulls intact. Avoid any that are soft, shriveled or moldy.

Wash berries before removing hulls.

One pint of strawberries yields 1-1/2 to 2 cups sliced.

Chair-Back Herb Bouquet

(Pictured at right)

NOT ONLY can fresh herbs flavor a variety of foods, they can provide a fabulous fragrance as well!

At your garden party, consider attaching easy Herb Bouquets to the backs of the guests' chairs.

First, tie onto the back of each chair a napkin that coordinates with your tablecloth.

For the Herb Bouquets, gather an assortment of fresh herbs, such as mint, sage and thyme. Tie with a ribbon and tuck into the knot of the napkin.

These aromatic bouquets can also serve as party favors.

Creamy Strawberry Salad Dressing

My family can't resist a sweet spinach and strawberry salad topped with this lovely dressing. Every bite smacks of summer.
—Kimberly Klindworth, Olathe, Kansas

1 cup sliced fresh strawberries
1/2 cup orange juice
2 tablespoons Strawberry Vinegar (recipe on opposite page) *or* raspberry vinegar
2 tablespoons olive oil
4 teaspoons honey
1/4 teaspoon salt
Baby spinach, red onion rings, orange segments, toasted sliced almonds and additional fresh strawberries

In a blender, combine the first six ingredients. Cover and process until pureed. Refrigerate until serving. In a salad bowl or on individual salad plates, combine the spinach, onion, orange, almonds and additional strawberries. Serve with dressing. **Yield:** 1-1/2 cups.

Fall Entertaining

Take Time Out to Tailgate

IS IT up to you to tackle the task of cooking a meal that your husband and his buddies can take to the big game this fall?

There's no need to fumble around the kitchen if you turn to this make-ahead menu!

Jumbo Greek Sub is just the sandwich for satisfying hearty appetites. Pass the platter and watch slices disappear!

For a side dish that's teeming with colorful produce and winning flavor, you can't go wrong with a cool Dressed-Up Vegetable Salad.

Then score extra points with the guys by packing a big batch of Chocolate Mint Delights. (All recipes shown at right.)

Outdoor Eating

(Top to bottom)

Chocolate Mint Delights (p. 141)

Dressed-Up Vegetable Salad (p. 142)

Jumbo Greek Sub (p. 140)

Jumbo Greek Sub

(Pictured on page 139)

It's nice to make just one sandwich that generously feeds six people. This meal from our Test Kitchen is easy to transport to a tailgate party or potluck.

- **2 boneless skinless chicken breast halves (6 ounces *each*)**
- **1 cup olive oil vinaigrette salad dressing, *divided***
- **1 tablespoon olive oil**
- **1 loaf (1 pound) unsliced Italian bread**
- **1/4 cup crumbled basil and tomato-flavored feta *or* plain feta cheese**
- **1/4 cup sliced ripe olives**
- **1 jar (7-1/4 ounces) roasted red peppers, drained**
- **15 to 20 cucumber slices (1/8 inch thick)**

Flatten chicken to 1/4-in. thickness. Place in a large resealable plastic bag. Add 3/4 cup salad dressing; seal and turn to coat. Refrigerate for 3 hours.

Drain and discard marinade. In a skillet, cook chicken in oil for 5 minutes on each side or until juices run clear. Cool. Cut the top third off the loaf of bread. Carefully hollow out top and bottom, leaving a 1/2-in. shell (discard removed bread or save for another use). Brush remaining salad dressing on cut sides of bread. Sprinkle feta and olives in bottom half of bread. Top with chicken, red peppers and cucumber. Replace bread top. Wrap tightly in plastic wrap; refrigerate for at least 2 hours. **Yield:** 6-8 servings.

Grilled Glazed Drummies

My family prefers these mild-tasting chicken wings more than the traditional hot wings. They are great for any gathering.
—Laura Mahaffey, Annapolis, Maryland

- **1 cup ketchup**
- **1/3 cup soy sauce**
- **4 teaspoons honey**
- **3/4 teaspoon ground ginger**
- **1/2 teaspoon garlic powder**
- **3 pounds chicken drumettes (about 24)**

In a bowl, combine the ketchup, soy sauce, honey, ginger and garlic powder; mix well. Pour 1 cup marinade into a large resealable plastic bag; add the chicken. Seal bag and turn to coat; refrigerate for at least 4 hours or overnight. Cover and refrigerate remaining marinade for basting.

Drain and discard marinade from chicken. Grill chicken, covered, over medium heat for 5 minutes. Turn and baste with reserved marinade. Grill 10-15 minutes longer or until juices run clear, turning and basting occasionally. **Yield:** 2 dozen.

Chocolate Mint Delights

(Pictured at right and on page 139)

I tuck a chocolate-covered peppermint patty into every one of these rich cookies. The drizzle on top adds a nice touch. I revised a brownie recipe to create these take-along treats.
—Heather Sandberg
Waukesha, Wisconsin

1 cup butter, softened
1 cup sugar
1 egg
1 teaspoon vanilla extract
1-3/4 cups all-purpose flour
1/2 cup baking cocoa
1-1/2 teaspoons baking powder
1/4 teaspoon salt
24 bite-size chocolate-covered peppermint patties

ICING:
18 bite-size chocolate-covered peppermint patties
4-1/2 teaspoons butter

In a mixing bowl, cream butter and sugar. Beat in egg and vanilla. Combine the flour, cocoa, baking powder and salt; gradually add to creamed mixture. Cover and refrigerate for 30 minutes or until easy to handle. Shape dough into two 6-in. rolls; wrap each in plastic wrap. Refrigerate for 2 hours or until firm.

Unwrap dough and cut into 1/4-in. slices. Place one slice on waxed paper; top with a peppermint patty and a second dough slice. Press edges of dough together to completely cover the peppermint patty. Repeat.

Place 2 in. apart on ungreased baking sheets. Bake at 325° for 11-13 minutes or until set, watching carefully. Cool for 5 minutes before removing to wire racks. For icing, in a microwave, melt peppermint patties and butter; stir until smooth. Drizzle over cookies. **Yield:** 2 dozen.

Editor's Note: This recipe was tested with Pearson's Mint Patties.

Country Ribs with Ginger Sauce

This recipe comes from my church kitchen. It's appeared on many menus through the years because the ribs have such mass appeal.
—Evangeline Jones, Standfordville, New York

3 pounds boneless country-style pork ribs
1/4 cup sugar
1/2 teaspoon salt
1/2 cup soy sauce
1/2 cup ketchup
3 tablespoons brown sugar
2 teaspoons minced fresh gingerroot

Sprinkle ribs with sugar and salt; rub into both sides of meat. Refrigerate for 2 hours. In a small bowl, combine the soy sauce, ketchup, brown sugar and ginger. Spoon half of the sauce over both sides of ribs; refrigerate for 1 hour. Set remaining sauce aside for basting.

Place ribs on a greased rack in a 15-in. x 10-in. x 1-in. baking pan. Bake at 450° for 15 minutes; drain. Reduce heat to 350°; bake 1-1/2 hours longer or until meat is tender, basting with remaining sauce every 15 minutes. **Yield:** 8-12 servings.

Dressed-Up Vegetable Salad

(Pictured on page 139)

If taking our Test Kitchen's marinated veggie salad to a picnic, simply place it in a covered plastic container and pop it into your cooler for easy transporting.

2 cups fresh broccoli florets
1 medium sweet yellow pepper, cut into 1-inch pieces
1 medium sweet orange pepper, cut into 1-inch pieces
1/2 medium red onion, cut into 1/4-inch wedges
1 cup halved cherry tomatoes
DRESSING:
6 tablespoons olive oil
3 tablespoons red wine vinegar
1-1/2 teaspoons Dijon mustard
2 to 3 garlic cloves, minced
1 teaspoon dried oregano
3/4 teaspoon sugar
1/4 teaspoon salt
1/8 teaspoon pepper

In a salad bowl, combine the vegetables. In a jar with a tight-fitting lid, combine the dressing ingredients; shake well. Drizzle over vegetables and toss to coat. Cover and refrigerate for at least 1 hour. Toss before serving. **Yield:** 8 servings.

Buying and Storing Broccoli

BROCCOLI comes from the Latin word brachium, which means branch or arm.

When purchasing broccoli, look for bunches that have a deep green color, tightly closed buds and crisp leaves. Store in a resealable plastic bag in the refrigerator for up to 4 days. Wash just before using.

One pound of broccoli yields about 2 cups florets.

Chip 'n' Dip Burgers

(Pictured at right)

French onion dip and potato chips top these special hamburgers. They're so delicious, no other toppings are needed!
—Diane Hixon, Niceville, Florida

1-1/2 cups crushed potato chips, *divided*
1-1/2 cups French onion dip, *divided*
1/4 cup dill pickle relish
1-1/2 pounds ground beef
6 hamburger buns, toasted

In a bowl, combine half of the potato chips and half of the dip; add relish. Crumble beef over the mixture and mix well. Shape into six patties. Grill, covered, over medium heat for 6 minutes on each side or until meat is no longer pink. Serve on buns; top with remaining chips and dip. **Yield:** 6 servings.

Stuffed Gouda Spread

I have fun experimenting with different cheeses in my cooking. I don't know a busy who doesn't appreciate make-ahead appetizers like this!
—Sally Halfaker, St. Charles, Missouri

1 package (7 ounces) Gouda cheese
1/4 cup beer *or* nonalcoholic beer
2 tablespoons butter, cubed
1 teaspoon Dijon mustard
1-1/2 teaspoons snipped fresh dill *or* 1/2 teaspoon dill weed
Crackers *or* pretzels

Carefully slice off the top of the waxed coating on the cheese round. Scoop out the cheese; set waxed shell aside. Place cheese in a food processor. Add the beer, butter and mustard; cover and process until smooth. Stir in dill. Spoon into the reserved shell. Refrigerate until serving. Serve with crackers or pretzels. **Yield:** 1-1/3 cups.

Hearty Party Meatballs

This flavorful, filling appetizer is similar to Swedish meatballs. They always disappear when I make them for parties.
—Sue Graham, Kansas City, Missouri

- **4 bacon strips, diced**
- **2 teaspoons beef bouillon granules**
- **2 cups boiling water**
- **1 egg**
- **1/4 cup dry bread crumbs**
- **3/4 teaspoon salt, *divided***
- **Dash pepper**
- **1 pound lean ground beef**
- **2 medium onions, sliced and separated into rings**
- **1/4 cup all-purpose flour**
- **1 can (12 ounces) beer *or* 1-1/2 cups beef broth**
- **2 teaspoons brown sugar**
- **2 teaspoons white vinegar**
- **1/2 teaspoon dried thyme**
- **1/4 to 1/2 teaspoon browning sauce, optional**

In a small skillet, cook bacon over medium heat until crisp; remove to paper towels. Drain, reserving drippings. In a small bowl, dissolve bouillon in boiling water. In a large bowl, combine the egg, 1/4 cup of bouillon, bread crumbs, 1/4 teaspoon salt and pepper. Crumble beef over mixture and mix well. Shape into 1-in. balls.

In a large skillet, brown meatballs in 1 tablespoon of reserved bacon drippings; drain. With a slotted spoon, transfer to a greased 11-in. x 7-in. x 2-in. baking dish. In the same skillet, saute onions until tender; drain. Place over meatballs.

In a saucepan, combine flour and 2 tablespoons of reserved drippings until smooth. Gradually stir in beer or broth and remaining bouillon. Add the brown sugar, vinegar, thyme and remaining salt. Bring to a boil; cook and stir for 2 minutes or until thickened. Stir in browning sauce if desired. Pour over meatballs. Cover and bake at 350° for 40-45 minutes or until meat is no longer pink. Sprinkle with bacon. **Yield:** 2 dozen.

Oatmeal Pecan Bars

These chewy bars took first place in the bar cookie division at our county fair in 2001. Topping them with a coconut-pecan frosting is a tasty twist.
—Leslie Duncan, Hayden, Idaho

- **2 cups all-purpose flour**
- **2 cups old-fashioned oats**
- **1-1/2 cups packed brown sugar**
- **1 teaspoon baking soda**
- **1 cup cold butter**
- **1 can (15 ounces) coconut pecan frosting**
- **1 cup (6 ounces) semisweet chocolate chips**
- **1/2 cup chopped pecans**

In a large bowl, combine the flour, oats, brown sugar and baking soda. Cut in butter until mixture resembles coarse crumbs. Set aside 2 cups for topping. Press remaining crumb mixture into a greased 15-in. x 10-in. x 1-in. baking pan. Bake at 350° for 8-10 minutes or until set.

In a microwave-safe bowl, heat frosting for 30-45 seconds or until softened; stir well. Spread over crust. Sprinkle with chocolate chips and pecans. Top with reserved crumb mixture. Bake for 14-18 minutes or until frosting is bubbly and top is golden brown. Cool completely on a wire rack; cut into squares. **Yield:** 40 servings.

Black Bean Dip

(Pictured at right)

With black beans, avocados, corn, peppers and cilantro, this family-favorite bean dip has lots of flavor and texture. This dip came about when I was experimenting with a similar recipe one day.
—Cheryl Anderson, Lincolnville, Maine

2 medium ripe avocados, peeled and diced
2 tablespoons lime juice
1 can (15-1/4 ounces) whole kernel corn, drained
1 can (15 ounces) black beans, rinsed and drained
1 medium sweet red pepper, chopped
6 green onions, chopped
2 tablespoons minced fresh cilantro
3 garlic cloves, minced
2 tablespoons olive oil
1 teaspoon red wine vinegar
1/2 teaspoon salt
1/4 teaspoon pepper
Tortilla chips

In a bowl, combine avocados and lime juice; let stand for 10 minutes. In a large bowl, combine the corn, beans, red pepper, onions, cilantro and garlic. In a small bowl, whisk the oil, vinegar, salt and pepper. Drizzle over corn mixture; toss to coat. Gently fold in the avocado mixture. Cover and refrigerate for at least 2 hours or until chilled. Serve with tortilla chips. **Yield:** 4-1/2 cups.

Cutting Kernels from Corncobs

WHEN making Black Bean Dip (above), you can use 1-3/4 cups fresh corn kernels instead of canned corn.

To cut kernels from a corncob, stand one end of the cob on a cutting board. Starting at the top, run a sharp knife down the cob, cutting deeply to remove whole kernels.

One medium cob yields about 1/2 cup kernels.

Zesty Smoked Links

These flavorful sausages prepared in a slow-cooker are great when entertaining. Men in the family can't resist these basic but good snacks.
—Jackie Boothman, La Grande, Oregon

1 bottle (12 ounces) chili sauce
1 cup grape jelly
2 tablespoons lemon juice
2 packages (1 pound *each*) miniature smoked sausage links *and/or* hot dogs

In a large skillet, combine chili sauce, jelly and lemon juice; cook over medium-low heat until jelly is melted. Stir in sausages. Reduce heat; cover and cook for 30 minutes or until heated through, stirring occasionally. Serve immediately or keep warm in a slow cooker. **Yield:** about 32 servings.

Great Tips for Tailgating

YOU'RE guaranteed a successful tailgate party with these winning helpful hints:

- Keep the menu simple. Guests aren't expecting a seven-course meal at this kind of casual get-together. Three to four homemade dishes should be the maximum. Fill in with purchased items like chips and dip if necessary.
- When selecting foods, look for ones that are easy to eat while standing up or sitting in a lawn chair. Also, dishes made without perishable ingredients (such as mayonnaise) travel best. Rely on foods that can be made ahead and brought to the event or that can be cooked there on the grill. When transporting, remember to keep hot foods hot and cold foods cold.
- If you're feeling ambitious, handle all the food yourself and divide the cost among the group. Or assign a food item to each person attending.
- To get an early start in the morning, pack the car the night before with nonperishable food, chairs and tables. Don't forget supplies like a blanket or tablecloth to spread over the tailgate and a variety of paper products (plates, napkins, utensils, paper towels, trash bags, resealable plastic bags, etc.).
- True tailgaters proudly show their support of the team, so dress in team colors or jerseys!
- Just before heading out, pack the food and beverage coolers. Covered plastic containers work great for all kinds of food because they prevent leaks and won't break during transport.
- When you get to the parking lot, fly a team banner so other tailgaters in your group can find you. Or keep in contact with cell phones.
- Plan on eating at least 45 minutes before the game starts. This gives you time to clean up and pack things away.
- Before heading into the game, make note of your parking location so you're not lost in a sea of cars afterward.
- Instead of fighting traffic jams when the game is over, linger in the parking lot for an hour or so. Rehash the highlights of the game over a snack or dessert.

Sweet 'n' Salty Snack Mix

(Pictured at right)

When my children were growing up, they enjoyed making—and eating!—this snack mix, especially on Halloween. Now my grandchildren love it as well.
—Ann Brown, Bolivar, Missouri

2-1/2 quarts popped popcorn
2 cups salted peanuts
2 cups miniature pretzels
2 cups raisins
1 cup plain M&M's
1 cup candy corn
1/2 cup sunflower kernels

In a large bowl, combine all of the ingredients; mix well. Store in an airtight container. **Yield:** about 4 quarts.

Sub Salad

Salami, ham, pepperoni and cheeses make this hearty salad a favorite of hungry folks. I sometimes serve this in a bread bowl.
—Dana Pletz, Wilmington, Delaware

8 ounces hard salami, diced
8 ounces fully cooked ham, diced
8 ounces pepperoni, diced
4 ounces provolone cheese, diced
4 ounces American cheese, diced
2 medium tomatoes, chopped
1 medium red onion, chopped
1/2 cup mayonnaise
1 tablespoon olive oil
1/2 teaspoon garlic salt
1/4 teaspoon dried oregano
French bread slices

In a 2-1/2-qt. glass serving bowl, combine the first seven ingredients. In a small bowl, combine the mayonnaise, oil, garlic salt and oregano. Pour over meat mixture and toss to coat. Cover and refrigerate until serving. Serve with French bread. **Yield:** 8-10 servings.

FALL *Entertaining*

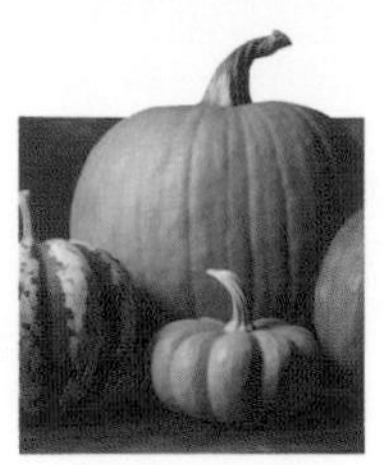

Eerie Halloween Evening

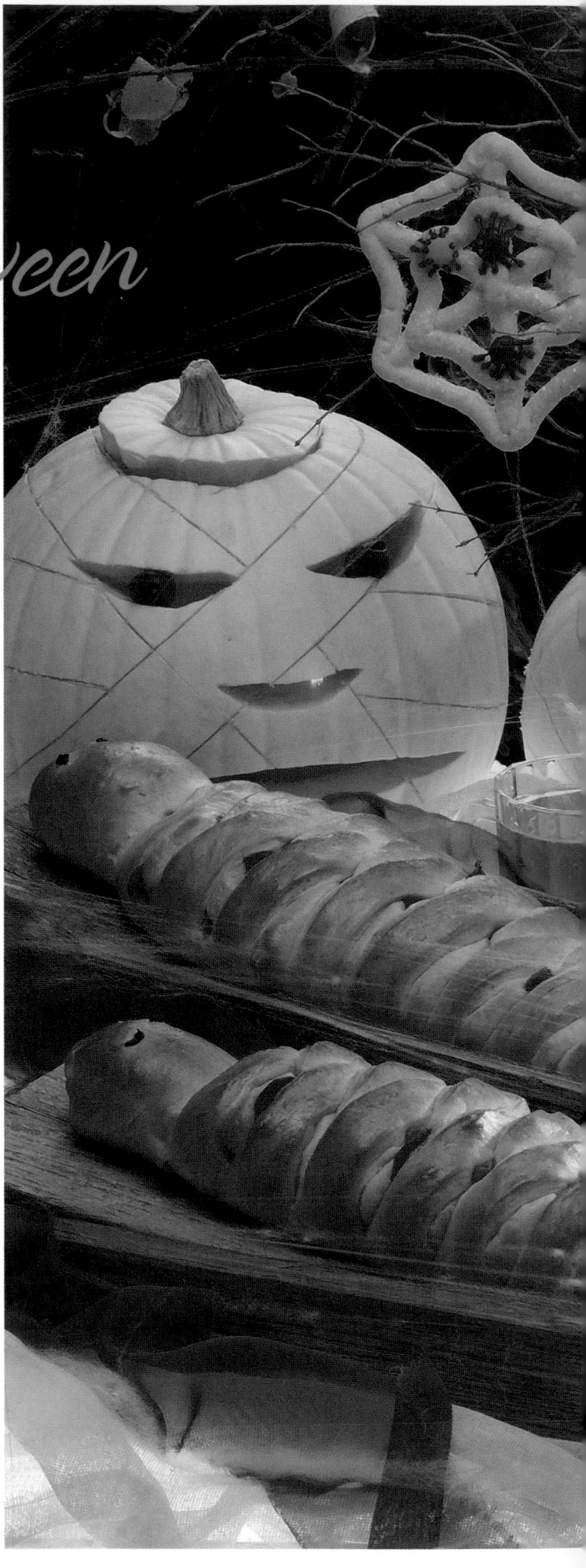

SCARE UP your favorite ghouls and goblins on October 31 for a haunting Halloween filled with frighteningly good food and fun!

Get the party jumping with Witch's Caviar appetizer and bubbling Magic Potion Punch.

Then bewitch hungry guests by laying Yummy Mummy Calzones upon your spine-tingling table.

You can fill these tasty Italian-inspired turnovers with any of your favorite pizza toppings.

Licorice Caramels shaped like tombstones are a spooky sweet sure to invoke the Halloween spirit in everyone.

Or put a spin on standard sugar cookies and serve Spiderweb Cookies! (Recipes shown at right.)

Creepy Cuisine

Yummy Mummy Calzones

(Pictured on page 148)

Family-favorite pizza toppings are the not-so-spooky surprise inside these clever calzones from our Test Kitchen. If you serve these on wood "coffins" like we did in the photo on page 148, be sure to line the surface with plastic wrap or waxed paper.

2 loaves (1 pound *each*) frozen bread dough, thawed
1-1/2 cups (6 ounces) shredded mozzarella cheese
1/2 cup pizza sauce
50 pepperoni slices
1/2 cup chopped green pepper
1 egg, beaten
2 ripe olive slices, cut in half

Roll out each piece of dough into a rounded triangle shape, about 14 in. long and 11 in. wide at the base of the triangle. Place each on a parchment-lined baking sheet with the tip of the triangle toward you. Lightly score a 4-in.-wide rectangle in the center of the triangle 2 in. from the top and bottom. On each long side, cut 1-in.-wide strips at an angle up to the score line, leaving a triangle in the top center of the wide end for the head.

Inside the scored rectangle in the center, layer cheese, pizza sauce, pepperoni and green pepper. Shape the top center triangle into a head. Starting at the head, fold alternating strips of dough at an angle across filling, stopping at the last strip on each side. Fold the bottom dough tip up over the filling, then fold the remaining two strips over the top; press down firmly.

Brush dough with egg. Cover and let rise for 15 minutes. For eyes, press olive pieces into head. Bake at 350° for 25-28 minutes or until golden brown. Let stand for 5 minutes before slicing. **Yield:** 8-10 servings.

Making Yummy Mummy Calzones

1. Form the bread dough into a rounded triangle shape and score a 4-in.-wide rectangle in the center. On each long side, cut 1-in.-wide strips at an angle up to the score line. Layer toppings in the rectangle.

2. Starting at the wide end, fold alternating strips of dough at an angle across the filling, leaving one strip on the bottom of each side. Continue with the recipe as directed.

Spiderweb Cookies

(Pictured at right and on page 148)

A clever design puts a new spin on standard sugar cookies in this recipe from our Test Kitchen.

1 cup butter, softened
1 cup confectioners' sugar
1 egg
1 tablespoon grated orange peel
2-1/4 cups all-purpose flour
Clear edible glitter
1/4 cup milk chocolate chips, melted
Brown and green milk chocolate M&M's
Orange nonpareils

In a large mixing bowl, cream butter and confectioners' sugar. Beat in egg and orange peel. Gradually add flour; mix well. Transfer dough to a pastry bag fitted with a large round pastry tip. Pipe spiderwebs (about 4 in. high x 4 in. wide) onto foil-lined baking sheets. With a pastry brush, gently brush each web with water. Lightly sprinkle with edible glitter. Bake at 375° for 8-10 minutes or until set but not browned. Cool for 1 minute before removing from pans to wire racks to cool completely.

Fill a small resealable plastic bag with melted chocolate; cut a small hole in a corner of bag. For spiders, attach two or three M&M's on each web with melted chocolate; pipe eight spider legs around each. For spider eyes, attach nonpareils with melted chocolate. **Yield:** 1-1/2 dozen.

Witch's Caviar

(Pictured on page 149)

I like to serve this dip with triangle-shaped tortillas because they look like pointy witch hats.
—Darlene Brenden, Salem, Oregon

2 cans (4-1/4 ounces *each*) chopped ripe olives, undrained
2 cans (4 ounces *each*) chopped green chilies, undrained
2 medium tomatoes, seeded and chopped
3 green onions, chopped
2 garlic cloves, minced
1 tablespoon red wine vinegar
1 tablespoon olive oil
1/2 teaspoon pepper
Dash seasoned salt
Tortilla chips

In a bowl, combine the first nine ingredients. Cover and refrigerate overnight. Serve with tortilla chips. **Yield:** 4 cups.

Magic Potion Punch

(Pictured on page 149)

At a Halloween party, the more creepy the food, the better!
I like to tuck gummy worms into an ice ring when I make this great green punch.
—Michelle Thomas, Bangor, Maine

2 packages (3 ounces *each*) lime gelatin
1/2 cup sugar
1 cup boiling water
3 cups cold water
1 quart noncarbonated lemon-lime drink, chilled
1-1/2 quarts lemon-lime soda, chilled

Dissolve gelatin and sugar in boiling water; add cold water. Transfer to a punch bowl. Stir in lemon-lime drink and soda. **Yield:** about 4 quarts.

Gummy Worm Ice Ring

TO KEEP Magic Potion Punch cold during your party, chill it with a gummy worm ice ring. Here's how:

Fill a ring mold halfway with water. Freeze until solid. Top with gummy worms; add enough water to almost cover. Freeze until solid.

To unmold, wrap the bottom of the ring with a hot, damp dishcloth. Turn out onto a baking sheet; place in a punch bowl.

Evil Eye Truffles

A few years ago, I hosted a Halloween bash with a variety of foods.
These were a fun addition to the table and so tasty!
—Linda Fete, Massillon, Ohio

1 cup chunky peanut butter
1/4 cup butter, softened
2 cups crisp rice cereal
1 cup confectioners' sugar
12 ounces white candy coating
2 tablespoons shortening
36 green *and/or* blue milk chocolate M&M's
1 tube red decorator icing
1 tube black decorator icing

In a large bowl, combine peanut butter and butter. Stir in cereal and confectioners' sugar until well combined. With buttered hands, form into 1-in. balls. In a microwave, melt candy coating and shortening until smooth. Dip balls into coating; allow excess to drip off. Place on a waxed paper-lined baking sheet. Before coating is cool, press an M&M into the center of each ball. Cool completely.

Using a small round pastry tip and red icing, pipe small wavy lines on the sides of balls to resemble bloodshot eyes. Use black icing frosting and a small round pastry tip to add a dot in the center of M&M for pupil. **Yield:** 3 dozen.

Ghoulish Fingers

(Pictured at right)

We serve this fun finger food at our annual Halloween party alongside sandwich rolls and condiments.
—Marilee Davieau
Allentown, Pennsylvania

- 3 **packages (8 ounces *each*) assorted lunch meat**
- 1 **package (3 ounces) cream cheese, softened**
- 12 **grape tomatoes, halved lengthwise**

Roll up each slice of lunch meat; spread a small amount of cream cheese at seam to secure roll. Insert a tomato half at one end of each roll to resemble a fingernail; secure tomato in place with a small amount of cream cheese. Place seam side down on a platter. Cover and refrigerate until serving. **Yield:** 2 dozen.

Harvest Snack Mix

Candy corn makes this a natural snack for fall gatherings. The sweet and salty flavors are irresistible.
—Marlene Harguth, Maynard, Minnesota

- 2 **cups pretzel sticks**
- 1 **cup mixed nuts**
- 1/2 **cup sunflower kernels**
- 6 **tablespoons butter, melted**
- 1/2 **teaspoon ground cinnamon**
- 1/8 **teaspoon ground cloves**
- 8 **cups popped popcorn**
- 1 **cup candy corn**
- 1 **cup chocolate bridge mix**

In a large bowl, combine the pretzels, nuts and sunflower kernels. Combine the butter, cinnamon and cloves. Drizzle a third of butter mixture over pretzel mixture; toss to coat. Transfer to a greased 15-in. x 10-in. x 1-in. baking pan. Bake at 300° for 15 minutes.

Place popcorn in a large bowl; drizzle with remaining butter mixture and toss to coat. Stir into pretzel mixture. Bake 15 minutes longer or until heated through. Cool; transfer to a large bowl. Add candy corn and bridge mix; toss to combine. **Yield:** 3 quarts.

Licorice Caramels

(Pictured on page 149)

Fans of black licorice won't be able to stop eating these gooey caramels. I appreciate their ease of preparation.
—Donna Higbee, Riverton, Utah

1 teaspoon plus 1 cup butter, ***divided***
2 cups sugar
1-1/2 cups light corn syrup
1 can (14 ounces) sweetened condensed milk
1/2 teaspoon salt
2 teaspoons anise extract
1/4 teaspoon black food coloring

Line an 8-in. square pan with heavy-duty foil and grease the foil with 1 teaspoon butter; set aside. In a heavy saucepan, combine the sugar, corn syrup, milk, salt and remaining butter; bring to a boil over medium heat. Cook and stir until a candy thermometer reads 244° (firm-ball stage).

Remove from the heat; stir in extract and food coloring (keep face away from mixture as odor is very strong). Pour into prepared pan (do not scrape saucepan). Cool completely before cutting. Using foil, lift candy out of pan. Discard foil; cut into 1-in.-wide rectangles. Using finger, round tops of caramels, forming tombstones. Wrap each in waxed paper. **Yield:** about 5 dozen.

Editor's Note: We recommend that you test your candy thermometer before each use by bringing water to a boil; the thermometer should read 212°. Adjust your recipe temperature up or down based on your test.

Creepy Spiders

Cake mix gives these chocolate sandwich cookies a head start. You can even have kids help assemble the "spiders!"
—Nella Parker, Hersey, Michigan

1 package (18-1/4 ounces) chocolate fudge cake mix
1/2 cup butter, melted
1 egg
1 can (16 ounces) chocolate frosting
Black shoestring licorice, cut into 1-1/2 inch pieces
1/4 cup red-hot candies

In a large mixing bowl, combine the cake mix, butter and egg (dough will be stiff). Shape into 1-in. balls. Place 2 in. apart on ungreased baking sheets. Bake at 350° for 10-12 minutes or until set. Cool for 1 minute before removing from pans to wire racks.

Spread a heaping teaspoonful of frosting over the bottom of half of the cookies. Place four licorice pieces on each side of cookies for spider legs; top with remaining cookies. For eyes, attach two red-hot candies with frosting to top edge of spider. **Yield:** about 2 dozen.

Goblin Eyeballs

(Pictured at right)

Our home economists had great vision when creating these devilish deviled eggs. Guests at your Halloween party will be "goblin" them up!

12 eggs
Red food coloring
3/4 cup mayonnaise
1 tablespoon prepared mustard
Salt and pepper to taste
12 large stuffed olives, halved widthwise

Place eggs in a single layer in a large saucepan; add enough cold water to cover eggs by 1 in. Bring to a boil over high heat. Reduce heat; cover and simmer for 15 minutes. Drain; let stand until cool enough to handle. Gently crack eggs (do not peel).

Fill a large bowl with hot water; add food coloring to tint water a dark red. Add eggs, making sure they are completely covered by water; let stand for 30 minutes. Remove eggs from water; peel (eggs should have a veined appearance).

Cut eggs in half widthwise; place yolks in a bowl. Set whites aside. Mash yolks with a fork; stir in the mayonnaise, mustard, salt and pepper. To make eggs stand better on serving plate, slice a small piece from the bottom of egg white halves. Stuff with yolk mixture. Place an olive half in the center of each to resemble an eyeball. Refrigerate until serving. **Yield:** 2 dozen.

Carnival Caramel Apples

With four kids (and one child whose birthday is November 1), we celebrate Halloween in style around our house. These caramel apples are a tried-and-true favorite year after year.
—Gail Prather, Bethel, Minnesota

1/2 cup butter
2 cups packed brown sugar
1 cup corn syrup
Dash salt
1 can (14 ounces) sweetened condensed milk
1 teaspoon vanilla extract
10 to 12 Popsicle sticks
10 to 12 medium tart apples, washed and dried
1 cup salted peanuts, chopped

In a large heavy saucepan, melt butter; add the brown sugar, corn syrup and salt. Cook and stir over medium heat until mixture comes to a boil, about 10-12 minutes. Stir in milk. Cook and stir until a candy thermometer reads 248° (firm-ball stage). Remove from the heat; stir in vanilla.

Insert Popsicle sticks into apples. Dip each apple into hot caramel mixture; turn to coat. Dip end of apples into peanuts. Set on buttered waxed paper to cool. **Yield:** 10-12 apples.

Editor's Note: We recommend that you test your candy thermometer before each use by bringing water to a boil; the thermometer should read 212°. Adjust your recipe temperature up or down based on your test.

Spiderweb Dip with Bat Tortilla Chips

Every year, our daughter and her friends anticipate our annual Halloween party. Among the menu items is this taco dip with bat-shaped tortilla chips.
—Sonia Candler, Edmonton, Alberta

20 chipotle chili and pepper tortillas *or* flour tortillas (7 inches)
3/4 teaspoon garlic salt
3/4 teaspoon ground coriander
3/4 teaspoon paprika
1/4 teaspoon plus 1/8 teaspoon pepper
DIP:
1 package (8 ounces) cream cheese, softened
3/4 cup salsa
1/2 cup prepared guacamole
1 to 2 tablespoons sour cream

Cut tortillas into bat shapes with a 3-3/4-in. cookie cutter. Place tortillas on baking sheets coated with nonstick cooking spray. Spritz tortillas with nonstick cooking spray. Combine the garlic salt, coriander, paprika and pepper; sprinkle over tortillas. Bake at 350° for 5-8 minutes or until edges just begin to brown.

In a small mixing bowl, combine cream cheese and salsa. Spread into a 9-in. pie plate. Carefully spread guacamole to within 1 in. of edges. Place sour cream in a small resealable plastic bag; cut a small hole in a corner of bag. Pipe thin concentric circles an inch apart over guacamole. Beginning with the center circle, gently pull a knife through circles toward outer edge. Wipe knife clean. Repeat to complete spiderweb pattern. Serve with tortilla bats. **Yield:** about 1-1/2 cups dip and about 7 dozen chips.

Pumpkin Mummies

(Pictured at right)

FOR a mummy-themed Halloween party, ordinary jack-'o-lanterns just won't do. Instead, carve out a niche for yourself by making these frightful Pumpkin Mummies!

Purchase white pumpkins in a variety of shapes and sizes. Carefully cut a circle around the pumpkin stem, lift off the lid and remove the seeds from the lid and inside the pumpkin.

With a knife, cut two narrow horizontal openings for the eyes, one opening for the nose and one opening for the mouth. Score the outside of the pumpkin to look like wrappings of a mummy. Set a black marble in each eye opening. Set a tea light candle inside the pumpkin and light.

Gauze-Covered Pumpkin Mummy

PUMPKIN MUMMIES will make a memorable impression on the guests at your ghoulish gathering. For even more fun, wrap self-adhesive athletic wrap or self-sticking first aid gauze around the outside of the pumpkin, allowing the black marble "eyes" to peek out.

A Mad Scientist Halloween Scene

GET in the spine-tingling spirit this Halloween by hosting a hair-raising bash in a spooky science lab that even Dr. Frankenstein would envy.

Go out on a limb and concoct a formula for fun with some revolting recipes.

For an enticing experiment, inject a mouth-watering marinade into drumsticks to create the electrifying Spicy Turkey Legs.

Visitors to your loony lab will bolt for the buffet table to scoop up eye-catching Creepy-Crawly Pasta Salad.

Mad Scientist Punch was developed by doctoring up frozen pineapple-orange juice concentrate with sherbet and soda for a batty brew. (All recipes are shown at right.)

Spine-Tingling Supper

(Pictured above)

Spicy Turkey Legs (p. 166)

Creep-Crawly Pasta Salad (p. 164)

Mad Scientist Punch (p. 166)

Fried Bolts

(Pictured at far right, bottom)

Our home economists' nuts-and-bolts appetizers feature mushroom caps and zucchini sticks. Assemble them earlier in the day and chill until ready to deep fry.

16 medium fresh mushrooms
2 small zucchini
2 eggs
2 tablespoons water
1/2 cup all-purpose flour
1/2 teaspoon chili powder
1/4 teaspoon salt
1/4 teaspoon sugar
1/4 teaspoon garlic powder
1/4 teaspoon cayenne pepper
1/4 teaspoon ground cumin
Oil for frying
Sweet-and-sour sauce, optional

Remove stems from mushrooms. Cut a thin layer from the top of mushroom caps; cut mushroom edges, forming a hexagon shape. Cut zucchini lengthwise into quarters, then into 2-in. pieces. Trim one end to fit into mushroom caps.

Insert a toothpick through the top of the mushroom into the zucchini, leaving about 1 in. of toothpick to use as a handle for dipping.

In a small shallow bowl, beat the eggs and water. In another bowl, combine the flour, chili powder, salt, sugar, garlic powder, cayenne and cumin. Dip zucchini-mushroom bolts in egg mixture, then coat with flour mixture.

In an electric skillet, heat 1 in. of oil to 375°. Fry bolts in batches for 2-3 minutes or until golden brown on all sides. Drain on paper towels. Serve warm with sweet-and-sour sauce if desired. **Yield:** 16 appetizers.

Buggy Snack Mix

Chocolate-covered raisin "bugs" are a tasty surprise in this sweet and crunchy snack mix from our Test Kitchen. Candy corn adds a bit of color.

1 can (3 ounces) chow mein noodles
1 cup unsalted cashews
1 cup salted peanuts
1/2 cup packed brown sugar
1/4 cup butter
2 tablespoons light corn syrup
1/8 teaspoon salt
1/4 teaspoon baking soda
1 cup candy corn
1 cup chocolate-covered raisins

In a large heatproof bowl, combine the chow mein noodles, cashews and peanuts; set aside. In a microwave-safe bowl, combine the brown sugar, butter, corn syrup and salt. Microwave, uncovered, on high for 2 minutes or until sugar is dissolved and syrup is bubbly, stirring frequently. Stir in baking soda; microwave 20 seconds longer or until mixture begins to foam.

Carefully pour over chow mein noodle mixture; stir to coat. Transfer to a greased 15-in. x 10-in. x 1-in. baking pan. Bake at 300° for 25-30 minutes, stirring every 10 minutes. Spread on waxed paper; cool for at least 30 minutes.

Place snack mix in a large bowl. Add candy corn and raisins; gently toss. Store in an airtight container. **Yield:** 6 cups.

Editor's Note: This recipe was tested in a 1,100-watt microwave.

Backbone Roll-Ups

(Pictured at right, top)

These roll-ups from our Test Kitchen are sliced thick, then stacked slightly askew to resemble a backbone. Feel free to use other fillings.

3/4 cup garlic-herb cheese spread
6 flour tortillas (8 inches)
1 cup fresh baby spinach
6 thin slices deli ham
12 thin slices hard salami
6 slices provolone cheese
1/2 cup chopped green pepper
1/2 cup chopped sweet red pepper

Spread 2 tablespoons of cheese spread over each tortilla. Layer with spinach, ham, salami and cheese. Sprinkle with peppers. Roll up tightly and wrap in plastic wrap. Refrigerate for 1 hour or until firm.

Unwrap and cut each into six slices. On a serving plate, stack roll-ups to resemble a spine. **Yield:** 3 dozen.

Body-Parts Party Game

HAVE the guests at your Halloween party gather 'round for a fun game that focuses on feeling frightfully fun foods. Place the "body parts" listed here in separate, large resealable plastic bags, then place in paper bags.

Dim the lights and have everyone sit in a circle. Tell guests to pass around the bags one at a time, reach into each bag without looking and guess the body parts. Here's what you need for a howling good time:

- Hot dog chunks (noses)
- Whole cooked, chilled cauliflower (brain)
- Peeled grapes (eyeballs)
- Cooked spaghetti noodles (intestines)
- Latex glove filled with warm water, tied and frozen (hand)
- Dried apple rings, cut in half (ears)
- Slab of gelatin (liver)
- Nut shells (toenails)
- Pieces of chalk (teeth)

Chunky Chili

(Pictured at far right)

My family (especially my dad) loves chili. After experimenting with several recipes, I came up with my own version that uses ground turkey and is conveniently prepared in a slow cooker.
—Jolene Britten, Gig Harbor, Washington

1 pound ground turkey *or* beef
1 medium onion, chopped
2 medium tomatoes, cut up
1 can (16 ounces) kidney beans, rinsed and drained
1 can (15 ounces) chili beans, undrained
1 can (15 ounces) tomato sauce
1 cup water
1 can (4 ounces) chopped green chilies
1 tablespoon chili powder
2 teaspoons salt
1 teaspoon ground cumin
3/4 teaspoon pepper
Sour cream and sliced jalapenos, optional

In a large skillet, cook turkey and onion over medium heat until meat is no longer pink; drain. Transfer to a 3-1/2-qt. slow cooker.

Stir in the tomatoes, beans, tomato sauce, water, chilies, chili powder, salt, cumin and pepper. Cover and cook on low for 5-6 hours or until heated through. Garnish with sour cream and jalapenos if desired. **Yield:** 6-8 servings (about 2 quarts).

Apple Peanut Butter Cookies

These spiced peanut butter cookies are great for fall gatherings. They're crisp outside and soft inside.
—Marjorie Benson, New Castle, Pennsylvania

1/2 cup shortening
1/2 cup chunky peanut butter
1/2 cup sugar
1/2 cup packed brown sugar
1 egg
1/2 teaspoon vanilla extract
1/2 cup grated peeled apple
1-1/2 cups all-purpose flour
1/2 teaspoon baking soda
1/2 teaspoon salt
1/2 teaspoon ground cinnamon

In a large mixing bowl, cream the shortening, peanut butter and sugars. Beat in egg and vanilla. Stir in apple. Combine the dry ingredients; gradually add to creamed mixture.

Drop by rounded tablespoonfuls 2 in. apart onto greased baking sheets. Bake at 375° for 10-12 minutes or until golden brown. Cool for 5 minutes before removing to wire racks. **Yield:** about 2-1/2 dozen.

Editor's Note: Reduced-fat or generic brands of peanut butter are not recommended for this recipe.

Breadstick Bones

(Pictured at right)

Our home economists lightly season refrigerated breadsticks, then tie the ends into knots to create these Breadstick Bones.

1 tube (11 ounces) refrigerated breadsticks
1 tablespoon butter, melted
2 tablespoons grated Parmesan cheese
1/4 teaspoon garlic salt

Unroll and separate breadsticks. Carefully stretch dough and tie the ends of each breadstick into a knot. With a scissors, snip a small notch in the center. Place on an ungreased baking sheet; brush with butter.

Combine Parmesan cheese and garlic salt; sprinkle over dough. Bake at 375° for 10-12 minutes or until golden brown. Serve warm. **Yield:** 1 dozen.

Fruity Eyeball Salad

A light mint dressing nicely coats assorted fruity "eyeballs" in this recipe from our Test Kitchen. Just watch this salad disappear from the buffet table!

2 cups watermelon balls
2 cups cantaloupe balls
2 cups honeydew balls
1 cup seedless red grapes
1 cup seedless green grapes
DRESSING:
1/3 cup unsweetened apple juice
1 tablespoon honey
2 teaspoons minced fresh mint

In a large bowl, combine the melon balls and grapes. In a small bowl, combine the dressing ingredients. Pour over fruit and toss to coat. Cover and refrigerate until chilled. **Yield:** 8 servings.

Creepy-Crawly Pasta Salad

(Pictured on page 159)

As a change of pace from pasta salads featuring Italian salad dressing or mayonnaise, our home economists developed a delicious sweet-and-sour dressing.

8 ounces uncooked fusilli *or* tricolor rotini pasta
1 medium zucchini, julienned
1 cup cherry tomatoes
1 cup fresh cauliflowerets
1 cup colossal ripe olives, halved
3/4 cup pimiento-stuffed olives
1 small green pepper, chopped
1/2 cup chopped red onion

DRESSING:

1/4 cup ketchup
2 tablespoons sugar
2 tablespoons white vinegar
1/2 small onion, cut into wedges
1 garlic clove, peeled
1 teaspoon paprika
1/4 teaspoon salt
1/4 cup vegetable oil

Cook pasta according to package directions; drain and rinse in cold water. Place in a large bowl; add the zucchini, tomatoes, cauliflower, olives, green pepper and red onion.

In a blender, combine the ketchup, sugar, vinegar, onion, garlic, paprika and salt; cover and process until blended. While processing, gradually add oil in a steady stream; process until thickened. Pour over pasta salad and toss to coat. Cover and refrigerate for at least 2 hours before serving. **Yield:** 13 servings.

Spooktacular Science Lab

TRY these tricks for creating an eerie lab where Frankenstein would be happy biding his tormented time! For many of these eye-popping props, we headed to a local science and surplus store.

- A spooky sterile environment starts with a simple stainless steel table. Concoct creepy serving containers from stainless steel baking pans and mixing bowls.
- Use stainless steel cooking instruments for serving and a meat cleaver to cut the Frankenstein Cake (see photo above right).
- Spine-tingling table toppers include beakers in various shapes and sizes, tall test tubes to display chocolate candy eyeballs, chains and Shrunken Apple Heads (see page 167).
- Tint water a yellow-green color and pour into assorted test tubes and beakers. Carefully add a little dry ice if desired.
- A white lab coat and skeleton in the background is an alarming addition.
- For a monstrous mood, dim the lights and fire up drippy candles on an inexpensive candelabra.

Frankenstein Cake

(Pictured at right)

Convenience items like a cake mix and canned frosting make this clever dessert a breeze to prepare. It always elicits oohs and aahs at Halloween parties.
—Nancy Bresler, Kinde, Michigan

1 package (18-1/4 ounces) chocolate cake mix
1 package (8 ounces) cream cheese, softened
1/2 cup sour cream
1/2 cup sugar
1 egg
1/2 teaspoon vanilla extract
1 carton (8 ounces) frozen whipped topping, thawed
Moss green paste food coloring
1 can (16 ounces) chocolate frosting
1 Swiss cake roll *or* Ho Ho

Prepare cake batter according to package directions. Pour into a greased and waxed paper-lined 13-in. x 9-in. x 2-in. baking pan. In a small mixing bowl, beat the cream cheese, sour cream, sugar, egg and vanilla until smooth. Drop by tablespoonfuls about 1 in. apart onto batter.

Bake at 350° for 40-45 minutes or until center is firm when lightly touched. Cool for 10 minutes before removing from pan to a wire rack to cool completely.

To make Frankenstein, cut a piece of cake for the head (about 10 in. x 7-3/4 in.) and neck (about 2-1/2 in. x 4-1/2 in.). Cut two pieces for ears (about 2-3/4 in. x 1/2 in.). Save remaining cake for another use. Position head, neck and ears on a covered board.

Place 1/4 cup whipped topping in a small bowl; tint dark green with moss green food coloring. Cut a small hole in the corner of a small plastic bag; insert round pastry tip #3 and fill with tinted topping. Set aside.

Tint remaining whipped topping moss green. Frost face, neck and ears, building up areas for the forehead, nose and cheeks. With reserved dark green topping, pipe mouth, stitches on neck and forehead, and eyes with pupils.

Cut a hole in the corner of a pastry or plastic bag; insert pastry tip #233. Fill with chocolate frosting; pipe hair 1-1/4 in. from top of head to forehead and about 4 in. down sides of head. Cut cake roll in half widthwise; place on each side of neck for bolts. Store in the refrigerator. **Yield:** 12-15 servings.

Spicy Turkey Legs

(Pictured on page 158)

Guests at your Halloween party will get a kick out of these flavorful turkey legs from our Test Kitchen. For less spicy flavor, reduce the amount of hot sauce and inject 1/2 ounce into each leg.

- **2/3 cup Louisiana-style hot sauce**
- **5 tablespoons vegetable oil**
- **1 tablespoon chili powder**
- **1 tablespoon soy sauce**
- **2 teaspoons ground mustard**
- **1 teaspoon garlic powder**
- **1 teaspoon poultry seasoning**
- **1 teaspoon onion powder**
- **1 teaspoon celery salt**
- **1/2 teaspoon white pepper**
- **1/2 teaspoon hot pepper sauce, optional**
- **6 turkey drumsticks (1 pound *each*)**

In a small bowl, combine the first 11 ingredients; set aside 1/4 cup for basting. Draw remaining marinade into a flavor injector. In several areas of each drumstick, inject a total of 2 tablespoons (or 1 oz.) of marinade into the meat while slowly pulling out the needle.

Place drumsticks on a foil-lined 15-in. x 10-in. x 1-in. baking pan. Cover and bake at 375° for 30 minutes. Uncover; bake 45-55 minutes longer or until a meat thermometer reads 180°, basting occasionally with reserved marinade. **Yield:** 6 servings.

Editor's Note: Flavor injectors can be found in the outdoor cooking section of your favorite home or cooking store or through numerous Internet sources.

Using Flavor Injectors

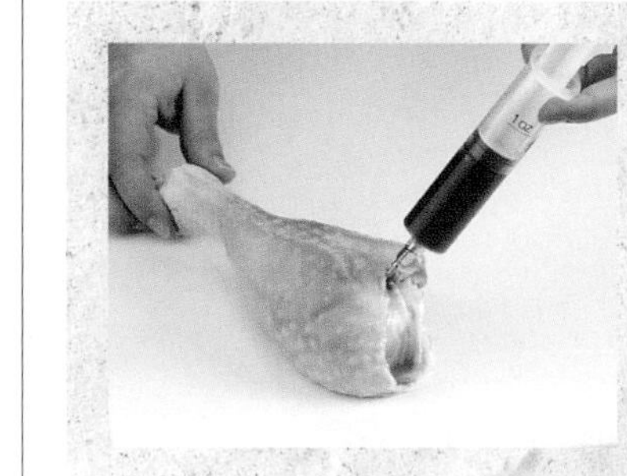

FILL the flavor injector with the marinade. With one hand holding the turkey leg, inject the marinade into the meat, slowly pull out the needle. Inject into several other areas of the meat.

Mad Scientist Punch

(Pictured on page 158)

Our home economists concocted this "potion" with kitchen staples such as juice concentrate, soft drink mix, soda and sherbet. It appeals to kids of all ages!

- **2 cans (12 ounces *each*) frozen pineapple-orange juice concentrate, thawed**
- **2 cups water**
- **1 envelope unsweetened orange soft drink mix**
- **2 liters lemon-lime soda, chilled**
- **1 pint orange sherbet, softened**

In a punch bowl, combine the juice concentrate, water and soft drink mix; stir in soda. Top with scoops of sherbet. Serve immediately. **Yield:** 16 servings (4 quarts).

Shrunken Apple Heads

(Pictured at right)

USE your noggin when decorating for your Halloween bash by fashioning foul faces from ordinary apples. Tuck these haunted "heads" around the food on your buffet table or stack them on candleholders.

With a paring knife remove the skin from large, medium and small Golden Delicious apples. (Note that the apples will shrink in size as they dry.)

Immediately dip the peeled apples into lemon juice to prevent browning.

Cut away the bottom of the apple to form a rounded chin. Carve a nose. Hollow out two circles for eyes and a single circle for a mouth.

Dip the carved apple in lemon juice again and sprinkle with non-iodized table salt.

Place the apples on a rack in a low-sided pan. Set aside in a warm, dry place away from direct sunlight until completely dry. (This may take up to three weeks.)

When dry, the apple heads can also be hung up for display. With a long, hand-sewing needle, insert nylon thread through the center of apples and tie a knot at the bottom end.

Tasty Turkey Day Dinner

GOLDEN roasted turkey, fluffy mashed potatoes, savory gravy, delectable desserts...no other holiday seems to center on a spread of fabulous food quite like Thanksgiving.

The menu featured here is just the thing for folks who favor traditional fare but want to add a tasty twist.

A slightly sweet, simple-to-prepare glaze flavors Maple-Butter Turkey with Gravy. (We also offer two other turkey recipes for you to try.)

In addition to your standard mashed potatoes, prepare a deliciously different side dish, such as Mushrooms au Gratin.

And a unique fruit gives new life to dessert in Persimmon Squash Pie. (All recipes are shown at right.)

A Feast for the Eyes

(Clockwise from top right)

Maple-Butter Turkey with Gravy (p. 172)

Mushrooms au Gratin (p. 176)

Persimmon Squash Pie (p. 173)

Thanksgiving Dinner Timeline

A Few Weeks Before:

- Prepare two grocery lists—one for nonperishable items to purchase now and one for perishable items to purchase a few days before Thanksgiving Day.
- Order a fresh turkey or buy and freeze a frozen turkey.
- Purchase a container for the Cornucopia Centerpiece (page 177).

Four Days Before:

- Thaw the frozen turkey in a pan in the refrigerator. (Allow 24 hours of thawing for every 5 pounds.)

Two Days Before:

- Buy remaining grocery items, including the fresh turkey if you ordered one.
- Make the Pomegranate Cranberry Relish up to the point of adding the chopped walnuts and grated orange peel.

The Day Before:

- Set the table.
- Purchase flowers for the centerpiece and assemble.
- Prepare the Persimmon Squash Pie; chill.
- Bake Scalloped Apples for 20 minutes. (Don't top with bread crumbs or bake longer.) Cover and refrigerate.
- If using the recipe for Maple-Butter Turkey with Gravy, make the maple butter. Cover and chill.

Thanksgiving Day:

- In the morning, peel and cube the potatoes for Traditional Mashed Potatoes; place in a bowl of cold water and refrigerate.
- Roast the turkey according to one of the following recipes: Maple-Butter Turkey with Gravy (p. 172), Seasoned Roast Turkey (p. 175) or Citrus-Rosemary Rubbed Turkey (p. 176).
- A few hours before guests arrive, prepare the Apple Cranberry Cider in a slow cooker.
- Assemble the Pecan Sweet Potato Casserole; add to the oven during the last 45 minutes of the turkey's baking time.
- Remove Scalloped Apples from the refrigerator 30 minutes before baking. Top with buttered bread crumbs.
- Prepare the Traditional Mashed Potatoes.
- Make Mushrooms au Gratin.
- Let the cooked turkey stand for 20 minutes before carving. Prepare the gravy if desired.
- Bake Scalloped Apples for 15 minutes or until tender and heated through.
- Reheat the Pomegranate Cranberry Relish; stir in the chopped walnuts and grated orange peel.
- Serve slices of Persimmon Squash Pie for dessert.

Pecan Sweet Potato Casserole

(Pictured at right)

This convenient casserole calls for canned sweet potatoes, so preparation time is minimal. The nutty, brown sugar topping adds a bit of crunch.
—Anita Briner, Etters, Pennsylvania

2 cans (40 ounces *each*) sweet potatoes, drained
8 eggs
1/2 cup sugar
1/4 cup all-purpose flour
2 teaspoons vanilla extract
1 teaspoon salt

TOPPING:

1 cup packed brown sugar
1/3 cup all-purpose flour
1 cup chopped pecans
1/4 cup cold butter

In a large mixing bowl, mash the sweet potatoes. Add the eggs, sugar, flour, vanilla and salt; beat until smooth. Transfer to a greased 13-in. x 9-in. x 2-in. baking dish.

In a small bowl, combine the brown sugar, flour and pecans; cut in butter until crumbly. Sprinkle over sweet potato mixture. Bake, uncovered, at 325° for 60-70 minutes or until a knife inserted near the center comes out clean. Refrigerate leftovers. **Yield:** 12 servings.

Apple Cranberry Cider

(Pictured at far right)

This fruity cider can be made ahead, then kept warm in a slow cooker so people can serve themselves.
—Kathy Wells, Brodhead, Wisconsin

3 cinnamon sticks (3 inches), broken
1 teaspoon whole cloves
2 quarts apple cider *or* juice
3 cups cranberry juice
2 tablespoons brown sugar

Place cinnamon sticks and cloves on a double thickness of cheesecloth; bring up corners of cloth and tie with string to form a bag. Place the cider, cranberry juice and brown sugar in a 5-qt. slow cooker; add spice bag. Cover and cook on high for 2 hours or until cider reaches desired temperature. Discard spice bag before serving. **Yield:** 11 cups.

Maple-Butter Turkey with Gravy

(Pictured on page 169)

Thyme, sage and marjoram blend beautifully with apple cider and maple syrup in this recipe from our Test Kitchen. The maple butter can be prepared 1 to 2 days in advance.

2 cups apple cider *or* juice
1/3 cup maple syrup
3/4 cup butter, cubed
2 tablespoons minced fresh thyme *or* 2 teaspoons dried thyme
1 tablespoon minced fresh sage *or* 1 teaspoon dried sage leaves
2 teaspoons dried marjoram
1 teaspoon salt
1 teaspoon pepper
1 turkey (14 to 16 pounds)
2 to 2-1/2 cups chicken broth
3 tablespoons all-purpose flour

For maple butter, in a small heavy saucepan, bring cider and syrup to a boil. Cook until reduced to 1/2 cup, about 20 minutes. Remove from the heat; stir in the butter, thyme, sage, marjoram, salt and pepper. Transfer to a bowl; cover and refrigerate until set.

With fingers, carefully loosen the skin from both sides of turkey breast. Rub 1/2 cup maple butter under turkey skin. Refrigerate remaining maple butter. Skewer turkey openings; tie drumsticks together. Place on a rack in a roasting pan.

Cover with foil and bake at 325° for 2 hours. Brush top with 1/3 cup maple butter. Bake, uncovered, 1 to 1-1/2 hours longer or until a meat thermometer reads 180°, basting occasionally with pan drippings. (Cover loosely with foil if turkey browns too quickly.) Remove turkey to a serving platter and keep warm. Cover and let stand for 20 minutes before carving.

Pour drippings and loosened brown bits into a 4-cup measuring cup. Skim and discard fat. Add enough broth to drippings to measure 3 cups. In a large saucepan, combine flour and broth mixture until smooth. Stir in remaining maple butter. Bring to a boil; cook and stir for 2 minutes or until thickened. Serve with turkey. **Yield:** 14-16 servings (3-1/3 cups gravy).

Persimmon Squash Pie

(Pictured on page 168 and at right)

I created this recipe for our local persimmon festival, using homegrown squash. I like to make two pies and use more toffee bits and pecans for garnish.
—Betty Milligan, Bedford, Indiana

1 unbaked pastry shell (9 inches)
1/4 cup buttermilk
1/2 cup mashed cooked butternut squash
1/2 cup mashed ripe persimmon pulp
3/4 cup sugar
1/4 cup packed brown sugar
3 tablespoons all-purpose flour
1/2 teaspoon ground cinnamon
1/4 teaspoon baking powder
1/4 teaspoon baking soda
1/4 teaspoon salt
2 eggs
1/4 cup heavy whipping cream
1/4 cup butter, melted
1 teaspoon vanilla extract

CARAMEL TOPPING:
30 caramels
2 tablespoons milk
1/3 cup chopped pecans
1/3 cup English toffee bits *or* almond brickle chips

Bake unpricked pastry shell at 450° for 5-6 minutes or until lightly browned; cool on a wire rack. Reduce heat to 350°.

In a blender, combine the buttermilk, squash and persimmon pulp; cover and process until smooth. In a large bowl, combine the sugars, flour, cinnamon, baking powder, baking soda and salt. In a small bowl, combine the eggs, cream, butter, vanilla and squash mixture; stir into dry ingredients just until moistened.

Pour into pastry shell. Bake for 40-45 minutes or until a knife inserted near the center comes out clean.

In a small saucepan, combine caramels and milk. Cook and stir over medium heat until melted and smooth. Pour over hot pie. Sprinkle with pecans and toffee bits. Cool completely on a wire rack. Store in the refrigerator. **Yield:** 8 servings.

Persimmon Pointers

THE PERSIMMON is an exotic fruit with yellow-orange skin, which is at its sweetest when very ripe. To ripen firm fruit, place it in a paper bag at room temperature for 1 to 3 days. When ripe, store in the refrigerator for up to 3 days.

When ready to eat or to use in cooking, cut off the top, scoop out the pulp and discard the seeds.

Pomegranate Cranberry Relish

(Pictured at far right, bottom)

I was inspired to develop this recipe one evening when I was making my usual cranberry relish and my husband was eating a pomegranate. It's so tasty when served alongside chicken or turkey.
—Donna Rivera, Pleasant Hill, California

- **1 package (12 ounces) fresh *or* frozen cranberries**
- **1 medium navel orange, peeled and sectioned**
- **3/4 cup sugar**
- **3 tablespoons honey**
- **1/2 cup pomegranate seeds**
- **1/2 cup chopped walnuts**
- **2 to 3 teaspoons grated orange peel**

In a large saucepan, combine the cranberries, orange, sugar and honey. Cook and stir over medium heat for 15-20 minutes or until berries pop and mixture is thickened. Stir in pomegranate seeds; cook 2 minutes longer.

Remove from the heat; stir in walnuts and orange peel. Serve warm or chilled. **Yield:** 2-1/2 cups.

Pomegranate Seed Secret

THE SEEDS and surrounding juice sacs (arils) are the only parts of the pomegranate that are edible. One medium pomegranate (about 8 ounces) yields roughly 3/4 cup arils.

Traditional Mashed Potatoes

It's just not Thanksgiving without mashed potatoes! In this version, our home economists stir in half-and-half, sour cream and chives.

- **12 medium potatoes, peeled and cubed**
- **1-1/4 to 1-1/2 cups half-and-half cream**
- **1/3 cup sour cream**
- **1/2 cup butter, cubed**
- **1 teaspoon salt**
- **1/2 teaspoon pepper**
- **1 tablespoon minced chives, optional**

Place potatoes in a Dutch oven and cover with water. Bring to a boil. Reduce heat; cover and cook for 15-20 minutes or until tender. Drain; transfer to a large mixing bowl. Add the cream, sour cream, butter, salt and pepper; beat until light and fluffy. Sprinkle with chives if desired. **Yield:** 16-18 servings.

Scalloped Apples

(Pictured at right, top)

When preparing my first Thanksgiving dinner years ago, I wanted to add a special side dish and came up with this recipe. It's been a part of our traditional dinner ever since.
—Kellie Erwin, Westerville, Ohio

10 cups thinly sliced peeled Golden Delicious apples (about 8)
1 cup sugar
1/2 teaspoon ground cinnamon
1/2 teaspoon ground cloves
6 tablespoons butter, *divided*
2 cups soft bread crumbs (about 4 slices)

In a large bowl, combine the apples, sugar, cinnamon and cloves. Transfer to a greased 13-in. x 9-in. x 2-in. baking dish. Dot with 2 tablespoons butter. Bake, uncovered, at 325° for 25 minutes or until apples are crisp-tender.

Meanwhile, in a small skillet, melt remaining butter. Add bread crumbs; cook and stir for 3-5 minutes or until crispy and golden brown. Sprinkle over apple mixture. Bake 10-15 minutes longer or until apples are tender. Serve warm. **Yield:** 8 servings.

Seasoned Roast Turkey

Rubbing the skin with melted butter keeps this simply seasoned turkey moist and tender.
—Nancy Reichert, Thomasville, Georgia

2 teaspoons salt
2 teaspoons garlic powder
2 teaspoons seasoned salt
1-1/2 teaspoons paprika
1 teaspoon ground ginger
3/4 teaspoon pepper
1/2 teaspoon dried basil
1/4 teaspoon cayenne pepper
1 turkey (13 to 15 pounds)
1/4 cup butter, melted

In a small bowl, combine the first eight ingredients. Place turkey, breast side up, on a rack in a roasting pan; pat dry. Brush with butter. Sprinkle with herb mixture.

Bake, uncovered, at 325° for 2-3/4 to 3-1/4 hours or until a meat thermometer reads 180°, basting occasionally with pan drippings. (Cover loosely with foil if turkey browns too quickly.) Cover and let stand for 20 minutes before carving. **Yield:** 13-15 servings.

Mushrooms au Gratin

(Pictured on page 168)

This easy-to-prepare side dish brings me rave reviews whenever I prepare it for the holidays. Even when I double the recipe, my family eats every bite.
—Tina McFarland, Elko, Nevada

- **2 pounds sliced fresh mushrooms**
- **1/4 cup butter, cubed**
- **1/2 cup white wine *or* chicken broth**
- **2 tablespoons all-purpose flour**
- **2/3 cup sour cream**
- **1 teaspoon pepper**
- **1/4 teaspoon ground nutmeg**
- **1 cup (4 ounces) shredded Gruyere *or* Swiss cheese**
- **2 tablespoons minced fresh parsley**

In a large skillet, saute mushrooms in butter until tender. Add wine or broth. Bring to a boil. Reduce heat; simmer, uncovered, for 4 minutes.

Combine the flour, sour cream, pepper and nutmeg until smooth; stir into mushrooms. Cook and stir for 1-2 minutes or until bubbly. Transfer to a shallow serving dish. Sprinkle with cheese and parsley. **Yield:** 8 servings.

Citrus-Rosemary Rubbed Turkey

While recovering from hip surgery, I wrote my family for some of their favorite recipes to compile into a cookbook. This seasoned turkey is timeless.
—Della Stamp, Long Beach, California

- **2 tablespoons minced fresh rosemary *or* 2 teaspoons dried rosemary, crushed**
- **1-1/2 teaspoons grated fresh *or* dried orange peel**
- **1-1/2 teaspoons grated fresh *or* dried lemon peel**
- **1 teaspoon salt**
- **1 teaspoon onion powder**
- **1 teaspoon garlic powder**
- **1 teaspoon pepper**
- **1/4 cup olive oil**
- **1 turkey (13 to 15 pounds)**

In a small bowl, combine the first seven ingredients. Place turkey, breast side up, on a rack in a roasting pan; pat dry. Brush with oil; sprinkle with rosemary mixture.

Bake, uncovered, at 325° for 2-3/4 to 3-1/4 hours or until a meat thermometer reads 180°, basting occasionally with pan drippings. (Cover loosely with foil if turkey browns too quickly.) Cover and let stand for 20 minutes before carving. **Yield:** 13-15 servings.

Cornucopia Centerpiece

(Pictured above)

CORNUCOPIA is a Latin term derived from two words: "cornu" (meaning horn) and "copia" (meaning plenty).

According to Greek mythology, after Zeus accidentally broke off a horn from the goat, Amalthea, he promised that the horn would always be filled with whatever fruits the goat desired.

A symbol of abundance, the horn of plenty is an appropriate centerpiece for Thanksgiving, where friends and family gather to celebrate around a beautiful table overflowing with home-cooked foods, lively conversation and cherished friends and family.

To create the cornucopia shown above, we purchased a metal, cone-shaped container, filled it with floral foam and added water.

Our fresh flower choices included: wheat-like green grass, liatris, Blue Mountain thistle, myrtle, green button mums, dusty miller, green solidaster and eucalyptus pods.

Sweet Treats Fit for Fall

WHEN the sun starts sinking in the sky and the breeze becomes a bit more brisk, give your family a warm welcome home by dishing out a homemade dessert at dinner.

Packed with seasonal produce like pumpkin, cranberries and nuts, the delectable desserts featured in this chapter are fitting finales for all of your fall menus, including Thanksgiving dinner.

In addition to serving ever-popular pumpkin pie, consider making crowd-pleasing Marbled Pumpkin Cheesecake.

Fruity treats like Individual Cranberry Trifles and Berry Nut Tarts will also become favorites with your family. (All recipes shown at right.)

Seasonal Treats

(Clockwise from top left)

Marbled Pumpkin Cheesecake (p. 180)

Individual Cranberry Trifles (p. 181)

Berry Nut Tarts (p. 182)

Marbled Pumpkin Cheesecake

(Pictured on page 178)

A gingersnap crust pairs well with the pumpkin and cream cheese filling.
—Judy Shatzer, Upper Strasburg, Pennsylvania

1 cup finely crushed gingersnaps (about 20 cookies)
3 tablespoons butter, melted

FILLING:

4 packages (8 ounces *each*) cream cheese, softened
1 cup sugar
3 tablespoons cornstarch, *divided*
1 cup (8 ounces) sour cream
1-1/2 teaspoons vanilla extract
1/4 teaspoon salt
3 eggs
1 teaspoon lemon juice
3/4 cup canned pumpkin
3 tablespoons dark brown sugar
1 tablespoon molasses
2 teaspoons ground cinnamon
3/4 teaspoon ground ginger
1/2 teaspoon ground nutmeg
1/8 teaspoon ground cloves

In a small bowl, combine cookie crumbs and butter. Press onto the bottom of a greased 9-in. springform pan. Place pan on a baking sheet. Bake at 325° for 10-15 minutes or until set. Cool on a wire rack.

In a large mixing bowl, beat the cream cheese, sugar and 2 tablespoons cornstarch until smooth. Beat in the sour cream, vanilla and salt. Add eggs; beat on low speed just until combined. Remove 3-1/2 cups filling to a bowl; stir in lemon juice and set aside. Add the pumpkin, brown sugar, molasses, spices and remaining cornstarch to the remaining filling; set aside 1/2 cup. Pour half of the remaining pumpkin filling over crust; top with half of the plain filling. Repeat layers. Dot with spoonfuls of the reserved pumpkin filling. Cut through filling with a knife to swirl.

Place pan on a double thickness of heavy-duty foil (about 16 in. square); securely wrap foil around pan. Place pan in a large baking pan. Add 1 in. of hot water to larger pan. Bake at 325° for 70-75 minutes or until center is almost set. Remove springform pan from water bath. Cool on a wire rack for 10 minutes. Carefully run a knife around edge of pan to loosen; cool 1 hour longer. Remove foil. Refrigerate overnight. Remove sides of pan. Refrigerate leftovers. **Yield:** 12-14 servings.

Making Cheesecakes in Advance

COOL AND CREAMY cheesecakes are a rich, filling dessert that feed a crowd. So, usually no other dessert is needed. Best of all, cheesecakes can be made in advance, meaning there's one less thing to do on the day you're entertaining.

Cheesecakes can be covered and refrigerated for up to 3 days. For even more convenience, bake a cheesecake weeks in advance and freeze it! Here's how:

Place a whole cheesecake or individual slices on a baking sheet; freeze until firm. Wrap in plastic wrap and place in a heavy-duty resealable plastic bag. Freeze for up to 2 months. Defrost whole cheesecakes in the refrigerator overnight. Individual pieces can be defrosted in the refrigerator or at room temperature for 30 minutes before serving.

Individual Cranberry Trifles

(Pictured at right and on page 179)

If you don't have enough individual parfaits, you can make this dessert from our Test Kitchen in a trifle bowl. Either way, it's sure to bring you rave reviews.

1 package (16 ounces) angel food cake mix
2 packages (8 ounces *each*) cream cheese, softened
2 cups confectioners' sugar
1 cup (8 ounces) sour cream
1 teaspoon vanilla extract
1 carton (12 ounces) frozen whipped topping, thawed
2 cans (16 ounces *each*) whole-berry cranberry sauce
2 tablespoons sugar
2 to 3 teaspoons grated orange peel
Fresh cranberries and mint, optional

Prepare, bake and cool angel food cake according to package directions. Cut into 1-in. cubes; set aside. In a large mixing bowl, combine cream cheese, confectioners' sugar, sour cream and vanilla; beat until smooth. Fold in whipped topping. In a bowl, combine the cranberry sauce, sugar and orange peel.

In individual parfait glasses or a 3-qt. trifle bowl, layer half of the cake cubes, cranberry mixture and whipped topping mixture. Repeat layers. Refrigerate until serving. Garnish with cranberries and mint if desired. **Yield:** 14-16 servings.

Berry Nut Tarts

(Pictured on page 178)

Cranberries are a delicious addition to this spin on individual pecan pies. Folks have a hard time eating only one.
—Lena Ehlert, Vancouver, British Columbia

1/2 cup butter, softened
1 package (3 ounces) cream cheese, softened
1 cup all-purpose flour
FILLING:
1-1/2 cups packed brown sugar
2 tablespoons butter, melted
2 eggs, lightly beaten
2 teaspoons vanilla extract
2/3 cup finely chopped cranberries
1/3 cup chopped pecans

In a small mixing bowl, beat the butter and cream cheese; add flour and mix well. Cover and refrigerate for 1 hour or until easy to handle.

Cut dough into 12 portions. Press onto the bottom and all the way up the sides of greased muffin cups. In a bowl, combine the brown sugar, butter, eggs and vanilla. Stir in the cranberries and pecans. Spoon into prepared crusts.

Bake at 350° for 25-30 minutes or until edges are golden brown. Cool for 5 minutes before removing from pan to a wire rack to cool completely. Store in the refrigerator. **Yield:** about 1 dozen.

Bread Pudding with Lemon Sauce

This bread pudding is a little lighter than most and is enhanced by a lovely lemon sauce. I've also served the sauce over slices of angel food cake.
—Margaret Anderson, Salmon, Idaho

2 cups milk
4 eggs
1/2 cup sugar
5 slices white bread, cut into 1-inch cubes
1/3 cup semisweet chocolate chips
1/8 teaspoon ground cinnamon
LEMON SAUCE:
1 cup sugar
1/2 cup butter, melted
1/4 cup water
2 tablespoons lemon juice
1 egg yolk
1 teaspoon grated lemon peel

In a large bowl, combine the milk, eggs and sugar. Stir in bread cubes; let stand for 5 minutes, stirring occasionally. Pour into a greased 1-1/2-qt. baking dish. Sprinkle with chocolate chips and cinnamon. Bake at 350° for 55-60 minutes or until a knife inserted near the center comes out clean.

For sauce, combine the sugar, butter, water and lemon juice in a saucepan. Whisk in egg yolk. Bring to a boil over medium heat, stirring constantly. Cook and stir for 1 minute. Remove from the heat; stir in lemon peel. Serve over pudding. **Yield:** 8 servings.

Maple Pecan Cookies

(Pictured at right)

When I bake cookies for the annual youth ski trip, I try at least one new recipe. When I received recipe requests for these frosted goodies, I knew I had a winner.
—Nancy Johnson, Laverne, Oklahoma

1 cup shortening
1/2 cup butter, softened
2 cups packed brown sugar
2 eggs
1 teaspoon vanilla extract
1 teaspoon maple flavoring
3 cups all-purpose flour
2 teaspoons baking soda
1 package (10 to 12 ounces) vanilla *or* white chips
1/2 cup chopped pecans

FROSTING:

1/4 cup butter, softened
4 cups confectioners' sugar
1 teaspoon maple flavoring
3 to 5 tablespoons milk
1-1/2 cups pecan halves

In a large mixing bowl, cream the shortening, butter and brown sugar. Add eggs, one at a time, beating well after each addition. Beat in vanilla and maple flavoring. Combine flour and baking soda; gradually add to the creamed mixture. Stir in vanilla chips and pecans.

Drop by tablespoonfuls 2 in. apart onto ungreased baking sheets. Bake at 350° for 9-11 minutes or until golden brown. Cool for 2 minutes before removing to wire racks.

In a mixing bowl, cream the butter, confectioners' sugar, maple flavoring and enough milk to achieve spreading consistency. Frost each cookie with 1 teaspoon frosting; top with a pecan half. **Yield:** 7 dozen.

Hickory Nut Cake

As a girl, I'd help my dad and grandpa gather hickory nuts for Grandma's classic cake. We could hardly wait for dinner to be over so we could indulge in a generous slice.
—Gloria Fee, McArthur, Ohio

1/2 cup butter, softened
1-1/2 cups sugar
1 teaspoon vanilla extract
2 cups cake flour
2 teaspoons baking powder
1/2 teaspoon salt
3/4 cup milk
1 cup finely chopped hickory nuts *or* walnuts, toasted
4 egg whites
BUTTER FROSTING:
3/4 cup butter, softened
5 cups confectioners' sugar
1/2 teaspoon vanilla extract
1/8 teaspoon salt
4 to 5 tablespoons half-and-half cream

In a large mixing bowl, cream the butter, sugar and vanilla. Combine the flour, baking powder and salt; add to creamed mixture alternately with milk. Stir in nuts. In a small mixing bowl, beat egg whites on high speed until soft peaks form; fold into batter. Pour into two greased and floured 9-in. round baking pans. Bake at 350° for 25-30 minutes or until a toothpick inserted near the center comes out clean. Cool for 10 minutes before removing from pans to wire racks to cool completely.

For frosting, in a large mixing bowl, beat butter and sugar on low speed for 1 minute. Beat in the vanilla, salt and enough cream until a fluffy consistency is achieved. Spread between layers and over top and sides of cake. **Yield:** 12-16 servings.

Spiced Butterscotch Fudge

This butterscotch fudge is a nice change from the more typical chocolate varieties. When I have a craving for a little sweet, this fits the bill.
—Cathy Steinkuhler, Burr, Nebraska

1 tablespoon plus 3/4 cup butter, *divided*
3 cups sugar
1 can (5 ounces) evaporated milk
1/2 cup canned pumpkin
1/2 teaspoon ground cinnamon
1/2 teaspoon ground nutmeg
1 package (11 ounces) butterscotch chips
1 jar (7 ounces) marshmallow creme
1 cup chopped pecans, optional
1 teaspoon vanilla extract

Line a 13-in. x 9-in. x 2-in. pan with foil and grease the foil with 1 tablespoon butter; set aside. In a large saucepan, combine the sugar, milk, pumpkin, cinnamon, nutmeg and remaining butter. Bring to a boil over medium heat, stirring constantly. Reduce heat; cook until a candy thermometer reaches 238° (soft-ball stage), stirring occasionally.

Remove from the heat. Stir in chips until melted. Stir in marshmallow creme, pecans if desired and vanilla. Spread into prepared pan. Cool to room temperature; cover and refrigerate. Using foil, lift fudge out of pan. Discard foil; cut fudge into 1-in. squares. **Yield:** about 3-1/4 pounds.

Editor's Note: We recommend that you test your candy thermometer before each use by bringing water to a boil; the thermometer should read 212°. Adjust your recipe temperature up or down based on your test.

Mincemeat Pumpkin Pie

(Pictured at right)

Instead of serving separate pumpkin and mincemeat pies one Thanksgiving, I served this one pie that combines those wonderful flavors. It was a hit!
—Joann Frazier Hensley
McGaheysville, Virginia

2 cups prepared mincemeat
1 unbaked pastry shell (9 inches)
1 egg
1 cup canned pumpkin
1/3 cup sugar
1/2 teaspoon ground cinnamon
1/4 teaspoon ground ginger
1/4 teaspoon ground nutmeg
1/8 teaspoon salt
1/8 teaspoon ground cloves
3/4 cup evaporated milk

Spread mincemeat over the bottom of pastry shell. In a large mixing bowl, beat the egg, pumpkin, sugar, cinnamon, ginger, nutmeg, salt and cloves just until smooth. Gradually stir in milk. Pour over mincemeat. Bake at 400° for 55-60 minutes or until a knife inserted near the center comes out clean. Cool on a wire rack. Store in the refrigerator. **Yield:** 6-8 servings.

Ginger Pear Pie

This recipe comes from my grandmother, who had lots of pear trees on her land. A gingersnap crust complements the pleasant taste of pears.
—Mildred Sherrer, Bay City, Texas

1 unbaked pastry shell (9 inches)
1/2 cup gingersnap crumbs (about 9 cookies)
1/4 cup sugar
1/4 cup packed brown sugar
1 tablespoon all-purpose flour
1/2 teaspoon salt
1/2 teaspoon ground cinnamon
1/4 cup cold butter
5 cups thinly sliced peeled pears (about 5 medium)

Line unpricked pastry shell with a double thickness of heavy-duty foil. Bake at 450° for 8 minutes. Remove foil; bake 5 minutes longer. Cool on a wire rack.

In a bowl, combine gingersnap crumbs, sugars, flour, salt and cinnamon. Cut in butter until crumbly. Place half of the pear slices in crust. Top with half of the crumb mixture. Repeat layers. Cover edges loosely with foil. Bake at 350° for 55-60 minutes or until golden. Cool on a wire rack. Store in the refrigerator. **Yield:** 6-8 servings.

Pear Pointers

PURCHASE pears that are firm, fragrant and free of blemishes or soft spots.

To ripen pears, place them in a paper bag at room temperature for several days. When the pears give in slightly to pressure, store in the refrigerator. Pears used for cooking should be a little more firm.

Before cooking pears, use a vegetable peeler or paring knife to remove the skin, which turns dark and tough when exposed to heat.

One pound of pears equals about 3 medium or 3 cups sliced.

To prevent pear slices from discoloring, toss with a little lemon juice.

Peanut Butter Maple Ice Cream Pie

Homemade pie can't get any easier than this! The recipe makes two pies, so you can enjoy one now and keep the other in the freezer for drop-in guests.
—Linda Markauskas, Walkerton, Ontario

2 quarts vanilla ice cream, softened
1 cup maple syrup
3/4 cup peanut butter
2 graham cracker crusts (9 inches)
1/2 cup finely chopped peanuts

In a large mixing bowl, combine the ice cream, syrup and peanut butter until smooth. Transfer half into each crust. Cover and freeze for 2-3 hours. Just before serving, sprinkle with peanuts. **Yield:** 2 pies (6-8 servings each).

Raisin Pumpkin Bars

(Pictured at right)

Chocolate-covered raisins are a fun surprise inside these moist pumpkin bars. The traditional cream cheese frosting never fails to please.
—Margaret Wilson, Hemet, California

2 cups sugar
3/4 cup vegetable oil
4 eggs
2 cups canned pumpkin
2 cups all-purpose flour
2 teaspoons baking powder
1 teaspoon baking soda
1 teaspoon ground cinnamon
1 teaspoon ground nutmeg
1/2 teaspoon ground ginger
1/4 teaspoon ground cloves
1 cup chopped walnuts
1 cup chocolate-covered raisins for baking

FROSTING:

1/3 cup butter, softened
1 package (3 ounces) cream cheese, softened
2 cups confectioners' sugar
1 tablespoon milk
1 teaspoon orange extract
Decorator sprinkles, optional

In a large mixing bowl, beat sugar and oil. Add eggs, one at a time, beating well after each addition. Add pumpkin; mix well. Combine the flour, baking powder, baking soda and spices; gradually add to the pumpkin mixture. Stir in walnuts and chocolate-covered raisins. Pour into a greased 15-in. x 10-in. x 1-in. baking pan. Bake at 350° for 25-30 minutes or until a toothpick inserted near the center comes out clean. Cool on a wire rack.

For frosting, in a mixing bowl, cream the butter, cream cheese and confectioners' sugar. Add milk and orange extract; beat until smooth. Frost bars. Decorate with sprinkles if desired. Cut into bars. Store in the refrigerator. **Yield:** 4 dozen.

An Elegant Thanksgiving Dinner

GATHER with your family this Thanksgiving for a distinguished dinner that pleases the eye as well as the stomach!

For an attractive entree that guests will be wild about, roast a succulent Mandarin Goose. Then set this golden bird on a bed of beautiful Roasted Autumn Vegetables.

Crimson-colored cranberries—a favorite fall fruit—shine in both Cranberry Tossed Salad and Cran-Apple Pie. (All recipes shown at right.)

Complement this lovely autumn dinner with two other splendid sides—Gingered Long Grain and Wild Rice, and Cornmeal Pan Rolls.

A Memorable Meal

(Clockwise from top left)

Cranberry Tossed Salad (p. 191)

Mandarin Goose with Roasted Autumn Vegetables (p. 192)

Cran-Apple Pie (p. 193)

Thanksgiving Dinner Agenda

A Few Weeks Before:

- Order a 12- to 14-pound domestic goose from your butcher.
- Prepare two grocery lists—one for non-perishable items to purchase now and one for perishable items to purchase a few days before Thanksgiving.
- Bake Cornmeal Pan Rolls; cool. Freeze in heavy-duty resealable plastic bags.

A Few Days Before:

- Buy the goose and any remaining grocery items, including fruit for the Sugared Fruit Centerpiece (see page 194).
- Toast bread cubes for Gingered Long Grain and Wild Rice. Cool and store in an airtight container at room temperature.

The Day Before:

- Set the table.
- For Cranberry Tossed Salad, make the dressing; cover and chill. Wash and dry salad greens; refrigerate in a resealable plastic bag. Wash and chop broccoli and cauliflower; place in a resealable plastic bag and chill.
- Bake Cran-Apple Pie. Store loosely covered at room temperature.
- Later in the day, make the Sugared Fruit Centerpiece.

Thanksgiving Day:

- In the morning, peel sweet potatoes for Roasted Autumn Vegetables and cut into wedges. Cover with cold water and refrigerate.
- Thaw Cornmeal Pan Rolls at room temperature.
- Assemble Gingered Long Grain and Wild Rice; cover and chill. Remove from the refrigerator 30 minutes before baking as directed.
- Bake the Mandarin Goose.
- Assemble Roasted Autumn Vegetables; bake as directed.
- Remove salad dressing from the refrigerator 30 minutes before dinner; combine all salad ingredients. Just before serving, shake dressing and drizzle over the salad; toss.
- Let the cooked goose stand for 10 to 15 minutes before carving. Meanwhile, make the gravy.
- Set out the Cornmeal Pan Rolls.
- Serve Cran-Apple Pie for dessert.

Gingered Long Grain and Wild Rice

Although I just recently added this recipe to my collection, it's already a favorite.
—Paula Magnus, Republic, Washington

2 slices bread, cut into 1/2-inch cubes
2 packages (6 ounces *each*) long grain and wild rice mix
4 celery ribs, chopped
1 medium onion, chopped
1 tablespoon minced fresh gingerroot
6 tablespoons butter
1/4 cup chicken broth
1 can (8 ounces) water chestnuts, drained, chopped

Place bread cubes on a baking sheet. Bake at 250° for 35 minutes or until toasted. Meanwhile, prepare rice according to package directions. In a skillet, saute the celery, onion and ginger in butter until tender. Add to the rice.

Stir in broth, water chestnuts and bread cubes. Transfer to a greased shallow 3-qt. baking dish. Bake, uncovered, at 350° for 30-35 minutes or until heated through. **Yield:** 10-12 servings.

Cranberry Tossed Salad

(Pictured at right and on page 188)

Dinner guests rave about this salad's poppy seed dressing.
—Marilyn Bue, Princeton, Minnesota

10 cups torn mixed salad greens
1 cup chopped broccoli
1 cup chopped cauliflower
1 cup (4 ounces) crumbled blue cheese
1 cup dried cranberries

DRESSING:

1/3 cup sugar
1/3 cup vegetable oil
2 tablespoons chopped onion
2 tablespoons cider vinegar
1 tablespoon jellied cranberry sauce
1/2 teaspoon salt
1/2 teaspoon Dijon mustard
1/4 teaspoon poppy seeds

In a large salad bowl, combine the first five ingredients. In a blender, combine the sugar, oil, onion, vinegar, cranberry sauce, salt and mustard; cover and process until blended. Add poppy seeds; cover and pulse for 5-10 seconds. Drizzle over salad; toss to coat. Serve immediately. **Yield:** 12 servings.

Mandarin Goose

(Pictured on page 189)

With mountains to the east, west and south of us and Canada to the north, we have ample opportunity to hunt. This succulent goose is one of our favorite dishes.
—Paula Magnus, Republic, Washington

- **1 domestic goose (12 to 14 pounds)**
- **Salt**
- **1 tablespoon all-purpose flour**
- **1 tablespoon ground mustard**
- **1/2 cup port wine *or* 1/4 cup grape juice plus 1/4 cup chicken broth**
- **1/4 cup orange juice**
- **1 medium onion, quartered**
- **1/4 cup plum *or* red raspberry jam**
- **2 tablespoons cornstarch**
- **2 tablespoons cold water**
- **1 can (11 ounces) mandarin oranges, drained**

Sprinkle inside of goose with salt. Prick skin well; place breast side up on a rack in a large shallow roasting pan. In a small bowl, combine the flour and mustard; stir in wine and orange juice until smooth. Pour over goose. Add onion to pan. Bake, uncovered, at 350° for 3 to 3-1/2 hours or until a meat thermometer reads 180° (cover with foil during the last hour to prevent overbrowning).

Discard onion. Cover goose and let stand 10-15 minutes before carving. Pour pan drippings into a 2-cup measuring cup; skim off fat. Add enough water to measure 2 cups. In a saucepan, combine juices and jam. Combine cornstarch and water until smooth; add to juices. Bring to a boil; cook and stir for 2 minutes or until thickened. Stir in oranges. Serve with goose. **Yield:** 8-10 servings.

Roasted Autumn Vegetables

(Pictured on page 189)

This colorful vegetable dish with mild garlic flavor was developed in our Test Kitchen. It conveniently bakes at the same temperature as the Mandarin Goose.

- **1 medium whole garlic bulb, peeled**
- **1/2 cup butter, melted**
- **1 tablespoon minced fresh thyme *or* 1 teaspoon dried thyme**
- **1/2 teaspoon salt**
- **1/4 teaspoon pepper**
- **4 medium sweet potatoes, peeled and cut into wedges**
- **1 pound fresh brussels sprouts, halved**
- **2 medium onions, cut into 1/2-inch wedges**

Separate garlic bulb into cloves. Mince two cloves; place in a small bowl. Add the butter, thyme, salt and pepper. In a large bowl, combine the sweet potatoes, brussels sprouts, onions and remaining garlic cloves. Drizzle with butter mixture; toss to coat.

Transfer to a greased 13-in. x 9-in. x 2-in. baking dish. Cover and bake at 350° for 30 minutes. Uncover; bake 40-45 minutes longer or until vegetables are tender. Stir before serving. **Yield:** 10 servings.

Cran-Apple Pie

(Pictured at right and on page 188)

Our home economists capture the flavor of fall in this pretty lattice fruit pie.

5 cups sliced peeled Golden Delicious apples
3/4 cup plus 2 tablespoons apple juice, *divided*
3/4 cup sugar
3/4 teaspoon ground cinnamon
1/4 teaspoon salt
1/4 teaspoon ground nutmeg
2 tablespoons plus 2 teaspoons cornstarch
2 cups cranberries

PASTRY:

2-3/4 cups all-purpose flour
3/4 teaspoon salt
3/4 cup plus 2 tablespoons shortening
8 to 9 tablespoons cold water
1 egg, lightly beaten
Additional sugar

In a saucepan, combine apples, 3/4 cup apple juice, sugar, cinnamon, salt and nutmeg; bring to a boil over medium heat, stirring occasionally. Combine cornstarch and remaining juice until smooth; add to saucepan. Return to a boil, stirring constantly. Cook and stir for 1 minute or until thickened. Remove from heat; cool to room temperature. Stir in cranberries.

In a bowl, combine the flour and salt; cut in shortening until crumbly. Gradually add cold water, tossing with a fork until dough forms a ball. Divide dough in half. Roll out one portion to fit a 9-in. pie plate. Transfer to pie plate. Trim pastry to 1 in. beyond edge of plate.

Pour fruit filling into crust. Divide the remaining dough in half. Roll out one portion; cut into six 1/2-in.-wide strips. Place three strips over filling in each direction, forming a lattice crust; trim edges of strips.

For decorative cutouts, roll out remaining dough and cut out with a 1-1/2-in. leaf-shaped cookie cutter. With a sharp knife, lightly score cutouts to resemble veins on leaves. Lightly brush lattice and edge of crust with egg. Overlap cutouts on the lattice and along edge of pie. Brush cutouts with egg; sprinkle lightly with sugar.

Cover edges loosely with foil coated with nonstick cooking spray. Bake at 400° for 20 minutes. Remove foil; bake 15-20 minutes longer or until crust is golden brown and filling is bubbly. Cool on a wire rack. **Yield:** 6-8 servings.

A Lovely Leaf-Topped Lattice Pie

1. Lightly brush lattice with beaten egg; overlap leaf cutouts on top.

2. Brush pie edge with beaten egg. Place leaf cutouts lengthwise along edge, overlapping slightly. Lightly press cutouts onto lattice and pie edge to secure.

Sugared Fruit Centerpiece

(Pictured at right and on page 189)

For an elegant table topper, create this centerpiece showcasing simple-to-make sugared fruit. It's not only eye-catching but edible as well!

15 to 20 pieces assorted fruit
3 envelopes unflavored gelatin
3/4 cup cold water
2 cups superfine sugar
Edible *or* silk leaves, optional

Scrub fruit in soapy water; rinse and dry completely. In a microwave-safe bowl, sprinkle gelatin over cold water; let stand for 1 minute. Microwave on high for 1-2 minutes, stirring every 20 seconds, until gelatin is completely dissolved. Whisk until slightly frothy.

Lightly brush mixture over all sides of fruit. Place on a wire rack over waxed paper. Sprinkle with sugar. Let stand at room temperature for up to 24 hours. Arrange as desired, adding leaves if desired.

Editor's Note: Fruit should not be refrigerated because the sugar will dissolve. This recipe was tested in a 1,100-watt microwave.

Making Sugared Fruit

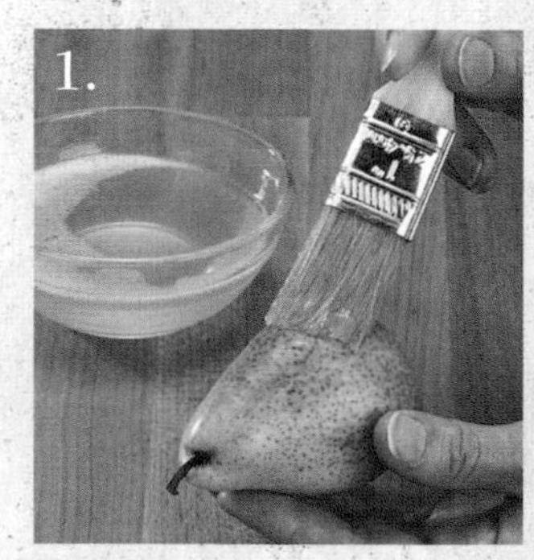

1. Working with one piece of fruit at a time, lightly brush gelatin mixture over entire surface with a pastry brush. Place on a wire rack over waxed paper.

2. With a spoon, sprinkle superfine sugar over all sides of the fruit until the desired look is achieved. Repeat with remaining fruit. Let dry completely before handling.

Secrets for Successful Sugared Fruit

A STUNNING Sugared Fruit Centerpiece is guaranteed if you review these helpful hints before beginning.

- You can sugar whole pieces of fruit as well as cut pieces. For cut pieces, it's best to use citrus—not fruits that turn brown when exposed to air, like apples and pears. Because cut fruit will be a bit juicy, the sugar may not adhere as well. Dab the cut side with paper towel and let air dry a few hours before brushing with the gelatin mixture and sprinkling with sugar.
- Sugared grape clusters become very stiff when dry. So if you would like them to have a little bend when arranging your centerpiece, drape the grapes over an inverted bowl until dry.
- If desired, you can sprinkle the fruits with additional sugar before completely dry to achieve a more dramatic effect.
- Sugar-coated fruit can be kept at room temperature for up to 24 hours; do not refrigerate.
- When arranging the centerpiece, handle fruit as little as possible so that the heat from your hands doesn't dissolve the sugar.

Cornmeal Pan Rolls

After I moved away from home, I realized I had better learn to cook if I wanted to enjoy wonderful meals like Mom used to make! Now my mom has me make these rolls every holiday. They're terrific topped with butter or jam.
—Sawyer Tremble, Bird Creek, Arkansas

1-2/3 cups milk
2/3 cup cornmeal
2/3 cup sugar
1/2 cup butter, cubed
1 teaspoon salt
2 tablespoons active dry yeast
1/4 cup warm water (110° to 115°)
2 eggs
1 cup whole wheat flour
3 cups all-purpose flour

In a saucepan, bring milk to a simmer. Gradually whisk in cornmeal; simmer for 3-4 minutes or until thickened. Stir in the sugar, butter and salt. Remove from the heat; cool to 110°-115°.

In a mixing bowl, dissolve yeast in warm water. Add cornmeal mixture, eggs and whole wheat flour; beat until smooth. Stir in enough all-purpose flour to form a soft dough (dough will be sticky). Do not knead. Place in a greased bowl, turning once to grease top. Cover and let rise in a warm place until doubled, about 1-1/4 hours.

Punch dough down. Turn onto a lightly floured surface; divide into 15 pieces. Shape each piece into a roll. Place in a greased 13-in. x 9-in. x 2-in. baking pan. Cover and let rise until doubled, about 30 minutes. Bake at 375° for 20-25 minutes or until golden brown. **Yield:** 15 rolls.

Winter Entertaining

St. Nick Celebration

ST. NICHOLAS was a fourth century bishop who would secretly give gifts to children in need. When Europeans settled in the United States, many brought with them the tradition of remembering his generous spirit on December 6.

The night before, kids hang up their stockings or put out their shoes. In the morning, they rush to see the fruits, nuts, candies or small gifts that St. Nick magically left for them.

Why not introduce this little-known holiday to friends by hosting a St. Nick party?

Slow Cooker Pizza Casserole, Herbed Garlic Bread and Colorful Caesar Salad is a mouthwatering meal that will appeal to young and old alike. (All recipes shown at right.)

For a fun, finger-licking dessert, have the kids decorate an array of tasty cupcakes. (See page 205 for inviting ideas.)

Family Fare

(Clockwise from bottom)

Slow Cooker Pizza Casserole (p. 200)

Colorful Caesar Salad (p. 203)

Herbed Garlic Bread (p. 200)

Herbed Garlic Bread

(Pictured on page 199)

No Italian meal is complete without bread. This garlic herb version comes from our home economists. If desired, sprinkle with shredded provolone cheese.

- **1/2 cup butter, softened**
- **1/4 cup grated Romano cheese**
- **2 tablespoons minced fresh basil *or* 2 teaspoons dried basil**
- **1 tablespoon minced fresh parsley**
- **3 garlic cloves, minced**
- **1 loaf (1 pound) French bread, halved lengthwise**
- **4 ounces provolone cheese, shredded, optional**

In a small bowl, combine the butter, Romano cheese, basil, parsley and garlic. Spread over cut sides of bread. Sprinkle with provolone cheese if desired.

Place on an ungreased baking sheet. Bake at 425° for 10-12 minutes or until cheese is melted. Slice and serve warm. **Yield:** 8 servings.

Slow Cooker Pizza Casserole

(Pictured on page 198)

A comforting casserole with mass appeal is just what you need when cooking for a crowd. For added convenience, it stays warm in a slow cooker.
—Virginia Krites, Cridersville, Ohio

- **1 package (16 ounces) rigatoni *or* large tube pasta**
- **1-1/2 pounds ground beef**
- **1 small onion, chopped**
- **4 cups (16 ounces) shredded part-skim mozzarella cheese**
- **2 cans (15 ounces *each*) pizza sauce**
- **1 can (10-3/4 ounces) condensed cream of mushroom soup, undiluted**
- **1 package (8 ounces) sliced pepperoni**

Cook pasta according to package directions. Meanwhile, in a skillet, cook beef and onion over medium heat until meat is no longer pink; drain.

Drain pasta; place in a 5-qt. slow cooker. Stir in the beef mixture, cheese, pizza sauce, soup and pepperoni. Cover and cook on low for 2-3 hours or until heated through and the cheese is melted. **Yield:** 12-14 servings.

Christmas Gelatin Cutouts

(Pictured at right)

Cool, fruity and creamy, these gelatin treats from our Test Kitchen are richer than plain gelatin and cut easily into whatever shape you want.

2 packages (6 ounces *each*) strawberry gelatin
2 packages (6 ounces *each*) lime gelatin
5 cups boiling water, *divided*
2 cups cold milk
2 packages (3.4 ounces *each*) instant vanilla pudding mix

In a large bowl, dissolve strawberry gelatin in 2-1/2 cups boiling water. In another bowl, dissolve lime gelatin in remaining boiling water; set both aside for 30 minutes.

In a bowl, whisk milk and pudding mixes until smooth, about 1 minute. Quickly pour half of the pudding into each bowl of gelatin; whisk until well blended. Pour into two 13-in. x 9-in. x 2-in. dishes coated with nonstick cooking spray. Chill for 3 hours or until set. Cut with 2-in. Christmas cookie cutters. **Yield:** 4 dozen.

Variations of Christmas Gelatin Cutouts

THE RECIPE for Christmas Gelatin Cutouts makes about 4 dozen. If a smaller yield is desired, use only one flavor of gelatin and half of the water, milk and pudding.

You can also use other flavors of red gelatin, such as cherry, cranberry and raspberry. If your family isn't fond of lime, just use all red gelatin.

Mandarin Fruit Dip

With all the heavy foods around the holidays, fruit is a refreshing change of pace. For more kid appeal, our home economists pair fruit with a sweet and creamy dip.

1 package (8 ounces) cream cheese, softened
1/4 cup confectioners' sugar
1 can (11 ounces) mandarin oranges, drained
1/2 teaspoon vanilla extract
1/2 teaspoon orange extract
1 cup whipped topping
Assorted fresh fruit

In a small mixing bowl, combine cream cheese, confectioners' sugar, oranges and extracts; beat on medium speed until combined. Fold in whipped topping. Transfer to a serving bowl. Refrigerate or serve immediately with fruit. **Yield:** 2 cups.

Bacon-Tomato Dip in a Bread Bowl

This tasty dip disappears whenever I serve it. I like that it is quick and can be made ahead.
—Laura Mahaffey, Annapolis, Maryland

1 package (8 ounces) cream cheese, softened
1/4 cup mayonnaise
1 medium tomato, peeled and chopped
8 bacon strips, cooked and crumbled
1/4 teaspoon dried basil
1/4 teaspoon pepper
1 round loaf (1/2 pound) unsliced sourdough bread
Assorted crackers

In a small mixing bowl, beat cream cheese and mayonnaise until smooth. Stir in the tomato, bacon, basil and pepper. Cover and refrigerate for 1 hour.

Cut a 1-1/2-in. thick slice off the top of bread; set aside. Carefully hollow out loaf, leaving a 1/2-in. shell. Cut removed bread into cubes. Fill bread shell with dip. Serve with crackers and bread cubes. **Yield:** 2 cups.

Making a Bread Bowl for Dip

YOU can't go wrong with a dip container that's both attractive and edible! First cut a thick slice off the top of the bread. Cut around the perimeter of the bread, about 1/2 inch from the crust.

Insert your fingers along the cut and loosen the bread from the bottom of loaf. Remove the bread; cut into cubes to serve with the dip. Fill the bread bowl with any savory dip of your choice.

Colorful Caesar Salad

(Pictured at right and on page 198)

We guarantee you'll enjoy our Test Kitchen's take on this classic salad. The dressing can be prepared up to 3 days in advance.

12 cups torn romaine
3 medium tomatoes, cut into wedges
1 medium cucumber, halved and sliced
3 hard-cooked eggs
6 anchovy fillets
1/4 cup red wine vinegar
2 tablespoons lemon juice
2 tablespoons Dijon mustard
1 tablespoon Worcestershire sauce
4 garlic cloves, minced
1 teaspoon sugar
1/2 teaspoon pepper
3/4 cup olive oil
1-1/2 cups Caesar salad croutons
3/4 cup shredded Parmesan cheese

In a large salad bowl, combine the romaine, tomatoes and cucumber. Slice eggs in half; remove yolks. (Refrigerate whites for another use.) In a blender, combine the anchovies, vinegar, lemon juice, mustard, Worcestershire sauce, garlic, sugar, pepper and egg yolks; cover and process until smooth. While processing, gradually add oil in a steady stream.

Drizzle desired amount of dressing over salad and toss to coat. Sprinkle with croutons and Parmesan cheese. Serve immediately. Refrigerate any leftover dressing for up to 3 days. **Yield:** 12 servings.

Creamy Hot White Chocolate

(Pictured at right)

We enjoy this hot beverage all year long but especially around the holidays. It's a nice change of pace from traditional hot chocolate.
—Karen Riordan, Fern Creek, Kentucky

6 cups half-and-half cream, *divided*
1-1/3 cups vanilla *or* white chips
2 cinnamon sticks (3 inches)
1/4 teaspoon ground cinnamon
Dash ground nutmeg
3 teaspoons vanilla extract

In a large saucepan, combine 1/2 cup cream, vanilla chips, cinnamon sticks, cinnamon and nutmeg. Cook and stir over low heat until chips are melted. Stir in remaining cream; heat through. Discard cinnamon sticks. Stir in vanilla. **Yield:** 8 servings.

Classic Chocolate Frosting

This fast, fudge-like frosting is so fantastic. It even makes cakes from a box mix taste like homemade!
—Karen Ann Bland, Gove, Kansas

1-2/3 cups confectioners' sugar
3/4 cup heavy whipping cream
4 squares (1 ounce *each*) unsweetened chocolate, chopped
2 teaspoons vanilla extract
6 tablespoons butter, softened

In a saucepan, combine confectioners' sugar and cream. Bring to a boil, stirring constantly. Remove from the heat; stir in chocolate until melted and smooth. Stir in vanilla. Cool until mixture is thickened, about 25 minutes, stirring occasionally.

In a mixing bowl, cream butter. Gradually beat in chocolate mixture until blended. Cover and refrigerate until ready to use. **Yield:** 1-1/2 cups.

Editor's Note: This recipe makes enough to frost 24 cupcakes or the top of a 13-inch x 9-inch cake. Recipe can be easily doubled.

Cupcake Decoration Station

(Pictured above)

WHEN hosting a party for children, there's no need for a fancy dessert. Just have some plain, baked cupcakes on hand!

As a fun food craft during the party, have kids frost the cupcakes, then decorate with assorted toppings, like colored sugar, sprinkles, chocolate jimmies and small candies.

Or for a little more creativity, have guests put on a happy holiday face by making St. Nick or Reindeer Cupcakes. Here's how:

St. Nick Cupcakes. Start with 2 cups (or one 16-ounce can) vanilla frosting. Place 2/3 cup in a bowl; tint with red food coloring.

Frost part of the cupcake top with white frosting for the face and the other part with red frosting for the hat. If desired, pipe white frosting to create the fur band of the hat. Press a miniature marshmallow on one side of the hat for pom-pom.

Add chocolate chips for the eyes and a red-hot candy for the nose. Gently press flaked coconut below the nose for the beard.

Reindeer Cupcakes. Frost cupcakes with Classic Chocolate Frosting or chocolate frosting of your choice. Add chocolate chips for the eyes and a red-hot candy for the nose. Break apart large pretzel twists; add two pieces for antlers.

For a mouth-watering centerpiece, display the decorated cupcakes in a tiered cupcake stand.

Holiday Fare Hints of Home

AT Canton, Ohio's House of Loreto nursing home, Sister Judith LaBrozzi and her food staff delight in providing residents with home-cooked meals throughout the year.

"Just like you and me, the residents here enjoy from-scratch food—not institutional fare—served at an attractive table," says Sister Judith.

So it's no wonder the mouth-watering feast presented at noon on Christmas Day is a favorite.

After starting with Appetizer Stuffed Mushrooms, residents dine on Roasted Beef Tenderloin, Special Twice-Baked Potatoes, Broccoli Tomato Cups and Lime-Pear Gelatin Bells. Saving room for Apricot Swan Cream Puffs and Ice Cream Snowballs is never a problem.

Laughs Sister Judith, "Many folks won't go out with their own families until *after* this dinner with their family at the home!"

Festive Feast

Roasted Beef Tenderloin (p. 208)

Special Twice-Baked Potatoes (p. 208)

Broccoli Tomato Cups (p. 212)

Apricot Swan Cream Puffs (p. 210)

Roasted Beef Tenderloin

(Pictured on page 206)

Beef tenderloin is a simple way to dress up a holiday dinner. This impressive entree is actually easy to make because it bakes in the oven unattended, allowing you to prepare other parts of the meal.

2 tablespoons Dijon mustard
1 garlic clove, minced
3/4 teaspoon coarsely ground pepper
1/2 teaspoon garlic salt
1/2 teaspoon onion salt
1 whole beef tenderloin (about 3-1/2 pounds), trimmed
1 cup beef broth

In a small bowl, combine the mustard, garlic, pepper, garlic salt and onion salt; brush over tenderloin. Place in a shallow roasting pan. Bake, uncovered, at 425° for 45 minutes or until meat reaches desired doneness (for rare, a meat thermometer should read 145°; medium, 160°; well-done, 170°).

Remove tenderloin from pan; let stand for 10-15 minutes before slicing. Meanwhile, add broth to pan drippings, stirring to loosen browned bits; heat through. Serve with sliced beef. **Yield:** 12 servings.

Special Twice-Baked Potatoes

(Pictured on page 207)

Twice-baked potatoes may take some time to prepare, but we know the residents really appreciate our efforts. This side dish pairs well with a variety of meaty entrees and is always a welcome sight on the holiday table.

12 large baking potatoes
1 cup butter *or* margarine, melted, *divided*
1 to 1-1/4 cups milk, warmed
8 bacon strips, cooked and crumbled
1 cup (4 ounces) shredded cheddar cheese
1/4 cup grated Parmesan cheese
2 tablespoons minced fresh parsley
1 teaspoon seasoned salt

Bake potatoes at 375° for 1 hour or until tender. Cool. Cut a thin slice off the top of each potato and discard; scoop out pulp, leaving a thin shell.

In a bowl, mash the pulp with 3/4 cup butter. Stir in milk, bacon, cheeses, parsley and seasoned salt. Spoon or pipe into potato shells. Place on a baking sheet. Drizzle with remaining butter. Bake at 425° for 25 minutes or until heated through. **Yield:** 12 servings.

Ice Cream Snowballs

(Pictured at right)

The House of Loreto residents agree there's no better way to enjoy this festive ice cream dessert than in the warm atmosphere of dinner with friends and family. For extra fun, we sometimes top each snowball with a lit red candle.

1/2 gallon vanilla ice cream
1 package (10 ounces) flaked coconut
Fresh mint, optional

Scoop ice cream into 12 balls. Place on a baking sheet and freeze until solid. Roll in coconut. Garnish with mint if desired. **Yield:** 12 servings.

Lime-Pear Gelatin Bells

For festive flair, I use bell-shaped molds for this gelatin salad, but use whatever molds you have on hand. It's such a refreshing way to ring in the holiday season.

1 package (6 ounces) lime gelatin
2 cups boiling water
2 cans (15-1/4 ounces *each*) sliced *or* halved pears, drained
12 ounces whipped cream cheese
1 cup whipping cream, whipped
Leaf lettuce
6 maraschino cherries, halved

In a bowl, dissolve gelatin in boiling water. Place pears in a blender or food processor; cover and process until smooth. Add cream cheese; process until smooth. Add to gelatin and stir well. Refrigerate until cool, about 15 minutes.

Fold in whipped cream. Pour into 12 individual bell-shaped molds or other molds coated with nonstick cooking spray. Refrigerate until firm. Unmold onto lettuce-lined plates. Place a piece of cherry at the end of each bell for clapper. **Yield:** 12 servings.

Apricot Swan Cream Puffs

(Pictured at right and on page 206)

Creating unusual desserts is a specialty of our food staff. We serve these pretty cream puffs many times through the year for special occasions or just simply to brighten someone's day.

1 cup water
1/2 cup butter (no substitutes)
1/4 teaspoon salt
1 cup all-purpose flour
4 eggs
FILLING:
1/3 cup sugar
2 tablespoons cornstarch
1/8 teaspoon salt
2 cups milk
2 egg yolks, beaten
2 tablespoons butter *or* margarine
1-1/2 teaspoons vanilla extract
1/4 teaspoon almond extract
About 3/4 cup chocolate syrup
2/3 cup apricot preserves
Confectioners' sugar

In a heavy saucepan over medium heat, bring water, butter and salt to a boil. Add flour all at once; stir until a smooth ball forms. Remove from the heat; let stand for 5 minutes. Add eggs, one at a time, beating well after each addition. Beat until smooth and shiny.

Cut a hole in the corner of a pastry or plastic bag; insert a #10 pastry tip. On a greased baking sheet, pipe twelve 3-in.-long S shapes for the swan necks, making a small dollop at the end for head. Bake at 400° for 8-10 minutes or until golden brown. Remove to wire racks to cool.

For each swan body, drop remaining batter by heaping teaspoonfuls 2 in. apart onto greased baking sheets. With a small icing knife or spatula, shape batter into 2-1/2-in. x 2-in. teardrops. Bake at 400° for 30-35 minutes or until golden brown. Cool on wire racks.

For filling, combine sugar, cornstarch and salt in a saucepan; gradually stir in milk until smooth. Bring to a boil over medium heat; cook and stir for 1-2 minutes or until thickened. Remove from the heat. Gradually stir a small amount of hot filling into egg yolks; return all to the pan, stirring constantly. Bring to a gentle boil; cook and stir for 2 minutes. Remove from the heat; stir in butter and extracts. Refrigerate until cool.

Just before serving, spoon about 1 tablespoon chocolate syrup onto serving plates. Cut off top third of swan bodies; set tops aside. Remove any soft dough inside. Spoon 1 tablespoon apricot preserves into bottoms of puffs; add filling. Set necks in filling. Cut reserved tops in half lengthwise to form wings; set wings in filling. Place swans on prepared plates. Dust with confectioners' sugar. **Yield:** 12 servings.

Making Swan Cream Puffs

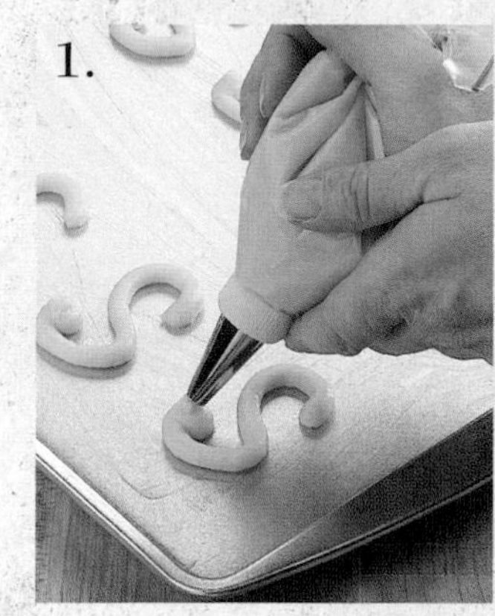
1.

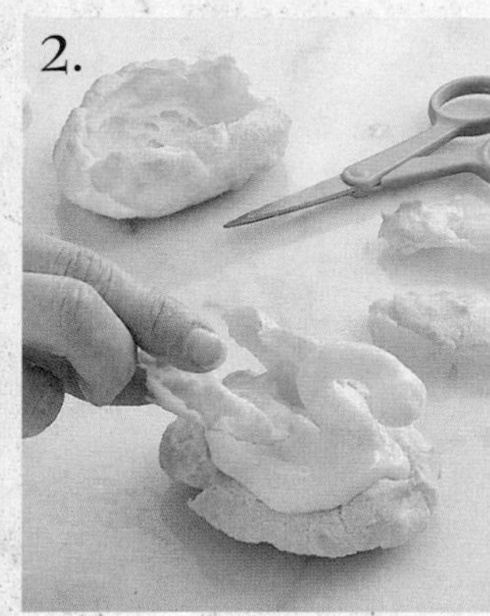
2.

1. To make swan necks, pipe dough into twelve 3-inch-long S shapes onto a greased baking sheet, making a small dollop at the end of each for the head. Bake as directed.

2. To assemble cream puffs, cut off the top third of swan bodies; cut tops in half lengthwise to form wings. Fill bottom of puffs with apricot preserves and filling. Place necks and wings in filling. Place swans on plates topped with chocolate sauce. Dust with confectioners' sugar.

Countdown to Christmas Day Dinner

A Few Weeks Before:

- Order a 3-1/2-pound whole beef tenderloin from your butcher.
- Make Tea Light Candle Centerpiece (see page 213).
- Assemble and freeze the Ice Cream Snowballs.
- Prepare two grocery lists—one for nonperishable items that can be purchased now and one for perishable items that need to be purchased a few days before Christmas.

Two Days Before:

- Buy remaining grocery items, including the beef tenderloin.
- Bake pastry for the Apricot Swan Cream Puffs and store in an airtight container at room temperature

Christmas Eve:

- Prepare Lime-Pear Gelatin Bells and Special Twice-Baked Potatoes and store in the refrigerator.
- Make the filling for the Apricot Swan Cream Puffs and refrigerate.
- Set the table.

Christmas Day:

- In the morning, assemble Appetizer Stuffed Mushrooms and Broccoli Tomato Cups. Cover (put a damp paper towel over the mushrooms) and refrigerate until baking time.
- Bake the Appetizer Stuffed Mushrooms as guests arrive.
- Prepare and bake the Roasted Beef Tenderloin. Bake the Broccoli Tomato Cups and Special Twice-Baked Potatoes as directed.
- Set out the Lime-Pear Gelatin Bells.
- For dessert, assemble the Apricot Swan Cream Puffs and serve with the Ice Cream Snowballs.

Broccoli Tomato Cups

(Pictured on page 207)

Red tomatoes stuffed with a green broccoli mixture make a colorful addition to the Christmas Day menu.

12 medium tomatoes
4 cups broccoli florets
4 tablespoons butter *or* margarine, melted, *divided*
1/4 cup seasoned bread crumbs

Cut a thin slice off the top of each tomato. Scoop out pulp, leaving a 1/2-in. shell (discard pulp or save for another use). Invert tomatoes onto paper towels to drain.

In a saucepan, place broccoli in a steamer basket over 1 in. of boiling water. Cover and steam for 5 minutes or until crisp-tender; set aside.

Brush inside of tomatoes with 2 tablespoons butter. Stuff broccoli into tomatoes. Toss bread crumbs and remaining butter; sprinkle over tops. Place in an ungreased baking dish. Bake, uncovered, at 425° for 15 minutes or until heated through. **Yield:** 12 servings.

Appetizer Stuffed Mushrooms

Heat-and-serve convenience foods are forbidden in the House of Loreto kitchen, and residents appreciate the "real" food we serve. Everyone reaches for seconds of these tasty morsels.

12 large fresh mushrooms
2 tablespoons finely chopped green onion
2 tablespoons finely chopped green pepper
1 tablespoon butter *or* margarine
1 slice bread, toasted and cut into small cubes
1/4 teaspoon onion salt
1/4 teaspoon garlic salt
1/8 teaspoon pepper
1/8 teaspoon dried thyme
Dash paprika
Grated Parmesan cheese

Remove stems from mushrooms; set caps aside. Finely chop stems; measure 1/2 cup (discard any remaining stems or save for another use). In a skillet, saute chopped mushrooms, onion and green pepper in butter until vegetables are tender and mushroom liquid has evaporated.

Add toast cubes, onion salt, garlic salt, pepper, thyme and paprika; mix well. Stuff into mushroom caps. Place on a greased baking sheet. Bake, uncovered, at 425° for 10 minutes or until heated through. Sprinkle with Parmesan cheese. **Yield:** 1 dozen.

Tea Light Candle Centerpiece

(Pictured at right)

IF HOLIDAY shopping has put your savings account in the red, take comfort in the fact that you don't have to spend a lot of "green" to present guests with a pretty dinner table!

For this eye-catching centerpiece, we simply wrapped pretty ribbon around inexpensive tea light candles (see instructions below) and set them on a tray along with red pillar candles and fresh cranberries.

Affordable tea light candles are easy to find in craft, department, discount and even grocery stores, especially around the holidays. Besides those with traditional metal bases, you may come across colored metal and clear or colored plastic bases. We chose white tea light candles for our centerpiece, but feel free to use whatever color you prefer.

Measure the height of the base of your tea light candles (5/8 inch is fairly standard) so you purchase the correct width of ribbon, then be creative! We used a solid green ribbon, but you can use a lace braid, plush velvet ribbon, beaded braid, sequin trim or any other decorative ribbon.

You can also mix and match ribbon colors by wrapping half the candles with patterned ribbon and the other half in a coordinating solid color. Make sure the color or colors work with your dishes and table linens.

In addition to making a centerpiece, scatter individual ribbon-wrapped tea lights on the dinner table or group them on smaller trays on other tables or the fireplace mantel.

(These decorated bases can be used even after the candles have burned away. Just remove candles from plain tea light bases and place them in the decorated bases.)

This candle centerpiece can be made weeks in advance. Before your guests arrive, add fresh cranberries and light the candles for a creative table topper.

It's a Wrap with Ribbon!

WRAP a piece of double-stick tape around the entire metal band on the outside of the tea light. (If you're using a lacy ribbon, be sure the tape is transparent.) Press one end of ribbon (we used 5/8-inch ribbon) onto the tape and wrap it around the tea light until it abuts the starting point. Trim excess ribbon.

Christmas Card-Writing Party

DURING the height of the holiday season, sending out Christmas cards can seem like just another chore on your list of things to do.

This year, address this sometimes daunting task by turning it into a card-writing party!

Invite a few close companions to your home one evening and have them bring along their cards, envelopes, address books, pens and postage stamps.

While writing out the cards at the dining room table, nibble on simple, special appetizers such as Pesto Crostini, Shrimp Napoleons and Antipasto Kabobs. (All recipes shown at right.)

Eating & Greeting

(Top to bottom)

Pesto Crostini (p. 217)

Shrimp Napoleons (p. 216)

Antipasto Kabobs (p. 217)

Creamy Buffalo Chicken Dip

This slightly spicy dip cleverly captures the flavor of buffalo chicken wings. Using canned chicken adds to the convenience.
—Allyson DiLascio, Saltsburg, Pennsylvania

1 package (8 ounces) cream cheese, softened
1 cup hot pepper sauce
1 cup ranch salad dressing
3 cans (4-1/2 ounces *each*) chunk white chicken, drained and shredded
1 cup (4 ounces) shredded cheddar cheese
Corn *or* tortilla chips

In a small mixing bowl, combine the cream cheese, hot pepper sauce and salad dressing. Stir in chicken. Spread into an ungreased 11-in. x 7-in. x 2-in. baking dish. Sprinkle with cheddar cheese. Bake, uncovered, at 350° for 20-22 minutes or until heated through. Serve with chips. **Yield:** 5 cups.

Editor's Note: This recipe was tested with Frank's Cayenne Pepper Sauce.

Use Your Slow Cooker!

CREAMY Buffalo Chicken Dip can be prepared, then heated in a slow cooker instead of baked. This will also keep the dip warm during a party.

Bacon Cheese Fondue

When I'm looking for an appetizer with mass appeal but want a change from the usual cheese spread, this is the recipe I make. Everyone enjoys the rich flavor.
—Bernice Morris, Marshfield, Missouri

4 to 5 bacon strips, diced
1/4 cup chopped onion
2 tablespoons all-purpose flour
1 pound process cheese (Velveeta), cubed
2 cups (16 ounces) sour cream
1 jalapeno pepper, seeded and chopped, optional
1 loaf (1 pound) French bread, cubed

In a large skillet, cook bacon over medium heat until crisp. Using a slotted spoon, remove to paper towels. In the drippings, saute onion until tender. Stir in flour until blended; cook and stir until thickened.

Reduce heat to low. Add cheese cubes; cook and stir until melted. Stir in sour cream, jalapeno if desired and bacon; cook and stir just until heated through. Transfer to a fondue pot and keep warm. Serve with bread cubes. **Yield:** 3-3/4 cups.

Editor's Note: When cutting or seeding hot peppers, use rubber or plastic gloves to protect your hands. Avoid touching your face.

Pear Pizza Wedges

(Pictured at right)

You won't be able to stop eating this sweet and savory appetizer. The recipe makes just the right amount for a smaller gathering.
—Mimi Merta, Dunedin, Florida

2 whole pita breads
2 teaspoons olive oil
1/2 cup crumbled Gorgonzola cheese
1 medium ripe pear, thinly sliced
1/4 cup coarsely chopped walnuts
1 tablespoon honey
1 teaspoon balsamic vinegar

Place pita breads on an ungreased baking sheet. Brush with oil; sprinkle with Gorgonzola cheese. Top with pear slices and walnuts. Bake at 400° for 12-15 minutes or until bread is crisp and cheese is melted. Combine honey and vinegar; drizzle over pitas. Cut each into four wedges. **Yield:** 8 appetizers.

Chutney Cheddar Spread

This is a quick appetizer to make with ingredients I have on hand in the kitchen.
—Regina Costlow, East Brady, Pennsylvania

4 ounces cheddar cheese, cubed
1/4 cup chutney
2 tablespoons butter, softened
1 tablespoon finely chopped onion
1/4 teaspoon Worcestershire sauce
Dash hot pepper sauce
Assorted crackers

In a food processor, combine the first six ingredients; cover and process until mixture achieves spreading consistency. Refrigerate until serving. Serve with crackers. **Yield:** about 1 cup.

Beef-Stuffed Crescents

My family loves these hearty appetizers year-round... not just during the Christmas season.
—Alene Knesel, Northome, Minnesota

3/4 pound ground beef
1/4 cup chopped onion
1 tablespoon sweet pickle relish
2 garlic cloves, minced
1/2 teaspoon salt
1/2 teaspoon chili powder
1/4 teaspoon pepper
Dash sugar
1 cup (4 ounces) shredded cheddar cheese
2 tubes (8 ounces *each*) refrigerated crescent rolls

In a large skillet, cook beef and onion over medium heat until meat is no longer pink; drain. Stir in the next seven ingredients; set aside.

Unroll crescent dough and separate into triangles. Cut each in half lengthwise, forming two triangles. Place 1 tablespoon beef mixture along the wide end of each triangle; carefully roll up. Place point side down 2 in. apart on ungreased baking sheets. Bake at 375° for 11-15 minutes or until golden brown. Serve warm. **Yield:** 32 appetizers.

Cheddar Onion Squares

When I was a child, my parents always served these appetizers before holiday meals. I like to use sharp cheddar cheese for more intense flavor.
—Debi Burrell-Thiem, Omaha, Nebraska

3/4 cup all-purpose flour
3/4 cup cornmeal
1/4 teaspoon salt
1/4 cup shortening
1/3 cup shredded cheddar cheese
1/4 cup water
TOPPING:
3 cups coarsely chopped onions
3 tablespoons butter
1/4 cup diced pimientos
1 egg, lightly beaten
1/2 cup sour cream
1/2 teaspoon salt
1/4 teaspoon paprika
1/4 teaspoon pepper
1 cup (4 ounces) shredded cheddar cheese

In a large bowl, combine the flour, cornmeal and salt. Cut in shortening until mixture resembles coarse crumbs. Stir in the cheese and water just until moistened. Press into a greased 13-in. x 9-in. x 2-in. baking pan. Bake at 400° for 5 minutes. Place pan on a wire rack. Reduce heat to 350°.

In a large skillet, saute onions in butter until tender. Stir in the pimientos. Spread over crust. Combine the egg, sour cream, salt, paprika and pepper; spread over onion layer. Bake for 20 minutes. Sprinkle with cheese. Bake 5 minutes longer or until cheese is melted. Cut into 1-1/2-in. squares. Serve warm. **Yield:** 4 dozen.

Ways to Reuse Christmas Cards

(Pictured above)

AS YOU PACK AWAY the holiday decorations after the new year, it's tempting to simply toss all the Christmas cards you received into the recycling bin.

Instead, read through those greeting cards one more time and put them in a box. Over the summer or in fall, pull out the cards and use them in the following creative ways:

Merry Markers. For beautiful bookmarks or gift tags, reach for the scissors and cut out images or words. Use a hole punch, then tie on a tassel. These homemade bookmarks make special stocking stuffers.

Pretty as a Picture. Framed photos of holiday scenes are a great way to liven up your decor at Christmastime, but they often can be costly. An easy and inexpensive alternative is to frame images from greetings cards. Use a traditional photo frame as a tabletop display. For an eye-catching wall hanging, purchase a larger matted frame.

Seasonal Stationery. The front, inside and even back of Christmas cards can have pretty images that would work well as postcards, note cards and recipe cards. (Be sure to check with your local post office regarding postcard size restrictions.)

Host an Ornament Exchange!

LIKE most people, you and your friends probably add a new ornament or two to your collection every Christmas.

Add a twist to that tradition this year by throwing an ornament exchange party!

As guests unwrap their pretty packages and "ooh" and "aah" over their new treasures, they can nibble on some delectable desserts.

For a sweet spread, set out Layered Coffee Ice Cream Dessert, Gift-Wrapped Chocolate Cake and Cream Puffs with Raspberry Sauce. (All recipes shown at right.) Guests are sure to be impressed!

Best of all, each of these recipes has time-saving tricks that won't keep you in the kitchen for hours.

Delightful Desserts

(Clockwise from top)

Gift-Wrapped Chocolate Cake (p. 231)

Layered Coffee Ice Cream Dessert (p. 234)

Cream Puffs with Raspberry Sauce (p. 232)

Chocolate Bow

(Pictured on opposite page and page 229)

What a beautiful sight this is on top of your favorite cake! It takes some time to prepare but can be made a month in advance, then stored in an airtight container.
—Debbie Gauthier, Timmins, Ontario

1 cup plus 2 tablespoons vanilla *or* white chips, *divided*
4 teaspoons shortening
1/2 large marshmallow

Cut three 6-in. squares from freezer paper. Cut each square into six 1-in. strips. Set aside four strips. Place remaining strips shiny side up on a waxed paper-lined work surface.

In a microwave, melt 1 cup vanilla chips and shortening; stir until smooth. Working quickly with a few strips at a time, spread chocolate beyond three sides of the strips onto the waxed paper, leaving 1/2 in. at one short end.

Immediately peel each strip from work surface; place on clean waxed paper. Let strips dry just until barely set but still pliable, about 1 minute. (If chocolate strips become too stiff, warm in the microwave for a few seconds.)

With paper side out, press ends of chocolate strips together. Stand strips on edges on a waxed paper-lined baking sheet. Chill until set, about 10 minutes. Carefully remove freezer paper.

For ribbons, coat four reserved strips with chocolate; peel strips from work surface. On an inverted 9-in. x 1-1/2-in. round baking pan, place strips, chocolate side down, at 90-degree angles to each other and drape 1-1/4 in. over side of pan. (If necessary, use a drop of chocolate under the bottom edge to hold in place. With a toothpick, press the strip onto the dab of chocolate.) Chill until set; remove freezer paper.

Melt remaining chips in the microwave. Fill a plastic bag with melted chocolate; cut a small hole in the corner. Place marshmallow half, cut side down, in the center of a piece of waxed paper. Secure six chocolate loops around edge of marshmallow with melted chocolate; press ends down. Layer five more loops on top with ends touching. Secure with chocolate. Coat top of marshmallow with remaining chocolate; place remaining loops in center, pressing down. Let dry for 1 hour or overnight. Carefully peel waxed paper from bow. Place ribbons and bow on top of cake. **Yield:** 1 chocolate bow for a 9-in. round or springform cake.

Creating a Chocolate Bow

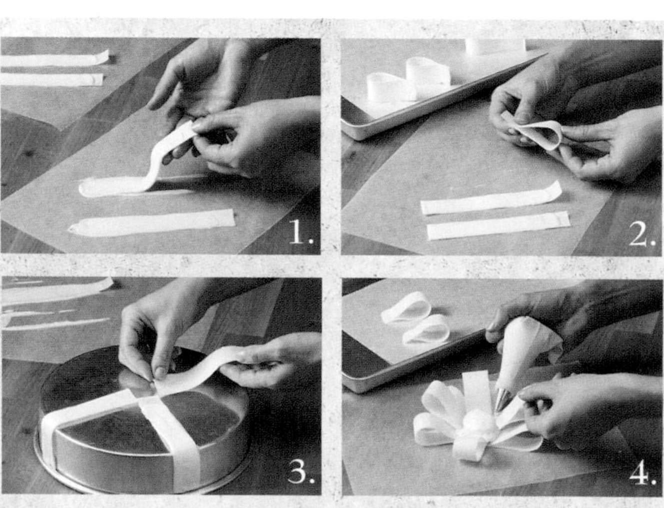

1. Spread chocolate onto strips of freezer paper. Immediately peel strips from work surface; place on clean waxed paper.

2. Press ends of strips together, paper side out. Stand on edges on a waxed paper-lined baking sheet.

3. Coat four reserved strips of freezer paper with chocolate. Peel from work surface. Place chocolate side down on an inverted 9-inch round baking pan.

4. Using additional melted chocolate, secure loops around the marshmallow.

Gift-Wrapped Chocolate Cake

(Pictured at right and on page 229)

Family and friends will be impressed when you present this rich, glazed cake from our Test Kitchen.

- **2 teaspoons plus 3/4 cup butter (no substitutes), softened, *divided***
- **1-1/2 cups sugar**
- **3 eggs, *separated***
- **3 tablespoons water**
- **3 tablespoons vegetable oil**
- **1-1/2 teaspoons vanilla extract**
- **1/2 cup all-purpose flour**
- **1/2 cup plus 1 tablespoon baking cocoa**
- **3/4 cup chopped pecans**
- **1/8 teaspoon cream of tartar**
- **1/8 teaspoon salt**

GLAZE:

- **8 squares (1 ounce *each*) semisweet chocolate, chopped**
- **1/2 cup heavy whipping cream**
- **Chocolate Bow (recipe on opposite page)**

Line the bottom of a 9-in. springform pan with foil; grease foil and sides of pan with 2 teaspoons butter; set aside. Melt remaining butter. In a mixing bowl, beat butter and sugar. Add egg yolks, one at a time, beating well after each. Beat in the water, oil and vanilla; mix well. Combine flour and cocoa; gradually add to egg mixture. Stir in pecans.

In another mixing bowl, beat egg whites on medium speed until foamy. Add cream of tartar and salt; beat on high until stiff peaks form. Fold into chocolate mixture. Pour into prepared pan. Bake at 350° for 45-50 minutes or until top begins to crack slightly and a toothpick comes out with moist crumbs. Cool on a wire rack for 10 minutes. Carefully run a knife around edge of pan to loosen; cool 1 hour longer. Refrigerate overnight.

To assemble, invert cake onto a waxed paper-lined baking sheet. Remove foil; set aside. In a heavy saucepan, heat chocolate and cream over very low heat until chocolate is melted (do not boil); stir until smooth. Remove from the heat. Cool if necessary until mixture reaches spreading consistency.

Slowly pour glaze over cake, smoothing sides with a metal spatula to evenly coat. Chill until set. Carefully transfer cake to a flat serving plate. Top with Chocolate Bow. Refrigerate leftovers. **Yield:** 10-12 servings.

Cream Puffs with Raspberry Sauce

(Pictured on page 228)

This is the most elegant dessert I make, and all who try it love it.
These cute little puffs filled with ice cream are perfect for any special occasion.
—Debbie Krygeris, Downers Grove, Illinois

1/2 cup water
1/4 cup plus 1 tablespoon butter (no substitutes), *divided*
1/2 cup all-purpose flour
2 eggs
3 cups vanilla ice cream, *divided*
1 package (10 ounces) frozen sweetened raspberries, thawed
2 squares (1 ounce *each*) semisweet chocolate
2 tablespoons milk
1/4 cup chopped pistachios

In a small saucepan, bring water and 1/4 cup butter to a boil. Add flour all at once and stir until a smooth ball forms. Remove from the heat; let stand for 5 minutes. Add eggs, one at a time, beating well after each addition. Continue beating until mixture is smooth and shiny.

Drop by rounded teaspoonfuls 2 in. apart onto greased baking sheets. Bake at 400° for 22-25 minutes or until golden brown. Remove to wire racks. Immediately split puffs open; remove tops and set aside. Discard soft dough from inside. Cool puffs. Fill puffs with 2-3/4 cups ice cream; replace tops. Cover tightly and freeze.

For sauce, place the raspberries in a blender or food processor; cover and process until smooth. Strain seeds. Stir in the remaining ice cream until melted. In a small saucepan, heat the chocolate, milk and remaining butter over low heat until melted, stirring constantly.

To serve, spoon 2 tablespoons raspberry sauce on each dessert plate; top with filled cream puffs. Drizzle with chocolate sauce; sprinkle with pistachios. **Yield:** 1-1/2 dozen.

Organizing an Ornament Exchange

WHETHER you host the event for close friends, co-workers or acquaintances, an ornament exchange is one of the easiest parties to organize. All you need to do is purchase an ornament and make a little food...a good time is guaranteed when the gift opening begins! Here's how an ornament exchange works:

- Ask each guest (the number depends on you) to bring one wrapped ornament. Specify a price range (often between $5 and $10).
- As the guests arrive, assign a number to each package and give the guests a number, making sure it's not the number attached to their gift. (For a fun way to attach the numbers and to display the lovely pile of presents, see the Pretty Packages Centerpiece on page 241.)
- In turn, each person opens the package corresponding to their number. For a little added fun, see if folks can guess who purchased each ornament.

Partridge in a Pear Tree Pie

(Pictured at right)

Delight guests and have a partridge in a pear tree make an appearance on your holiday table! The crimson cranberry filling makes this a fitting Christmas pie.
—Jill Rens, Champlin, Minnesota

1 can (15 ounces) pear halves, drained
1 package (12 ounces) fresh *or* frozen cranberries
1 can (8 ounces) crushed pineapple
1-1/2 cups sugar
3 tablespoons all-purpose flour
1/4 teaspoon salt
1/4 teaspoon ground cinnamon
Pastry for double-crust pie (9 inches)
Additional sugar, optional

Set aside five pear halves; chop remaining pears. In a saucepan, combine the chopped pears, cranberries, pineapple and sugar. Bring to a boil; cook and stir for 4-5 minutes or until some cranberries have popped. Cool for 30 minutes, stirring several times. In a bowl, combine the flour, salt and cinnamon. Stir in cooled cranberry mixture.

Line a 9-in. pie plate with bottom pastry; trim and flute edges. Spoon cranberry mixture into pastry shell; arrange pear halves on top. Bake at 400° for 35-40 minutes or until bubbly and crust is golden brown (cover edges with foil for last 15 minutes of baking if necessary). Cool on a wire rack.

Roll out remaining pastry. Using cookie cutters, cut out small leaves, small pears and a partridge. Place on an ungreased baking sheet; sprinkle with sugar if desired. Bake at 400° for 6-8 minutes or until golden brown. Place partridge in center of pie with leaves and pears around it. **Yield:** 6-8 servings.

Layered Coffee Ice Cream Dessert

(Pictured on page 229)

Family and friends won't believe it when you tell them this attractive layered dessert has only four ingredients. Our Test Kitchen home economists created this make-ahead recipe with your busy days in mind.

27 cream-filled chocolate sandwich cookies, crushed (about 2-1/2 cups)
6 tablespoons butter *or* margarine, melted
5 cups coffee ice cream, softened
1 cup prepared chocolate frosting
Chocolate-covered coffee beans, mint leaves and warm caramel ice cream topping, optional

Line the bottom and sides of a 9-in. x 5-in. x 3-in. loaf pan with heavy-duty foil. In a bowl, combine the crushed cookies and butter. Press half of the cookie mixture into the prepared pan. Gently spread half of the ice cream over the crumbs. Freeze for 15 minutes. Spread frosting over the ice cream, then carefully spread remaining ice cream over the top. Sprinkle with remaining crumb mixture and press down lightly. Cover and freeze overnight.

Remove from the freezer 5 minutes before serving. Invert dessert onto a serving platter. Discard foil. Garnish with coffee beans and mint if desired. Cut into slices. Serve with caramel topping if desired. **Yield:** 10 servings.

Celebration Cranberry Cake

After I've served this cake, guests never leave my house without requesting the recipe. The sweetness of the butter cream sauce balances beautifully with the cake's tart cranberries.
—Jeri Clayton, Sandy, Utah

3 tablespoons butter (no substitutes), softened
1 cup sugar
1 cup evaporated milk
2 cups all-purpose flour
3 teaspoons baking powder
1 teaspoon salt
2 cups fresh *or* frozen cranberries, halved
BUTTER CREAM SAUCE:
1/2 cup butter
1 cup sugar
1 cup heavy whipping cream
1 teaspoon vanilla extract

In a mixing bowl, cream butter and sugar; beat in milk. Combine the flour, baking powder and salt; gradually add to creamed mixture. Stir in cranberries. Pour into a greased 9-in. square baking pan. Bake at 350° for 40-45 minutes or until a toothpick inserted near the center comes out clean. Cool on a wire rack.

For sauce, melt butter in a saucepan. Stir in the sugar and cream; bring to a boil, stirring often. Boil for 8-10 minutes or until slightly thickened. Remove from the heat; stir in vanilla. Serve warm with cake. **Yield:** 9 servings.

Raspberry Sponge Torte

(Pictured at right)

This lovely three-layer cake is moist, tender and light. It rivals any cake from the finest bakery. I use black walnuts to add a more distinctive flavor.
—Janet Zoz, Alvo, Nebraska

1/2 cup butter *or* margarine, softened
1/2 cup shortening
2 cups sugar
5 eggs, *separated*
1-1/2 teaspoons vanilla extract
2 cups all-purpose flour
1 teaspoon baking soda
1 cup buttermilk
1 cup finely chopped walnuts, toasted
1/2 cup flaked coconut
1/2 teaspoon cream of tartar
FILLING/FROSTING:
1 cup raspberry preserves, warmed
2 packages (one 8 ounces, one 3 ounces) cream cheese, softened
3/4 cup butter *or* margarine, softened
6-1/2 cups confectioners' sugar
2 teaspoons vanilla extract
1/2 cup chopped walnuts

In a large mixing bowl, cream butter, shortening and sugar. Add egg yolks, one at a time, beating well after each addition. Beat in vanilla. Combine the flour and baking soda; add to creamed mixture alternately with buttermilk. Stir in nuts and coconut.

In another mixing bowl, beat egg whites and cream of tartar until stiff peaks form. Fold into cake batter. Pour into three greased and floured 9-in. round baking pans. Bake at 350° for 28-30 minutes or until a toothpick inserted near the center comes out clean. Cool for 10 minutes before removing from pans to wire racks to cool completely.

Spread raspberry preserves over the top of two cake layers. Refrigerate for 30 minutes. Meanwhile, in a mixing bowl, beat the cream cheese, butter and confectioners' sugar until fluffy. Beat in vanilla. Spread between layers and over the top and sides of cake. Sprinkle with nuts. Store in the refrigerator. **Yield:** 12-16 servings.

Keeping a Cake Plate Pretty

TO HELP KEEP the serving plate clean when frosting a cake, try this trick. Tuck several 3-inch strips of waxed paper slightly under the cake, covering the plate's edge. Frost as desired, then carefully remove the waxed paper.

Orange Coconut Custard

These pretty parfaits are perfect for weekend guests as well as for the family during the week. I sometimes add banana slices for more tropical flavor.
—Suzanne Cleveland, Lyons, Georgia

1/4 cup sugar
1 tablespoon all-purpose flour
Dash salt
1 cup milk
4 egg yolks, beaten
1 teaspoon vanilla extract
1/4 teaspoon orange extract
1 cup heavy whipping cream, whipped
Fresh orange sections
1/4 cup flaked coconut, toasted

In a saucepan, combine the sugar, flour and salt. Gradually add the milk; stir until smooth. Bring to a boil; cook and stir for 2 minutes or until thickened. Remove from the heat. Stir a small amount of hot filling into egg yolks; return all to the pan, stirring constantly. Bring to a gentle boil; cook and stir for 1-2 minutes. Remove from the heat; cool slightly. Stir in extracts.

In four individual dessert glasses or bowls, layer the custard, whipped cream, orange sections and coconut. Refrigerate until serving. **Yield:** 4 servings.

Double-Crust Creamy Raisin Pie

Old-fashioned pudding pie never goes out of fashion. I got the recipe from a boyfriend's mother when I was 16 years old. One pie never lasts long around my house.
—Janene Curtis, West Valley City, Utah

2 cups all-purpose flour
3/4 teaspoon salt
3/4 cup butter-flavored shortening
1/4 cup cold water
FILLING:
1-1/2 cups water
1 cup raisins
3/4 cup sugar
3 tablespoons cornstarch
1/4 teaspoon salt
1-1/2 cups heavy whipping cream
1 teaspoon vanilla extract

In a bowl, combine flour and salt; cut in shortening until crumbly. Gradually add water, tossing with a fork until dough forms a ball. Divide dough in half. Roll out one portion to fit a 9-in. pie plate; place pastry in pie plate and trim even with edge of plate.

In a large saucepan, bring water and raisins to a boil. Reduce heat; simmer, uncovered, for 10 minutes. In a small bowl, combine the sugar, cornstarch and salt; stir in cream until smooth. Add to raisin mixture. Bring to a boil; cook and stir for 2 minutes or until thickened. Remove from the heat; stir in vanilla. Pour into pastry shell.

Roll out remaining pastry to fit top of pie. Place over filling; trim, seal and flute edges. Cut slits in top. Bake at 350° for 35-40 minutes or until crust is golden brown. Cool completely on a wire rack. Store in the refrigerator. **Yield:** 6-8 servings.

Mocha Meringue Cups

(Pictured at right)

No one can resist a rich mocha filling sitting on top of a crisp, chewy meringue cup. My clan expects me to make these treats for many special occasions throughout the year.
—Helen Davis, Waterbury, Vermont

3 egg whites
1/4 teaspoon cream of tartar
Dash salt
1 cup sugar
CHOCOLATE FILLING:
2 cups milk chocolate chips
1 cup heavy whipping cream
1 teaspoon instant coffee granules
1 teaspoon vanilla extract

In a small mixing bowl, beat the egg whites, cream of tartar and salt on medium speed until soft peaks form. Gradually beat in sugar, 1 tablespoon at a time, on high until stiff peaks form. Spoon meringue into eight mounds on parchment-lined baking sheets. Shape into 3-in. cups with the back of a spoon. Bake at 275° for 45-50 minutes. Turn oven off; leave meringues in oven for 1 hour. Remove from the oven and cool on baking sheet. When completely cooled, remove meringues from the paper and store in an airtight container at room temperature.

For filling, in a heavy saucepan, melt the chocolate chips, cream and coffee granules; stir until smooth. Remove from the heat; stir in vanilla. Transfer to a small mixing bowl; refrigerate until chilled. Beat until stiff peaks form. Immediately spoon into a pastry bag or plastic bag with a #20 star tip. Pipe filling into meringue cups. Refrigerate until serving. **Yield:** 8 servings.

Cream Cheese Cherry Dessert

When I'm anticipating a busy day, I make this pretty dessert the night before. You don't need a very big piece to satisfy a sweet tooth.
—Jeanne Krab, Paxton, Nebraska

3 cups Rice Chex, crushed
3/4 cup packed brown sugar
1 cup chopped walnuts
1/2 cup flaked coconut
1/2 cup butter *or* margarine, melted
2 packages (8 ounces *each*) cream cheese, softened
1 cup sugar
1 teaspoon vanilla extract
2 eggs
2 cans (21 ounces *each*) cherry pie filling
1 carton (8 ounces) frozen whipped topping, thawed

In a large bowl, combine the cereal, brown sugar, walnuts, coconut and butter; set aside 1 cup for topping. Press remaining crumb mixture into a greased 13-in. x 9-in. x 2-in. baking dish; set aside.

In a mixing bowl, beat the cream cheese, sugar and vanilla. Add eggs, one at a time, beating well after each addition. Pour over the crust. Bake at 350° for 25-30 minutes or until center is almost set. Cool completely on a wire rack.

Spread pie filling over cream cheese layer; top with whipped topping. Sprinkle with reserved crumb mixture. Refrigerate for at least 1 hour before serving. **Yield:** 18-20 servings.

Mini Pineapple Upside-Down Cakes

These individual pineapple upside-down cakes are an eye-catching addition to my holiday dessert table. A boxed cake mix makes them easy to bake anytime.
—Cindy Colley, Othello, Washington

2/3 cup packed brown sugar
1/3 cup butter *or* margarine, melted
2 cans (20 ounces *each*) sliced pineapple
1 package (18-1/4 ounces) yellow cake mix
3 eggs
1/3 cup vegetable oil
12 maraschino cherries, halved

In a bowl, combine the brown sugar and butter; mix well. Spoon into 24 greased muffin cups. Drain pineapple, reserving the juice. Trim pineapple to fit the muffin cups; place one ring in each cup.

In a mixing bowl, combine the cake mix, eggs, oil and 1-1/4 cups of the reserved pineapple juice; mix well. Spoon over pineapple, filling each cup two-thirds full. Bake at 350° for 20-25 minutes or until a toothpick inserted near the center comes out clean. Immediately invert onto wire racks to cool. Place a cherry in the center of each pineapple ring. **Yield:** 2 dozen.

Frosty Ginger Pumpkin Squares

(Pictured at right)

My family loves getting together to sample good food. While pumpkin makes it perfect for the holidays, this ice cream dessert is requested year-round.
—Kathryn Reeger, Shelocta, Pennsylvania

- **1/4 cup butter *or* margarine, melted**
- **1 cup crushed graham crackers (about 16 squares)**
- **1 cup crushed gingersnaps (about 18 cookies)**
- **2 cups canned pumpkin**
- **1 cup sugar**
- **1/2 to 1 teaspoon ground cinnamon**
- **1/2 teaspoon salt**
- **1/2 teaspoon ground ginger**
- **1/4 teaspoon ground nutmeg**
- **1 cup chopped walnuts**
- **2 quarts vanilla ice cream, softened slightly**

In a bowl, combine the butter and crushed graham crackers and gingersnaps. Press half of the crumb mixture into an ungreased 13-in. x 9-in. x 2-in. dish. In a bowl, combine the pumpkin, sugar, cinnamon, salt, ginger and nutmeg. Stir in walnuts. Fold in ice cream. Spoon over crust. Sprinkle with remaining crumb mixture. Freeze until firm, about 3 hours. **Yield:** 12-15 servings.

Pumpkin Pecan Bites

This recipe makes a lot, so I like sharing the bite-size treats at potlucks. To easily frost them, try putting the frosting in a pastry bag and piping it on top of the cupcakes.
—Carol Beyerl, Ellensburg, Washington

1 package (18-1/4 ounces) spice cake mix
1 can (15 ounces) solid-pack pumpkin
3 eggs
1/2 cup vegetable oil
1 tablespoon ground cinnamon
1 teaspoon baking soda
1/4 teaspoon ground cloves
36 pecan halves, cut into halves
CREAM CHEESE FROSTING:
1/2 cup butter *or* margarine, softened
4 ounces cream cheese, softened
1 teaspoon vanilla extract
3-3/4 cups confectioners' sugar
2 to 3 tablespoons milk
Ground cinnamon

In a large mixing bowl, combine the cake mix, pumpkin, eggs, oil, cinnamon, baking soda and cloves. Beat on medium speed for 2 minutes. Fill paper-lined miniature muffin cups two-thirds full. Press a pecan piece into each. Bake at 350° for 17-20 minutes or until a toothpick inserted near the center comes out clean. Cool for 5 minutes before removing from pans to wire racks to cool completely.

In a small mixing bowl, cream the butter, cream cheese and vanilla. Gradually add confectioners' sugar. Add enough milk to achieve spreading consistency. Frost cupcakes. Sprinkle with cinnamon. **Yield:** about 6 dozen.

Editor's Note: This recipe can be prepared in 2 dozen regular-size muffin cups. Bake for 22-26 minutes.

Coconut Trifle

The friend who shared this recipe is a great cook who never fails to come up with terrific dishes. The fast-to-fix dessert tastes like coconut cream pie.
—Betty Claycomb, Alverton, Pennsylvania

1 prepared angel food cake (8 inches), cut into 1-inch cubes
2 cups cold milk
2 packages (3.4 ounces *each*) instant coconut cream pudding mix
1 quart vanilla ice cream, softened
1 carton (8 ounces) frozen whipped topping, thawed
1/4 cup flaked coconut, toasted

Place cake cubes in a large bowl. In a bowl, whisk milk and pudding mixes for 2 minutes. Let stand for 2 minutes or until soft-set. Stir in ice cream until well mixed. Pour over cake cubes; stir just until combined. Transfer to a 5-qt. trifle bowl. Spread with whipped topping and sprinkle with coconut. Cover and refrigerate for at least 30 minutes before serving. **Yield:** 20 servings.

Pretty Packages Centerpiece

(Pictured above)

WHEN HOSTING an ornament exchange, let the wrapped boxes and gift bags brought by guests serve as your centerpiece. The various shapes of boxes and bags and the variety of wrapping paper will add visual appeal and color in an instant.

Because most of the boxes brought to the party will likely be small, you may want to wrap a large empty box to serve as the anchor for the display.

Before the party, cut a long ribbon for each guest you're expecting. Then attach a number to each of the ribbons. Put the same amount of numbers on a separate piece of paper in a container and set aside.

As guests arrive, tie a numbered ribbon to each of the packages. Have guests select a number from the container (be sure it's not the same number you just assigned to their gift!). Set the boxes and bags around your large wrapped box. Position the ribbons so the numbers are visible.

When you're ready to begin the ornament exchange, have each guest look for their number and follow the ribbon to their gift. Have each person take a turn to unwrap their new ornament.

Gift-Wrapping Dessert Party

THE TASK of wrapping all of the Christmas gifts you purchased can seem like a daunting task. So why not make a fun night of it by inviting over a few close friends for a gift-wrapping party?

In addition to their gifts, have each guest bring along wrapping paper, ribbons and bows. (For a Yuletide twist, see "It's a Wrap!" on page 253 for non-traditional gift-wrapping ideas.)

Let guests know you'll supply plenty of tape, scissors, pens and gift tags.

Avoid the temptation to go all out on the food...keep the celebration simple by offering a stunning dessert, such as Chocolate-Mint Present Cake (pictured at right).

Pretty Presentation

(Pictured above)

Chocolate-Mint Present Cake (p. 244)

Chocolate-Mint Present Cake

(Pictured on page 243)

The flavor of crushed peppermint candies infuses every forkful of this outstanding chocolate cake from our home economists. It's a tasty surprise during the holidays.

1-1/3 cups baking cocoa
2-2/3 cups boiling water
1-1/3 cups butter, softened
3-1/3 cups sugar
6 eggs
1 teaspoon vanilla extract
4 cups all-purpose flour
2-1/2 teaspoons baking soda
2 teaspoons salt
1/2 teaspoon baking powder
1 cup crushed peppermint candies

FROSTING:
1-2/3 cups butter, softened
15 cups confectioners' sugar
1 cup plus 2 tablespoons milk, *divided*
2-1/2 teaspoons peppermint extract

FONDANT:
1/4 cup shortening
3-3/4 cups confectioners' sugar
9 tablespoons light corn syrup
Red paste food coloring
4 pieces ribbon candy (4 inches x 1 inch)
Assorted round candies, optional

In a small bowl, combine cocoa and water until smooth; cool completely. In a large mixing bowl, cream butter and sugar until light and fluffy. Add eggs, one at a time, beating well after each. Beat in vanilla. Combine the flour, baking soda, salt and baking powder; add to creamed mixture alternately with cocoa mixture. Beat until smooth. Fold in peppermint candies.

Pour into four greased and floured 9-in. square baking pans. Bake at 350° for 25-30 minutes or until a toothpick inserted near the center comes out clean. Cool for 10 minutes before removing from the pans to wire racks to cool completely.

For frosting, in a large mixing bowl, cream butter. Add confectioners' sugar, 1 cup milk and extract; beat on low until combined. Beat on medium for 1 minute or until frosting achieves spreading consistency, adding remaining milk if necessary.

Place one cake layer on a serving plate; spread with frosting. Repeat three times. Frost sides of cake.

For fondant, in a large mixing bowl of a heavy-duty stand mixer, cream shortening until light and fluffy. Beat in confectioners' sugar until crumbly. Gradually beat in corn syrup on low speed (mixture will be stiff).

Divide in half; tint one portion red and one portion pink. For ribbon, on a work surface dusted with confectioners' sugar, roll out red portion into a 19-in. x 4-in. rectangle; cut in half lengthwise. Carefully arrange over cake, draping ends down the sides. On a work surface dusted with confectioners' sugar, roll out pink portion into a 19-in. x 2-in. rectangle; cut in half lengthwise. Carefully position over red ribbon, draping ends down the sides.

Just before serving, break ribbon candies in half; place over ribbon on top of cake, creating a bow. Decorate with round candies if desired. **Yield:** 24 servings.

Toasted Butter Pecan Cake

(Pictured at right and on front cover)

If you like butter pecan ice cream, you'll love this cake. Loads of nuts are folded into the batter and toasted pecans are sprinkled over a delectable cream cheese frosting. Irresistible!
—Phyllis Edwards, Fort Valley, Georgia

1-1/4 cups butter, softened, *divided*
2 cups chopped pecans
2 cups sugar
4 eggs
2 teaspoons vanilla extract
3 cups all-purpose flour
2 teaspoons baking powder
1/2 teaspoon salt
1 cup milk

FROSTING:

2 packages (8 ounces *each*) cream cheese, softened
1 cup butter, softened
1 package (2 pounds) confectioners' sugar
2 teaspoons vanilla extract
2 to 3 tablespoons milk
2/3 cup chopped pecans, toasted

In a small heavy skillet, melt 1/4 cup butter. Add pecans; cook over medium heat until toasted, about 4 minutes. Spread on foil to cool.

In a large mixing bowl, cream sugar and remaining butter. Add eggs, one at a time, beating well after each addition. Beat in vanilla. Combine the flour, baking powder and salt; add to creamed mixture alternately with milk. Beat just until combined. Fold in pecans. Pour into three greased 9-in. round baking pans. Bake at 350° for 25-30 minutes or until a toothpick inserted near the center comes out clean. Cool for 10 minutes before removing from pans to wire racks to cool completely.

For frosting, in a large mixing bowl, beat the cream cheese, butter, confectioners' sugar and vanilla. Beat in enough milk to achieve spreading consistency. Spread frosting between layers and over top and sides of cake. Sprinkle with pecans. Store in the refrigerator. **Yield:** 12-16 servings.

Mint Dip with Brownies

(Pictured at far right, bottom)

My sister shared the simple, refreshing dip recipe with me many years ago. It also tastes terrific with fresh strawberries.
—Carol Klein, Franklin Square, New York

1 package fudge brownie mix (8-inch square pan size)
3/4 cup sour cream
2 tablespoons brown sugar
2 tablespoons green creme de menthe

Prepare and bake brownies according to package directions. Cool completely on a wire rack. Meanwhile, in a small bowl, combine the sour cream, brown sugar and creme de menthe; cover and refrigerate until serving.

Cut brownies into 1-in. diamonds. Serve with dip. **Yield:** 1 dozen (3/4 cup dip).

Cranberry Cake Roll

This low-fat angel food cake roll is a guilt-free indulgence, which is much-appreciated during the Christmas season.
—Paige Kowolewski, Topton, Pennsylvania

9 egg whites
1-1/2 teaspoons vanilla extract
3/4 teaspoon cream of tartar
1/4 teaspoon salt
1 cup plus 2 tablespoons sugar
3/4 cup cake flour

FILLING:

2-1/3 cups fresh *or* frozen cranberries
1 cup sugar
6 tablespoons water, *divided*
2 tablespoons cornstarch

Place egg whites in a large mixing bowl; let stand at room temperature for 30 minutes. Meanwhile, line a greased 15-in. x 10-in. x 1-in. baking pan with waxed paper; grease the paper and set aside.

Add vanilla, cream of tartar and salt to egg whites; beat on medium speed until soft peaks form. Gradually beat in sugar, 2 tablespoons at a time, on high until stiff glossy peaks form and sugar is dissolved. Fold in flour, about 1/4 cup at a time.

Carefully spread into prepared pan. Bake at 350° for 15-20 minutes or until cake springs back when lightly touched. Cool for 5 minutes. Turn cake onto a kitchen towel dusted with confectioners' sugar. Gently peel off waxed paper. Roll up cake in the towel jelly-roll style, starting with a long side. Cool completely on a wire rack.

For filling, in a large saucepan, combine the cranberries, sugar and 1/4 cup water. Bring to a boil. Reduce heat; simmer, uncovered, for 5-6 minutes or until berries pop. Mash berries; strain, reserving juice and discarding pulp. Return juice to the pan. Combine cornstarch and remaining water until smooth; gradually add to cranberry juice. Bring to a boil; cook and stir for 2 minutes or until thickened. Chill.

Unroll cake and spread filling to within 1/2 in. of edges. Roll up again. Cover and refrigerate for 1 hour before serving. Refrigerate leftovers. **Yield:** 12 servings.

Mint Ice Cream Torte

(Pictured at right, top)

Wouldn't it be great to have an impressive dessert on hand for unexpected company over the Christmas season? Try our Test Kitchen's recipe for a from-the-freezer favorite!

- **20 cream-filled chocolate sandwich cookies, crushed**
- **1/4 cup butter, melted**
- **10 mint Andes candies, melted**
- **1/2 gallon mint chocolate chip ice cream, *divided***
- **1 jar (11-3/4 ounces) hot fudge ice cream topping**

In a small bowl, combine the cookie crumbs and butter. Press half of the mixture into a greased 9-in. springform pan. Spread melted candies over crust. Top with half of the ice cream.

Place 1/4 cup hot fudge topping in a small bowl; cover and refrigerate until serving. In another bowl, combine remaining topping and crumb mixture; spread over ice cream. Cover and freeze for 2 hours or until firm.

Top with remaining ice cream. Cover and freeze for 8 hours or overnight until firm. Remove from the freezer 5 minutes before serving. Warm reserved fudge topping and use to garnish torte. **Yield:** 12 servings.

Cutting Ice Cream Cake

TO CUT frozen Mint Ice Cream Torte, use a long straight-edged knife. Dip it often into hot water for easier slicing.

Caramel Tassies

(Pictured at far right)

Buttery cookie cups with a caramel filling make a nice addition to a dessert tray.
—Jane Bricker, Scottdale, Pennsylvania

1 cup butter, softened
2 packages (3 ounces *each*) cream cheese, softened
2 cups all-purpose flour
FILLING:
1 package (14 ounces) caramels
1/4 cup plus 3 tablespoons evaporated milk
FROSTING:
2 tablespoons shortening
2 tablespoons butter, softened
1 cup confectioners' sugar
1 tablespoon evaporated milk

In a large mixing bowl, cream butter and cream cheese. Gradually beat in flour. Cover and refrigerate for 1 hour or until easy to handle.

Roll dough into 1-in. balls; press onto the bottom and up the sides of ungreased miniature muffin cups. Prick bottoms with a fork. Bake at 375° for 15-17 minutes or until golden. Cool for 5 minutes; remove from pans to wire racks.

In a large heavy saucepan over low heat, melt caramels with milk. Remove from the heat; cool slightly. Transfer to a heavy-duty resealable plastic bag; cut a small hole in a corner of the bag. Pipe filling into pastry cups. Cool to room temperature.

For frosting, in a small mixing bowl, beat shortening and butter until smooth. Gradually beat in confectioners' sugar and milk until fluffy. Pipe onto filling. Store in the refrigerator. **Yield**: 4 dozen.

Cherry-Nut Brownie Bars

I created these bars by accident one day, but now I make a point of preparing them often.
—Richell Welch, Buffalo, Texas

3 cups all-purpose flour
2 cups sugar
1 cup baking cocoa
1/2 teaspoon baking powder
1/2 teaspoon baking soda
1/2 teaspoon salt
2 eggs
1 cup butter, melted
3 teaspoons vanilla extract
1 can (21 ounces) cherry pie filling
1 cup chopped walnuts
1/2 cup vanilla *or* white chips
1 tablespoon milk

In a large mixing bowl, combine the first six ingredients. In another bowl, whisk the eggs, butter and vanilla; add to dry ingredients. Beat until well blended (mixture will be thick).

Set aside 1 cup dough for topping. Press remaining dough into a greased 13-in. x 9-in. x 2-in. baking dish. Spread evenly with pie filling. Crumble reserved dough over the top; sprinkle with walnuts.

Bake at 350° for 35-40 minutes or until top is dry and nuts are golden brown. Cool completely on a wire rack.

In a microwave-safe bowl, melt vanilla chips at 70% power; stir in milk until smooth. Drizzle over bars. **Yield:** about 2 dozen.

Fancy Phyllo Cups

(Pictured at right)

Phyllo dough is great for making eye-catching desserts with little work. Experiment with other preserves for a tasty twist.
—Cody Geisler, Minnetonka, Minnesota

- 8 sheets phyllo dough (14 inches x 9 inches)
- 1/3 cup butter, melted
- 1/2 cup confectioners' sugar
- 1/2 cup vanilla *or* white chips
- 2 tablespoons milk
- 1 package (8 ounces) cream cheese, softened
- 1 carton (8 ounces) frozen whipped topping, thawed
- 1/2 cup seedless raspberry preserves, room temperature

White chocolate curls, optional

Place one sheet of phyllo dough on a work surface (keep remaining phyllo covered with plastic wrap and a damp towel to prevent it from drying out); brush sheet with butter and dust with confectioners' sugar. Top with a second sheet of phyllo; brush with butter and dust with sugar.

Cut into 12 squares. Place one square on top of a second square, alternating corner points; press into a greased muffin cup. Repeat with remaining 10 squares, filling five more muffin cups. Repeat the process three times with remaining phyllo dough, butter and sugar.

Bake at 350° for 5-6 minutes or until lightly browned. Carefully remove from pans to wire racks to cool.

In a microwave-safe bowl, heat vanilla chips and milk at 70% power until chips are melted; stir until smooth. In a large mixing bowl, beat cream cheese and melted chip mixture until smooth. Fold in whipped topping.

Spoon or pipe into phyllo cups; drizzle with raspberry preserves. Cover and refrigerate until serving. Garnish with chocolate curls if desired. **Yield:** 2 dozen.

Butterscotch Cake

I get lots of compliments and recipe requests whenever I make this delicious, rich cake. The filling is similar to German chocolate cake.
—Judy Lamon, Louisville, Tennessee

2/3 cup butterscotch chips
1/4 cup water
1/2 cup shortening
3/4 cup sugar
3/4 cup packed brown sugar
3 eggs
2-1/4 cups all-purpose flour
1 teaspoon baking soda
1/2 teaspoon baking powder
1/2 teaspoon salt
1 cup buttermilk

FILLING/TOPPING:

1/2 cup sugar
1 tablespoon cornstarch
1/2 cup evaporated milk
1/3 cup water
1 egg yolk, lightly beaten
1/3 cup butterscotch chips
2 tablespoons butter
1 cup pecans, chopped
1 cup flaked coconut
2 to 3 cups buttercream frosting

Line two greased 9-in. round baking pans with waxed paper; set aside. In a saucepan, melt butterscotch chips with water over low heat, stirring occasionally. Cool to room temperature.

In a large mixing bowl, cream shortening and sugars. Add eggs, one at a time, beating well after each addition. Beat in butterscotch mixture. Combine the flour, baking soda, baking powder and salt; add to creamed mixture alternately with buttermilk (do not overbeat).

Pour into prepared pans. Bake at 375° for 30-35 minutes or until a toothpick inserted near the center comes out clean. Cool for 10 minutes before removing from pans to wire racks to cool completely.

In a large saucepan, combine sugar and cornstarch. Stir in evaporated milk and water until smooth. Cook and stir over medium heat until thickened and bubbly. Reduce heat; cook and stir 2 minutes longer. Remove from the heat. Stir a small amount of hot filling into egg yolk; return all to the pan, stirring constantly. Bring to a gentle boil; cook and stir 2 minutes longer.

Remove from the heat. Gently stir in chips and butter. Stir in pecans and coconut. Cool to room temperature without stirring.

Place one cake layer on a serving plate; spread with half of the filling. Top with second layer and remaining filling. Frost sides with buttercream frosting. Store in the refrigerator. **Yield:** 12 servings.

Basic Buttercream Frosting

IN a large mixing bowl, cream 1/2 cup softened butter until light and fluffy. Beat in 4-1/2 cups confectioners' sugar and 1-1/2 teaspoons vanilla extract. Add 5 to 6 tablespoons milk until desired consistency is reached. **Yield:** about 3 cups.

Raspberry-Cream Chocolate Torte

(Pictured at right)

This spectacular torte looks and tastes like it came from a European bakery. Although it takes some time to make, each step is actually very easy.
—Mary Beth Jung
Hendersonville, North Carolina

2/3 cup butter, softened
1 cup sugar
3 eggs
2 teaspoons vanilla extract
2 cups all-purpose flour
3/4 cup baking cocoa
1-1/2 teaspoons baking powder
1/2 teaspoon baking soda
1-1/3 cups milk

FILLING:

1 package (10 ounces) frozen unsweetened raspberries, thawed
1 envelope unflavored gelatin
1 cup heavy whipping cream
1/4 cup confectioners' sugar
1/2 teaspoon vanilla extract

GANACHE:

1/2 cup semisweet chocolate chips
3 tablespoons heavy whipping cream

In a large mixing bowl, cream butter and sugar. Beat in eggs and vanilla. Combine the flour, cocoa, baking powder and soda; add to creamed mixture alternately with milk.

Line a greased 15-in. x 10-in. x 1-in. baking pan with waxed paper; grease the paper. Spread batter evenly into pan. Bake at 350° for 15-20 minutes or until cake springs back when lightly touched in center. Cool for 10 minutes before removing from pan to a wire rack; carefully remove paper. Cool completely.

For filling, puree raspberries in a food processor. Strain, reserving juice and discarding seeds. Place juice in a small saucepan. Sprinkle with gelatin; let stand for 1 minute. Cook and stir over low heat until gelatin is completely dissolved. Cool to room temperature.

In a small mixing bowl, beat cream until it begins to thicken. Add confectioners' sugar and vanilla; beat until stiff peaks form. Gently fold into raspberry mixture.

Trim edges from cake. Cut into four 7-1/2-in. x 4-1/2-in. rectangles. Place one rectangle on a serving platter; spread with a third of the filling. Repeat layers twice. Top with remaining rectangle.

For ganache, place chocolate chips and cream in a small saucepan. Cook and stir over low heat until chocolate is melted. Cool until thickened, about 10 minutes. Spread over torte. Refrigerate for 2 hours before serving. **Yield:** 8-10 servings.

Mocha Parfait Dessert

I found this recipe in an old cookbook from my Dad. It's wonderful after a big meal.
—Robin Lamar, North Easton, Massachusetts

- **1 package (9 ounces) devil's food cake mix**
- **1 envelope unflavored gelatin**
- **1 cup milk, *divided***
- **1/2 cup sugar**
- **4 teaspoons instant coffee granules**
- **1/8 teaspoon salt**
- **1 cup heavy whipping cream**
- **3/4 cup chopped walnuts, toasted, *divided***

Prepare and bake cake according to package directions, using a 9-in. round baking pan. Cool the cake for 10 minutes before removing it from pan to a wire rack to cool completely.

In a small bowl, sprinkle gelatin over 1/4 cup milk; let stand for 1 minute. In a small saucepan, combine the sugar, coffee granules, salt and remaining milk. Cook and stir until bubbles form around edge of pan. Add gelatin mixture; stir until dissolved. Transfer to a bowl. Refrigerate until slightly thickened, about 1-1/4 hours.

In a chilled mixing bowl, beat cream until soft peaks form. Fold whipped cream and 1/2 cup walnuts into gelatin mixture.

Line the bottom of a greased 9-in. round pan with waxed paper. Pour gelatin mixture into pan; carefully place cooled cake layer on top. Refrigerate for at least 3 hours.

Just before serving, invert dessert onto a serving platter; gently peel off waxed paper. Garnish with remaining walnuts. **Yield:** 8-10 servings.

Cream Puffs in a Cloud

We entertain family and friends often, and this dessert is always a hit.
—Donna Austin, Abbotsford, British Columbia

- **1 cup water**
- **1/2 cup butter, cubed**
- **2 tablespoons sugar**
- **1/2 teaspoon salt**
- **1 cup all-purpose flour**
- **4 eggs**
- **1 cup confectioners' sugar**
- **3 tablespoons baking cocoa**
- **2 to 3 tablespoons boiling water**
- **1 pint fudge ripple, chocolate *or* vanilla ice cream**
- **Whipped cream in a can**

In a large saucepan, bring the water, butter, sugar and salt to a boil. Add flour all at once; stir until a smooth ball forms. Remove from the heat; let stand for 5 minutes. Add eggs, one at a time, beating well after each addition. Continue beating until smooth and shiny.

Drop batter by heaping teaspoonfuls 1 in. apart onto greased baking sheets. Bake at 400° for 20-25 minutes or until golden brown, dry and firm to the touch. Remove to wire racks. Immediately split puffs open; remove tops and set aside. Discard soft dough from inside. Cool puffs.

For glaze, in a bowl, combine the confectioners' sugar, cocoa and boiling water; stir until smooth. Fill each puff with a small scoop of ice cream; replace tops. Drizzle with glaze. Place three or four puffs in each dessert dish; pipe whipped cream around puffs to resemble a cloud. Serve immediately. **Yield:** 12-16 servings.

It's a Wrap!

(Pictured above)

THINK outside the box when wrapping Christmas gifts this holiday season with these clever ideas:

Go Beyond Gift Wrap. On some of our pretty packages, we used white butcher block paper, faux suede and tulle. Other ideas include felt, flannel, dish towels, newspaper, magazine pages and brown paper bags.

Get Rid of Ribbon. Secure a wrapped bottle of wine with a girl's ponytail or wrap a necktie around a box (both ideas shown above.) You can also use twine, raffia, gold wire and upholstery trim. For a little girl, tie on a new jump rope!

Easy Embellishments. Dress up a wrapped gift with inexpensive things like pom-poms or feathers. Other finishing touches include pine sprigs, pinecones, small jingle bells and cinnamon sticks.

You can even add a little extra gift on the outside of the package. Tie on a silver key ring (as we did), a cookie cutter or candy canes.

Delightful Holiday Hors d'oeuvres

THERE'S no better way to welcome friends and neighbors into your holiday home than with a lovely table decked out in appealing appetizers!

For merry munching, offer an assortment of hot appetizers (such as Veggie Wonton Quiches and Peach-Glazed Meatballs) as well as cold choices (Beef Canapes with Cucumber Sauce, fruit and cheese, for instance).

A refreshing beverage like Fruity Rum Punch rounds out the evening. (All recipes are shown at right.)

To cater to a large number of people, use a buffet-style setup. Guests can easily help themselves, leaving you lots of time to meet and greet all those who've gathered.

Seasonal Snacking

(Pictured above)

Beef Canapes with Cucumber Sauce (p. 257)

Veggie Wonton Quiches (p. 256)

Peach-Glazed Meatballs (p. 256)

Fruity Rum Punch (p. 258)

Veggie Wonton Quiches

(Pictured on page 255)

With green broccoli and red pepper, these mini quiches from our home economists are a fitting finger food for Christmas. Crispy wonton cups make a tasty "crust."

24 wonton wrappers
1 cup finely chopped fresh broccoli
3/4 cup diced fresh mushrooms
1/2 cup diced sweet red pepper
1/4 cup finely chopped onion
3 eggs
1 tablespoon water
2 teaspoons dried parsley flakes
1/4 teaspoon salt
1/4 teaspoon dried thyme
1/4 teaspoon white pepper
Dash cayenne pepper
3/4 cup shredded cheddar cheese

Gently press wonton wrappers into miniature muffin cups coated with nonstick cooking spray. Lightly coat wontons with nonstick cooking spray. Bake at 350° for 5 minutes. Remove wontons from cups; place upside down on baking sheets. Lightly coat with nonstick cooking spray. Bake 5 minutes longer or until light golden brown.

Meanwhile, in a nonstick skillet, cook the broccoli, mushrooms, red pepper and onion over medium heat for 4-5 minutes or until crisp-tender. In a bowl, whisk eggs and water; stir in the parsley, salt, thyme, white pepper and cayenne. Add to vegetable mixture; cook over medium heat for 4-5 minutes or until eggs are completely set.

Remove from the heat; stir in cheese. Spoon about 1 tablespoonful into each wonton cup. Bake for 5 minutes or until filling is heated through. Serve warm. **Yield:** 2 dozen.

Peach-Glazed Meatballs

(Pictured on page 255)

When my daughter and her husband come to visit over the holidays, we enjoy nibbling on these mouth-watering meatballs while playing games. Water chestnuts add a bit of crunch.
—Christine Martin, Durham, North Carolina

2 eggs, lightly beaten
1 can (8 ounces) water chestnuts, drained and chopped
3/4 cup dry bread crumbs
1 tablespoon beef bouillon granules
1-1/2 pounds ground beef
1 jar (16 ounces) peach preserves
1 bottle (12 ounces) chili sauce
1 envelope onion soup mix

In a large bowl, combine the eggs, water chestnuts, bread crumbs and bouillon. Crumble beef over mixture and mix well. Shape into 1-in. balls. In a large skillet, cook meatballs in batches until no longer pink; drain. Return all to the skillet.

In a small saucepan, combine the preserves, chili sauce and soup mix. Cook over medium-low heat for 5 minutes. Pour over meatballs. Simmer, uncovered, for 10 minutes or until heated through. **Yield:** about 4-1/2 dozen.

Beef Canapes With Cucumber Sauce

(Pictured at right and on page 254)

A homemade cucumber yogurt sauce complements tender slices of beef in this recipe from our Test Kitchen. Both the meat and sauce are conveniently made in advance.

- **4 cups (32 ounces) plain yogurt**
- **1 whole beef tenderloin (1-1/2 pounds)**
- **2 tablespoons olive oil,** ***divided***
- **1 teaspoon salt,** ***divided***
- **1/4 teaspoon plus 1/8 teaspoon white pepper,** ***divided***
- **1 medium cucumber, peeled, seeded and diced**
- **1 tablespoon finely chopped onion**
- **1 garlic clove, minced**
- **1 tablespoon white vinegar**
- **1 French bread baguette, cut into 36 thin slices**
- **1 cup fresh arugula**

Line a fine mesh strainer with two layers of cheesecloth; place over a bowl. Place yogurt in strainer. Cover and refrigerate for at least 4 hours or overnight.

Rub tenderloin with 1 tablespoon oil. Sprinkle with 1/2 teaspoon salt and 1/4 teaspoon white pepper. In a large skillet, cook tenderloin over medium-high heat until browned on all sides. Transfer to a shallow roasting pan. Bake at 400° for 25-30 minutes or until a meat thermometer reads 145°. Cool on a wire rack for 1 hour. Cover and refrigerate.

Transfer yogurt from strainer to another bowl (discard yogurt liquid). Add the cucumber, onion, garlic and remaining salt and white pepper. In a small bowl, whisk the vinegar and remaining oil; stir into yogurt mixture.

Thinly slice the tenderloin. Spread yogurt mixture over bread slices; top with beef and arugula. Serve immediately or cover and refrigerate until serving. **Yield:** 3 dozen.

Fruity Rum Punch

(Pictured on page 255)

Our Test Kitchen home economists stirred together this sweet punch by combining four kinds of juice. Feel free to omit the rum for a kid-friendly option.

2 cups unsweetened apple juice
1-1/2 cups unsweetened pineapple juice
1 can (12 ounces) frozen cranberry juice concentrate, thawed
1 can (6 ounces) frozen orange juice concentrate, thawed
1 cup gold rum
4 cups club soda, chilled
Ice cubes

In a pitcher or punch bowl, combine the apple juice, pineapple juice, cranberry juice concentrate, orange juice concentrate and rum. Refrigerate until chilled. Just before serving, add club soda. Serve over ice. **Yield:** 10 servings (2-1/2 quarts).

Olive-Onion Cheese Squares

This rich appetizer goes a long way so it's perfect for potlucks and parties. I've relied on this recipe for more than 20 years, and it hasn't failed me yet!
—Sharon Ambrose, Mason, Michigan

1 package (16 ounces) hot roll mix
1 cup warm water (120° to 130°)
2 tablespoons butter, softened
1 egg, beaten
1 tablespoon minced chives
4 cups (16 ounces) shredded part-skim mozzarella cheese
1 cup mayonnaise
1/2 cup chopped green onions
1/4 cup chopped pimiento-stuffed olives
Grated Parmesan cheese

In a large bowl, combine the contents of hot roll mix and yeast packet. Stir in the warm water, butter, egg and chives until dough pulls away from sides of bowl. Turn onto a lightly floured surface; knead until smooth and elastic, about 5 minutes. Place in a greased bowl, turning once to grease top. Cover and let rest for 5 minutes.

Turn dough onto a lightly floured surface. Roll into a 15-in. x 10-in. rectangle. Transfer to a greased 15-in. x 10-in. x 1-in. baking pan.

In a large bowl, combine the mozzarella cheese, mayonnaise, onions and olives; spread over dough to within 1/2 in. of edges. Sprinkle with Parmesan cheese. Bake at 375° for 25-30 minutes or until lightly browned. Cut into 1-1/4-in. squares; serve warm. **Yield:** 8 dozen.

Chicken Satay

(Pictured at right)

Our home economists came up with this Asian-style dish featuring a simple-to-prepare peanut sauce. It's a hearty addition to an appetizer buffet.

2 pounds boneless skinless chicken breasts
1/3 cup soy sauce
1 green onion, sliced
2 tablespoons sesame oil
1 tablespoon brown sugar
1 tablespoon honey
2 garlic cloves, minced
1/2 teaspoon ground ginger

PEANUT SAUCE:

1/2 cup salted peanuts
1/4 cup chopped green onions
1 garlic clove, minced
3 tablespoons chicken broth
3 tablespoons butter, melted
2 tablespoons soy sauce
1 tablespoon lemon juice
1 tablespoon honey
1/2 teaspoon ground ginger
1/4 to 1/2 teaspoon crushed red pepper flakes

Flatten chicken to 1/4-in. thickness; cut lengthwise into 1-in.-wide strips. In a large resealable plastic bag, combine the soy sauce, onion, sesame oil, brown sugar, honey, garlic and ginger; add chicken. Seal bag and turn to coat; refrigerate for 4 hours.

In a food processor or blender, combine the peanuts, onions and garlic; cover and process until mixture forms a paste. Add the broth, butter, soy sauce, lemon juice, honey, ginger and pepper flakes; cover and process until smooth. Transfer to a bowl. Refrigerate until serving.

Drain and discard marinade. Thread chicken strips onto soaked wooden skewers. Broil 6 in. from the heat for 2-4 minutes on each side or until chicken is no longer pink. Serve with peanut sauce. **Yield:** 10-12 servings.

Get Creative with Cream Cheese!

THE CHRISTMAS SEASON often includes spur-of-the-moment gatherings with friends and neighbors. You'll eagerly open your door to drop-in guests with these made-in-minutes munchies that start with convenient cream cheese and other items you can keep on hand.

1.

2.

3.

4.

1. Confetti Cheese Balls. Beat a 3-ounce package of softened cream cheese with 1 cup finely shredded cheddar cheese. Stir in 2 to 3 tablespoons each of chopped ripe olives, chopped pimiento and chopped green pepper. Shape mixture into 1-in. balls; roll half in chopped pecans and the other half in fresh minced parsley. Serve with crackers or breadsticks.

2. Pesto-Cream Cheese Spread. Cut an 8-ounce package of cream cheese in half diagonally. Turn one piece around and arrange both pieces with long sides touching to form a triangular "tree." Place a piece of a cinnamon stick at the base for the trunk. Spoon 1/2 cup of prepared pesto sauce over the cream cheese. Cut a 1-in. star out of red pepper and place it at the top of the tree. Serve with assorted crackers.

3. Hot Pizza Dip. Spread 8 ounces of softened cream cheese in a 9-in. pie plate. Top with 1/2 cup pizza sauce, shredded mozzarella cheese and pizza toppings like chopped onion, chopped green pepper, sliced ripe olives, sliced mushrooms and chopped pepperoni. Bake at 350° for 15-20 minutes. Serve with soft or hard breadsticks.

4. Speedy Taco Spread. Pour salsa over an 8-ounce block of cream cheese. (If desired, first cut the block into four sections and stagger on the plate.) Sprinkle with your favorite taco toppings such as shredded cheddar cheese, sliced green onion, chopped tomato and sliced ripe olives. Serve with corn or tortilla chips.

Shrimp Salad On Endive

(Pictured at right)

Our home economists make a simple-to-prepare shrimp salad and serve it on endive leaves for a from-the-sea version of lettuce wraps.

1/3 cup mayonnaise
1/2 teaspoon lemon juice
1/4 teaspoon dill weed
1/4 teaspoon seafood seasoning
1/8 teaspoon salt
1/8 teaspoon pepper
1/2 pound cooked shrimp, chopped
1 green onion, sliced
2 tablespoons chopped celery
1 tablespoon diced pimientos
2 heads Belgian endive, separated into leaves

In a small bowl, combine the first six ingredients. Stir in the shrimp, onion, celery and pimientos. Spoon 1 tablespoonful onto each endive leaf; arrange on a platter. Refrigerate until serving. **Yield:** about 1-1/2 dozen.

Cappuccino Punch

I first had this coffee-flavored punch at my baby shower, and it's been my favorite ever since. The beverage rivals any coffeehouse variety.
—Angela Schwartz, Marietta, Georgia

3-1/2 quarts water
2-1/3 cups sugar
3/4 cup instant coffee granules
1/2 cup chocolate syrup
1 gallon vanilla ice cream
1 pint coffee ice cream

In a large kettle, bring water to a boil. Remove from the heat. Stir in the sugar, coffee and chocolate syrup until sugar is dissolved. Cool to room temperature. Transfer to four half-gallon containers. Cover and refrigerate for 4 hours or overnight.

Just before serving, pour coffee mixture into a punch bowl. Add scoops of vanilla and coffee ice cream; stir until partially melted. **Yield:** about 2 gallons.

Italian Christmas Eve Feast

IN OLD-TIME Italian tradition, Christmas Eve is a major celebration and features the Feast of the Seven Fishes.

Traditionally, this seafood supper is served after midnight mass and includes seven kinds of fish. (The number symbolizes Catholicism's seven sacraments.)

"My family has adhered to this custom for years," says Weda Mosellie of Phillipsburg, New Jersey. "I'm pleased to share the following six dishes with you."

You'll net compliments with Classic Antipasto Platter, Tomato Clam Chowder and Angel Hair Pasta with Tuna. (All recipes pictured at right.)

Round out the meal with Weda's Crabmeat Spread, Sicilian Fig Pastries and Tender Italian Sugar Cookies.

From-the-Sea Celebration

(Top to bottom)

Tomato Clam Chowder (p. 265)

Classic Antipasto Platter (p. 264)

Angel Hair Pasta with Tuna (p. 264)

Angel Hair Pasta with Tuna

(Pictured on page 263)

When my summer garden is in full bloom, I'll make homemade puree with fresh tomatoes. Instead of tuna steaks, you can use two 10-ounce cans of chunk white tuna.

4 garlic cloves, minced
2 tablespoons olive oil
2 cans (29 ounces *each*) tomato puree
1/2 cup dry red wine *or* chicken broth
2 tablespoons minced fresh basil
1 to 1-1/2 teaspoons crushed red pepper flakes
1 teaspoon salt
2 to 2-1/2 pounds tuna steaks
2 packages (16 ounces *each*) angel hair pasta
1/2 cup grated Parmesan cheese

In a large saucepan, saute garlic in oil for 2-3 minutes or until tender. Stir in the tomato puree, wine or broth, basil, pepper flakes and salt. Bring to a boil. Reduce heat; simmer, uncovered, for 35-45 minutes or until flavors are blended.

In a large skillet coated with nonstick cooking spray, cook tuna over medium-high heat for 6-8 minutes on each side or until fish flakes easily with a fork. Flake tuna into large chunks; add to sauce. Cook pasta according to package directions; drain. Top with sauce; sprinkle with Parmesan cheese. **Yield:** 12 servings.

Classic Antipasto Platter

(Pictured on page 262)

This is a real favorite on our Christmas Eve buffet table. The large platter of fish, cheese, olives and vegetables disappears quickly.

1 pound fresh mozzarella cheese, sliced
1 jar (16 ounces) pickled pepper rings, drained
1 jar (10 ounces) colossal Sicilian olives, drained
4 large tomatoes, cut into wedges
6 hard-cooked eggs, sliced
1 medium cucumber, sliced
1 medium sweet red pepper, julienned
1 can (3-3/4 ounces) sardines, drained
1 can (2 ounces) anchovy fillets, drained
1/4 cup olive oil
1 teaspoon grated Parmesan cheese
1 teaspoon minced fresh oregano
1/8 teaspoon salt
1/8 teaspoon pepper

On a large serving platter, arrange the first nine ingredients. In a small bowl, combine oil, Parmesan cheese, oregano, salt and pepper; drizzle over antipasto. **Yield:** 14-16 servings.

Tomato Clam Chowder

(Pictured at right and on page 263)

Steaming bowls of this Manhattan-style clam chowder really warm guests when they come in from the cold on Christmas Eve.

5 to 6 medium potatoes, peeled and diced
6 bacon strips, diced
1 small onion, finely chopped
2 celery ribs, chopped
1 garlic clove, minced
2 cans (6 ounces *each*) minced clams
2 cups water
1 can (15 ounces) tomato sauce
1 can (14-1/2 ounces) diced tomatoes, undrained
1/2 to 1 teaspoon pepper
1/4 teaspoon salt
2 teaspoons minced fresh parsley

Place the potatoes in a soup kettle or Dutch oven and cover with water. Bring to a boil. Reduce heat; cover and cook for 10-15 minutes or until tender.

Meanwhile, in a large skillet, cook bacon over medium heat until crisp. Using a slotted spoon, remove to paper towels; drain, reserving 2 tablespoons drippings. In the drippings, saute the onion, celery and garlic until tender.

Drain clams, reserving liquid; set clams aside. Drain potatoes and return to the pan. Add onion mixture, bacon and reserved clam liquid. Stir in the water, tomato sauce, tomatoes, pepper and salt. Bring to a boil. Reduce heat; simmer, uncovered, for 30-35 minutes or until heated through. Add clams and parsley; simmer 5 minutes longer. **Yield:** 11 servings (2-3/4 quarts).

Sicilian Fig Pastries

(Pictured at far right, bottom)

These fig-filled desserts have true European flavor. They add just the right amount of sweetness to the buffet table.

4 cups all-purpose flour
3/4 cup shortening
1/4 teaspoon salt
1/3 cup sugar
1/2 cup warm water
1 egg, beaten
1/4 teaspoon vanilla extract

FILLING:

1/2 pound dried figs, chopped
2/3 cup chopped walnuts
1 tablespoon water
1 tablespoon grape jelly
1/2 teaspoon grated orange peel
1/8 teaspoon ground cinnamon
1 egg, beaten
2 tablespoons sugar

In a food processor, combine the flour, shortening and salt; cover and process until mixture resembles coarse crumbs. In a bowl, dissolve sugar in warm water; stir in egg and vanilla. Gradually add to crumb mixture; pulse until dough forms a ball. Cover and let rest for 10 minutes.

In a food processor, combine the figs, walnuts, water, grape jelly, orange peel and cinnamon; cover and process until blended. Set aside.

Separate dough into six portions. On a lightly floured surface, roll each portion into a 12-in. x 8-in. rectangle (dough will be very thin). Cut into 4-in. x 2-in. rectangles. Place a teaspoon of fig mixture on one short side of each rectangle; fold dough over filling. Press edges with a fork to seal.

Place 1 in. apart on ungreased baking sheets. Brush with egg and sprinkle with sugar. Bake at 375° for 15-17 minutes or until golden brown. Remove from pans to wire racks. **Yield:** 3 dozen.

Crabmeat Spread

This versatile crab spread can be served warm or cold. Either way, it's delicious!

1/4 cup mayonnaise
2 tablespoons sour cream
1 tablespoon sweet pickle relish
1 teaspoon lemon juice
1 pound canned crabmeat, drained, flaked and cartilage removed
1 small onion, finely chopped
1 celery rib, finely chopped
Paprika and pimiento-stuffed olives, optional
Assorted crackers *or* Italian bread slices

In a bowl, whisk the mayonnaise, sour cream, pickle relish and lemon juice until blended. Stir in the crab, onion and celery. Transfer to a serving bowl. Garnish with paprika and olives if desired. Serve with crackers.

Or spread on slices of bread. Place on a baking sheet; broil 4-6 in. from the heat for 1-2 minutes or until heated through. **Yield:** 3 cups.

Tender Italian Sugar Cookies

(Pictured at right, top)

These traditional cookies are moist and tender. To tie into the colors of the Italian flag, you could tint the icing red, green and white.

3/4 cup shortening
3/4 cup sugar
3 eggs
1 teaspoon vanilla extract
3 cups all-purpose flour
3 teaspoons baking powder
1/8 teaspoon salt

ICING:

1/4 cup milk
2 tablespoons butter, melted
1/2 teaspoon vanilla extract
2-1/2 cups confectioners' sugar
Food coloring and colored sugar, optional

In a large mixing bowl, cream shortening and sugar. Beat in eggs and vanilla. Combine the flour, baking powder and salt; gradually add to creamed mixture and mix well.

Shape dough into 1-1/2-in. balls. Place 1 in. apart on ungreased baking sheets. Bake at 400° for 8-10 minutes or until lightly browned. Remove to wire racks to cool.

For icing, in a small bowl, combine the milk, butter, vanilla and confectioners' sugar until smooth. Tint with food coloring if desired. Dip the tops of cookies in icing. Sprinkle with colored sugar if desired. Place on waxed paper until set. **Yield:** 3 dozen.

Christmas Eve Timeline

A Few Weeks Before:

- Prepare two grocery lists—one for nonperishable items to purchase now and one for perishable items to purchase a few days before Christmas Eve.
- Purchase any items for Dressed-Up Dishes (opposite page).
- Bake Sicilian Fig Pastries and Tender Italian Sugar Cookies (don't ice the sugar cookies). Freeze.

Two Days Before:

- Buy remaining grocery items.
- Assemble Dressed-Up Dishes and set the table.
- Make the Crabmeat Spread; cover and chill.
- Prepare Tomato Clam Chowder; cover and refrigerate.
- Hard boil the eggs for the Classic Antipasto Platter; chill.

The Day Before:

- For Angel Hair Pasta with Tuna, make the marinara sauce. Cook and flake the tuna. Store sauce and tuna in separate containers; chill.
- Thaw the Sicilian Fig Pastries and Tender Italian Sugar Cookies at room temperature. Ice the sugar cookies.

Christmas Eve:

- Early in the day, assemble the Classic Antipasto Platter; refrigerate.
- For Angel Hair Pasta with Tuna, reheat marinara sauce; add tuna and heat through. Cook pasta; serve with sauce.
- Reheat the Tomato Clam Chowder. If desired, use a slow cooker.
- Set out the Classic Antipasto Platter.
- Make Crabmeat Spread canapes or serve cold.
- For dessert, serve Sicilian Fig Pastries and Tender Italian Sugar Cookies.

Dressed-Up Dishes

(Pictured above)

CHRISTMAS GUESTS will ask you to take a bow for presenting these pretty place settings!

First, set a dinner plate on a charger of your choice. (Options include gold, silver, wicker and colored.) Make sure the dinner plate fits in the indentation of the charger. Top with a coordinating salad plate.

Unwrap your creativity and tie a wide ribbon around the stack. Then make a bow. (Or attach a purchased, pre-made bow.)

This place setting cleverly ties into the gift-giving season.

Embossed Place Card

ADD even more elegance to your tabletop by making embossed place cards (as shown in the photo above).

Stop at your local craft store for plain place cards, a rubber stamp in the design of your choice, embossing ink, an embossing pen and embossing powder.

Stamp the front of the card with embossing ink. While still wet, sprinkle the stamped area with embossing powder. Tap to remove any excess powder. Heat with a heat gun until the embossing powder melts; let cool.

Use the embossing pen to write guests' names on each place card. Sprinkle with the embossing powder; heat and cool as directed above.

A Merry Christmas Morning

ON CHRISTMAS MORNING, it's hard to know what folks will anticipate more...opening presents or sitting down to the breath-taking breakfast pictured at right!

An early-day Yuletide gathering is easy when you make Fruit Salad with Citrus Yogurt Sauce and Mini Cherry Muffins. That's because both of these dishes can be prepared the night before.

And with the flurry of the day's activity, folks won't have to scramble to prepare Cheese and Sausage Strudels. See the make-ahead features for this recipe on page 273.

So make mugs of your favorite hot chocolate and call your hungry clan to the table on Christmas morning with this bright-eyed brunch!

EARLY-DAY DINING

Cheese and Sausage Strudels (p. 273)

Mini Cherry Muffins (p. 272)

Fruit Salad with Citrus Yogurt Sauce (p. 272)

Fruit Salad with Citrus Yogurt Sauce

(Pictured at right and on page 271)

Making this fruit salad the night before gives me one less thing to think about during the rush of gift opening on Christmas morning.
—Wanda Peterson, Lindsay, Ontario

3/4 cup water
1/2 cup sugar
1/2 cup orange juice
1/4 cup lemon juice
1 teaspoon grated orange peel
2 tablespoons orange liqueur, optional
2 medium kiwifruit, peeled, sliced and halved
2 medium ripe pears, peeled and chopped
2 medium Red Delicious apples, chopped
2 medium navel oranges, peeled and sectioned
2 cups seedless red grapes, halved
1 medium pink grapefruit, peeled and sectioned

CITRUS YOGURT SAUCE:
1 cup plain yogurt
2 tablespoons brown sugar
2 tablespoons sour cream
1 teaspoon grated orange peel
1/2 teaspoon vanilla extract

For syrup, combine the first five ingredients in a large saucepan; bring to a boil. Reduce heat; simmer, uncovered, for 10 minutes. Cool; stir in orange liqueur if desired.

In a large bowl, combine the kiwi, pears, apples, oranges, grapes and grapefruit; add syrup and gently toss. Cover and refrigerate overnight. In a small bowl, combine sauce ingredients. Cover and refrigerate overnight.

Serve fruit salad with a slotted spoon; drizzle with yogurt sauce. **Yield:** 8-10 servings.

Mini Cherry Muffins

(Pictured above right and on page 271)

These pretty muffins from our Test Kitchen are perfect for Christmas morning. Make them the night before and keep on the counter in an airtight container.

3/4 cup butter, softened
3/4 cup sugar
1 egg
1/2 cup plain yogurt
1/2 teaspoon almond extract
1 cup all-purpose flour
1/4 teaspoon baking soda
1/4 teaspoon salt
1/2 cup red candied cherries, chopped

In a small mixing bowl, cream butter and sugar. Beat in the egg, yogurt and extract. Combine the flour, baking soda and salt; stir into creamed mixture just until moistened. Fold in cherries.

Fill greased or paper-lined miniature muffin cups two-thirds full. Bake at 350° for 15-17 minutes or until a toothpick comes out clean. Cool for 5 minutes before removing from pans to wire racks. **Yield:** about 2 dozen.

Cheese and Sausage Strudels

(Pictured at right and on page 271)

Instead of a typical egg bake, our Test Kitchen home economists came up with this elegant entree. Each phyllo dough strudel features a flavorful cheese sauce and hearty pork sausage.

1/4 cup butter
1/4 cup all-purpose flour
2 cups milk
2/3 cup shredded Swiss cheese
1/4 cup grated Parmesan cheese
1 teaspoon salt
1/4 teaspoon ground nutmeg
Dash pepper
1/2 pound bulk pork sausage
10 eggs, well beaten
1 teaspoon dried thyme
2 teaspoons dried parsley flakes
PASTRY:
20 sheets phyllo dough (14 inches x 9 inches)
1 cup butter, melted
1/2 cup dry bread crumbs
TOPPING:
1/4 cup grated Parmesan cheese
Minced fresh parsley

In a large saucepan, melt butter. Stir in flour until smooth; gradually add milk. Bring to a boil; cook and stir for 2 minutes or until thickened. Stir in the cheeses, salt, nutmeg and pepper. Cook and stir until cheese is melted; set aside.

Crumble sausage into a skillet; cook over medium heat until no longer pink. Drain. Add eggs and thyme; cook and stir gently until eggs are completely set. Stir into cheese sauce; add parsley. Cool completely.

Carefully unroll phyllo dough. Place one sheet of phyllo on a sheet of waxed paper (keep remaining dough covered with plastic wrap to avoid drying out). Brush with butter; sprinkle lightly with bread crumbs. Top with a second sheet of phyllo; brush with butter. Spread 1/2 cup egg mixture along the short side of dough to within 1 in. of edges. Beginning from the filled end, fold short side over filling. Fold in sides and roll up. Place seam side down on an ungreased baking sheet. Repeat nine times.

For topping, combine Parmesan cheese and parsley. Brush each roll with remaining butter; sprinkle with topping. Bake at 350° for 15-20 minutes or until crisp and lightly browned. Serve immediately. **Yield:** 10 servings.

Secrets to Speedy Strudels

CHEESE and Sausage Strudels have several make-ahead features.

The night before, prepare the cheese sauce as directed; cool, cover and refrigerate. Reheat in a saucepan over low heat before combining with the sausage mixture.

Early in the morning, finish assembling the strudels. Cover with plastic wrap; refrigerate for up to 2 hours before baking as directed.

Egg 'n' Pepperoni Bundles

My family calls these "one more gift to open" because it's the last present they unwrap on Christmas morning. Everyone's mouth waters when they break open these delicious bundles.
—Helen Meadows, Trout Creek, Montana

10 sheets phyllo dough (14 inches x 9 inches)
1/2 cup butter, melted
8 teaspoons dry bread crumbs
2 ounces cream cheese, cut into 8 cubes
4 eggs
24 slices pepperoni, quartered *or* 1-1/2 ounces Canadian bacon, diced
1/3 cup shredded provolone cheese
2 teaspoons minced chives

Place one sheet of phyllo dough on a work surface; brush with butter. Top with another sheet of phyllo; brush with butter. Repeat five times. Cut phyllo in half widthwise, then cut in half lengthwise.

Carefully place stacks in four greased jumbo muffin cups. Brush edges of dough with butter. Sprinkle 2 teaspoons of bread crumbs onto the bottom of each cup. Top each with two cubes of cream cheese.

Break each egg separately into a custard cup; gently pour egg over cream cheese. Sprinkle with pepperoni, provolone cheese and chives. Pinch corners of phyllo together to seal. Bake at 400° for 13-17 minutes or until golden brown. Serve warm. **Yield:** 4 servings.

Fluffy French Toast

My family can't wait for golden slices of this French toast to come off the griddle. We prefer the homemade Molasses Syrup to any store-bought variety.
—Julie Sterchi, Flora, Illinois

1-1/2 cups all-purpose flour
2 teaspoons baking powder
1 teaspoon salt
3 eggs
1-1/2 cups milk
10 slices day-old bread, halved

MOLASSES SYRUP:
3 cups sugar
3/4 cup water
3 tablespoons molasses
1 teaspoon vanilla extract
1 teaspoon maple flavoring

In a shallow bowl, combine the flour, baking powder and salt. Combine eggs and milk; add to dry ingredients and mix well. Dip bread into batter, coating both sides; cook on a greased hot griddle until golden brown on both sides and cooked through.

Meanwhile, for syrup, in a large saucepan, combine the sugar, water and molasses. Bring to a boil; boil for 1 minute. Stir in vanilla and maple flavoring. Serve with French toast. **Yield:** 5 servings.

Asparagus Cheese Quiche

(Pictured at right)

The fluffy texture of this quiche practically melts in your mouth! The green asparagus and red tomatoes on top make this a natural for the holidays.
—Sheryl Long
Lincolnton, North Carolina

1/2 pound fresh asparagus, trimmed and halved lengthwise
1 cup (8 ounces) sour cream
1 cup (8 ounces) small-curd cottage cheese
2 egg whites
1 egg
2 tablespoons butter, melted
5 tablespoons grated Parmesan cheese, *divided*
1/4 cup all-purpose flour
1/2 teaspoon baking powder
1/4 teaspoon salt
1 plum tomato, sliced

In a large saucepan, bring 4 cups water to a boil. Add asparagus; cover and boil for 3 minutes. Drain and immediately place asparagus in ice water. Drain and pat dry. Arrange half of the spears in a spoke pattern in a greased 9-in. pie plate.

In a blender, combine the sour cream, cottage cheese, egg whites, egg and butter; cover and process until smooth. Add 3 tablespoons Parmesan cheese, flour, baking powder and salt; cover and process until smooth. Carefully pour over asparagus. Arrange remaining asparagus in a spoke pattern over the top. Sprinkle with remaining Parmesan cheese.

Bake at 350° for 25-30 minutes or until a knife inserted near the center comes out clean. Garnish with tomato slices. Let stand for 10 minutes before slicing. **Yield:** 6 servings.

Bacon Popovers

This recipe proves that simple ingredients oftentimes result in the best-tasting dishes. These popovers are a nice change from ordinary toast or muffins.
—Donna Gaston, Coplay, Pennsylvania

3 bacon strips, diced
1 cup all-purpose flour
2 tablespoons grated Parmesan cheese
1/4 teaspoon salt
2 eggs
1 cup milk

In a skillet, cook bacon over medium heat until crisp; remove to paper towels to drain. Grease cups of popover pan with bacon drippings.

In a mixing bowl, combine the flour, Parmesan cheese and salt. Add eggs and milk; beat just until smooth and blended (do not overbeat). Stir in bacon. Place prepared popover pan in a 450° oven for 3 minutes. Carefully remove and fill cups half full with batter. Bake for 20 minutes.

Reduce heat to 350° (do not open oven door). Bake 20 minutes longer or until very firm and golden brown (do not underbake). Cut a slit in each popover to allow steam to escape. Serve immediately. **Yield:** 6 servings.

Popover Pointers

SUCCESS with popovers is easy with these tips:

- In order for popovers to reach the maximum height while baking, all ingredients should be brought to room temperature before mixing.
- Place the oven rack in the lowest position.
- Generously grease the popover pan cups.
- Don't open the oven door while baking or the popovers will fall.
- After removing popovers from the oven, prick the tops with the point of a sharp knife, allowing steam to escape.

Warm Spiced Citrus Punch

I serve this drink every year during the holidays. It's one of my most requested recipes. It can be doubled if you're entertaining an even larger group.
—Edie DeSpain, Logan, Utah

2-1/2 quarts water, *divided*
1-1/2 cups sugar
1 can (6 ounces) frozen orange juice concentrate, thawed
3/4 cup lemon juice
1 teaspoon almond extract
1 teaspoon vanilla extract
1/8 teaspoon *each* ground allspice, cinnamon and cloves

In a large kettle, bring 1 qt. of water and sugar to a boil; stir until sugar is dissolved. Stir in the remaining water. Add the orange juice concentrate, lemon juice, extracts and spices; cook and stir over medium heat until hot (do not boil). Serve warm. Refrigerate leftovers. **Yield:** 16 servings (3 quarts).

Coffee Ripple Coffee Cake

(Pictured at right)

I love presenting oven-fresh coffee cakes to the guests in our bed and breakfast. This moist coffee cake recipe really has coffee in it!
—Sandy Znetko, Flagstaff, Arizona

1 cup chopped walnuts
1/4 cup sugar
1/4 cup packed brown sugar
2 teaspoons instant coffee granules
2 teaspoons ground cinnamon

CAKE:

4 teaspoons instant coffee granules
2 teaspoons hot water
1/2 cup butter, softened
1-1/2 cups packed brown sugar
3 eggs
1 cup (8 ounces) sour cream
1/2 cup unsweetened applesauce
1/4 cup buttermilk
1 teaspoon vanilla extract
3 cups all-purpose flour
1-1/2 teaspoons baking powder
1 teaspoon baking soda

GLAZE:

2/3 cup confectioners' sugar
3 to 4 teaspoons brewed coffee
1 teaspoon butter, melted

In a small bowl, combine the walnuts, sugars, coffee granules and cinnamon; set aside. For cake, in a small bowl, dissolve coffee granules in water; set aside. In a large mixing bowl, cream the butter and brown sugar. Add eggs, one at a time, beating well after each addition. Combine the sour cream, applesauce, buttermilk, vanilla and coffee. Combine the flour, baking powder and baking soda; gradually add to creamed mixture alternately with sour cream mixture.

Pour half of the batter into a greased and floured 10-in. fluted tube pan. Sprinkle with walnut mixture. Top with remaining batter.

Bake at 350° for 45-50 minutes or until a toothpick inserted near the center comes out clean. Cool for 10 minutes before removing from pan to a wire rack to cool completely. Combine glaze ingredients until smooth; drizzle over cake. **Yield:** 12 servings.

Artichoke Tartlets

Refrigerated pie pastry gives me a head start in this wonderful recipe. You can also serve these bite-size quiches as a special appetizer.
—Kelly Thornberry, La Porte, Indiana

2 packages (15 ounces *each*) refrigerated pie pastry
3 eggs
1-1/2 cups heavy whipping cream
1/2 teaspoon salt
12 pitted ripe olives
2 jars (6-1/2 ounces *each*) marinated artichoke hearts, drained and chopped
1 cup (4 ounces) shredded Swiss cheese
Coarsely ground pepper

Roll each pastry sheet into a 10-in. x 8-in. rectangle. Using a 2-1/2-in. round cookie cutter, cut out 12 circles from each rectangle. Press pastry rounds into the bottom and up the sides of ungreased miniature muffin cups; set aside.

In a small bowl, whisk the eggs, cream and salt. Cut each olive into four slices. Place 1 heaping teaspoonful of artichokes in each prepared cup; top with an olive slice and 1 teaspoon of cheese. Pour egg mixture into cups to within 1/4 in. of the top.

Sprinkle with pepper. Bake at 375° for 22-26 minutes or until a knife inserted near the center comes out clean. Serve warm. **Yield:** 4 dozen.

Spinach Egg Bake

This potluck pleaser showcases mouth-watering Wisconsin cheddar cheese. I first made this egg bake for an after-church breakfast. The big pan disappeared in a hurry!
—Genny Derer, Madison, Wisconsin

4 bunches green onions, finely chopped
1/4 cup butter
1 pound fresh spinach, trimmed
6 tablespoons minced fresh parsley
12 eggs
1/2 cup sour cream
1/2 teaspoon salt
1-1/2 cups (6 ounces) shredded cheddar cheese
1/2 cup grated Parmesan cheese

In a large skillet, saute onions in butter for 2 minutes. Add spinach and parsley; saute 3 minutes longer. Remove from the heat. In a large mixing bowl, beat the eggs, sour cream and salt. Stir in the spinach mixture and cheddar cheese. Pour into a greased 15-in. x 10-in. x 1-in. baking pan. Sprinkle with Parmesan cheese.

Bake, uncovered, at 350° for 25-30 minutes or until a knife inserted near the center comes out clean. Cut into squares. **Yield:** 15 servings.

A Bright Brunch Table

(Pictured at right)

ON A CRISP and snowy Christmas morning, the bold color of red is stunning against a wintry white table.

For the vibrant floral arrangement pictured at right, we purchased an assortment of red and white flowers (such as daisies, carnations, roses and tulips) as well as some vibrant greens. (We first filled the vase with hydrated water polymer crystals to give an icy effect. See the tip box below.)

We then tied a sheer red ribbon around the vase and tucked in a large candy cane. (We carried this cute candy cane theme onto individual mugs of hot chocolate. These small candy canes make sweet stirrers!)

If you're serving a brunch buffet, consider making some handy cutlery bundles by tying a knife, fork and spoon together with the same sheer red ribbon as used on the vase and mugs.

What Are Water Polymer Crystals?

YOU CAN FIND water polymer crystals at any large craft store. The crystals will look like hard pellets (see photo, left). But when you hydrate them as instructed on the package, they soften and take on the look of crystal (see photo, right).

Place the hydrated crystals in a vase and arrange flowers as desired. Water polymer crystals can be dried and hydrated over and over again.

Regal Christmas Dinner

ON CHRISTMAS DAY, the house is decked out in your most festive decorations...everyone is dressed in their finest fashions ...the table is adorned with sparkling china and crystal.

On this holy holiday, the meal should match the importance of the occasion.

Treat your family like royalty and prepare Stuffed Crown Roast of Pork. It's an impressive entree when served alongside the simply delicious Green Beans with Cashews and Herb Potato Rolls.

Dinner guests will sing your praises when pretty Poached Pears in Raspberry Sauce appear on the table. (All of these recipes are shown at right.)

Fare Fit for a King

(Clockwise from left)

Stuffed Crown Roast of Pork (p. 282)

Green Beans with Cashews (p. 285)

Herb Potato Rolls (p. 283)

Poached Pears in Raspberry Sauce (p. 286)

Stuffed Crown Roast of Pork

(Pictured on page 280)

Folks may be intimidated to prepare an elegant crown roast of pork, but it's actually an easy entree. Our four grown sons and their families expect this every Christmas.
—Mary Ann Balam, Tujunga, California

1 pork crown roast (16 ribs and about 10 pounds)
2 garlic cloves, slivered
2 tablespoons olive oil
Salt and pepper to taste
2 cups apple juice *or* cider
APPLE RAISIN STUFFING:
1 cup raisins
1 cup boiling water
1 cup chopped onion
1 cup chopped celery
1 garlic clove, minced
3/4 cup butter
5 cups soft bread crumbs
3 cups chopped peeled tart apples
1/4 cup minced fresh parsley
1 teaspoon salt
1/4 teaspoon paprika

Cut slits in the bottom of each rib; insert garlic slivers. Rub oil over entire roast; sprinkle with salt and pepper. Place in a shallow roasting pan. Cover rib ends with foil. Pour apple juice into pan. Bake, uncovered, at 350° for 1 hour, basting occasionally.

Meanwhile, for stuffing, place the raisins in a small bowl; pour boiling water over raisins. Let stand for 2 minutes; drain and set aside. In a skillet, saute the onion, celery and garlic in butter until tender. Add the bread crumbs, apples, parsley, salt, paprika and raisins; mix well.

Carefully spoon stuffing into center of roast. Bake 1 to 1-1/2 hours more or until a meat thermometer reads 160°-170° and juices run clear. Let stand for 10 minutes. Remove foil and stuffing. Cut between ribs. **Yield:** 12-16 servings.

Sweet Potato Bake

This sweet and savory casserole is part of our traditional Christmas dinner. It goes great with any meaty entree.
—Lynn McAllister, Mt. Ulla, North Carolina

2-1/2 pounds sweet potatoes
1/2 cup sugar
1/2 cup milk
1/2 cup butter, melted, *divided*
2 eggs, beaten
1/4 cup all-purpose flour
1/2 teaspoon salt
1/2 teaspoon vanilla extract
3/4 cup chopped pecan *or* walnuts
3/4 cup packed brown sugar
1 teaspoon ground cinnamon

Place unpeeled sweet potatoes in a large kettle; cover with water. Cover and bring to a gentle boil; cook for 30-40 minutes or until potatoes can easily be pierced with a sharp knife. Drain and cool slightly; peel and cube.

In a large bowl, mash the sweet potatoes. Add sugar, milk, 1/4 cup butter, eggs, flour, salt and vanilla. Pour into a greased 1-1/2-qt. baking dish. Combine the nuts, brown sugar, cinnamon and remaining butter; sprinkle over the top. Bake, uncovered, at 350° for 40-45 minutes or until golden brown. **Yield:** 8 servings.

Herb Potato Rolls

(Pictured at right and on page 281)

My grandma always made these rolls. She herself enjoyed them as a child in Germany. I practiced for years before I finally perfected the recipe!
—Lonna Smith, Woodruff, Wisconsin

5 to 5-1/2 cups all-purpose flour
1 cup mashed potato flakes
2 packages (1/4 ounce *each*) active dry yeast
1 tablespoon sugar
1 tablespoon minced chives
2 teaspoons salt
2 teaspoons minced fresh parsley
2 cups milk
1/2 cup sour cream
2 eggs

In a large mixing bowl, combine 3 cups flour, potato flakes, yeast, sugar, chives, salt and parsley. In a saucepan, heat milk and sour cream to 120°-130°. Add to dry ingredients; beat just until moistened. Add the eggs; beat until smooth. Stir in enough remaining flour to form a soft dough.

Turn onto a floured surface; knead until smooth and elastic, about 6-8 minutes. Place in a greased bowl, turning once to grease top. Cover and let rise in a warm place until doubled, about 45 minutes.

Punch dough down. Turn onto a lightly floured surface; divide into 24 pieces. Shape each into a roll. Place in a greased 13-in. x 9-in. x 2-in. baking pan. Cover and let rise until doubled, about 35 minutes. Bake at 375° for 30-35 minutes or until golden brown. Remove to wire racks. **Yield:** 2 dozen.

Christmas Day Timeline

A Few Weeks Before:

- Prepare two grocery lists—one for non-perishable items to purchase now and one for perishable items to purchase a few days before Christmas Day.
- From your butcher, order a pork crown roast (16 ribs and about 10 pounds).
- Bake Herb Potato Rolls; cool. Freeze in a single layer in heavy-duty resealable plastic bags.
- Gather boxes for the Blooming Gift Boxes (page 287). Wrap and decorate with ribbon as desired.

Two Days Before:

- Buy your remaining grocery items, including the crown roast you ordered. Also pick up flowers for the centerpiece.
- Set the table.
- Finish assembling the Blooming Gift Boxes.

Christmas Eve:

- Assemble Sweet Potato Bake; cover and refrigerate.
- Clean and trim the 2 pounds of fresh green beans for the Green Beans with Cashews. Store in a plastic bag in your refrigerator's crisper drawer.
- Prepare Marinated Cauliflower Salad; cover and chill.

Christmas Day:

- In the morning, poach pears; cool. Place pears in a large serving dish or in individual dishes. Cover with plastic wrap and chill. Make the raspberry sauce; cool. Cover and refrigerate.
- Thaw the Herb Potato Rolls at room temperature.
- Bake the Stuffed Crown Roast of Pork as directed.
- Remove Sweet Potato Bake from the refrigerator 30 minutes before baking. (Please note if you refrigerate this casserole overnight, you may need to bake it a little longer than the recipe specifies.)
- If desired, wrap the rolls in foil and reheat in a 350° oven for 15-20 minutes.
- While the roast is standing, make Green Beans with Cashews.
- Set out rolls with butter and the Marinated Cauliflower Salad.
- For dessert, reheat raspberry sauce in a saucepan over low heat if desired. Serve Poached Pears in Raspberry Sauce.

Marinated Cauliflower Salad

(Pictured at right)

I often serve this as an appetizer alongside a meat and cheese tray. But it can also be a side dish.
—Stephanie Hase, Lyons, Colorado

1/4 cup red wine vinegar
1/4 cup olive oil
2 tablespoons water
1 bay leaf
1 garlic clove, minced
1/4 teaspoon salt
1/4 teaspoon coarsely ground pepper
5 cups fresh cauliflowerets
1/2 cup shredded carrot
1/4 cup chopped red onion
1/4 cup minced fresh parsley
1/4 teaspoon dried basil

In a small saucepan, bring the vinegar, oil and water just to a boil. Meanwhile, place the bay leaf, garlic, salt, pepper and cauliflower in a large heat-proof bowl. Add hot oil mixture; toss to combine. Cover and refrigerate for at least 6 hours or overnight, stirring occasionally.

Add the carrot, onion, parsley and basil; toss to coat. Cover and refrigerate for 2 hours. Discard bay leaf. Serve with a slotted spoon. **Yield:** 10-12 servings.

Green Beans with Cashews

(Pictured on page 281)

This nice, simple side dish is dressed up with salted whole cashews. Frozen whole green beans can be used instead of fresh beans. Just cook according to package directions.
—Cathleen Bushman, Geneva, Illinois

2 pounds fresh green beans, trimmed
1/4 cup butter, cubed
1 tablespoon dried parsley flakes
3/4 teaspoon salt
1/2 teaspoon pepper
3/4 cup salted whole cashews

Place the beans in a large saucepan and cover with water. Bring to a boil. Reduce heat; simmer, uncovered, for 8-10 minutes or until crisp-tender. Drain and return beans to the pan. Add the butter, parsley, salt and pepper. Cook, uncovered, over medium heat until heated through. Sprinkle with cashews. **Yield:** 8 servings.

Poached Pears in Raspberry Sauce

(Pictured at right and on page 281)

This fruity recipe is just right for anyone who loves elegant desserts, but not the extra pounds associated with so many of them.

—Clara Coulston
Washington Court House, Ohio

8 medium Bosc pears
2 cups pear juice
1 cinnamon stick (3 inches)
1-1/2 teaspoons minced fresh gingerroot
1 teaspoon whole cloves
1/4 teaspoon ground nutmeg
1 tablespoon cornstarch
1/2 cup cranberry juice
2 cups fresh raspberries *or* 1 package (12 ounces) frozen unsweetened raspberries, thawed
2 tablespoons maple syrup

Core pears from the bottom, leaving stems intact. Peel pears. If necessary, cut 1/4 in. from bottom so pears will sit flat. Place in a Dutch oven. Add the pear juice, cinnamon stick, ginger, cloves and nutmeg. Cover and bring to a boil. Reduce heat; simmer for 25-30 minutes or until pears are tender.

Remove the pears and place in serving dishes. Discard cinnamon stick and cloves from poaching liquid. In a small bowl, combine cornstarch and cranberry juice until smooth; stir into liquid. Bring to a boil; cook and stir for 2 minutes or until thickened. Add raspberries and syrup. Remove from the heat; cool slightly.

In a blender or food processor, puree raspberry sauce in batches until smooth. Strain and discard seeds. Pour sauce over pears. Serve warm, at room temperature or chilled. **Yield:** 8 servings.

Coring Pears Like a Pro

TO CORE a fresh pear, insert an apple corer into the bottom of the pear to within 1 in. of its top. Twist the corer to cut around the core, then slowly pull the corer out of the pear to remove the core.

If you don't have an apple corer, use a sharp knife or vegetable peeler to cut the core from the bottom of the pear.

Blooming Gift Boxes

(Pictured above)

BY DINNERTIME on Christmas Day, all of the packages under the tree have been opened and the pretty wrappings have been discarded.

Enjoy the sight of pretty packages a while longer by creating this lovely arrangement.

First, chose a color theme for the wrapping paper, ribbons and flowers, making sure the colors work with your dishes and table linens.

For an elegant look, we chose green and gold wrapping paper and ribbons. Then we selected pretty paperwhites to pop out of the packages.

Next, look for boxes in varying sizes. We made three stacks with two boxes each. The largest boxes were used in the center of the display.

Then find narrow glasses or vases that are roughly the same height as each stack of boxes.

For each stack of boxes, wrap the top and bottom of the largest box separately. Then wrap the bottom only of the next largest box. Set the smaller boxes on top of the larger boxes.

With tape or a stapler, secure ribbons at the top and bottom on each side of the stacks.

With a utility knife, cut a large "X" in the bottom of the top box and through the lid of the bottom box.

Carefully fill each glass or vase with floral marbles if desired and water. Insert the glass or vase into each stack of boxes, making sure it's resting within the bottom box. Add flowers.

In the top box of each stack, fill in with tissue paper and gold angel hair or raffia, covering the glass or vase as much as possible.

To continue with the gift box theme, we set smaller decorated boxes at each place setting. The boxes could be empty or filled with a party favor, such as an ornament or candy.

Come for Cheesecake & Coffee!

THE HOLIDAYS are hectic and there's often not a moment to spare. So if time doesn't allow you to plan an entire sit-down dinner party, consider a simple, elegant get-together featuring cheesecakes and coffee.

Although cheesecakes do take some time to prepare, they're conveniently made the day before and simply served on party day. Best of all, cheesecakes will surely impress all of your guests!

For a superb assortment of flavorful crusts, creamy fillings and tasty toppings, you can rely on Chocolate Macadamia Cheesecake, Cranberry Cheesecake and Apricot Swirl Cheesecake (shown at right).

To round out your dazzling dessert party, see our suggestions for setting up an unforgettable coffee service.

CHEERS FOR CHEESECAKE

(Left to right)

Chocolate Macadamia Cheesecake (p. 290)

Cranberry Cheesecake (p. 292)

Apricot Swirl Cheesecake (p. 291)

Chocolate Macadamia Cheesecake

(Pictured on page 288)

When one of my co-workers turned 50, I created this recipe for her birthday. There wasn't a crumb left on the platter when I left for home that day!
—Bob Weaver, University Place, Washington

1-1/4 cups chocolate wafer crumbs (about 25 wafers)
1/4 cup ground macadamia nuts
2 tablespoons sugar
3 tablespoons butter *or* margarine, melted
1/8 teaspoon almond extract

FILLING:
8 squares (1 ounce *each*) white baking chocolate
4 packages (8 ounces *each*) cream cheese, softened
3/4 cup sugar
3 tablespoons all-purpose flour
5 eggs
1 teaspoon vanilla extract
1/3 cup milk chocolate chips

TOPPING:
8 squares (1 ounce *each*) semisweet chocolate
7 tablespoons whipping cream
White chocolate shavings and chopped macadamia nuts

In a bowl, combine wafer crumbs, nuts and sugar; stir in butter and almond extract. Press onto the bottom of a greased 10-in. springform pan. Bake at 350° for 10 minutes. Cool on a wire rack. Reduce heat to 325°.

In a saucepan over low heat, melt white chocolate, stirring frequently until smooth. Cool. In a mixing bowl, beat cream cheese and sugar until smooth. Add flour; mix well. Add eggs and vanilla; beat on low speed just until combined. Remove 1 cup and set aside. Stir melted white chocolate into remaining cream cheese mixture; beat just until combined. Pour over crust.

Melt chocolate chips; cool slightly. Stir in reserved cream cheese mixture; drop by spoonfuls over filling. Cut through filling with a knife to swirl chocolate mixture.

Place pan on a baking sheet. Bake at 325° for 55-60 minutes or until center is almost set. Cool on a wire rack for 10 minutes. Carefully run a knife around edge of pan to loosen. Cool 1 hour longer.

In a saucepan over low heat, melt semisweet chocolate with cream; stir until smooth. Cool slightly. Spread over cheesecake. Refrigerate for 4 hours or overnight. Remove sides of pan. Garnish with chocolate shavings and macadamia nuts. **Yield:** 12 servings.

Preventing Cracked Cheesecakes

SOMETIMES a "cracked" cheesecake is unavoidable. But these steps can help prevent the top from slitting open.

- Let cream cheese and eggs stand at room temperature for 30 minutes before mixing.
- After adding the eggs, beat mixture on low speed. (If too much air is beaten into the mixture, it will puff during baking, then collapse and split when cooled.)
- Grease the sides of the pan so the cake easily pulls away as it cools.
- Prevent drafts by opening the oven door as seldom as possible during baking.
- Don't use a knife to test for doneness because it may create a crack. The center of the cheesecake (about the size of a walnut) should not be completely set and will jiggle slightly.

Apricot Swirl Cheesecake

(Pictured at right and on page 289)

I've always loved to cook and try new dishes. But there are just some recipes—like this fancy cheesecake—that I turn to time after time. This is a favorite of family and friends.
—Ardyth Voss, Rosholt, South Dakota

1/2 cup finely ground almonds
1 cup dried apricots
1 cup water
1 tablespoon grated lemon peel
3 packages (8 ounces *each*) cream cheese, softened
1 cup sugar
2 tablespoons all-purpose flour
4 eggs
1/2 cup whipping cream
1 cup apricot preserves
Whipped cream and toasted sliced almonds

Grease the bottom and sides of a 10-in. springform pan; sprinkle with ground almonds and set aside. In a saucepan over medium heat, cook apricots and water for 15 minutes or until the water is nearly absorbed and apricots are tender, stirring occasionally. Stir in lemon peel. Cool slightly; pour into a blender. Cover and process until smooth; set aside.

In a mixing bowl, beat cream cheese and sugar until smooth. Add flour; mix well. Add eggs; beat on low speed just until combined. Beat in cream just until blended. Stir 1 cup into pureed apricots; set aside. Pour remaining mixture into prepared pan. Drop apricot mixture by 1/2 teaspoonfuls over filling. Cut through filling with a knife to swirl apricot mixture.

Place pan on a baking sheet. Bake at 350° for 50-55 minutes or until center is almost set. Cool on a wire rack for 10 minutes. Carefully run a knife around edge of pan to loosen. Cool 1 hour longer.

In a small saucepan, heat preserves. Press through a strainer (discard pulp). Spread over cheesecake. Refrigerate overnight. Remove sides of pan. Garnish with whipped cream and sliced almonds. **Yield:** 12 servings.

Cranberry Cheesecake

(Pictured at right and on page 289)

Refreshing cranberries, lemon juice and orange peel complement the cheesecake's sweet filling. This is my favorite Christmas dessert to make as gifts. It really appeals to people who don't care for chocolate.

—Joy Monn, Stockbridge, Georgia

1-1/2 cups cinnamon graham cracker crumbs (about 24 squares)
1/4 cup sugar
1/3 cup butter *or* margarine, melted

FILLING:

4 packages (8 ounces *each*) cream cheese, softened
1 can (14 ounces) sweetened condensed milk
1/4 cup lemon juice
4 eggs
1-1/2 cups chopped fresh *or* frozen cranberries
1 teaspoon grated orange peel
Sugared cranberries and orange peel strips, optional

In a bowl, combine cracker crumbs and sugar; stir in butter. Press onto the bottom of a greased 9-in. springform pan; set aside.

In a mixing bowl, beat cream cheese and milk until smooth. Beat in lemon juice until smooth. Add eggs; beat on low speed just until combined. Fold in cranberries and orange peel. Pour over the crust. Place pan on a baking sheet. Bake at 325° for 60-70 minutes or until center is almost set. Cool on a wire rack for 10 minutes.

Carefully run a knife around edge of pan to loosen. Cool 1 hour longer. Refrigerate for at least 6 hours or overnight. Remove sides of pan. Garnish with sugared cranberries and orange peel if desired. **Yield:** 12 servings.

Fun with Fruit

TO MAKE the sugared cranberries and orange peel garnishing the Cranberry Cheesecake, combine several orange peel strips, 1/3 cup fresh cranberries and 1/2 cup sugar. Stir gently to combine. Cover and refrigerate for 1 hour. Arrange orange peel strips and cranberries on top of the cheesecake just before serving.

Chocolate Chip Cookie Cheesecake

(Pictured at right)

Our daughter first astounded us with her cooking talents when she made this cheesecake at 13 years of age. With a unique cookie crumb crust and extra-creamy filling, people think this dessert was made by a gourmet baker!
—Kathleen Gualano, Cary, Illinois

2 cups chocolate chip cookie crumbs (about 28 cookies)
3 tablespoons sugar
5 tablespoons butter *or* margarine, melted

FILLING:

5 packages (8 ounces *each*) cream cheese, softened
1-1/4 cups sugar
3 tablespoons all-purpose flour
5 eggs
2 egg yolks
1/4 cup sour cream
1 teaspoon grated orange peel
1/2 teaspoon vanilla extract
1 cup miniature semisweet chocolate chips

TOPPING:

1 cup (8 ounces) sour cream
2 tablespoons sugar
1 teaspoon vanilla extract
1 tablespoon chocolate chip cookie crumbs

In a bowl, combine cookie crumbs and sugar; stir in butter. Press onto the bottom and 2 in. up the sides of a greased 9-in. springform pan; set aside.

In a mixing bowl, beat cream cheese and sugar until smooth. Add flour; mix well. Add eggs and egg yolks; beat on low speed just until combined. Beat in sour cream, orange peel and vanilla just until combined. Stir in chocolate chips. Pour over crust. Place pan on a baking sheet.

Bake at 325° for 65-75 minutes or until center is almost set. Remove from the oven; let stand for 5 minutes. Combine the sour cream, sugar and vanilla; spread over filling. Return to the oven for 8 minutes. Cool on a wire rack for 10 minutes. Carefully run a knife around edge of pan to loosen. Cool 1 hour longer. Refrigerate overnight. Remove sides of pan. Garnish with cookie crumbs. **Yield:** 12-14 servings.

Caramel Cashew Cheesecake

When a friend served this luscious cheesecake at a birthday party, I left with the recipe. Every time I make it, rave reviews and recipe requests come my way.
—Pat Price, Bucyrus, Ohio

1/4 cup cold butter *or* margarine
1/2 cup all-purpose flour
3/4 cup chopped unsalted cashews
2 tablespoons confectioners' sugar
Pinch salt
FILLING:
4 packages (8 ounces *each*) cream cheese, softened
1-1/4 cups sugar
1 tablespoon vanilla extract
5 eggs
2 tablespoons whipping cream
TOPPING:
1 cup sugar
3 tablespoons water
3/4 cup whipping cream
1 cup coarsely chopped unsalted cashews

In a bowl, cut butter into flour until mixture resembles coarse crumbs. Stir in cashews, confectioners' sugar and salt. Press onto the bottom and 1/2 in. up the sides of a greased 9-in. springform pan. Bake at 350° for 15 minutes. Cool on a wire rack. Reduce heat to 325°.

In a mixing bowl, beat cream cheese, sugar and vanilla until smooth. Add eggs and cream; beat on low speed just until combined. Pour over crust. Place pan on a baking sheet. Bake at 325° for 55-60 minutes or until center is almost set. Cool on a wire rack for 10 minutes. Carefully run a knife around edge of pan to loosen. Cool 1 hour longer.

In a saucepan, combine sugar and water. Cook over medium-low heat until sugar is dissolved. Bring to a boil over medium-high heat; cover and boil for 2 minutes. Uncover; boil until mixture is golden brown and a candy thermometer reads 300° (hard-crack stage), about 8 minutes.

Remove from the heat. Stir in cream until smooth, about 5 minutes (mixture will appear lumpy at first). Add cashews; cool to lukewarm. Carefully spoon over cheesecake. Refrigerate overnight. Remove sides of pan. **Yield:** 12 servings.

Company Cheesecake

This plain cheesecake is anything but ordinary! The marvelously rich filling is terrific with the pecan-laden crust. My brother gave me the recipe.
—Donna Bucher, Tirane, Albania

3/4 cup all-purpose flour
1/4 cup sugar
1/4 cup finely chopped pecans
1 teaspoon grated lemon peel
6 tablespoons cold butter (no substitutes)
1 egg yolk
1/2 teaspoon vanilla extract

FILLING:
5 packages (8 ounces *each*) cream cheese, softened
1-3/4 cups sugar
3 tablespoons all-purpose flour
1 teaspoon vanilla extract
1/4 teaspoon salt
4 eggs
2 egg yolks
1/4 cup whipping cream

In a bowl, combine the flour, sugar, pecans and lemon peel; cut in butter until crumbly. Combine egg yolk and vanilla; stir into flour mixture. Press onto the bottom of a greased 10-in. springform pan. Bake at 400° for 9-11 minutes or until edges are lightly browned. Cool on a wire rack.

Fill a 13-in. x 9-in. x 2-in. baking dish with 8 cups water; place on lowest oven rack. Reduce heat to 325°.

In a mixing bowl, beat cream cheese until smooth. Gradually beat in sugar. Add the flour, vanilla and salt. Combine eggs and egg yolks; add to cream cheese mixture just until combined. Beat in cream just until combined. Pour over crust.

Bake on middle rack at 325° for 70-75 minutes or until center is almost set (top of cheesecake will crack). Cool on a wire rack for 10 minutes. Carefully run a knife around edge of pan to loosen. Cool 1 hour longer. Refrigerate overnight. Remove sides of pan. **Yield:** 12 servings.

Setting Up A Coffee Service

(Pictured at right)

WHEN OFFERING an assortment of rich desserts—like the cheesecakes in this chapter—it's nice to serve guests a hot beverage. Here are hints for successfully serving coffee.

- For guests to dress up individual cups of coffee, set out bowls of cream, sugar cubes, red-hot candies, cinnamon sticks, purchased chocolate stirrers, vanilla and almond extracts and ground cinnamon, nutmeg or ginger.

  Other stir-in ideas include grated chocolate, whipped cream, cocoa powder, chocolate syrup or orange and peppermint extracts.

- To flavor an entire pot of coffee, sprinkle coffee grounds with orange or lemon peel or ground cinnamon, nutmeg and ginger before brewing.
- The flavor of coffee begins to diminish within an hour after it's made, and leaving coffee on the heating element accelerates the problem. To keep coffee fresh and hot, transfer it to a carafe or thermos that's been preheated with hot water.
- Only make as much coffee as needed and avoid reheating coffee, which can make it bitter. For 12 people, you need about 1/4 pound of coffee and 3 quarts water. For 25 people, you need about 1/2 pound of coffee and 1-1/2 gallons water. For best flavor, start with cold, fresh tap water. If your tap water has an off-taste, use bottled water instead.

After-Sledding Snacks

WHEN THE winter blues settle in, it's easy to lift spirits with the promise of food and fun!

Start by inviting family and friends to meet at your favorite toboggan hill for an afternoon of splendid sledding.

When everyone's had their share of spills and thrills, head back home for a savory spread of hot and cold appetizers and thirst-quenching beverages.

Rich and hearty Savory Appetizer Cheesecake, Chicken Ham Pinwheels and Bacon Water Chestnut Wraps will squelch hunger in a hurry. With their fresh flavor, Fruit 'n' Cheese Kabobs and Vegetable Wreath with Dip make appealing accompaniments. (All shown at right.)

But don't limit your buffet to the recipes mentioned above. You'll find a host of innovative appetizers and beverages on the following pages.

Winter Warm-Ups

(Clockwise from top left)

Savory Appetizer Cheesecake (p. 298)

Chicken Ham Pinwheels (p. 302)

Bacon Water Chestnut Wraps (p. 300)

Fruit 'n' Cheese Kabobs (p. 303)

Vegetable Wreath with Dip (p. 305)

Appetizer and Beverage Basics

AN APPETIZER and beverage buffet is a fun twist on entertaining and lends itself to a less formal atmosphere than a traditional sit-down dinner. But don't be intimidated by such an undertaking...these helpful hints make it a snap!

- For an appetizer buffet that serves as the meal, offer five or six different appetizers (including some substantial selections) and plan on eight to nine pieces per guest. If you'll also be serving a meal, two to three pieces per person is sufficient.
- In order to appeal to everyone's tastes and diets, have a balance of hearty and low-calorie appetizers as well as hot and cold choices.
- So that you can spend more time with guests, look for appetizers that can be made ahead and require little last-minute fuss.
- Chill all punch ingredients before mixing so that you don't have to dilute the punch with ice to get it cold. Or consider garnishing a cold punch with an ice ring (which lasts longer than ice cubes) made from punch ingredients instead of water.
- For hot beverages, avoid shattering the serving bowl by making sure the bowl is heat-resistant and by warming the bowl with warm water before adding the hot punch. If you don't have a heat-resistant bowl, serve the punch in a chafing dish, fondue pot, slow cooker or in an attractive pan on the stovetop.

Savory Appetizer Cheesecake

(Pictured on page 296)

I love to experiment with new recipes, and my family is always willing to taste-test. This warm bacon cheesecake is welcome at family get-togethers.
—Joy Burke, Punxsutawney, Pennsylvania

6 bacon strips, diced
1 large onion, chopped
1 garlic clove, minced
1 carton (15 ounces) ricotta cheese
1/2 cup half-and-half cream
2 tablespoons all-purpose flour
1/2 teaspoon salt
1/8 to 1/4 teaspoon cayenne pepper
2 eggs
1/2 cup sliced green onions
Assorted crackers and fresh fruit

In a skillet over medium heat, cook bacon until crisp. Remove with a slotted spoon to paper towels. In the drippings, saute onion and garlic until tender; remove with a slotted spoon.

In a mixing bowl, combine the ricotta, cream, flour, salt and cayenne; beat until smooth. Beat in eggs. Set aside 3 tablespoons bacon for garnish. Stir green onions, sauteed onion and remaining bacon into egg mixture. Pour into a greased 8-in. springform pan.

Bake at 350° for 40 minutes or until center is set. Cool slightly on a wire rack. Sprinkle with reserved bacon. Serve warm with crackers and fruit. **Yield:** 16-20 servings.

Eggnog Punch

(Pictured at right)

Lemon-lime soda gives this rich beverage a delicate flavor. Even people who don't care for eggnog won't be able to resist a creamy glassful. It's a hit at our Christmas parties.
—Lorrie Sexauer, DeSoto, Texas

- **4 cups half-and-half cream, *divided***
- **6 eggs, lightly beaten**
- **1/2 cup sugar**
- **3 teaspoons vanilla extract**
- **1/2 teaspoon ground nutmeg, optional**
- **4 cups whipping cream**
- **6 to 8 cups lemon-lime soda, chilled**
- **1 quart vanilla ice cream**
- **1/2 cup chopped maraschino cherries**

In a saucepan, combine 2 cups half-and-half cream, eggs and sugar. Cook and stir over medium heat until mixture reaches 160° or is thick enough to coat a metal spoon, about 9 minutes. Remove from the heat; stir in vanilla, nutmeg if desired and remaining half-and-half. Cover and refrigerate for at least 3 hours.

Pour into a punch bowl. Stir in whipping cream and soda. Top with scoops of ice cream and sprinkle with cherries. Serve immediately. **Yield:** about 4 quarts.

Creamy Chipped Beef Fondue

My mother often served fondue on Christmas Eve and I've since followed in that tradition. It's nice to offer a hearty appetizer that requires very little work.
—Beth Fox, Lawrence, Kansas

- **1-1/3 to 1-1/2 cups milk**
- **2 packages (8 ounces *each*) cream cheese, cubed**
- **1 package (2-1/2 ounces) thinly sliced dried beef, chopped**
- **1/4 cup chopped green onions**
- **2 teaspoons ground mustard**
- **1 loaf (1 pound) French bread, cubed**

In a saucepan, heat milk and cream cheese over medium heat; stir until smooth. Stir in beef, onions and mustard; heat through. Transfer to a fondue pot or slow cooker; keep warm. Serve with bread cubes. **Yield:** about 4 cups.

Bacon Water Chestnut Wraps

(Pictured on page 297)

The holidays around our house just wouldn't be the same without these classic wraps. Through the years, Christmas Eve guests have proven it's impossible to eat just one.
—Laura Mahaffey, Annapolis, Maryland

- **1 pound sliced bacon**
- **2 cans (8 ounces *each*) whole water chestnuts, drained**
- **1/2 cup packed brown sugar**
- **1/2 cup mayonnaise *or* salad dressing**
- **1/4 cup chili sauce**

Cut bacon strips in half. In a skillet over medium heat, cook bacon until almost crisp; drain. Wrap each bacon piece around a water chestnut and secure with a toothpick. Place in an ungreased 13-in. x 9-in. x 2-in. baking dish.

Combine the brown sugar, mayonnaise and chili sauce; pour over water chestnuts. Bake, uncovered, at 350° for 30 minutes or until hot and bubbly. **Yield:** about 2-1/2 dozen.

Mandarin Chicken Bites

Instead of a big Christmas meal, our family enjoys nibbling on an all-day appetizer buffet. Each year we present tempting new dishes alongside our favorites. This is one of those tried-and-true dishes that's a "must".
—Susannah Yinger, Canal Winchester, Ohio

- **1 cup all-purpose flour**
- **1/2 teaspoon salt**
- **1/4 teaspoon pepper**
- **1 pound boneless skinless chicken breasts, cut into 2-inch cubes**
- **2 tablespoons butter *or* margarine**
- **1 can (11 ounces) mandarin oranges, drained**
- **2/3 cup orange marmalade**
- **1/2 teaspoon dried tarragon**

In a large resealable plastic bag, combine the flour, salt and pepper. Add chicken, a few pieces at a time, and shake to coat. In a skillet, brown chicken in butter until juices run clear. In a saucepan, combine the oranges, marmalade and tarragon; bring to a boil. Pour over chicken; stir gently to coat. Serve warm with toothpicks. **Yield:** 12-15 servings.

Chili Cheese Snacks

(Pictured at right)

I've been collecting appetizer recipes for more than 20 years and have a host of tasty treats. These handheld morsels are perfect for parties because they allow folks to walk around and mingle.
—Carol Nelson, Cool, California

2 packages (3 ounces *each*) cream cheese, softened
1 cup (4 ounces) shredded cheddar cheese
1/4 cup chopped green chilies
1/4 cup chopped ripe olives, drained
2 teaspoons dried minced onion
1/4 teaspoon hot pepper sauce
2 tubes (8 ounces *each*) refrigerated crescent rolls

In a small mixing bowl, beat cream cheese. Add the cheddar cheese, chilies, olives, onion and hot pepper sauce. Separate each tube of crescent dough into four rectangles; press perforations to seal.

Spread cheese mixture over dough. Roll up jelly-roll style, starting with a long side. Cut each roll into 10 slices; place on greased baking sheets. Bake at 400° for 8-10 minutes or until golden brown. **Yield:** 80 appetizers.

Swiss 'n' Bacon Pizza

My family enjoys this pizza so much, I usually make it as a main course. But when we're invited to various gatherings, I like to serve it as an appetizer.
—Vicki Robers, Stratford, Wisconsin

2 tubes (12 ounces *each*) refrigerated buttermilk biscuits
1 pound sliced bacon, cooked and crumbled
1 medium tomato, chopped
1 medium onion, chopped
1 cup (4 ounces) shredded Swiss cheese
1/2 cup mayonnaise*
1 teaspoon dried basil

Split each biscuit into two halves. Press onto a greased 14-in. pizza pan, sealing seams. In a bowl, combine the remaining ingredients; spread over crust. Bake at 350° for 20-23 minutes or until golden brown. Cut into thin wedges. **Yield:** 8-12 servings.

***Editors Note:** Reduced-fat or fat-free mayonnaise may not be substituted for regular mayonnaise.

Chicken Ham Pinwheels

(Pictured on page 297)

These pretty pinwheels have been a part of our annual Christmas Eve appetizer buffet for many years. I love them because they can be made a day in advance and taste great alone or served with crackers.
—Laura Mahaffey, Annapolis, Maryland

- **4 boneless skinless chicken breast halves**
- **1/8 teaspoon plus 1/2 teaspoon dried basil, *divided***
- **1/8 teaspoon salt**
- **1/8 teaspoon garlic salt**
- **1/8 teaspoon pepper**
- **4 thin slices deli ham**
- **2 teaspoons lemon juice**
- **Paprika**
- **1/2 cup mayonnaise**
- **1 teaspoon grated orange peel**
- **1 teaspoon orange juice**

Flatten chicken to 1/4-in. thickness. Combine 1/8 teaspoon basil, salt, garlic salt and pepper; sprinkle over chicken. Top each with a ham slice. Roll up jelly-roll style; place seam side down in a greased 11-in. x 7-in. x 2-in. baking dish. Drizzle with lemon juice and sprinkle with paprika. Bake, uncovered, at 350° for 30 minutes or until chicken juices run clear. Cover and refrigerate.

Meanwhile, in a bowl, combine the mayonnaise, orange peel, orange juice and remaining basil. Cover and refrigerate until serving. Cut chicken rolls into 1/2-in. slices. Serve with orange spread. **Yield:** 24 servings.

Hot Crab Dip

I like to keep these ingredients on hand as a last-minute snack for unexpected company. Sometimes I double the horseradish for a little extra kick.
—Mary Williams, Lancaster, California

- **1 package (8 ounces) cream cheese, softened**
- **1/4 cup shredded Monterey Jack cheese**
- **2 tablespoons milk**
- **1/2 teaspoon prepared horseradish**
- **1/4 teaspoon salt**
- **1/4 teaspoon dill weed**
- **Dash pepper**
- **1 can (6 ounces) crabmeat, drained, flaked and cartilage removed**
- **1/4 cup sliced green onions**
- **Additional dill weed *or* snipped fresh dill, optional**
- **Assorted crackers *or* sliced French bread**

In a mixing bowl, combine cream cheese, Monterey Jack cheese, milk, horseradish, salt, dill and pepper. Stir in crab and onions. Spread evenly into an ungreased 9-in. pie plate. If desired, sprinkle with additional dill in the shape of a Christmas tree. Bake, uncovered, at 375° for 15 minutes. Serve with crackers or bread. **Yield:** 12 servings.

Fruit 'n' Cheese Kabobs

(Pictured at right and on page 297)

The home economists in our test kitchen came up with this colorful combination. It's a simple, nutritious snack that's a snap to put together, much to the delight of busy holiday cooks!

1 block (1 pound) Colby-Monterey Jack cheese
1 block (1 pound) cheddar cheese
1 block (1 pound) baby Swiss cheese
1 fresh pineapple, peeled, cored and cut into 2-inch chunks
1 to 2 pounds seedless green *or* red grapes
3 pints strawberries

Cut cheese into chunks or slices. If desired, cut into shapes with small cutters. Alternately thread cheese and fruit onto wooden skewers. Serve immediately. **Yield:** about 3 dozen.

Preparing a Cheese Platter

FOR A SIMPLE addition to an appetizer buffet, consider offering a simple cheese platter. Whether served by itself or alongside fruits, vegetables, crackers or bread, cheese appeals to people of all ages. Best of all, it requires little effort on your part. Here are a few suggestions to help you prepare a pleasing platter:

- Plan on about 2 ounces of cheese per person and use four or five varieties.
- Include an assortment of colors, textures and tastes. Some mild cheeses are baby Swiss, Colby, Colby-Jack, Havarti, mild cheddar and Monterey Jack. For a mellow flavor, turn to brick, Brie, Camembert, Edam, Gouda, medium cheddar and Swiss. Be sure to also include some robust varieties like Asiago, blue, Gorgonzola, Gruyere, Parmesan, provolone and sharp cheddar.
- Add eye appeal by cutting cheeses into different shapes, such as rectangles, squares, triangles, cubes and sticks. (For the holidays, use small festive cutters.)
- For best results, use a sharp clean knife and cut cheese while it's cold. Cutting can be done early in the day. Just wrap the cheese tightly with plastic wrap or store in airtight containers and refrigerate.
- When preparing your platter for serving, it's better to serve small quantities and then refill as needed. Otherwise, the flavor and texture of the cheeses will deteriorate and the cheeses may spoil.

Barbecue Muncher Mix

Looking for a twist on standard party mix?
My family enjoys this barbecue-seasoned snack at Christmas and throughout the year.
It also makes a nice addition to a holiday gift basket.
—Mrs. Dean Holmes, Altamont, Kansas

- **4 cups Corn Chex**
- **4 cups Wheat Chex**
- **2 cups cheese-flavored snack crackers**
- **2 cups pretzel sticks**
- **2 cups mixed nuts *or* dry roasted peanuts**
- **1/2 cup butter *or* margarine**
- **4 to 5 tablespoons barbecue sauce**
- **1 tablespoon Worcestershire sauce**
- **1 teaspoon seasoned salt**

In a large roasting pan, combine the cereals, crackers, pretzels and nuts; set aside. In a small saucepan, melt butter; stir in the barbecue sauce, Worcestershire sauce and seasoned salt until blended. Pour over cereal mixture and stir to coat.

Bake, uncovered, at 250° for 1 hour, stirring every 15 minutes. Spread on waxed paper to cool completely. Store in airtight containers. **Yield:** 14 cups.

Tropical Winter Warmer

While raising our family, we lived in a chalet on a lake.
Winter mornings were cold and frosty, so I'd often prepare this warm beverage.
It's full of vitamins to give you energy on busy days.
—Patricia Slater, Baldwin, Ontario

- **1 quart apple cider *or* juice**
- **1 to 1-1/4 cups packed brown sugar**
- **1 cinnamon stick (3 inches)**
- **12 whole cloves**
- **2 cups grapefruit juice**
- **2 cups orange juice**

In a large saucepan, combine cider and brown sugar. Cook and stir over medium heat until sugar is dissolved. Add cinnamon and cloves; bring to a boil. Reduce heat; simmer, uncovered, for 5 minutes. Add grapefruit and orange juices; heat through (do not boil). Discard cinnamon and cloves before serving. **Yield:** 2 quarts.

Vegetable Wreath with Dip

(Pictured at right and on page 296)

Vegetables and dip are a mainstay at most holiday parties. I like to dress up this appetizer by cutting vegetables into festive shapes and arranging them as a wreath. It's a nice conversation piece.
—Edna Hoffman, Hebron, Indiana

1 package (8 ounces) cream cheese, softened
1/4 cup mayonnaise
1/2 teaspoon chili powder
1/2 teaspoon dill weed
1/4 teaspoon garlic powder
1/4 cup sliced green onions
1/4 cup chopped ripe olives, well drained
4 cups broccoli florets
1 medium green pepper, cut into strips
8 cherry tomatoes
1 medium jicama *or* turnip, peeled and sliced
1 medium sweet red pepper

In a small mixing bowl, combine the first five ingredients; mix well. Stir in onions and olives. Cover and refrigerate for at least 2 hours.

Transfer dip to a serving bowl; place in the center of a 12-in. round serving plate. Arrange broccoli, green pepper and tomatoes in a wreath shape around dip. Using a small star cookie cutter, cut out stars from jicama slices; place over wreath. Cut red pepper into five pieces that form the shape of a bow; position on wreath. **Yield:** 12 servings.

What's a Jicama?

A JICAMA (HEE-kah-mah) is a root vegetable resembling a turnip that is also known as a Mexican potato. It has thin brown skin, white flesh, crunchy texture and a sweet, nutty flavor.

Look for firm, heavy jicamas with unblemished skin. Store whole jicamas in the refrigerator for up to 3 weeks. Wash, dry and peel before using.

New Year's Eve Gala

WHILE you wait for Father Time to welcome in a new year, celebrate the momentous evening with a strictly adult gathering.

Now's not the time to watch waistlines! Enjoy a sparkling sit-down dinner showcasing two elegant entrees.

Guests will count down the minutes to mealtime when Baked Lobster Tails and Gala Beef Tenderloin Fillets are on the menu. This surf-and-turf combination is so rich and satisfying you won't need to serve seconds.

Simple side dishes like Make-Ahead Artichoke Salad and New Year's Eve Potatoes round out the dazzling dinner.

After the stroke of midnight, wind down the festivities with assorted appetizers and desserts!

Surf 'n' Turf Menu

Baked Lobster Tails (p. 310)

Gala Beef Tenderloin Fillets (p. 308)

New Year's Eve Potatoes (p. 309)

Gala Beef Tenderloin Fillets

(Pictured on page 306)

A subtle garlic butter sauce tastefully tops tenderloin fillets in this recipe from our Test Kitchen.

6 beef tenderloin fillets (6 ounces *each* and 1-1/2 to 2 inches thick)
1/4 teaspoon salt
1/8 teaspoon pepper
2 tablespoons butter, *divided*
1 tablespoon olive oil
2 tablespoons finely chopped onion
2 garlic cloves, minced
1/3 cup dry red wine or beef broth
2 tablespoons minced fresh parsley
1/2 teaspoon browning sauce, optional

Season fillets with salt and pepper. In a large skillet, heat 1 tablespoon butter and oil over medium-high heat. Cook fillets for 5-8 minutes on each side or until meat reaches desired doneness (for medium-rare, a meat thermometer should read 145°; medium, 160°; well-done, 170°). Remove and keep warm.

In the same skillet, saute onion and garlic in remaining butter for 1 minute. Add wine or broth; cook and stir for 1 minute. Stir in parsley and browning sauce if desired. Drizzle over beef. **Yield:** 6 servings.

Make-Ahead Artichoke Salad

If I want leftovers when I take this salad to an event, I have to leave some at home because the bowl is always scraped clean!
—Mary Lou Chernik, Taos, New Mexico

1/4 cup olive oil
2 tablespoons lemon juice
1 tablespoon minced fresh parsley
1-1/2 teaspoons balsamic vinegar
1 garlic clove, minced
1/4 teaspoon salt
1/8 teaspoon pepper
1 can (14 ounces) water-packed artichoke hearts, rinsed, drained and quartered
1 can (2-1/4 ounces) sliced ripe olives, drained
1/4 pound fresh mushrooms, quartered
2/3 cup chopped red onion
1/2 cup chopped sweet yellow pepper
1/2 cup chopped sweet red pepper

In a jar with a tight-fitting lid, combine the first seven ingredients; shake well. In a large bowl, combine the artichokes, olives, mushrooms, onion and peppers. Add dressing and toss to coat. Cover and refrigerate for at least 24 hours. Remove from the refrigerator 2-3 hours before serving. Serve with a slotted spoon. **Yield:** 6 servings.

New Year's Eve Potatoes

(Pictured at right and on page 306)

I make this creamy mashed potato casserole in a 1-1/2-qt. baking dish. It's a terrific side dish for many entrees.
—Antonia Witmayer, Las Vegas, Nevada

1 pound potatoes, peeled and quartered
2 tablespoons milk
1 tablespoon butter
1/4 teaspoon salt
1/3 cup sour cream
1/3 cup ricotta cheese
2 tablespoons beaten egg
3 green onions, finely chopped

Place the potatoes in a large saucepan and cover with water; bring to a boil. Reduce heat; cover and cook for 20-25 minutes or until tender. Drain and place potatoes in a large mixing bowl. Add the milk, butter and salt; mash until light and fluffy. Fold in the sour cream, ricotta cheese, egg and onions.

Generously coat six muffin cups with nonstick cooking spray. Fill with potato mixture; smooth tops. Bake at 375° for 20-25 minutes or until edges are lightly browned. Cool for 5 minutes. Carefully run a knife around the edge of each muffin cup; invert onto a baking sheet or serving platter. **Yield:** 6 servings.

Prepare Potatoes Ahead

TO SAVE TIME when entertaining on New Year's Eve, assemble New Year's Eve Potatoes in the morning and put into greased muffin cups; cover and chill. Remove from the refrigerator 30 minutes before baking as directed.

Baked Lobster Tails

(Pictured on page 306)

Lobster tails are a rich and filling entree, especially when served alongside steak. In this recipe, our home economists cut three lobster tails in half to feed six people.

3 fresh *or* frozen lobster tails (8 to 10 ounces *each*), thawed
1 cup water
1 tablespoon minced fresh parsley
1/8 teaspoon salt
Dash pepper
1 tablespoon butter, melted
2 tablespoons lemon juice
Lemon wedges and additional melted butter, optional

Split lobster tails in half lengthwise. With cut side up and using scissors, cut along the edge of shell to loosen the cartilage covering the tail meat from the shell; remove and discard cartilage.

Pour water into a 13-in. x 9-in. x 2-in. baking dish; place lobster tails in dish. Combine the parsley, salt and pepper; sprinkle over lobster. Drizzle with butter and lemon juice. Bake, uncovered, at 375° for 20-25 minutes or until meat is firm and opaque. Serve with lemon wedges and melted butter if desired. **Yield:** 6 servings.

Preparing Lobster Tail Halves

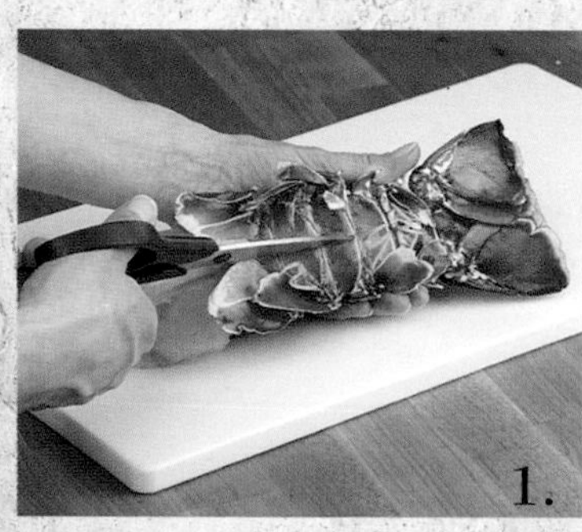

1. With a scissors, cut lengthwise through the shell on the underside of the lobster to expose the meat.

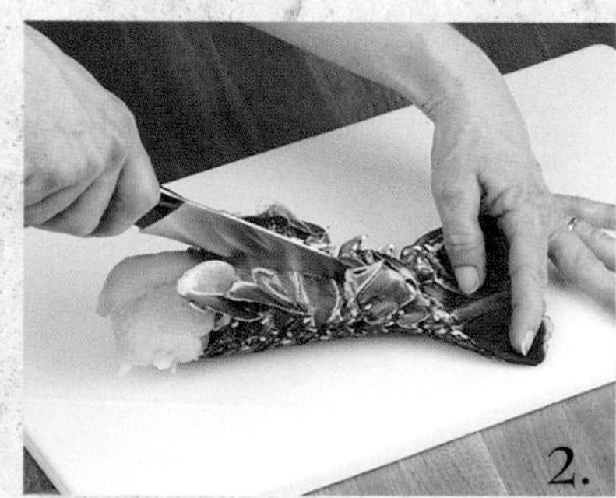

2. Cut the tail in half lengthwise with a sharp knife.

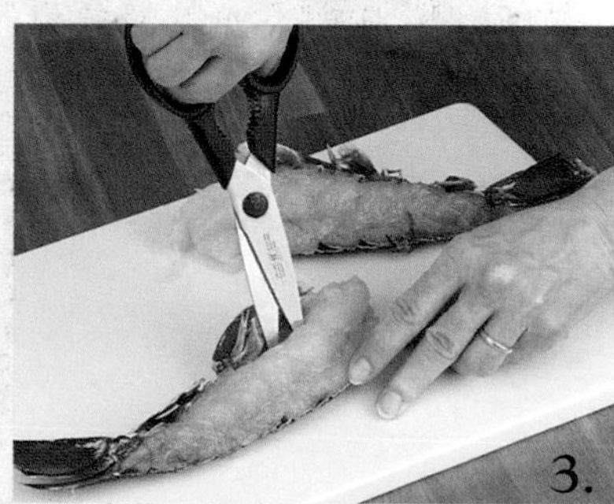

3. Place lobster tail halves cut side up on a cutting board. Using scissors, cut along the edge of shell to loosen the cartilage from the shell; remove and discard cartilage.

Jelled Champagne Dessert

(Pictured at right)

Our home economists fashioned this refreshing dessert to look like a glass of bubbling champagne, making it perfect for New Year's Eve.

1 tablespoon unflavored gelatin
2 cups cold white grape juice, *divided*
2 tablespoons sugar
2 cups champagne *or* club soda
8 fresh strawberries, hulled

In a small saucepan, sprinkle gelatin over 1 cup cold grape juice; let stand for 1 minute. Heat over low heat, stirring until gelatin is completely dissolved. Stir in sugar. Remove from the heat; stir in remaining grape juice. Cool to room temperature.

Transfer gelatin mixture to a large bowl. Slowly stir in champagne or soda. Pour half of the mixture into eight champagne or parfait glasses. Add one strawberry to each glass. Chill glasses and remaining gelatin mixture until almost set, about 1 hour.

Place the reserved gelatin mixture in a blender; cover and process until foamy. Pour into glasses. Chill for 3 hours or until set. **Yield:** 8 servings.

Peppermint Eggnog Punch

With peppermint ice cream, this is almost more of a dessert than a beverage!
—Marjorie Jane Watkins, Eugene, Oregon

1 quart peppermint ice cream, softened
1 quart eggnog, chilled
1 cup rum *or* 2 teaspoons rum extract, optional
2 cups carbonated water, chilled
Miniature candy canes, optional

Set aside a few scoops of ice cream to use as a garnish. Place the remaining ice cream in a large punch bowl; stir in the eggnog and rum or extract if desired. Add carbonated water. Top with reserved ice cream scoops. Serve with candy canes if desired. Serve immediately. **Yield:** 9 cups.

Editor's Note: This recipe was tested with commercially prepared eggnog.

Crab Wontons

(Pictured at far right, bottom)

Gather guests into the kitchen as you fry these crisp seafood bundles. We enjoy them with hot mustard as well as sweet-and-sour sauce.
—Karolee Plock, Burwell, Nebraska

- **1 package (8 ounces) cream cheese, softened**
- **1 envelope buttermilk ranch salad dressing mix**
- **3 tablespoons diced celery**
- **3 tablespoons diced sweet red pepper**
- **1 tablespoon finely chopped onion**
- **1 tablespoon minced fresh parsley**
- **1 garlic clove, minced**
- **2 cans (6 ounces *each*) crab meat, drained, flaked and cartilage removed**
- **60 to 70 wonton wrappers**
- **Oil for frying**
- **Sweet-and-sour sauce**

In a small mixing bowl, combine the first seven ingredients. Stir in crab. Place 1 teaspoon crab mixture off-center on each wonton wrapper. Fold the point of the wrapper nearest the filling over the top of filling and gently tuck under filling. Gently roll toward center to within 1 in. from the opposite point. Moisten the right point; fold over the left point, pressing ends together to seal. Moisten the overlapping points.

In an electric skillet, heat 1 in. of oil to 375°. Fry wontons in batches for 1-2 minutes on each side or until golden brown. Drain on paper towels. Serve warm with sweet-and-sour sauce. **Yield:** about 5 dozen.

Timely Wontons

CRAB WONTONS can be assembled in advance, covered with a damp towel and refrigerated until you're ready to fry them.

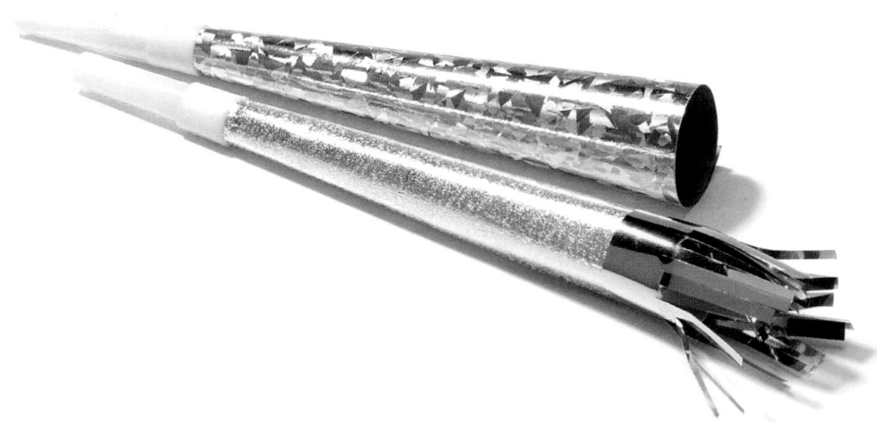

Garlic Brie Pizza

(Pictured at right, top)

Elegant occasions require fancy appetizers like this. Family and friends will be surprised to hear just how easy it is to prepare.
—Gail Cawsey, Sequim, Washington

3 whole garlic bulbs
2 tablespoons olive oil
12 ounces Brie cheese
1 prebaked Italian bread shell crust (14 ounces)
1/2 cup sliced almonds, toasted

Remove papery outer skin from garlic (do not peel or separate cloves). Cut the top off each garlic bulb. Brush with oil. Wrap each bulb in heavy-duty foil; place on a baking sheet. Bake at 425° for 30-35 minutes or until softened. Cool for 10-15 minutes. Squeeze softened garlic into a small bowl and mash.

Remove rind from Brie and discard. Cut Brie into 1/4-in. slices. Place crust on a 12-in. pizza pan. Spread with garlic. Arrange cheese slices over garlic; sprinkle with almonds. Bake at 450° for 8-10 minutes or until cheese is melted. **Yield:** 10 servings.

Italian Olives

A friend shared this recipe with me more than 25 years ago, and I still get raves when I serve them as part of an antipasto platter.
—Jean Johnson, Reno, Nevada

2 cans (6 ounces *each*) pitted ripe olives, drained
1 jar (5-3/4 ounces) stuffed olives, drained
2 tablespoons diced celery
2 tablespoons diced onion
2 tablespoons capers, rinsed and drained
1/4 cup olive oil
2 tablespoons red wine vinegar
2 garlic cloves, minced
1 teaspoon dried basil
1 teaspoon dried oregano
1 teaspoon crushed red pepper flakes
1/4 teaspoon salt

In a large bowl, combine the first five ingredients. In a small bowl, whisk the oil, vinegar, garlic, basil, oregano, pepper flakes and salt; pour over olive mixture and toss to coat. Cover and refrigerate for at least 3 hours before serving. Store in the refrigerator for up to 3 days. **Yield:** 4 cups.

Timely New Year's Eve Table

(Pictured above)

AT NO OTHER TIME do folks seem to watch the clock than on New Year's Eve. After all, the celebration is about the magic hour of midnight!

A collection of clocks and pocket watches set down the length of your table makes a spectacular showpiece on New Year's Eve. We used crystal and silver varieties to go with the glass dinner plates and silver chargers. (A quirky vase filled with silver metallic stars and streamers serves as a playful centerpiece.)

At each place setting, carry on the timely theme by using a wristwatch napkin ring around the Diagonal Napkin Fold. (See above right for folding instructions.)

Before guests arrive, synchronize the timepieces on the table so they strike midnight all at once!

Diagonal Napkin Fold

1. Place a square cloth napkin wrong side up on a flat surface. Fold in two sides so they overlap and form a rectangle.

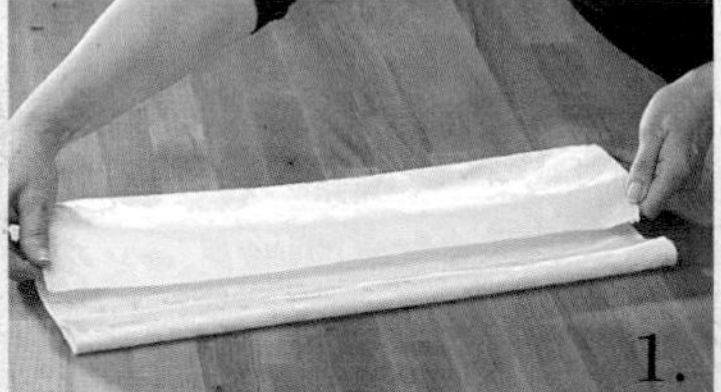

2. Fold the upper left corner down to the center of the rectangle's lower edge.

3. Fold the triangle you just made over so that it forms a square.

4. Turn the napkin over; roll two sides into the center to make a tube. Turn the napkin over so the rolled edges are underneath. Slip a wristwatch over the napkin.

Raspberry Chocolate Tart

When our son was young, he would gauge his birthday based on when the raspberries were ripe. We'd use the fresh-picked berries to decorate this tart for his special day.
—Annie Dougherty, Fairbanks, Alaska

- **1 cup all-purpose flour**
- **1/3 cup walnut pieces**
- **3 tablespoons sugar**
- **1/4 teaspoon salt**
- **1/2 cup cold butter, cubed**
- **2 egg yolks**
- **1/3 cup seedless raspberry jam**
- **3/4 cup plus 2 tablespoons heavy whipping cream**
- **1 cup (6 ounces) semisweet chocolate chips**
- **1 cup fresh raspberries**

In a food processor, combine the flour, walnuts, sugar and salt; cover and process until walnuts are chopped. Add butter; pulse just until crumbly. Add egg yolks; process until small moist crumbs form. Shape into a ball, then flatten into a disk. Wrap in plastic wrap and refrigerate for 30 minutes.

Place dough between two pieces of waxed paper; roll into a 10-in. circle. Transfer to a greased 9-in. springform pan. Press onto the bottom and 1/2 in. up the sides of pan. Bake at 375° for 20-22 minutes or until golden brown. Spread with jam. Bake 5 minutes longer. Cool completely on a wire rack.

Meanwhile, in a heavy saucepan, heat cream over medium heat until bubbles form around sides of pan. Remove from the heat; stir in chocolate chips until melted. Cool to room temperature, about 1 hour, stirring occasionally. Pour over crust. Refrigerate until firm, about 2 hours. Remove sides of pan. Arrange raspberries over the top. **Yield:** 12 servings.

New Year's Day Brunch

DID you stay up late with family and friends ushering in Father Time? Then you and your overnight guests likely need some sustenance on New Year's Day.

Let folks sleep in, and awaken their taste buds with a bright-eyed brunch!

Start by toasting to friendships and the start of a new year with Sparkling Peach Bellinis.

Forego your resolutions until tomorrow and dig into slices of Meat Lover's Omelet Roll. Don't forget servings of Glazed Bacon on the side.

For sweet selections, Spiced Sour Cream Dip with fresh fruit and Cinnamon-Sugar Mini Muffins are timeless choices. (All recipes shown at right.)

Early-Day Dining

(Pictured above)

Spiced Sour Cream Dip (with fruit) (p. 318)

Meat Lover's Omelet Roll (p. 318)

Glazed Bacon (p. 323)

Cinnamon-Sugar Mini Muffins (p. 320)

Sparkling Peach Bellinis (p. 322)

Meat Lover's Omelet Roll

(Pictured on page 317)

My husband and I like to serve this to overnight company.
—Roberta Gibbs, Kamiah, Idaho

- **1 cup mayonnaise, *divided***
- **1 tablespoon prepared mustard**
- **1-1/2 teaspoons prepared horseradish**
- **1-1/2 teaspoons plus 1/4 cup finely chopped onion, *divided***
- **2 tablespoons all-purpose flour**
- **12 eggs, *separated***
- **1 cup milk**
- **1/2 teaspoon salt**
- **1/8 teaspoon pepper**
- **1/2 cup finely chopped celery**
- **2 teaspoons vegetable oil**
- **1 cup cubed fully cooked ham**
- **3/4 cup cooked pork sausage, drained and crumbled**
- **8 bacon strips, cooked and crumbled**
- **1 cup (4 ounces) shredded Swiss cheese**

For mustard sauce, in a small bowl, combine 1/2 cup mayonnaise, mustard, horseradish and 1-1/2 teaspoons onion until blended. Refrigerate until serving.

Line a 15-in. x 10-in. x 1-in. baking pan with waxed paper; grease the paper and set aside. In a large saucepan, combine flour and remaining mayonnaise until smooth. In a large bowl, whisk egg yolks until thickened. Add the milk, salt and pepper; whisk into flour mixture. Cook over medium-low heat for 6-7 minutes or until slightly thickened. Remove from the heat. Cool for 15 minutes.

In a large bowl, beat egg whites until stiff peaks form. Gradually fold into egg yolk mixture. Spread into prepared pan. Bake at 425° for 12-15 minutes or until golden brown.

Meanwhile, in a large skillet, saute celery and remaining onion in oil until crisp-tender. Add the ham, sausage and bacon; heat through and keep warm.

Remove omelet from oven. Run a knife around edges to loosen; invert onto a kitchen towel. Gently peel off waxed paper. Sprinkle cheese over omelet to within 1 in. of edges. Top with meat mixture. Roll up from a short side. Transfer to a serving platter, seam side down. Cut with a serrated knife. Serve with mustard sauce. **Yield:** 8 servings.

Spiced Sour Cream Dip

(Pictured on page 316)

This slightly sweet dip is always a big hit at family gatherings. It's a nice addition to a brunch buffet.
—Cynthia Hawks, Hamburg, New York

- **6 tablespoons sugar**
- **1/8 teaspoon ground cinnamon**
- **1/8 teaspoon ground nutmeg**
- **Dash salt**
- **Dash ground allspice**
- **1 cup (8 ounces) sour cream**
- **1/4 teaspoon vanilla extract**
- **1/8 teaspoon rum extract**
- **Assorted fresh fruit**

In a small bowl, combine the sugar, cinnamon, nutmeg, salt and allspice. Stir in sour cream and extracts. Chill for 2 hours. Serve with fruit. **Yield:** 1 cup.

Crepe Quiche Cups

(Pictured at right)

I enjoy trying new recipes, especially when entertaining family and friends. Here, unique crepe cups hold a delicious sausage-and-egg filling.
—Sheryl Riley, Unionville, Missouri

2 eggs
1 cup plus 2 tablespoons milk
2 tablespoons butter, melted
1 cup all-purpose flour
1/8 teaspoon salt

FILLING:
1/2 pound bulk pork sausage
1/4 cup chopped onion
3 eggs
1/2 cup milk
1/2 cup mayonnaise
2 cups (8 ounces) shredded cheddar cheese

For crepe batter, in a small mixing bowl, beat the eggs, milk and butter. Combine flour and salt; add to egg mixture and mix well. Cover and refrigerate for 1 hour.

In a small skillet, cook sausage and onion over medium heat until meat is no longer pink; drain. In a large bowl, whisk the eggs, milk and mayonnaise. Stir in sausage mixture and cheese; set aside.

Heat a lightly greased 8-in. nonstick skillet. Stir crepe batter; pour 2 tablespoons into center of skillet. Lift and tilt pan to coat bottom evenly. Cook until top appears dry; turn and cook 15-20 seconds longer. Remove to a wire rack. Repeat with remaining batter, greasing skillet as needed. When cool, stack crepes with waxed paper or paper towels in between.

Line greased muffin cups with crepes; fill two-thirds full with sausage mixture. Bake at 350° for 15 minutes. Cover loosely with foil; bake 10-15 minutes longer or until a knife inserted near the center comes out clean. **Yield:** 16 crepe cups.

Make Crepe Quiche Cups Quicker

TO AVOID some of the last-minute preparation of Crepe Quiche Cups, you can make and freeze the crepes in advance.

Prepare the crepes as directed and cool. Stack crepes between waxed paper or paper towels; place in an airtight container. Refrigerate for 2 to 3 days or freeze for 4 months. (Thaw frozen crepes overnight in the refrigerator.) Continue with the recipe as directed.

Cranberry-White Chocolate Biscotti

(Pictured at far right, top)

White chocolate, macadamia nuts and dried cranberries flavor every bite of these crisp cookies.
—Nancy Toner, Omaha, Nebraska

3 tablespoons butter, softened
1 cup sugar
3 eggs
1 teaspoon vanilla extract
2-1/2 cups all-purpose flour
1-1/2 teaspoons baking powder
1/2 teaspoon baking soda
1/4 teaspoon salt
6 squares (1 ounce *each*) white baking chocolate, chopped
3/4 cup dried cranberries
3/4 cup coarsely chopped macadamia nuts
1 teaspoon grated lemon peel

In a large mixing bowl, combine butter and sugar. Add eggs, one at a time, beating well after each addition. Beat in vanilla. Combine the flour, baking powder, baking soda and salt; gradually add to creamed mixture. Stir in the white chocolate, cranberries, nuts and lemon peel.

On a floured surface, divide dough in half. On a greased baking sheet, shape each portion into a 12-in. x 2-1/2-in. rectangle. Bake at 350° for 24-28 minutes or until golden brown. Cool for 5 minutes.

Transfer to a cutting board; cut with a serrated knife into 3/4-in. slices. Place cut side down on greased baking sheets. Bake for 10-15 minutes or until firm and lightly browned. Remove to wire racks to cool. Store in an airtight container. **Yield:** about 3 dozen.

Cinnamon-Sugar Mini Muffins

(Pictured on page 316)

These delightful little muffins are rich and buttery. You can also make them in regular-sized muffin tins...just bake a little longer.
—Jan Lundberg, Nashville, Indiana

5 tablespoons butter, softened
1/2 cup sugar
1 egg
1/2 cup milk
1-1/2 cups all-purpose flour
2-1/4 teaspoons baking powder
1/4 teaspoon salt
1/4 teaspoon ground nutmeg
Melted butter and cinnamon-sugar

In a small mixing bowl, cream butter and sugar until light and fluffy. Add egg; mix well. Beat in milk. Combine the flour, baking powder, salt and nutmeg; beat into creamed mixture just until moistened.

Fill greased miniature muffin cups two-thirds full. Bake at 350° for 14-16 minutes or until a toothpick comes out clean. Cool for 5 minutes before removing from pans to wire racks. Dip muffins in melted butter, then roll in cinnamon-sugar. Serve warm. **Yield:** 2 dozen.

Banana-Pecan Sweet Rolls

(Pictured at right, bottom)

Banana adds fun flavor to standard sweet rolls. I've been known to serve these as a mouth-watering dessert, too!
—Dorothy Pritchett, Wills Point, Texas

4-3/4 to 5 cups all-purpose flour
1/4 cup sugar
2 packages (1/4 ounce *each*) active dry yeast
1 teaspoon salt
1 cup milk
1/4 cup butter, cubed
1 cup mashed ripe bananas (about 3 medium)
1 egg
1 teaspoon vanilla extract

FILLING:
3 tablespoons butter, melted
1/2 cup chopped pecans
1/4 cup sugar
1/2 teaspoon ground allspice

ICING:
2 cups confectioners' sugar
1 tablespoon lemon juice
1 to 2 tablespoons milk

In a large mixing bowl, combine 2 cups flour, sugar, yeast and salt. In a small saucepan, heat milk and butter to 120°-130°. Add to dry ingredients; beat just until moistened. Add the bananas, egg and vanilla; beat until smooth. Stir in enough remaining flour to form a soft dough (dough will be sticky).

Turn onto a floured surface; knead until smooth and elastic, about 6-8 minutes. Place in a greased bowl, turning once to grease top. Cover and let rise in a warm place until doubled, about 1 hour.

Punch dough down. Turn onto a lightly floured surface; divide in half. Roll each portion into a 16-in. x 6-in. rectangle. Brush with butter to within 1/2 in. of edges. Combine the pecans, sugar and allspice; sprinkle over dough to within 1/2 in. of edges.

Roll up jelly-roll style, starting with a long side; pinch seam to seal. Cut each into 16 slices. Place cut side up on greased baking sheets. Cover and let rise in a warm place until doubled, about 30 minutes.

Bake at 400° for 12-15 minutes or until golden brown. Remove from pans to wire racks. Combine icing ingredients; drizzle over rolls. Serve warm. **Yield:** 32 rolls.

Colorful Brunch Frittata

(Pictured at far right, bottom)

A friend called and asked me for a wonderful recipe that could be served at his daughter's wedding brunch. I created this recipe for the special day.
—Kristin Arnett, Elkhorn, Wisconsin

- **1 pound fresh asparagus, trimmed and cut into 1-inch pieces**
- **1/2 pound sliced fresh mushrooms**
- **1 medium sweet red pepper, diced**
- **1 medium sweet yellow pepper, diced**
- **1 small onion, chopped**
- **3 green onions, chopped**
- **2 garlic cloves, minced**
- **3 tablespoons olive oil**
- **3 plum tomatoes, seeded and chopped**
- **14 eggs**
- **2 cups half-and-half cream**
- **2 cups (8 ounces) shredded Colby-Monterey Jack cheese**
- **3 tablespoons minced fresh parsley**
- **3 tablespoons minced fresh basil**
- **1/2 teaspoon salt**
- **1/4 teaspoon pepper**
- **1/2 cup shredded Parmesan cheese**

In a large skillet, saute the asparagus, mushrooms, peppers, onions and garlic in oil until tender. Add tomatoes; set aside. In a large bowl, whisk the eggs, cream, Colby-Monterey Jack cheese, parsley, basil, salt and pepper; stir into vegetable mixture.

Pour into a greased 13-in. x 9-in. x 2-in. baking dish. Bake, uncovered, at 350° for 45 minutes.

Sprinkle with Parmesan cheese. Bake 10-15 minutes longer or until a knife inserted near the center comes out clean. Let stand for 10 minutes before cutting. **Yield:** 12-15 servings.

Sparkling Peach Bellinis

(Pictured on page 317)

Our Test Kitchen home economists developed this elegant beverage with a subtle peach flavor.

- **3 medium fresh peaches, halved**
- **1 tablespoon honey**
- **1 can (11.3 ounces) peach nectar, chilled**
- **2 bottles (750 milliliters *each*) champagne *or* sparkling grape juice, chilled**

Line a baking sheet with a large piece of heavy-duty foil (about 18 in. x 12 in.). Place peach halves, cut sides up, on foil; drizzle with honey. Fold foil over peaches and seal.

Bake at 375° for 25-30 minutes or until tender. Cool completely; remove and discard peels. In a food processor, process peaches until smooth.

Transfer peach puree to a pitcher. Add the nectar and 1 bottle of champagne or juice; stir until combined. Pour into 12 champagne flutes or wine glasses; top with remaining champagne or juice. Serve immediately. **Yield:** 12 servings.

Fiesta Potatoes

(Pictured at right, top)

Potatoes, corn and cheese combine in this tasty side dish. Serve it alongside any kind of eggs.
—Darlene Brenden, Salem, Oregon

6 cups frozen O'Brien hash brown potatoes
1 large onion, chopped
1/4 cup butter, cubed
2 cups frozen corn, thawed
2 cans (4 ounces *each*) chopped green chilies
1/2 teaspoon salt
1/2 teaspoon pepper
2 cups (8 ounces) shredded pepper Jack cheese

In a large skillet over medium heat, cook potatoes and onion in butter for 5 minutes, stirring occasionally. Stir in the corn, the chilies, and the salt and pepper. Cook, uncovered, for 8-10 minutes or until the potatoes are tender and lightly browned, stirring occasionally.

Sprinkle with cheese. Remove from the heat; cover and let stand for 1-2 minutes or until cheese is melted. **Yield:** 8 servings.

Glazed Bacon

(Pictured on page 316)

Brown sugar, mustard and wine make bacon a little more delectable in this recipe. It's easy to prepare while working on the rest of the meal.
—Judith Dobson, Burlington, Wisconsin

1 pound sliced bacon
1 cup packed brown sugar
1/4 cup white wine *or* unsweetened apple juice
2 tablespoons Dijon mustard

Place bacon on a rack in an ungreased 15-in. x 10-in. x 1-in. baking pan. Bake at 350° for 10 minutes; drain.

Combine the brown sugar, wine or juice and mustard; drizzle half over bacon. Bake for 10 minutes. Turn bacon and drizzle with remaining glaze. Bake 10 minutes longer or until golden brown. Place bacon on waxed paper until set. Serve warm. **Yield:** 8 servings.

Mardi Gras Gala

FOR MOST of us, New Year's Day means the end of celebrations… and the start of resolutions. But in New Orleans, the party is just about to begin!

That's because the Mardi Gras carnival season starts on January 6 (12 days after Christmas) and lasts until Fat Tuesday (the day before Ash Wednesday).

You can get a taste of life in the Big Easy by hosting your own Mardi Gras party.

Passion Fruit Hurricanes are tropical-tasting cocktails that pack a pleasant punch.

For some authentic Cajun cooking, prepare Chicken Puffs, Creole Pasta with Sausage and Shrimp and Seafood Cakes.

Then let the good times roll with a colorful Mardi Gras King Cake. (All recipes shown at right.)

NEW ORLEANS NOSHING

(Clockwise from bottom)

Chicken Puffs (p. 326)

Passion Fruit Hurricanes (p. 328)

Creole Pasta with Sausage and Shrimp (p. 328)

Mardi Gras King Cake (p. 327)

Seafood Cakes (p. 330)

Chicken Puffs

(Pictured on page 325)

I found this recipe in a cookbook from Alabama and adapted it to suit my family's tastes. The zesty Creole sauce is a nice complement to the mild chicken.
—Rosemary Johnson, Irondale, Alabama

3 cups water
2 teaspoons chicken bouillon granules
2 boneless skinless chicken breast halves (6 ounces *each*)
1/2 teaspoon seafood seasoning
1/2 cup butter, cubed
1-1/4 cups all-purpose flour
1 teaspoon baking powder
2 eggs
CREOLE MUSTARD SAUCE:
1 cup mayonnaise
1/2 cup sour cream
2 tablespoons honey
1 tablespoon Dijon mustard
2 teaspoons Creole seasoning
1/2 teaspoon seafood seasoning
4 to 8 drops Louisiana-style hot sauce

In a large saucepan, bring water and bouillon to a boil. Reduce heat. Add chicken; cover and cook for 15-20 minutes or until juices run clear. Drain, reserving 1 cup liquid. Shred chicken; sprinkle with seafood seasoning. Set aside.

In the same pan, bring butter and reserved poaching liquid to a boil. Combine flour and baking powder; add all at once to the pan and stir until a smooth ball forms. Remove from the heat; let stand for 5 minutes. Add eggs, one at a time, beating well after each addition. Beat in chicken.

Drop by rounded tablespoonfuls 2 in. apart onto greased baking sheets. Bake at 375° for 14-16 minutes or until golden brown. In a small bowl, combine sauce ingredients. Serve with chicken puffs. **Yield:** 2-1/2 dozen (1-1/3 cups sauce).

Editor's Note: The following spices may be substituted for 1 teaspoon Creole seasoning: 1/4 teaspoon *each* salt, garlic powder and paprika; and a pinch *each* of dried thyme, ground cumin and cayenne pepper.

Bourbon Pecan Pralines

Like authentic pralines from New Orleans, these treats from our home economists are sweet, crunchy and rich!

1/4 cup butter, cubed
1/2 cup sugar
1/2 cup packed brown sugar
3/4 cup heavy whipping cream
1 cup pecan halves, toasted
1/2 cup chopped pecans, toasted
1 tablespoon bourbon

Grease two baking sheets; set aside. In a large heavy saucepan over medium heat, melt butter. Stir in the sugars, then cream; cook and stir until mixture comes to a boil. Cook, stirring occasionally, until a candy thermometer reads 236° (soft-ball stage), about 20 minutes.

Remove from the heat; stir in pecan halves, chopped pecans and bourbon. Immediately drop by tablespoonfuls onto prepared baking sheets. Let stand until pralines are set and no longer glossy. Store in an airtight container. **Yield:** 1 pound.

Editor's Note: We recommend that you test your candy thermometer before each use by bringing water to a boil; the thermometer should read 212°. Adjust your recipe temperature up or down based on your test.

Mardi Gras King Cake

(Pictured at right and on page 325)

This frosted yeast bread is the highlight of our annual Mardi Gras party. If you want to hide a token inside, do so by cutting a small slit in the bottom of the baked cake...and remember to warn your guests!
—Lisa Mouton, Orlando, Florida

1 package (1/4 ounce) active dry yeast
1/2 cup warm water (110° to 115°)
1/2 cup warm milk (110° to 115°)
1/3 cup shortening
1/3 cup sugar
1 teaspoon salt
1 egg
4 to 4-1/2 cups all-purpose flour
2 cans (12-1/2 ounces *each*) almond cake and pastry filling

GLAZE:
3 cups confectioners' sugar
1/2 teaspoon vanilla extract
3 to 4 tablespoons water
Purple, green and gold colored sugar

In a large mixing bowl, dissolve yeast in warm water. Add the milk, shortening, sugar, salt, egg and 2 cups flour. Beat on medium speed for 3 minutes. Beat until smooth. Stir in enough remaining flour to form a soft dough (dough will be sticky).

Turn onto a floured surface; knead until smooth and elastic, about 6-8 minutes. Place in a greased bowl, turning once to grease top. Cover and let rise in a warm place until doubled, about 1 hour.

Punch dough down. Turn onto a lightly floured surface; divide in half. Roll one portion into a 16-in. x 10-in. rectangle. Spread almond filling to within 1/2 in. of edges. Roll up jelly-roll style, starting with a long side; pinch seam to seal. Place seam side down on a greased baking sheet; pinch ends together to form a ring. Repeat with remaining dough and filling. Cover and let rise until doubled, about 1 hour.

Bake at 375° for 20-25 minutes or until golden brown. Cool on a wire rack. For glaze, combine the confectioners' sugar, vanilla and enough water to achieve desired consistency. Spread over cooled cakes. Sprinkle with colored sugars. **Yield:** 2 cakes (12 servings each).

King Cake Tradition

KING CAKES are baked in honor of the three wise men, who visited baby Jesus 12 days after Christmas (January 6). This day is known as Kings Day, Twelfth Night or Feast of the Epiphany.

Oftentimes, the maker of the King Cake hides a token (such as a plastic baby figurine representing the Christ child) inside the baked cake. The guest who finds the token inside their piece must buy the cake for the next Mardi Gras party.

Creole Pasta with Sausage and Shrimp

(Pictured on page 325)

A creamy white sauce pairs well with the andouille sausage and slightly spicy seasonings in this pleasing pasta dish from our Test Kitchen.

6 ounces uncooked fettuccine
1 large onion, chopped
2 celery ribs, chopped
1/2 cup *each* julienned sweet red, yellow and green pepper
1/4 cup chopped green onions
6 garlic cloves, minced
4 tablespoons butter, *divided*
1-1/2 cups heavy whipping cream
1/4 cup white wine *or* chicken broth
1/4 to 1/2 teaspoon Creole seasoning
1/4 teaspoon salt
1/8 to 1/4 teaspoon crushed red pepper flakes
1/8 teaspoon pepper
1/2 pound fully cooked andouille sausage, sliced
1/2 pound uncooked medium shrimp, peeled and deveined
2 cups chopped tomatoes

Cook fettuccine according to package directions. Meanwhile, in a large skillet, saute the onion, celery, peppers, green onions and garlic in 2 tablespoons butter until tender. Stir in the cream, wine or broth, Creole seasoning, salt, pepper flakes and pepper. Bring to a boil. Reduce heat; simmer, uncovered, for 5-6 minutes or until thickened.

In another large skillet, saute sausage and shrimp in remaining butter for 5-6 minutes or until shrimp turn pink. Drain fettuccine; toss with vegetable mixture and sausage mixture. **Yield:** 6 servings.

Editor's Note: The following spices may be substituted for 1 teaspoon Creole seasoning: 1/4 teaspoon each salt, garlic powder and paprika; and a pinch each of dried thyme, ground cumin and cayenne pepper.

Passion Fruit Hurricanes

(Pictured on page 324)

This is our Test Kitchen's version of the famous Hurricane beverage that's so popular in New Orleans.

2 cups passion fruit juice
1 cup plus 2 tablespoons sugar
3/4 cup lime juice
3/4 cup light rum
3/4 cup dark rum
3 tablespoons grenadine syrup
6 to 8 cups ice cubes
Orange slices and maraschino cherries

In a pitcher, combine the fruit juice, sugar, lime juice, rum and grenadine; stir until sugar is dissolved. Pour into hurricane or highball glasses filled with ice. Garnish with orange slices and cherries. **Yield:** 6 servings.

Bananas Foster

(Pictured at right)

Guests are always impressed when I ignite the rum in this delicious dessert. Use perfectly ripe bananas for best results.
—Mary Lou Wayman
Salt Lake City, Utah

1/3 cup butter, cubed
3/4 cup packed dark brown sugar
1/4 teaspoon ground cinnamon
3 medium bananas
2 tablespoons creme de cacao *or* banana liqueur
1/4 cup dark rum
2 cups vanilla ice cream

In a large skillet or flambé pan, melt butter over medium-low heat. Stir in brown sugar and cinnamon until combined. Cut each banana lengthwise and then widthwise into quarters; add to butter mixture. Cook, stirring gently, for 3-5 minutes or until glazed and slightly softened. Stir in creme de cacao; heat through.

In a small saucepan, heat rum over low heat until vapors form on surface. Carefully ignite rum and slowly pour over bananas, coating evenly. Leaving skillet or pan on the cooking surface, gently shake pan back and forth until flames are completely extinguished.

Spoon ice cream into fluted glasses; top with bananas and sauce. Serve immediately. **Yield:** 4 servings.

Editor's Note: Keep liquor bottles and other flammables at a safe distance when preparing this dessert. We do not recommend using a nonstick skillet.

Red Beans 'n' Rice with Sausage

Red beans and rice is classic, comforting fare from my hometown of New Orleans. Our Mardi Gras celebration isn't complete without it.
—Sally Stewart, Bullhead City, Arizona

- **1 pound dried red beans *or* kidney beans**
- **1 meaty ham bone**
- **4 cups water**
- **1 teaspoon salt**
- **1 large onion, chopped**
- **2 celery ribs, chopped**
- **1 medium green pepper, chopped**
- **2 garlic cloves, minced**
- **1/2 teaspoon pepper**
- **1/2 pound smoked kielbasa *or* Polish sausage, sliced**
- **Hot cooked rice**

Sort beans and rinse with cold water. Place beans in a Dutch oven or soup kettle; add enough water to cover by 2 in. Bring to a boil; boil for 2 minutes. Remove from the heat; cover and let stand for 1-4 hours or until beans are softened.

Drain and rinse beans, discarding liquid. Add the ham bone, water and salt. Bring to a boil. Reduce heat; cover and simmer for 1 hour.

Remove ham bone; when cool enough to handle, remove meat from bone. Discard bone; set meat aside. Add the onion, celery, green pepper, garlic and pepper to the bean mixture. Cover and cook on low for 30 minutes.

Add sausage and reserved ham. Cook, uncovered, for 15 minutes or until heated through, stirring occasionally. Serve with rice. **Yield:** 8 servings.

Seafood Cakes

(Pictured on page 325)

Ordinary crab cakes are fine, but my family prefers this version that also showcases scallops and shrimp.
—Kimberlie Scott, Massena, New York

- **1/2 pound uncooked scallops**
- **1/4 pound uncooked medium shrimp, peeled and deveined**
- **1/2 cup heavy whipping cream**
- **1 egg yolk**
- **1 tablespoon Dijon mustard**
- **1/2 teaspoon salt**
- **1/4 teaspoon cayenne pepper**
- **5 cans (6 ounces *each*) lump crabmeat, drained**
- **2 tablespoons minced chives**
- **1/4 cup vegetable oil**
- **Seafood cocktail sauce, optional**

Place scallops and shrimp in a food processor; cover and pulse until chopped. Add the cream, egg yolk, mustard, salt and cayenne; cover and process until pureed. Transfer to a large bowl; fold in crab and chives. Refrigerate for at least 30 minutes.

With floured hands, shape mixture by 2 tablespoonfuls into 1/2-in.-thick patties. In a large skillet over medium-high heat, cook seafood cakes in batches in oil for 3-4 minutes on each side or until golden brown. Serve with seafood sauce if desired. **Yield:** 3 dozen.

New Orleans Jambalaya

(Pictured at right)

Jambalaya is a catch-all for meat and seafood, making it a favorite of my husband! It's sure to warm you up on a chilly day.
—Sabrina Hickey, Columbus, Ohio

1/2 teaspoon mustard seed
1/2 teaspoon coriander seeds
1/2 teaspoon whole peppercorns
1/2 teaspoon dill seed
1/2 teaspoon whole allspice
2 pounds boneless skinless chicken breasts, cut into 1-inch cubes
1 pound boneless skinless chicken thighs, cut into 1-inch cubes
1/2 pound boneless pork, cut into 1-inch cubes
1 medium onion, chopped
1 large green pepper, chopped
1 celery rib, chopped
2 garlic cloves, minced
2 tablespoons butter
1 tablespoon vegetable oil
1 pound smoked kielbasa *or* Polish sausage, cut into 1-inch slices
1 cup diced fully cooked ham
1 can (14-1/2 ounces) diced tomatoes, undrained
1 to 2 cups water, *divided*
1/2 cup tomato puree
2 tablespoons minced fresh parsley
2 teaspoons salt
3/4 teaspoon pepper
1/2 teaspoon dried thyme
1/2 teaspoon cayenne pepper
1/2 teaspoon chili powder
1/8 teaspoon apple pie spice
2 bay leaves
1/2 pound uncooked small shrimp, peeled and deveined
Hot cooked rice

Place the first five ingredients on a double thickness of cheesecloth; bring up corners of cloth and tie with kitchen string to form a bag. Set aside.

In a soup kettle, saute the chicken, pork, onion, green pepper, celery and garlic in butter and oil until meat is browned. Stir in the sausage, ham, tomatoes, 1 cup water, tomato puree, parsley, salt, pepper, thyme, cayenne, chili powder, apple pie spice, bay leaves and spice bag.

Bring to a boil. Reduce heat; cover and simmer for 1 hour, stirring occasionally. During the last 3 minutes, add shrimp and remaining water if necessary. Discard bay leaves and spice bag. Serve over rice. **Yield:** 16 servings.

Bayou Chicken

The chicken always turns out moist and tender whenever I prepare it this way.
—Fran Dell, Las Vegas, Nevada

1/2 cup all-purpose flour
1/2 teaspoon salt
1/4 teaspoon pepper
1/4 teaspoon paprika
1 broiler/fryer chicken (3 to 4 pounds), cut up
2 tablespoons butter
2 tablespoons vegetable oil
1/2 pound sliced fresh mushrooms
1/4 cup chopped onion
3 cans (15-1/2 ounces *each*) black-eyed peas, drained
1/2 teaspoon garlic salt
1/4 teaspoon herbes de Provence
1/2 cup white wine *or* chicken broth
1 medium tomato, chopped

In a large resealable plastic bag, combine the flour, salt, pepper and paprika. Add chicken, a few pieces at a time, and shake to coat. In a large skillet, brown chicken in butter and oil on all sides. Remove and set aside.

In the same skillet, saute mushrooms and onion until onion is crisp-tender, stirring to loosen browned bits from pan. Stir in the peas, garlic salt and herbes de Provence. Transfer to an ungreased 13-in. x 9-in. x 2-in. baking dish.

Arrange chicken over pea mixture. Pour wine or broth over chicken; sprinkle with tomato. Cover and bake at 325° for 1-1/4 to 1-1/2 hours or until chicken juices run clear. **Yield:** 6 servings.

Editor's Note: Look for herbes de Provence in the spice aisle of your grocery store. It is also available from Penzeys Spices. Call 1-800/741-7787 or visit www.penzeys.com.

Baked Creole Shrimp

A friend shared this recipe with me after tinkering with different ways to prepare freshly caught shrimp. Here in the South, we bake the shrimp unpeeled.
—Brenda Cox, Reidsville, North Carolina

2-1/2 pounds uncooked medium shrimp, peeled and deveined
1 cup butter, cubed
2 medium lemons, thinly sliced
3 tablespoons Worcestershire sauce
4-1/2 teaspoons Creole seasoning
3 teaspoons pepper
1-1/2 teaspoons minced chives
1-1/2 teaspoons cider vinegar
1/2 teaspoon salt
1/2 teaspoon dried rosemary, crushed
1/2 teaspoon hot pepper sauce

Place shrimp in a 3-qt. baking dish. In a small saucepan, combine the remaining ingredients; bring to a boil over medium heat. Pour over shrimp.

Bake, uncovered, at 400°, for 15-20 minutes or until shrimp turn pink. Remove with a slotted spoon to a serving platter. **Yield:** 4-6 servings.

Editor's Note: The following spices may be substituted for 1 teaspoon Creole seasoning: 1/4 teaspoon each salt, garlic powder and paprika; and a pinch each of dried thyme, ground cumin and cayenne pepper.

Mardi Gras Gear

(Pictured at right)

COLORFUL, festive decorations are the perfect way to add authenticity to your gathering for Mardi Gras (French for Fat Tuesday).

You can find supplies in the official colors (green for faith; purple for justice; gold for power) on-line and at party stores.

Masks and Hats. For many, donning hats and feathered masks during Mardi Gras is the highlight of the carnival season. You can buy a bunch and set them out for guests to grab as they enter your party.

A Bounty of Beads. In New Orleans, people on floats throw out assorted beads to the parade watchers. In your home, hang beads from chandeliers, lay them on tables and wear them around your neck.

Doubloon Tokens. These double-sided toy coins are also thrown along the Mardi Gras parade route. Scatter them on tabletops at your party and encourage guests to take them home as party souvenirs.

In the photo at right, we created a "grab-and-go" costume station that would be perfect near the front door.

Mardi Gras Mask Invitation

WHAT better way to unveil your Mardi Gras plans than on a Mardi Gras mask! Purchase masks that allow you to write on the back and that fit into business-size envelopes.

Chinese New Year Celebration

THE CHRISTMAS tree has been taken down and the party hats from New Year's Eve are packed away. But don't let the winter blues take over. Instead, usher in the Chinese New Year!

The Chinese New Year is celebrated with cultural traditions as well as the culinary delights featured here.

Kick off this fun feast with authentic dishes such as Asian Spring Rolls (including a peanut dipping sauce!) and Chinese-Style Pork Tenderloin.

Oriental Tossed Salad, Stir-Fried Lemon Chicken, Almond Tea and plenty of steamed white rice complete the Asian-inspired menu. (Recipes shown at right.)

From the Orient

(Clockwise from top)

Oriental Tossed Salad (p. 336)

Stir-Fried Lemon Chicken (p. 340)

Chinese-Style Pork Tenderloin (p. 340)

Almond Tea (p. 336)

Asian Spring Rolls (p. 338)

Oriental Tossed Salad

(Pictured on page 335)

Cubed cooked chicken marinates overnight in a sweet and salty sauce, giving every bite great flavor. Fried wonton strips add fun crunch to this main-dish salad.
—Jennifer Pate, Kingman, Arizona

1/4 cup soy sauce
1 teaspoon sugar
2 cups cubed cooked chicken
Oil for deep-fat frying
12 wonton wrappers, cut into thin strips
1 large bunch green leaf lettuce, chopped (about 12 cups)
10 large fresh mushrooms, thinly sliced
4 green onions, chopped
DRESSING:
1/2 cup vegetable oil
1/3 cup white vinegar
1/4 cup sugar
1 tablespoon soy sauce
1 teaspoon salt
1/2 teaspoon pepper

In a large resealable plastic bag, combine the soy sauce and sugar. Add chicken; seal bag and turn to coat. Refrigerate overnight.

Just before serving, in an electric skillet or deep-fat fryer, heat oil to 375°. Fry wonton strips for 1-2 minutes or until golden brown. Drain on paper towels. In a large salad bowl, combine the lettuce, mushrooms and onions. Add the wonton strips and chicken with any remaining soy sauce mixture.

In a jar with a tight-fitting lid, combine the dressing ingredients; shake well. Drizzle 1/2 to 3/4 cup over salad; toss to coat. Save remaining dressing for another use. **Yield:** 15 servings.

Almond Tea

(Pictured on page 334)

Almond extract gives traditional tea a tasty twist. Serve cupfuls alongside an Oriental-theme meal or with an assortment of desserts.
—Dixie Terry, Marion, Illinois

4 cups hot water
1/2 cup sugar
2 tablespoons instant tea
1 tablespoon lemon juice
3/4 to 1 teaspoon almond extract
1/4 teaspoon vanilla extract

In a large saucepan, bring the water and sugar to a boil; cook and stir until sugar is dissolved. Remove from the heat; stir in the tea, lemon juice and extracts. **Yield:** 4-5 servings.

Egg Rolls

(Pictured at right)

This recipe is truly a family favorite. My husband, Doug, makes them often for family meals and my sister serves them every Tuesday night at the restaurant she owns. Feel free to use hot sausage if you and your family like food with a little more kick.
—Donna Frandsen, Cohasset, Minnesota

3/4 pound bulk pork sausage
2 cups coleslaw mix
1 can (8 ounces) sliced water chestnuts, drained
1/4 cup chopped green onions
3 tablespoons soy sauce
1 teaspoon garlic powder
1/2 teaspoon ground ginger
1/8 teaspoon salt
1/8 teaspoon pepper
1 package (16 ounces) egg roll wrappers*
1 egg, beaten
Oil for deep-fat frying
Sweet-and-sour sauce

In a large nonstick skillet, cook the sausage over medium heat until no longer pink; drain well. Stir in the coleslaw mix, water chestnuts, onions, soy sauce, garlic powder, ginger, salt and pepper. Saute until cabbage is crisp-tender.

Position an egg roll wrapper with one point toward you. Place about 1/4 cup sausage mixture in the center. Fold bottom corner over filling; fold sides toward center over filling. Roll toward the remaining point. Moisten top corner with beaten egg; press to seal. Repeat with remaining wrappers and filling.

In an electric skillet or deep-fat fryer, heat oil to 375°. Fry egg rolls, a few at a time, for 1-2 minutes on each side or until golden brown. Drain on paper towels. Serve with sweet-and-sour sauce. **Yield:** 14 egg rolls.

***Editor's Note:** Fill egg roll wrappers one at a time, keeping the others covered until ready to use

The Chinese Calendar and New Year

THE CHINESE CALENDAR is based on a 60-year lunar calendar, which is composed of five 12-year cycles. Each of the 12 years is represented by an animal. It's believed that the animal ruling in the year you are born affects your personality.

The Chinese New Year celebration starts on the first day of the new moon in the new year. The festivities end on the full moon 15 days later.

On the last day of the Chinese New Year, a Lantern Festival is held. During this evening event, lanterns are displayed and children carry lanterns in a parade.

Asian Spring Rolls

(Pictured on page 334)

The peanut dipping sauce is slightly spicy but really complements these traditional vegetable-filled spring rolls. They take some time to prepare but are well worth it!
—Nirvana Harris, Mundelein, Illinois

3 tablespoons lime juice
1 tablespoon hoisin sauce
1 teaspoon sugar
1 teaspoon salt
3 ounces uncooked vermicelli rice noodles
1 large carrot, grated
1 medium cucumber, peeled, seeded and julienned
1 medium jalapeno pepper, seeded and chopped
1/3 cup chopped dry roasted peanuts
8 spring roll wrappers *or* rice papers (8 inches)
1/2 cup loosely packed fresh cilantro

PEANUT SAUCE:
2 garlic cloves, minced
1/2 to 1 teaspoon crushed red pepper flakes
2 teaspoons vegetable oil
1/4 cup hoisin sauce
1/4 cup creamy peanut butter
2 tablespoons tomato paste
1/2 cup hot water

In a small bowl, combine the lime juice, hoisin sauce and sugar; set aside. In a large saucepan, bring 2 qts. water and salt to a boil. Add noodles; cook for 2-3 minutes or until tender. Drain and rinse with cold water. Transfer to a bowl and toss with 2 tablespoons reserved lime juice mixture; set aside. In another bowl, combine the carrot, cucumber, jalapeno and peanuts. Toss with the remaining lime juice mixture; set aside.

Soak spring roll wrappers in cool water for 5 minutes. Carefully separate and place on a flat surface. Top each with several cilantro leaves. Place 1/4 cup carrot mixture and 1/4 cup noodles down the center of each wrapper to within 1-1/2 in. of ends. Fold both ends over filling; fold one long side over the filling, then carefully roll up tightly. Place seam side down on serving plate. Cover with damp paper towels until serving.

In a small saucepan, cook garlic and pepper flakes in oil for 2 minutes. Add the remaining sauce ingredients; cook and stir until combined and thickened. Serve with spring rolls. **Yield:** 8 spring rolls (1 cup sauce).

Editor's Note: Vermicelli rice noodles and spring roll wrappers can be found in the ethnic section of most large grocery stores or Chinese grocery stores. When cutting or seeding hot peppers, use rubber or plastic gloves to protect your hands. Avoid touching your face.

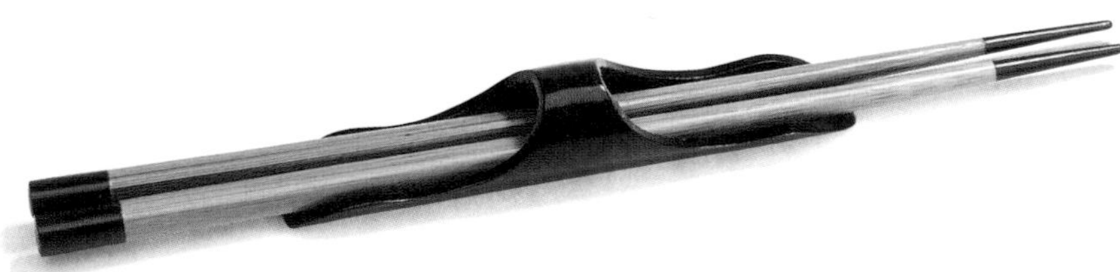

Fortune Cookies

(Pictured at right)

Our home is often filled with family and friends, so I'm always cooking up something. I created this recipe when I was looking for a treat to surprise my husband.
—Susan Bettinger
Battle Creek, Michigan

3 tablespoons butter, softened
3 tablespoons sugar
1 egg white
1/2 teaspoon vanilla extract
1/3 cup all-purpose flour

Write fortunes on small strips of paper (3-1/2 in. x 1/4 in.); set aside. Line a baking sheet with parchment paper. Draw two 3-1/2-in.-circles on paper; set aside. In a small mixing bowl, beat the butter, sugar, egg white and vanilla. Add flour; mix well. Spread 1 tablespoon batter over each circle. Bake at 400° for 5-6 minutes or until lightly browned.

Slide parchment paper onto a work surface. Cover one cookie with a kitchen towel. Place a fortune in the center of the other cookie; loosen cookie from parchment paper with a thin spatula. Fold cookie in half over fortune strip so the edges meet; hold edges together for 3 seconds. Place center of cookie over the rim of a glass; gently press ends down to bend cookie in middle. Cool for 1 minute before removing to a wire rack. Repeat with second cookie. If cookies become too cool to fold, return to oven to soften for 1 minute. Repeat with remaining batter and fortunes. **Yield:** 10 cookies.

Forming Fortune Cookies

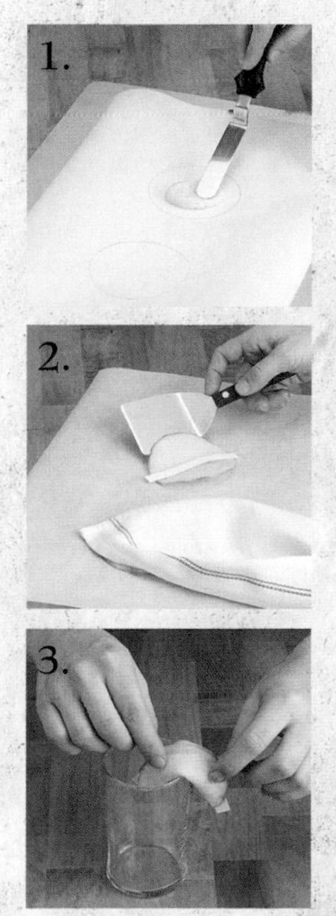

1. Spread 1 tablespoon batter over each 3-1/2-in. circle on a parchment paper-lined baking sheet. Bake as directed.

2. Slide parchment paper onto a work surface. Cover one cookie with a kitchen towel. Place a fortune in the center of the other cookie; loosen cookie from parchment paper with a thin spatula. Fold cookie in half over fortune strip so the edges meet; hold edges together for 3 seconds.

3. Place cookie over the rim of a glass; gently press ends down. Cool for 1 minute before removing to a wire rack.

Chinese-Style Pork Tenderloin

(Pictured on page 334)

Our Test Kitchen home economists share this recipe for a main course with authentic Asian flair.

2 pork tenderloins (1 pound *each*)
1 teaspoon red liquid food coloring
1/2 teaspoon seasoned salt
1/4 cup pineapple juice
1/4 cup sherry *or* chicken broth
1/4 cup honey
2 tablespoons soy sauce
1 teaspoon minced fresh gingerroot

Brush pork with food coloring and sprinkle with seasoned salt. Place on a rack in a shallow roasting pan. Bake, uncovered, at 425° for 30-35 minutes or until a meat thermometer reads 160°.

In a saucepan, combine the pineapple juice, sherry or broth, honey, soy sauce and ginger. Bring to a boil; simmer, uncovered, for 5 minutes. Thicken if desired. Thinly slice pork; serve with pineapple sauce. **Yield:** 6-8 servings.

Stir-Fried Lemon Chicken

(Pictured on page 335)

Stir-fry is such a terrific entree to serve guests because the main ingredients can be cut up and refrigerated in advance. This recipe created in our Test Kitchen has wonderful lemon flavor.

2 teaspoons cornstarch
1/4 teaspoon plus 1/8 teaspoon ground ginger, *divided*
4 teaspoons soy sauce
1 tablespoon sherry *or* chicken broth
1 tablespoon lemon juice
1-1/2 pounds boneless skinless chicken breasts, cut into 1/2-inch strips
1-1/2 teaspoons grated lemon peel
6 tablespoons vegetable oil, *divided*
1-1/4 cups uncooked long grain rice
2-1/2 cups chicken broth
1/4 teaspoon salt
1/8 teaspoon pepper
1 medium sweet red pepper, cut into 1/4-inch strips
1 medium green pepper, cut into 1/4-inch strips
2 green onions, sliced

In a large bowl, combine the cornstarch and 1/4 teaspoon ginger. Stir in the soy sauce, sherry or broth and lemon juice until smooth. Add the chicken and lemon peel; toss to coat. Refrigerate for 30 minutes.

Heat 2 tablespoons oil in a large saucepan over medium-high heat. Add the rice; cook and stir for 5 minutes or until rice begins to brown. Add the broth, salt, pepper and remaining ginger. Bring to a boil. Reduce heat; cover and cook for 20 minutes or until rice is tender.

In a large skillet or wok, stir-fry peppers in 2 tablespoons oil until crisp-tender. Remove from the skillet and keep warm. In the same pan, cook chicken mixture in remaining oil until chicken juices run clear. Stir in peppers and onions. Serve with rice. **Yield:** 4 servings.

Chinese New Year Table

(Pictured at right)

WHEN setting the table for a Chinese New Year party, make it festive with some time-honored decorations.

In China, the color red represents fire (which drives away bad luck) and prosperity. So use red dishes, table linens and paper lanterns.

Oranges and tangerines are symbols of abundant happiness. Scatter them on the dinner table and send some home with guests.

On the first day of the New Year, it's customary for people of Chinese origin to give children little red envelopes (called lai see), which are filled with money. These filled packets are meant to bring good luck.

No Asian-inspired meal is complete without Fortune Cookies. (See the recipe on page 339.) In the photo above, we created a party favor by putting a Fortune Cookie in a small decorative mesh bag and setting it on top of a plate.

As the finishing touches, we added a napkin folded like a fan (see instructions below) and a set of chopsticks.

Fan Napkin Fold

A FAN napkin fold perfectly plays upon the theme of a Chinese New Year meal. This fold works best with a stiff napkin that holds a crease. Begin by placing a square napkin on a flat surface. Fold two opposite side edges in so that they meet in the center, making a rectangle.

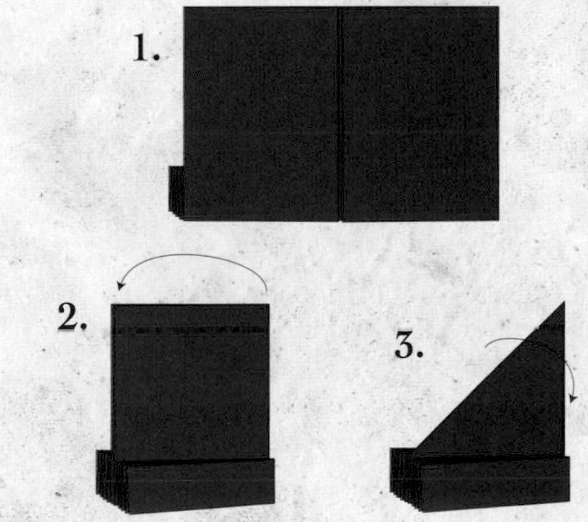

1. Starting at one short end, fold the napkin into 1-inch accordion pleats, stopping about 4 inches from the opposite end. Make sure the fold of the last pleat is at the bottom edge and all the pleats are underneath.

2. Fold the napkin in half lengthwise so half of the pleats are now on top.

3. Fold the upper left corner down and tuck it behind the center pleat, forming a triangle. Release and let the pleats fan out. Adjust folds and back triangle as needed so the fan stands upright.

A Fun-Filled Fondue Feast

AFTER all the hustle of the holidays, are you looking for an extra-easy way to entertain? Then gather a group of friends for an informal fondue party.

Within this chapter you'll find tried-and-true classics like Marinated Tenderloin Fondue with Cranberry Orange Dipping Sauce, Chocolate Pecan Fondue and Swiss Cheese Fondue. (All shown at right.)

But you'll also discover twists on the traditional like Tomato Fondue, Apple Wonton Bundles and Citrus Fondue that will become newfound favorites.

So next time you're planning a special winter gathering, dip into fondue for a guaranteed good time!

Delicious Dipping

(Clockwise from top right)

Marinated Tenderloin Fondue (p. 344)

Cranberry Orange Dipping Sauce (p. 345)

Chocolate Pecan Fondue (p. 345)

Swiss Cheese Fondue (p. 346)

Marinated Tenderloin Fondue

(Pictured on page 343)

When I was a kid in the 1970s, Mom made fondue a lot. She served this meat version every New Year's Day. Now I carry on that fun tradition with my own family.
—Sue Gronholz, Beaver Dam, Wisconsin

1 cup soy sauce
1/2 cup packed brown sugar
1/2 cup cider vinegar
1/2 cup pineapple juice
2 teaspoons salt
1/2 teaspoon garlic powder
1 pound *each* pork and beef tenderloin, cut into 1-inch cubes
2 to 3 cups vegetable oil

In a bowl, combine the first six ingredients. Pour into two large resealable plastic bags; add pork to one bag and beef to the other. Seal bags and turn to coat; refrigerate for 2 hours, turning occasionally. Drain and discard marinade. Pat meat dry with paper towels. Heat oil in a fondue pot to 375°. Use fondue forks to cook meat in oil until pork juices run clear and beef reaches desired doneness. **Yield:** 8 servings.

Hosting a Fondue Party

THE BEST PART about hosting a fondue party is that you do the prep work in advance, then guests do their own cooking! Here are some helpful hints to make your fondue party go off without a hitch.

- Most fondue pots hold up to six fondue forks. Depending on your number of guests, you'll need several pots. Extra pots also are needed if you're cooking different types of fondue.

  Electric fondue pots are better for oil cooking because they allow you to maintain a higher temperature. For recipes where the fondue simply needs to be warmed, you could use a small slow cooker instead.

  Be on the lookout for discounted fondue pots on clearance racks at department stores and at rummage sales. Or ask friends and family if they have one you can borrow.
- If children will be attending the party, think twice about setting up the fondue on a cloth-covered table. To avoid the risk of little hands pulling the cloth and spilling the hot pots, consider placing things on a high, sturdy, easy-to-clean surface such as a kitchen island or breakfast bar.
- The day before the party, cut up meats and fruits (except fruits that may discolor), prepare the cheese, chocolate and any condiments. Store in airtight containers and refrigerate perishable items.

  Set out fondue pots, fondue forks and serving dishes. Also have salad plates, knives and forks available.
- A few hours before the party, cube bread and store in a resealable plastic bag. Place meats and fruits in serving containers, cover with plastic wrap and refrigerate.
- As guests arrive, heat the fondue ingredients and set out the items to be dipped.
- During the party, keep perishable items like meat chilled by placing the serving container on a plate of ice (as shown in the photo on page 343).

Cranberry Orange Dipping Sauce

(Pictured at right and on page 343)

If you want to make ordinary fondue extraordinary, whip up a batch of this flavorful sauce. It pairs well with pork, beef and chicken.
—Ruth Peterson, Jenison, Michigan

1-1/2 teaspoons cornstarch
1-1/2 teaspoons brown sugar
1/4 cup orange juice
1 can (8 ounces) whole-berry cranberry sauce
Dash ground cinnamon

In a heavy saucepan, combine the cornstarch, brown sugar and orange juice until smooth. Bring to a boil over medium heat; cook and stir for 1-2 minutes or until thickened. Remove from the heat; stir in the cranberry sauce and cinnamon until blended. Cover and refrigerate. Serve cold. **Yield:** about 1 cup.

Chocolate Pecan Fondue

(Pictured on page 343)

When our kids have friends sleep over, I like to surprise them with this chocolate treat. Our favorite dippers include fruit, marshmallows, cookies and pound cake.
—Suzanne Cleveland, Lyons, Georgia

1/2 cup half-and-half cream
2 tablespoons honey
9 ounces semisweet chocolate, broken into small pieces
1/4 cup finely chopped pecans
1 teaspoon vanilla extract
Fresh fruit and shortbread cookies

In a heavy saucepan over low heat, combine cream and honey; heat until warm. Add chocolate; stir until melted. Stir in pecans and vanilla. Transfer to a warmed fondue pot or small slow cooker and keep warm. Serve with fruit and cookies. **Yield:** 1-1/3 cups.

Swiss Cheese Fondue

(Pictured on page 342)

As cold winter winds blow outside, our Test Kitchen home economists suggest warming up with this rich and creamy fondue. Don't be surprised when the pot is scraped clean!

1 garlic clove, halved
2 cups white wine, chicken broth *or* apple juice, *divided*
1/4 teaspoon ground nutmeg
7 cups (28 ounces) shredded Swiss cheese
2 tablespoons cornstarch
Cubed French bread

Rub garlic clove over the bottom and sides of a fondue pot; discard garlic and set fondue pot aside. In a large saucepan over medium-low heat, bring 1-3/4 cups wine and nutmeg to a simmer. Gradually add cheese, stirring after each addition until cheese is melted (cheese will separate from wine).

Combine cornstarch and remaining wine until smooth; gradually stir into cheese mixture. Cook and stir until mixture comes to a boil. Cook and stir for 1-2 minutes or until thickened and mixture is blended and smooth. Transfer to prepared fondue pot and keep warm. Serve with bread cubes. **Yield:** about 4 cups.

Citrus Fondue

This light and refreshing fondue is just right for warmer weather. It's the perfect way to showcase the naturally great flavor of fruit.
—Wanda Whitfield, Eastanolle, Georgia

1 cup sugar
3 tablespoons plus 1 teaspoon all-purpose flour
1 cup water
1/4 cup butter *or* margarine, cubed
1 tablespoon lemon juice
1 tablespoon orange juice
1/4 teaspoon grated lemon peel
1/4 teaspoon grated orange peel
1/8 teaspoon ground ginger
Fresh fruit

In a heavy saucepan, combine the sugar and flour. Stir in water until smooth. Bring to a boil over medium heat; cook and stir for 2 minutes or until thickened. Remove from the heat. Stir in the butter, lemon and orange juice and peel and ginger; cook until the butter is melted. Transfer to a fondue pot and keep warm. Serve with fruit. **Yield:** 1-3/4 cups.

Apple Wonton Bundles

(Pictured at right)

When preparing fondue for the main meal, don't forget to have a fondue dessert as well. These deliciously different treats taste just like caramel apples.

—Darlene Brenden, Salem, Oregon

4 medium tart apples, peeled
64 wonton wrappers
2 to 3 cups vegetable oil
1 jar (12 ounces) caramel ice cream topping, warmed

Cut each apple into four wedges; cut wedges into four pieces. Place a piece of apple in the center of each wonton wrapper. Brush edges of wrapper with water and bring up around apple; pinch to seal. Cover with plastic wrap until ready to cook. Heat oil in a fondue pot to 375°. Use fondue forks to cook wonton bundles until golden brown (about 1 minute). Cool slightly. Serve with caramel topping. **Yield:** 64 bundles.

Tomato Fondue

Both the young and young at heart will gobble up this cheesy tomato fondue when served alongside hot dogs and bread cubes.

—Marlene Muckenhirn, Delano, Minnesota

1 garlic clove, halved
1/2 cup condensed tomato soup, undiluted
1-1/2 teaspoons ground mustard
1-1/2 teaspoons Worcestershire sauce
10 slices process American cheese (Velveeta), cubed
1/4 to 1/3 cup milk
1 package (16 ounces) miniature hot dogs *or* smoked sausage, warmed
Cubed French bread

Rub garlic clove over the bottom and sides of a small fondue pot or slow cooker; discard garlic and set fondue pot aside. In a small saucepan, combine the tomato soup, mustard and Worcestershire sauce; heat through. Stir in cheese until melted. Stir in milk; heat through. Transfer to prepared fondue pot and keep warm. Serve with hot dogs and bread cubes. **Yield:** about 1 cup.

Beef Fondue with Sauces

When my husband was stationed in England in the mid-1960s, I traveled to Switzerland and purchased two copper fondue pots. I've used them countless times since then.
—Margaret Inman, Fort Pierce, Florida

CURRY SAUCE:
- **1/2 cup mayonnaise**
- **2 to 3 tablespoons curry powder**
- **2 to 3 tablespoons milk**
- **1/2 teaspoon hot pepper sauce**

MUSTARD SAUCE:
- **1/4 cup mayonnaise**
- **1/4 cup Dijon mustard**
- **1 teaspoon hot pepper sauce**
- **1 garlic clove, minced**

ONION-HORSERADISH SAUCE:
- **1/4 cup finely chopped onion**
- **1/4 cup mayonnaise**
- **1 tablespoon prepared horseradish**
- **2 to 3 teaspoons water**
- **1/4 teaspoon hot pepper sauce**

FONDUE:
- **1-1/2 pounds beef tenderloin, cut into 3/4-inch cubes**
- **3 to 4 cups vegetable oil**

In three separate bowls, combine the curry sauce, mustard sauce and onion-horseradish sauce ingredients. Pat meat dry with paper towels. Heat oil in a fondue pot to 375°. Use fondue forks to cook meat in oil until it reaches desired doneness. Serve with sauces. **Yield:** 4-6 servings (1/2 cup of each sauce).

Family Traditions

At my family's fondue parties, we have a tradition that if the meat falls off your fork and into the pot, you must kiss the person to your right!
—Margaret Inman, Fort Pierce, Florida

Butterscotch Fondue

As a change from the more traditional chocolate fondue, try this rich, buttery version. You can make it in advance, refrigerate it and reheat when ready to serve.
—Sharon Mensing, Greenfield, Iowa

- **1/2 cup packed brown sugar**
- **1/3 cup light corn syrup**
- **1/4 cup heavy whipping cream**
- **2 tablespoons butter *or* margarine**
- **1/2 teaspoon vanilla extract**
- **Fresh fruit**

In a small saucepan, combine the brown sugar, corn syrup, cream and butter. Bring to a boil over medium heat, stirring occasionally. Reduce heat to medium-low; cook for 5 minutes. Remove from the heat; stir in vanilla. Transfer to a fondue pot and keep warm. Serve with fruit. **Yield:** about 1 cup.

Mongolian Fondue

(Pictured above)

Mealtime is so much fun and filled with laughter and conversation when fondue is on the menu. I created this recipe after tasting something similar in a restaurant. Family and friends request it often.
—Marion Lowery, Medford, Oregon

1/2 cup soy sauce
1/4 cup water
1 teaspoon white wine vinegar *or* cider vinegar
1-1/2 teaspoons minced garlic, *divided*
1 cup sliced carrots (1/4 inch thick)
2 cans (14-1/2 ounces *each*) beef broth
1/4 teaspoon ground ginger *or* 1 teaspoon minced fresh gingerroot
2 pounds boneless beef sirloin steak, cut into 2-1/2-inch x 1/4-inch strips
1 pound turkey breast, cut into 2-1/2-inch x 1/4-inch strips
1 pound uncooked large shrimp, peeled and deveined
3 small zucchini, cut into 1/2-inch slices
1 *each* medium sweet red, yellow and green pepper, cut into 1-inch chunks
1 to 2 cups whole fresh mushrooms
1 cup cubed red onion (1-inch pieces)
1 jar (7 ounces) hoisin sauce
1 jar (4 ounces) Chinese hot mustard

In a saucepan, combine the soy sauce, water, vinegar and 1/2 teaspoon garlic; bring to a boil. Remove from the heat. Cover and refrigerate for at least 1 hour.

In a small saucepan, cook carrots in a small amount of water for 3 minutes or until crisp-tender; drain and pat dry. In a saucepan, bring the broth, ginger and remaining garlic to a boil. Transfer to a fondue pot and keep warm. Pat steak, turkey and shrimp dry with paper towels.

Use fondue forks to cook beef to desired doneness. Cook turkey until juices run clear. Cook shrimp until pink. Cook vegetables until they reach desired doneness. Serve with hoisin sauce, mustard sauce and reserved garlic-soy sauce. **Yield:** 6-8 servings.

Fireside Valentine's Day Dinner

INSTEAD of making reservations and heading to a restaurant for a mediocre meal on Valentine's Day, invite your one and only to a flavorful fireside supper at home!

You'll only have eyes for each other...until you catch a glimpse of Orange-Glazed Cornish Hens! These big birds feature a special seasoned stuffing and finger-licking-good citrus glaze.

You'll both fancy Raspberry Spinach Salad, which pairs berries, sugared almonds and a slightly sweet dressing.

Then show heartfelt affection for each other by sharing succulent Miniature Spiced Chocolate Cakes topped with hot fudge sauce. (All recipes shown at right.)

Table for Two

Orange-Glazed Cornish Hens (p. 352)

Raspberry Spinach Salad (p. 354)

Miniature Spiced Chocolate Cakes (p. 353)

Wild Rice Cheese Soup

The addition of chopped apple, beer and Gouda cheese makes this version of wild rice soup extra special.
—Christine Paulton, Phelps, Wisconsin

2 tablespoons finely chopped onion
2 tablespoons butter
1-1/4 cups chicken broth
1 cup chopped peeled apple
1/2 cup beer *or* additional chicken broth
1/2 cup cooked wild rice
1/4 teaspoon white pepper
8 ounces Gouda cheese, shredded
4 teaspoons all-purpose flour
2/3 cup half-and-half cream

In a saucepan, saute onion in butter until tender. Add the broth, apple, beer or additional broth, wild rice and pepper; bring to a boil. Reduce heat; simmer, uncovered, for 10 minutes.

In a bowl, combine cheese and flour; gradually add to soup. Bring to a boil, stirring constantly. Reduce heat to low; stir in cream. Cook for 2-3 minutes or until heated through. **Yield:** 4 servings.

Orange-Glazed Cornish Hens

(Pictured on pages 350 and 351)

When I make these succulent stuffed Cornish hens, my husband's only complaint is that he gets full before he's ready to quit eating!
—Cathy Broker, Meridian, Idaho

3 bacon strips, diced
1/2 cup finely shredded carrot
1/4 cup chopped onion
1-1/2 cups unseasoned stuffing cubes
2 tablespoons minced fresh parsley
1/4 teaspoon dried savory
Dash pepper
1/4 teaspoon plus 1/2 teaspoon chicken bouillon granules, *divided*
2 tablespoons hot water
2 Cornish game hens (22 ounces *each*)
1 tablespoon vegetable oil
1/4 cup white wine *or* apple juice
2 tablespoons plus 2/3 cup orange juice, *divided*
1 tablespoon butter
1 tablespoon brown sugar
1-1/2 teaspoons cornstarch

In a small skillet, cook bacon over medium heat until crisp. Remove with a slotted spoon to paper towels. In the drippings, saute carrot and onion until tender; transfer to a large bowl. Stir in the stuffing cubes, parsley, savory, pepper and bacon.

Dissolve 1/4 teaspoon bouillon in hot water; pour over stuffing mixture and gently toss to moisten. Spoon into hens. Tie legs of each hen together; turn wings under backs. Place on a greased rack in a roasting pan. Lightly brush hens with oil; loosely cover with foil. Bake at 375° for 30 minutes.

Meanwhile, in a saucepan, combine the wine or apple juice, 2 tablespoons orange juice and butter. Bring to a boil; remove from the heat. Set aside 1/4 cup for sauce and keep warm. Brush remaining glaze over hens. Bake 40-50 minutes longer or until meat juices run clear and a meat thermometer inserted into stuffing reads 165°, brushing every 15 minutes with glaze.

For sauce, in a small saucepan, combine the brown sugar, cornstarch, and remaining bouillon and orange juice until smooth. Stir in reserved glaze. Bring to a boil; cook and stir for 1-2 minutes or until thickened. Serve with hens. **Yield:** 2 servings.

Miniature Spiced Chocolate Cakes

(Pictured at right and on page 351)

In keeping with chocolate's association with Valentine's Day, our home economists created these individual chocolate cakes. Set out two forks and share this dessert with the one you love!

2/3 cup butter
7 ounces German sweet chocolate
1/2 teaspoon ground cardamom
1/2 teaspoon ground cinnamon
1/8 teaspoon white pepper
1/8 teaspoon ground cloves
3 eggs
3 egg yolks
1/2 teaspoon rum extract
1/2 teaspoon vanilla extract
1-1/2 cups confectioners' sugar
1/2 cup all-purpose flour
Additional confectioners' sugar
Hot fudge ice cream topping, warmed

In a heavy saucepan over low heat, melt the butter, chocolate, cardamom, cinnamon, pepper and cloves; stir until smooth. Remove from the heat; cool for 5 minutes. In a bowl, whisk the eggs, yolks and extracts. Whisk in confectioners' sugar until smooth and blended. Whisk in chocolate mixture. Add flour; whisk until blended.

Pour into four generously greased 6-oz. souffle dishes or custard cups to within 1/4 in. of the top. Place on a baking sheet. Bake at 425° for 15-17 minutes or until a thermometer inserted near the center reads 160°.

Cool on a wire rack for 5 minutes. Remove cakes from dishes to dessert plates. Dust with confectioners' sugar and drizzle with fudge topping. Serve immediately. **Yield:** 4 servings.

Raspberry Spinach Salad

(Pictured on pages 350 and 351)

Sugared almonds provide fun crunch in this slightly sweet spinach salad. You can easily double the recipe when entertaining a larger group.
—Lauri Mills, Mississauga, Ontario

2-1/4 teaspoons sugar
2 tablespoons slivered almonds
5 cups fresh baby spinach
1/2 cup fresh raspberries
DRESSING:
2 tablespoons vegetable oil
1 tablespoon raspberry vinegar
1 tablespoon sugar
3/4 teaspoon poppy seeds
1/2 teaspoon finely chopped onion
1/4 teaspoon Worcestershire sauce
Dash paprika

In a small heavy skillet, melt sugar over medium heat, stirring constantly. Add almonds; stir to coat. Spread on foil to cool; break apart. In a salad bowl, gently toss the spinach and raspberries.

In a jar with a tight-fitting lid, combine the dressing ingredients; shake well. Pour over salad. Sprinkle with sugared almonds; toss to coat. **Yield:** 4 servings.

Mediterranean Shrimp and Pasta

When our appetites are hearty, I double this dish. The shrimp and pasta are tossed in a light sauce.
—Charolette Westfall, Houston, Texas

4 ounces uncooked linguine
3 green onions, thinly sliced
2 garlic cloves, minced
2 tablespoons olive oil
1/2 cup sliced fresh mushrooms
3 plum tomatoes, chopped
1 jar (6 ounces) marinated artichoke hearts, drained
1/4 cup white wine *or* chicken broth
1 teaspoon Italian seasoning
1/4 teaspoon salt
1/8 teaspoon dried rosemary, crushed
1/8 teaspoon pepper
1/2 pound medium shrimp, peeled and deveined
Grated Parmesan cheese, optional

Cook linguine according to package directions. Meanwhile, in a skillet, saute onions and garlic in oil until tender. Add mushrooms and tomatoes; cook and stir for 3 minutes. Stir in the artichoke hearts, wine or broth, Italian seasoning, salt, rosemary and pepper. Bring to a boil. Reduce heat; simmer, uncovered, for 5 minutes or until mixture reaches desired thickness.

Add shrimp; cook and stir for 3 minutes or until shrimp turn pink. Drain linguine; top with shrimp mixture and toss to coat. Sprinkle with Parmesan cheese if desired. **Yield:** 2 servings.

Chocolate Cherry Heart

(Pictured at right)

My family enjoys this dessert so much that I make it throughout the year by simply using the pie pastry circles. Packaged products make it a snap to prepare.
—Jackie Hannahs, Fountain, Michigan

- **1 package (15 ounces) refrigerated pie pastry**
- **2 teaspoons all-purpose flour**
- **1 egg white, beaten**
- **1/4 cup ground almonds**
- **2 tablespoons sugar**
- **1 package (8 ounces) cream cheese, softened**
- **1 cup confectioners' sugar**
- **1/4 to 1/2 teaspoon almond extract**
- **1/2 cup heavy whipping cream**
- **1 jar (16 ounces) hot fudge ice cream topping**
- **2 cans (21 ounces *each*) cherry pie filling**

Let pastry stand at room temperature for 15-20 minutes. Unfold pastry and place each circle on an ungreased baking sheet. Sprinkle each with 1 teaspoon flour; turn over. Using a 9-in. paper heart pattern, cut out a heart from each circle. Prick pastries all over with a fork. Brush with egg white. Combine almonds and sugar; sprinkle over pastries. Bake at 450° for 7-9 minutes or until lightly browned. Carefully slide crusts onto wire racks to cool.

In a mixing bowl, combine the cream cheese, confectioners' sugar and almond extract; beat until smooth. Add cream; beat until thickened.

Place one crust on a serving plate; spread with half of the fudge topping. Carefully spread with half of the cream cheese mixture; top with half of the cherry pie filling. Top with remaining crust, fudge topping and cream cheese mixture. Spoon remaining cherry pie filling to within 1 in. of edges. Chill until set. Refrigerate leftovers. **Yield:** 6-8 servings.

Orange Fantasy Fudge

Orange and chocolate team up in this full-flavored fudge. My daughter, Melissa, created the recipe one day when experimenting in the kitchen.
—Marie Bickel, LaConner, Washington

1-1/2 teaspoons plus 1/2 cup butter, softened, *divided*
1-1/2 cups sugar
1 can (5 ounces) evaporated milk
2 cups (12 ounces) semisweet chocolate chips
1 jar (7 ounces) marshmallow creme
3 teaspoons orange extract
1 teaspoon vanilla extract

Line a 9-in. square pan with foil; grease the foil with 1-1/2 teaspoons butter and set aside. In a heavy saucepan, combine the sugar, milk and remaining butter. Cook and stir over medium heat until sugar is dissolved. Bring to a rapid boil; boil for 5 minutes, stirring constantly.

Reduce heat to low; stir in chocolate chips and marshmallow creme until melted and blended. Remove from the heat; stir in extracts. Pour into prepared pan. Refrigerate overnight or until firm.

Using foil, lift fudge out of pan; carefully peel off foil. Cut fudge into 1-in. squares. Store in the refrigerator. **Yield:** 2-1/4 pounds.

Crab-Stuffed Mushrooms

When my brother arrives at family gatherings, the first thing he asks is whether or not I brought this appetizer!
—Kelly English, Cogan Station, Pennsylvania

3 tablespoons butter, *divided*
1 tablespoon all-purpose flour
1/2 cup milk
2 slices bread, crusts removed and cubed
1-1/2 teaspoons Worcestershire sauce
1 teaspoon dried minced onion
1/2 cup mayonnaise
1 tablespoon lemon juice
1/2 teaspoon salt
1/8 teaspoon pepper
48 whole medium mushrooms
3 cans (6 ounces *each*) crabmeat, drained, flaked and cartilage removed
Paprika

In a large saucepan, melt 1 tablespoon butter. Stir in flour until smooth. Gradually stir in milk. Bring to a boil over medium heat; cook and stir for 2 minutes or until thickened. Reduce heat; stir in the bread cubes, Worcestershire sauce and onion. Remove from the heat; cool to room temperature. Stir in mayonnaise, lemon juice, salt and pepper; set aside.

Remove and chop the mushroom stems; set caps aside. In a skillet, saute chopped mushrooms and crab in the remaining butter. Using a slotted spoon, transfer to the sauce. Stuff 1 tablespoonful into each mushroom cap. Place on a greased baking sheet; sprinkle with paprika. Bake at 400° for 25-30 minutes or until mushrooms are tender. **Yield:** 4 dozen.

Heartthrob Cookies

(Pictured at right)

I've made these peppermint-flavored cookies for Valentine's Day as well as wedding receptions. I especially like that they don't require frosting.
—Luella Dirks, Emelle, Alabama

- **2 cups butter-flavored shortening**
- **2 cups sugar**
- **2 eggs**
- **2 teaspoons vanilla extract**
- **1/4 to 1/2 teaspoon peppermint extract**
- **4 cups all-purpose flour**
- **1 teaspoon baking powder**
- **1/4 teaspoon salt**
- **15 drops red food coloring**
- **Red decorating gel**

In a large mixing bowl, cream shortening and sugar. Add eggs, one at a time, beating well after each addition. Beat in extracts. Combine the flour, baking powder and salt; gradually add to the creamed mixture. Divide dough in half. Tint one portion pink; leave remaining dough white. Cover and refrigerate for 1 hour or until easy to handle.

On a floured surface, roll out each portion of dough to 1/4-in. thickness. Cut out hearts with a small heart-shaped cookie cutter dipped in flour.

For Heart-to-Heart Cookies: On an ungreased baking sheet, arrange hearts in groups of three in a straight line with sides of hearts touching. Bake at 375° for 8-10 minutes or until edges are lightly browned. Remove to wire racks to cool. Pipe Valentine phrases on cookies.

For Valentine Wreaths: On an ungreased baking sheet, arrange alternating colors of six small hearts in a circle with sides of hearts touching. Bake at 375° for 8-10 minutes or until edges are lightly browned. Remove to wire racks to cool. Pipe Valentine phrases on cookies. **Yield:** about 5-1/2 dozen (depending on size).

Almond French Toast Hearts

I like to surprise my family at breakfast by having heart-shaped French toast on the table. Confectioners' sugar, strawberries and almond butter tastefully top off each bite.
—Donna Cline, Pensacola, Florida

6 slices bread
2 eggs
1/4 cup milk
1-1/2 teaspoons almond extract, ***divided***
2 tablespoons plus 1 cup butter, ***divided***
3 tablespoons confectioners' sugar
Additional confectioners' sugar
Sliced fresh strawberries

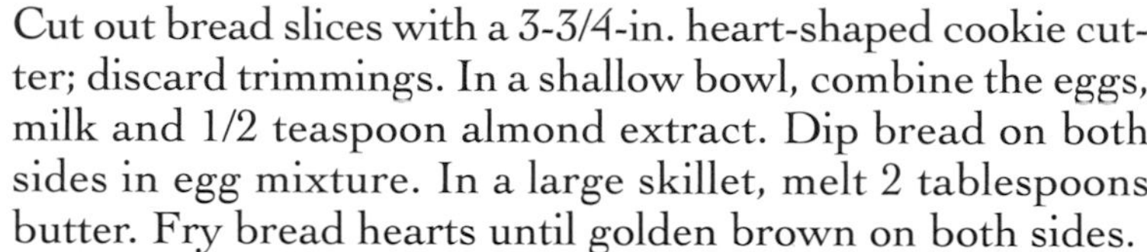

Cut out bread slices with a 3-3/4-in. heart-shaped cookie cutter; discard trimmings. In a shallow bowl, combine the eggs, milk and 1/2 teaspoon almond extract. Dip bread on both sides in egg mixture. In a large skillet, melt 2 tablespoons butter. Fry bread hearts until golden brown on both sides.

For almond butter, in a small mixing bowl, combine confectioners' sugar and remaining butter and extract; mix well. Sprinkle French toast with additional confectioners' sugar. Serve with almond butter and strawberries. **Yield:** 3 servings.

Crusts Make Great Croutons

INSTEAD of throwing away the trimmed bread pieces when making Almond French Toast Hearts, use them to make salad croutons!

Cube the bread trimmings and place on a baking pan. Drizzle with melted butter. Season with garlic powder and seasoned salt; toss to coat. Bake at 350° until lightly browned. Turn off the oven and let dry.

Coffee House Slush

Coffee drinks are all the rage these days. This slush rivals any from a gourmet coffee shop.
—Shannon Wade, Kansas City, Kansas

6 cups strong brewed coffee
2 cups sugar
2 quarts milk
1 quart half-and-half cream
4 teaspoons vanilla extract
Whipped cream

In a 5-qt. freezer container, stir coffee and sugar until sugar is dissolved. Stir in the milk, cream and vanilla. Cover and freeze overnight. To serve, thaw in the refrigerator for 8-10 hours or until slushy. Spoon into glasses; garnish with whipped cream. **Yield:** 5 quarts.

Romantic Table for Two

(Pictured at right)

CREATE a cozy atmosphere when making a special meal on Valentine's Day. Begin by draping the table in an elegant cloth with white and red hues. Place a lovely Heart-Shaped Napkin (instructions below) on top of each dinner plate.

Then add some ambiance by creating Rose Candleholders. Here's how:

Cut the stem off of a large rose, making sure the bottom is even. Use your fingers to fully open the rose. If necessary, remove some center petals so there's a small open area in the middle.

Place a tea light candle in a clear tea light holder; set inside the rose. Place the Rose Candleholder on a small saucer or candle base. To prevent wilting, make these flower candleholders just before sitting down to dinner.

Heart-Shaped Napkin

1.

2.

3.

4. 5.

1. Place a square napkin on a flat surface. Fold two opposite side edges in so that they meet in the center, making a rectangle.

2. Fold the rectangle in half lengthwise. Rotate the napkin so that the single fold is on the bottom

3. With your finger in the center of the rectangle, bring up one end of the napkin until it touches your finger.

4. Bring up the other end so that the two ends touch and a point is formed on the bottom.

5. Tuck under the two upper corners to create a heart shape.

YEAR-ROUND *Entertaining*

Teddy Bear Birthday Party

KIDS of all ages are crazy about teddy bears. So surprise your little one on their birthday with a fun-filled party centered on those furry friends!

Dessert is a bare necessity for kids. Your own bear cubs will be keen on the tasty assortment pictured at right.

To make tiny tummies growl with delight, have adorable Brown Bear Cake take center stage at the table.

Honey Snack Mix and Bear Claw Cookies fit the bill for energetic kids who crave on-the-go munchies that won't slow them down.

On the following pages, you'll find more main courses, appetizers and sides dishes just right for teddy-bear-loving tykes!

Birthday Bash

Brown Bear Cake (p. 364)

Honey Snack Mix (p. 367)

Bear Claw Cookies (p. 365)

Teddy Bear Birthday Party Planner

HOSTING a child's birthday party at home doesn't have to be a bear! Here are some tips to make your teddy bear party a success:

- Purchase teddy bear invitations. Or make your own by using festive paper and a bear or honey pot cookie cutter.
- On the invitations, encourage guests to bring along their favorite teddy bear or other stuffed animal.
- Plan on having the party last for 1-1/2 to 2 hours. Make it clear on the invitation if lunch or just dessert will be served so parents can feed their kids accordingly beforehand.
- Kids love to be involved, so have them help with the invitations, whether it be addressing them, stuffing them or simply putting them in the mailbox.
- For the party, set up two tables...one for the kids and one for their furry friends.
- Don't forget decorations like balloons, party hats and streamers.
- Get the party going with a bear-related game. (See page 368 for *Grrr*eat Teddy Bear Party Games!)
- For party favors, hand out treat bags filled with Honey Snack Mix (page 367) or gummy bears.

Brown Bear Cake

(Pictured on page 363)

Homemade chocolate frosting dresses up a boxed cake mix in this cute cake from our Test Kitchen home economists.

2 packages (18-1/4 ounces *each*) chocolate cake mix
4 ounces cream cheese, softened
1 tablespoon butter, softened
4 cups confectioners' sugar
1/3 cup baking cocoa
1/4 cup milk
3 cups flaked coconut, *divided*
Brown gel food coloring
5 chocolate-covered peppermint patties
16 brown milk chocolate M&M's
2 dark chocolate kisses
5 pieces red shoestring licorice

Prepare cake mixes according to package directions. Pour 3 cups batter into a greased and floured 2-qt. round baking dish. Pour 1-1/2 cups batter into a greased and floured 1-qt. ovenproof bowl. Using remaining batter, fill six greased jumbo muffin cups and four greased regular muffin cups two-thirds full.

Bake cupcakes for 18-20 minutes and cakes for 40-45 minutes at 350° or until a toothpick inserted near the center comes out clean. Cool cupcakes for 5 minutes and cakes for 10 minutes before removing from pans to wire racks to cool completely.

Level the top of the cakes, four jumbo cupcakes and two regular cupcakes. (Save the remaining cupcakes for another use.) Place large cake, top side down, on an 18-in. x 12-in. covered board. For teddy bear's head, place the small cake, top side down, above large cake. Position jumbo cupcakes, cut side up, for arms and legs. Place regular cupcakes on top of head for ears.

In a large mixing bowl, beat the cream cheese and butter until smooth. Add the confectioners' sugar, cocoa and milk;

beat until smooth. Frost tops and sides of cakes and cupcakes. Tint 2-1/4 cups coconut dark brown; tint remaining coconut light brown.

Sprinkle dark brown coconut over arms and legs. Leaving a 4-in. circle in center of bear's body, sprinkle dark brown coconut in a 1-in. circle around edge of cake. Sprinkle dark brown coconut in a 1/2-in. circle around edges of the head and ears. Press dark brown coconut into the sides of the body, head and ears. Sprinkle light brown coconut over the middle of the body, head and ears.

Position one peppermint patty on face for nose. Place one peppermint patty and four M&M's on each paw. Insert chocolate kisses point side down for eyes. Cut one licorice piece into two 2-in. strips; shape to form a mouth. Cut two licorice pieces into a 7-in. strip; place around neck. Shape the remaining licorice into a bow; place below neck. Store in the refrigerator. **Yield:** 18-20 servings.

Bear Claw Cookies

(Pictured at right and on page 363)

Kids can help add the "claws" to our Test Kitchen's clever cookies. Don't be surprised if they swipe a sample before party guests arrive!

- **1 cup butter, softened**
- **1-1/2 cups sugar**
- **2 eggs**
- **2 teaspoons vanilla extract**
- **2 cups all-purpose flour**
- **2/3 cup baking cocoa**
- **3/4 teaspoon baking soda**
- **1/2 teaspoon salt**
- **2-1/2 cups sweetened puffed wheat cereal**
- **3 tablespoons semisweet chocolate chips, melted**
- **2 tablespoons slivered almonds**

In a mixing bowl, cream butter and sugar. Add eggs, one at a time, beating well after each addition. Beat in vanilla. Combine the flour, cocoa, baking soda and salt; gradually add to creamed mixture. Stir in cereal. Cover and refrigerate for 1 hour or until easy to handle.

Roll into 1-in. balls. Place 2 in. apart on ungreased baking sheets. Flatten with a glass dipped in sugar. Bake at 350° for 9-11 minutes or until edges are firm. Remove to wire racks to cool completely.

Place melted chocolate in a pastry bag or resealable plastic bag; cut a small hole in corner of bag. For bear claws, pipe three small dabs of chocolate on each cookie; top each with an almond. **Yield:** 3 dozen.

Delicious Chicken Dippers

Our home economists coated chicken strips with a slightly sweet sauce before rolling them in a seasoned crumb mixture. Teriyaki sauce complements apricot preserves and honey.

3/4 cup apricot preserves
1/3 cup honey
2 tablespoons teriyaki sauce
1-1/2 teaspoons lemon juice
1-1/2 pounds boneless skinless chicken breasts, cut into 1-inch strips
1-1/2 cups crushed sesame crackers (about 38 crackers)
1/2 teaspoon ground ginger
1/4 teaspoon salt

In a bowl, combine the preserves, honey, teriyaki sauce and lemon juice. Set aside 1/2 cup to serve as a dipping sauce. Add chicken to remaining mixture and stir to coat. Let stand for 15 minutes.

In a large resealable plastic bag, combine the cracker crumbs, ginger and salt. With tongs, add chicken in batches to crumb mixture; shake to coat. Place in a single layer on greased baking sheets. Bake at 450° for 9-11 minutes or until juices run clear, turning once. Serve with reserved sauce. **Yield:** 6 servings.

Rainbow Gelatin Salad

This seven-layer gelatin salad will elicit oohs and aahs from all of your guests. It's well worth the time it takes to prepare.
—Dianna Badgett, St. Maries, Idaho

7 packages (3 ounces *each*) assorted flavored gelatin
4-1/2 cups boiling water, *divided*
4-1/2 cups cold water, *divided*
1 can (12 ounces) evaporated milk, chilled, *divided*

In a bowl, dissolve one package of gelatin in 3/4 cup boiling water. Stir in 3/4 cup cold water. Pour into a 13-in. x 9-in. x 2-in. dish coated with nonstick cooking spray; refrigerate until firm, about 1 hour.

Dissolve a second package of gelatin in 1/2 cup boiling water. Stir in 1/2 cup cold water and 1/2 cup milk. Spoon over the first layer. Chill until firm.

Repeat five times, alternating plain gelatin with creamy gelatin. Chill until each layer is firm before adding the next layer. Refrigerate overnight. Cut into squares. **Yield:** 16-20 servings.

Editor's Note: This salad takes time to prepare since each layer must be set before the next layer is added.

Swiss Swirl Ice Cream Cake

(Pictured at right)

With cake rolls, ice cream and hot fudge, this dessert suits anyone with a sweet tooth. Family and friends get a kick out of this treat's fun appearance.
—Danielle Hales, Baltimore, Maryland

10 to 12 Swiss Cake Rolls*
2 pints vanilla ice cream, softened
3/4 cup hot fudge ice cream topping
2 pints chocolate ice cream, softened

Line a 2-qt. bowl with plastic wrap. Cut each cake roll into eight slices; place in prepared bowl, completely covering the bottom and sides. Cover and freeze for at least 20 minutes or until cake is firm.

Spread vanilla ice cream over cake. Cover and freeze for at least 1 hour. Spread with fudge topping. Freeze for at least 1 hour. Spread with chocolate ice cream. Cover and freeze for up to 2 months. Just before serving, remove from the freezer and invert onto a serving plate. Remove bowl and plastic wrap. Cut into wedges. **Yield:** 12-14 servings.

***Editor's Note:** This recipe was tested with Little Debbie Swiss Cake Rolls.

Honey Snack Mix

(Pictured on page 363)

Little cubs can't resist gobbling up the crackers, cereal, raisins and candy in this sweet snack mix created in our Test Kitchen.

1 package (10 ounces) honey-flavored bear-shaped graham crackers (about 4 cups)
3 cups Honeycomb cereal
1-1/2 cups Reese's Pieces
1 cup chocolate-covered raisins

In a large bowl, combine all ingredients. Store in an airtight container. **Yield:** 9 cups.

Teddy Bear Sandwiches

A bear shape is cut out of the top bread slice revealing a special peanut butter filling in these cute sandwiches from our Test Kitchen. Make them ahead or have party guests assemble the sandwiches to their liking.

1-1/3 cups peanut butter
1/4 cup honey
16 slices bread
2 medium bananas, thinly sliced *or* 1/2 cup strawberry jam
24 raisins

In a bowl, combine peanut butter and honey. Spread over eight slices of bread; top with bananas or spread with jam. Using a 4-in. teddy bear cookie cutter, cut a bear shape in the center of the remaining slices of bread; remove centers and save for another use. Place cutout bread over peanut butter. Arrange three raisins on each for eyes and nose. **Yield:** 8 sandwiches.

Peanut Butter Cheese Ball

It's easy to encourage children to eat an apple a day when this creamy peanut butter spread is served with it! I've made this cheese ball for many occasions, and it's always well received.
—Tessie Hughes, Marion, Virginia

1 package (8 ounces) cream cheese, softened
1-1/2 cups peanut butter
1/2 cup confectioners' sugar
1 teaspoon vanilla extract
3/4 cup chopped peanuts
Apple slices

In a small mixing bowl, beat cream cheese until light. Add the peanut butter, confectioners' sugar and vanilla; beat until smooth. Shape into a ball; roll in peanuts. Wrap in plastic wrap. Refrigerate until serving. Serve with apples. **Yield:** 2-1/2 cups.

*GRRR*EAT TEDDY BEAR PARTY GAMES!

KIDS are always game for a little fun like these teddy bear-related ideas:

- **Pin the Bow Tie on the Bear.** Cut out a bear from brown construction paper and bow ties from red paper. Use bandanas for blindfolds. See which guest comes closest to taping their bow tie onto the bear's neck.
- **Honey Pot Guessing Game.** Fill a jar with yellow and black jelly beans (to look like bees). The child whose guess is closest to the actual amount wins and takes the jelly bean-filled jar home.
- **Pass the Teddy Bear.** Purchase an inexpensive stuffed bear. Have the kids sit in a circle. As the music plays, have them pass the bear around the circle. When the music stops, the child holding the bear bows out. The last one remaining wins the bear.

Raspberry Fruit Dip

(Pictured at right)

A cool, creamy raspberry dip enhances the naturally sweet flavor of fruit.
—Dolores Ann Thorp
Mechanicstown, Ohio

1 cup fresh *or* frozen unsweetened raspberries, thawed
1 package (8 ounces) cream cheese, softened
2 tablespoons sugar
Assorted fresh fruit

Place raspberries in a blender or small food processor; cover and process until pureed. Strain to remove seeds. In a small mixing bowl, beat cream cheese and sugar until smooth. Add raspberry puree; beat until well blended. Cover and refrigerate until serving. Serve with fruit. **Yield:** 1-1/2 cups.

Bacon Cheddar Dip

Give this recipe a try if you're looking for a deliciously different dip to serve with crackers, potato chips or vegetables. Ranch salad dressing adds a little zest.
—Kathy Westendorf, Westgate, Iowa

2 cups (16 ounces) sour cream
1 cup (4 ounces) finely shredded cheddar cheese
1 envelope ranch salad dressing mix
2 to 4 bacon strips, cooked and crumbled
Crackers, potato chips *or* fresh vegetables

In a bowl, combine the sour cream, cheddar cheese, salad dressing mix and bacon. Cover and refrigerate for at least 1 hour. Serve with crackers, chips or vegetables. **Yield:** 2-1/2 cups.

Thrill of the Grill

NO MATTER the season or occasion, people often head outside to cook great-tasting food on their grills. And it's no wonder...the food is always fabulous and the mess stays out of the kitchen!

Add a little sizzle to suppertime by preparing Apple-Butter Barbecued Chicken. The can-cooking method results in moist and tender, flavorful fare.

Looking to liven up ordinary side dishes? Check out Carrots on the Grill and Grilled Vegetable Medley. Then pass a basket of sliced Bacon Garlic Bread. (All recipes shown at right.)

From appetizers and sides to main dishes and even desserts, the dishes on the following pages provide everything you need for excellent outdoor dining.

Backyard Yummies

(Pictured above, left to right)

Bacon Garlic Bread (p. 374)

Apple-Butter Barbecued Chicken (p. 372)
with Grilled Vegetable Medley (p. 373)

Carrots on the Grill (p. 373)

Apple-Butter Barbecued Chicken

(Pictured on page 371)

I love cooking so much I sometimes think of recipes in my sleep and wake up to write them down! This dream-inspired dish is my family's favorite way to eat chicken.
—Holly Kilbel, Akron, Ohio

1 teaspoon salt
3/4 teaspoon garlic powder
1/4 teaspoon pepper
1/8 teaspoon cayenne pepper
1 roasting chicken (6 to 7 pounds)
1 can (11-1/2 ounces) unsweetened apple juice
1/2 cup apple butter
1/4 cup barbecue sauce

Combine the salt, garlic powder, pepper and cayenne; sprinkle over chicken.

Prepare grill for indirect heat, using a drip pan. Pour half of the apple juice into another container and save for another use. With a can opener, poke additional holes in the top of the can. Holding the chicken with legs pointed down, lower chicken over the can so it fills the body cavity. Place chicken on grill rack over drip pan.

Grill, covered, over indirect medium heat for 1-1/2 to 2 hours or until a meat thermometer reads 180°. Combine apple butter and barbecue sauce; baste chicken occasionally during the last 30 minutes. Remove chicken from grill; cover and let stand for 10 minutes. Remove chicken from can before carving. **Yield:** 6-8 servings.

Removing the Can from Grilled Chicken

THE trickiest part of can cooking is removing the chicken from the grill. Carefully slide a wide grilling spatula under the can while grasping the chicken with tongs.

Remember, the liquid in the can is hot, so allow the chicken and can to cool slightly before removing the can. Using tongs or insulated gloves, grasp the can and gently twist the chicken slightly while pulling upward to release from the can.

To make this grilling method easier and safer, you may want to invest in a manufactured grill helper that holds or replaces the can. They can range in price from $7 to $20.

Carrots on The Grill

(Pictured at right and on page 371)

Family and friends are surprised when I tell them these carrots are prepared on the grill. This side complements any meaty entree.
—Carol Gaus, Elk Grove Village, Illinois

1/4 cup soy sauce
1/4 cup vegetable oil
1 tablespoon minced fresh gingerroot
1 tablespoon cider vinegar
1 garlic clove, minced
1 pound large carrots, halved lengthwise

In a large bowl, combine the soy sauce, oil, ginger, vinegar and garlic. Add carrots; toss to coat.

With tongs, place carrots on grill rack. Grill, covered, over medium heat for 15-20 minutes or until tender, turning and basting frequently with soy sauce mixture. **Yield:** 4-6 servings.

Grilled Vegetable Medley

(Pictured on page 371)

A simple-to-make marinade flavors a blend of vegetables in this recipe from our home economists.

2 tablespoons Worcestershire sauce
2 tablespoons olive oil
2 tablespoons Dijon mustard
1 teaspoon herbes de Provence
1/4 teaspoon pepper
3 baby eggplants *or* 1 medium eggplant, cut lengthwise into 1/2-inch slices
3 small yellow summer squash, cut lengthwise into 1/2-inch slices
2 cups fresh sugar snap peas

In a large resealable plastic bag, combine the first five ingredients; add eggplant, squash and peas. Seal bag and turn to coat; refrigerate for 2 hours, turning once.

Drain and discard marinade. Place vegetables in a grill basket or disposable foil pan with slits cut in the bottom. Grill, covered, over medium heat for 5-7 minutes or until tender, stirring once. **Yield:** 4 servings.

Editor's Note: Look for herbes de Provence in the spice aisle of your grocery store. It is also available from Penzeys Spices. Call 1-800/741-7787 or visit www.penzeys.com.

Bacon Garlic Bread

(Pictured on page 371)

Guests at your next backyard barbecue will request our home economists' recipe for grilled garlic bread. Serve it as an appetizer or side dish.

- **1/3 cup butter, softened**
- **1/3 cup mayonnaise**
- **4 bacon strips, cooked and crumbled**
- **5 garlic cloves, minced**
- **1 loaf (1 pound) French bread, halved lengthwise**
- **1 cup (4 ounces) shredded Italian cheese blend**

In a small bowl, combine the butter, mayonnaise, bacon and garlic. Spread over cut sides of bread; reassemble loaf. Wrap in a large piece of heavy-duty foil (about 36 in. x 18 in.); seal tightly.

Grill, covered, over medium heat for 4-5 minutes on each side. Unwrap and separate bread halves. Sprinkle with cheese. Grill 5 minutes longer or until cheese is melted. **Yield:** 10-12 servings.

Ginger-Orange Pork Tenderloins

This fork-tender pork has a citrus, smoky flavor that my whole family loves. The combination of ingredients is unbeatable.
—Elaine Sweet, Dallas, Texas

- **1/2 cup orange juice concentrate**
- **2 tablespoons sherry *or* chicken broth**
- **2 tablespoons soy sauce**
- **1 tablespoon sesame oil**
- **2 tablespoons minced fresh thyme**
- **1 tablespoon minced fresh gingerroot**
- **3 garlic cloves, minced**
- **1 teaspoon pepper**
- **2 pork tenderloins (1 pound *each*)**

GLAZE:

- **1/4 cup orange juice concentrate**
- **2 tablespoons brown sugar**
- **2 tablespoons cider vinegar**
- **2 tablespoons molasses**
- **2 teaspoons minced fresh gingerroot**
- **1/2 teaspoon salt**
- **1/2 teaspoon pepper**

In a blender or food processor, combine the first eight ingredients; cover and process until smooth. Pour into a large resealable plastic bag; add the pork. Seal bag and turn to coat. Refrigerate for 8 hours or overnight.

In a small saucepan, combine the glaze ingredients. Cook and stir over medium heat until thickened.

Prepare grill for indirect heat. Coat grill rack with nonstick cooking spray before starting the grill. Drain and discard marinade. Grill pork, covered, over indirect medium heat for 10-13 minutes on each side or until a meat thermometer reads 160°, brushing with glaze during the last 10 minutes. Let stand for 5 minutes before slicing. Serve with any remaining glaze. **Yield:** 6-8 servings.

Appetizer Pizzas

(Pictured at right)

To keep a summer kitchen cool, our home economists suggest preparing pizzas on the grill! A variety of ingredients tops flour tortillas for three terrific tastes.

9 flour tortillas (6 inches)
3 tablespoons olive oil
TRADITIONAL PIZZAS:
1/3 cup chopped pepperoni
3/4 cup shredded Colby-Monterey Jack cheese
1 jar (14 ounces) pizza sauce
MEDITERRANEAN PIZZAS:
1/2 cup chopped seeded tomato
1/3 cup sliced ripe olives
3/4 cup crumbled feta cheese
1/4 cup thinly sliced green onions
1 carton (7 ounces) hummus
MARGHERITA PIZZAS:
9 thin slices tomato
1 package (8 ounces) small fresh mozzarella cheese balls, sliced
1 tablespoon minced fresh basil
1 cup prepared pesto

Brush one side of each tortilla with oil. Place oiled side down on grill rack. Grill, uncovered, over medium heat for 2-3 minutes or until puffed. Brush tortillas with oil; turn and top with pizza toppings.

For Traditional Pizzas: Top three grilled tortillas with pepperoni and cheese. Cover and grill for 2-3 minutes or until cheese is melted. Cut into wedges; serve with pizza sauce.

For Mediterranean Pizzas: Top three grilled tortillas with tomato, olives, feta cheese and onions. Cover and grill for 2-3 minutes or until the cheese is heated through. Cut into wedges; serve with hummus.

For Margherita Pizzas: Top three grilled tortillas with tomato slices, mozzarella cheese and basil. Cover and grill for 2-3 minutes or until cheese is melted. Cut into wedges; serve with pesto. **Yield:** 9 appetizer pizzas.

Curried Salmon

(Pictured at far right)

Until our daughter shared this recipe, my husband and I swore we didn't like salmon. But after one taste of this grilled version, we were converts!
—Carma Blosser, Livermore, Colorado

- **1/3 cup soy sauce**
- **1/3 cup vegetable oil**
- **1 teaspoon garlic powder**
- **1 teaspoon curry powder**
- **1 teaspoon lemon-pepper seasoning**
- **1 teaspoon Worcestershire sauce**
- **1/4 teaspoon Liquid Smoke, optional**
- **6 salmon fillets (8 ounces *each*)**

In a large resealable plastic bag, combine the soy sauce, oil, garlic powder, curry powder, lemon-pepper, Worcestershire sauce and Liquid Smoke if desired; add the salmon. Seal bag and turn to coat. Refrigerate for 1 hour.

Coat grill rack with nonstick cooking spray before starting the grill. Drain and discard marinade. Place salmon skin side down on rack. Grill, covered, over medium heat for 10-12 minutes or until fish flakes easily with a fork. **Yield:** 6 servings.

Grilled Peach-Berry Crisps

As dinner is winding down, put these individual fruit crisps from our Test Kitchen on the grill. A scoop of cold ice cream is the crowning touch.

- **3 cups chopped peeled fresh peaches**
- **1-1/2 cups fresh raspberries**
- **3 tablespoons sugar**
- **3 tablespoons plus 1/4 cup all-purpose flour, *divided***
- **1/4 teaspoon ground cinnamon**
- **1/2 cup quick-cooking oats**
- **2 tablespoons brown sugar**
- **2 tablespoons cold butter**
- **Vanilla ice cream, optional**

In a large bowl, combine the peaches, raspberries, sugar, 3 tablespoons flour and cinnamon. Divide mixture evenly among four 4-1/2-in. disposable foil tart pans coated with nonstick cooking spray; set aside.

In a small bowl, combine the oats, brown sugar and remaining flour; cut in the butter until crumbly. Sprinkle over the filling.

Prepare grill for indirect heat. Grill crisps, covered, over indirect medium heat for 15-20 minutes or until filling is bubbly. Serve warm with ice cream if desired. **Yield:** 4 servings.

Grilled Pineapple with Lime Dip

(Pictured above, left)

This fruit appetizer was created by our home economists. If desired, roll the pineapple wedges in flaked coconut before grilling.

1 fresh pineapple
1/4 cup packed brown sugar
3 tablespoons honey
2 tablespoons lime juice

LIME DIP:

1 package (3 ounces) cream cheese, softened
1/4 cup plain yogurt
2 tablespoons honey
1 tablespoon brown sugar
1 tablespoon lime juice
1 teaspoon grated lime peel

Peel and core the pineapple; cut into eight wedges. Cut each wedge into two spears. In a large resealable plastic bag, combine the brown sugar, honey and lime juice; add pineapple. Seal bag and turn to coat; refrigerate for 1 hour.

In a small mixing bowl, beat cream cheese until smooth. Beat in the yogurt, honey, brown sugar, lime juice and peel. Cover and refrigerate until serving.

Coat grill rack with nonstick cooking spray before starting the grill. Drain and discard marinade. Grill pineapple, covered, over medium heat for 3-4 minutes on each side or until golden brown. Serve with lime dip. **Yield:** 8 servings.

Tasty 'n' Tangy Baby Back Ribs

I doctor up bottled barbecue sauce with a blend of ingredients, including honey, mustard and red pepper flakes. Marinating the ribs makes them mouth-watering.
—Gladys Gibbs, Brush Creek, Tennessee

- **1 bottle (18 ounces) barbecue sauce**
- **1 cup honey**
- **1 can (6 ounces) tomato paste**
- **1/2 cup white vinegar**
- **1/2 cup lemon juice**
- **1/4 cup soy sauce**
- **1/4 cup Dijon mustard**
- **2 tablespoons Worcestershire sauce**
- **1 garlic clove, minced**
- **1 teaspoon crushed red pepper flakes**
- **1 teaspoon ground allspice**
- **2 teaspoons coarsely ground pepper, *divided***
- **4 to 5 pounds pork baby back ribs**
- **1 teaspoon salt**

In a large saucepan, combine the first 11 ingredients. Add 1 teaspoon pepper. Bring to a boil. Reduce heat; simmer, uncovered, for 15 minutes. Remove from the heat; set aside 2 cups of sauce for basting.

Brush ribs with the remaining sauce; place in two large resealable plastic bags. Seal and turn to coat; refrigerate for 30 minutes.

Prepare grill for indirect heat, using a drip pan. Drain and discard marinade. Sprinkle both sides of the ribs with the salt and remaining pepper. Place on grill rack over drip pan. Grill, covered, over indirect medium heat for 1 hour, turning occasionally.

Baste ribs with some of the reserved sauce. Grill 15 minutes longer or until juices run clear and meat is tender, turning and basting occasionally. **Yield:** 4 servings.

Herb Beef Burgers

You can prepare these patties ahead of time and keep them covered in the fridge until ready to grill.
—Pat Habiger, Spearville, Kansas

- **1 medium tomato, seeded and chopped**
- **1/3 cup canned chopped green chilies**
- **1/4 cup chopped ripe olives**
- **1/4 cup chopped onion**
- **2 garlic cloves, minced**
- **2 teaspoons chili powder**
- **2 teaspoons Dijon mustard**
- **1 teaspoon *each* minced fresh oregano, thyme, basil and parsley**
- **1/2 to 1 teaspoon minced fresh dill**
- **1/2 to 1 teaspoon grated lemon peel**
- **1 pound ground beef**
- **4 hamburger buns, split**
- **Sliced tomato, lettuce leaves and sliced onion, optional**

In a large bowl, combine the tomato, chilies, olives, onion, garlic, chili powder, mustard, herbs and lemon peel. Crumble beef over mixture and mix well. Shape into four patties.

Grill, covered, over medium heat for 5-7 minutes on each side or until no longer pink. Serve on buns with tomato, lettuce and onion if desired. **Yield:** 4 servings.

Planked Spicy Strip Steaks

(Pictured at right)

To infuse steaks with a sweet, smoky flavor, our home economists cook them on wood grilling planks. Simple seasonings are all you need.

2 maple grilling planks
4 New York strip steaks (about 12 ounces *each*), trimmed
1 tablespoon olive oil
3/4 teaspoon ground coriander
3/4 teaspoon chili powder
1/2 teaspoon ground allspice
1/2 teaspoon cayenne pepper

Soak grilling planks in water for 2-3 hours. Drizzle steaks with oil. Combine the coriander, chili powder, allspice and cayenne; rub over both sides of steaks. Grill, covered, over medium heat for 1-2 minutes on each side or until grill marks appear; remove.

Place planks on grill over direct medium heat. Cover and heat until planks create a light to medium smoke and begin to crackle (this indicates planks are ready), about 3 minutes. Turn planks over. Place steaks on planks. Grill, covered, for 15-20 minutes or until meat reaches desired doneness (for medium-rare, a meat thermometer should read 145°; medium, 160°; well-done, 170°). **Yield:** 4 servings.

Editor's Note: Steak may be known as strip steak, Kansas City steak, New York Strip steak, Ambassador Steak or boneless Club Steak in your region.

Cedar Plank Pointers

YOU CAN purchase packages of grill-ready cedar, maple and cherry or apple wood planks at grocery, hardware, specialty and kitchen stores. Another option is to buy untreated planks at a lumberyard and cut them into 1-inch thick sections. (NEVER cook with wood that has been chemically treated.)

To prevent the wood from burning while grilling, first immerse the plank in water and let it soak for several hours or overnight. (You may have to weigh it down with a soup can.) For even more flavor, add white wine, beer, apple cider or fresh herbs to the water.

When ready to cook, dry off the plank and grill as the recipe directs. Remove the cooked food from the plank. Let the plank cool on the grill grate before removing.

Family Game Night

SCHOOL...work...meetings... extra-curricular activities. With so many things to do, it's no wonder people find themselves away from home more often than they'd like.

So plot a strategy to bring your family back into focus by planning a fun-filled game night!

Get the evening rolling with Rack 'em Up Cheese Balls. This billiard-inspired snack can be served alongside clever breadstick "cues" as well as crackers and vegetable dippers.

For members of your clan who have a sweet tooth, Caramel Cereal Snack Mix is a sure bet. (Both recipes are shown at right.)

You don't need to be skilled in the kitchen to plan a game-time menu that plays into the theme of the evening. Just turn the page for other inspiring ideas.

PLAY FOODS
(Top to bottom)
Caramel Cereal Snack Mix (p. 384)
Rack 'em Up Cheese Balls (p. 382)

Rack 'em Up Cheese Balls

(Pictured on page 381)

With chipped beef and three kinds of cheese, this appetizer from our Test Kitchen appeals to everyone. Make ahead of time to blend the flavors.

1 package (8 ounces) cream cheese, softened
1 cup ricotta cheese
1 cup (8 ounces) sour cream
2 packages (2-1/2 ounces *each*) thinly sliced dried beef, finely chopped
2 cups (8 ounces) finely shredded cheddar cheese
1-1/4 cups crisp rice cereal, crushed
1/4 cup finely chopped white onion
1 tablespoon Worcestershire sauce

TOPPINGS:
Blue paste food coloring
1/2 cup finely shredded Swiss cheese, chopped
1/2 cup finely chopped white onion
1 can (2-1/4 ounces) chopped ripe olives
1/2 cup finely shredded cheddar cheese
1 package (2-1/2 ounces) thinly sliced dried beef
1/2 cup finely chopped red onion
1/2 cup finely chopped green onions (green tops only)
1/2 cup diced sweet yellow pepper
1/2 cup diced sweet red pepper
15 small water chestnut slices
2 tablespoons cream cheese, softened
1 teaspoon milk
Black paste food coloring
2 breadsticks
Assorted crackers

In a large mixing bowl, beat cream cheese, ricotta and sour cream; add beef. Beat in cheddar cheese, cereal, onion and Worcestershire sauce. Cover and chill for 30 minutes.

In a small shallow bowl, combine blue food coloring and Swiss cheese; set aside. Shape cheese mixture into 16 balls. Roll one ball in white onion for the cue ball. Roll another cheese ball in olives for the eight ball. Roll a third ball in colored Swiss cheese; make a stripe of colored Swiss cheese on a fourth ball.

With remaining cheese balls, make six solid-colored balls and six striped balls by rolling in the cheddar cheese, beef, red onion, green onions, yellow pepper and red pepper. Cover and refrigerate until serving.

Thoroughly pat water chestnuts dry with paper towels. In a small bowl, combine the cream cheese, milk and black food coloring. Cut a small hole in a corner of a pastry or plastic bag; insert round tip #4. Fill bag with cream cheese mixture. Write numbers on water chestnuts; lightly press one water chestnut onto each ball (except cue ball).

Arrange pool balls on a wooden cutting board. Use breadsticks for pool cues. Serve with crackers. **Yield:** 16 cheese balls (about 1/3 cup each).

Garlic-Filled Meatballs

(Pictured at right)

Family and friends will go wild for these "gourmet" meatballs. I also use the chutney to top baked chicken, steaks and burgers.
—Mary Beth Harris-Murphree
Tyler, Texas

4 whole garlic bulbs
1 tablespoon olive oil
1 egg, beaten
1/3 cup dry bread crumbs
1 teaspoon salt
1 teaspoon pepper
1-1/2 pounds ground beef
SWEET ONION CHUTNEY:
3 bacon strips, diced
1-1/4 cups thinly sliced sweet onion
1 to 2 tablespoons red wine vinegar
1-1/2 teaspoons sugar
Dash pepper
1/3 cup crumbled goat cheese
Toasted French bread slices (1/2 inch thick), optional

Remove papery outer skin from garlic (do not peel or separate cloves). Cut tops off bulbs. Brush with oil. Wrap each bulb in heavy-duty foil. Bake at 425° for 30-35 minutes or until softened. Cool for 10-15 minutes. Squeeze softened garlic into a bowl; set aside.

In a large bowl, combine the egg, bread crumbs, salt and pepper. Crumble beef over mixture and mix well. Divide into 18 portions; flatten. Top each with 1/2 teaspoon softened garlic; form beef mixture around garlic into meatballs. Set remaining garlic aside.

In a large skillet, cook meatballs in batches until browned on all sides and a meat thermometer reads 160°. Meanwhile, in a large saucepan, cook bacon over medium heat until crisp. Add onion; cook for 4-6 minutes or until tender. Reduce heat; stir in the vinegar, sugar, pepper and remaining roasted garlic. Cook for 2 minutes or until heated through.

Drain meatballs; top with chutney and goat cheese. Serve with toasted French bread if desired. **Yield:** 6 servings.

You'll Relish Roasted Garlic

WHEN garlic is roasted, it turns golden and buttery. Its flavor mellows and becomes slightly sweet and nutty. Roasted garlic is terrific in a variety of dishes (like Garlic-Filled Meatballs, above) or spread on bread and grilled meats.

You can roast garlic and refrigerate it in an airtight container for up to 1 week.

Caramel Cereal Snack Mix

(Pictured on page 380)

I like to share this sweet snack with neighbors, friends and co-workers. My husband gets upset if I don't leave enough at home for him!
—Carol Merkel, Yorkville, Illinois

8 cups Corn Pops
1 cup salted peanuts
2 cups packed brown sugar
1 cup butter, cubed
1/2 cup light corn syrup
1 teaspoon vanilla extract
1/2 teaspoon baking soda

In a large bowl, combine cereal and peanuts; set aside. In a large heavy saucepan, combine the brown sugar, butter and corn syrup; bring to a boil over medium heat, stirring constantly. Boil for 5 minutes, stirring occasionally.

Remove from the heat. Stir in vanilla and baking soda (mixture will foam). Immediately pour over cereal mixture and toss to coat.

Spread into two greased 15-in. x 10-in. x 1-in. baking pans. Bake at 250° for 1 hour, stirring every 20 minutes. Cool completely on wire racks. Store in airtight containers. **Yield:** 14 cups.

Successful Game Night Strategy

TURN off the television...unplug the phone ...ignore the "to do" list. Instead, focus on your family by planning a night filled with a winning combination of fun, food and games. (Kids have a skill for being silly, so be sure to include them in the planning!)

- First, pick a night when no one has to work and doesn't have mandatory meetings or events. If possible, try to make Family Game Night a regularly scheduled occasion.
- Use a score sheet from a game to write out "invitations." Send them along in briefcases, backpacks or lunchboxes. You can also place them on bed pillows, tape them to a mirror or set them on breakfast plates.
- Resist the temptation to include other families and just concentrate on having fun with your immediate family.
- For the winners of each game, have on hand inexpensive door prizes, such as decks of cards, hand-held games and books of crossword puzzles or sudoku.
- Plan your menu. For extra fun, use recipes (like the ones in this chapter) that tie into the theme.
- Use a game table to display the food (as shown on page 380). Or decorate a dining table with playing cards, dice, game pieces, game boards, etc.
- Starting with the youngest family member, let each person choose a game to play.
- Keep a running tally of the winners and post it on the refrigerator or family bulletin board. Award a larger prize (like a new board game) to the winner after a few weeks or months.

Clue Night Reuben Loaf

(Pictured at right)

My family loves Reubens but making so many sandwiches at once became daunting. So I came up with this recipe that serves several people.
—Laura Hagadorn, North Creek, New York

1 loaf (1 pound) frozen pizza dough, thawed
3/4 pound thinly sliced deli pastrami
1/2 cup Thousand Island salad dressing
1/2 pound sliced Swiss cheese
1-1/2 cups sauerkraut, rinsed and well drained
1 egg yolk
1 tablespoon cold water

On a greased baking sheet, roll pizza dough into a 15-in. x 12-in. rectangle. Arrange pastrami down the center third of rectangle; spread with dressing. Top with cheese and sauerkraut.

On each long side, cut 1-in.-wide strips about 1/2 in. into center. Starting at one end, fold alternating strips at an angle across filling. Pinch ends to seal. Beat egg yolk and water; brush over braid.

Bake at 350° for 35-38 minutes or until golden brown. Let stand for 5 minutes before slicing. **Yield:** 8-10 servings.

Stuffed Pepperoncinis

To reduce some of the juice in these spicy appetizers, I drain the pepperoncinis for about 3 hours on a paper towel before stuffing. This recipe makes a big batch, which is perfect for parties.
—Jeani Robinson, Weirton, West Virginia

1 cup grated Parmesan cheese
1 medium tomato, cut into wedges
1 can (2-1/4 ounces) sliced ripe olives, drained
1/2 cup chopped pepperoni
1/4 cup chopped salami
1/4 cup cubed fully cooked ham
1/4 cup shredded cheddar cheese
1/4 cup shredded Monterey Jack *or* pepper Jack cheese
1/4 cup zesty Italian salad dressing
2 jars (24 ounces *each*) whole pepperoncinis, drained
Additional grated Parmesan cheese

In a food processor, combine the first nine ingredients; cover and process until finely chopped. Cut off the stem end of each pepperoncini; remove seeds. Pipe or stuff pepperoncinis with cheese mixture. Dip exposed end into additional Parmesan cheese. Cover and refrigerate until serving. **Yield:** about 4 dozen.

Chili Cheese Dip

(Pictured at far right)

I would often make this delicious dip as an after-school snack for my children. They're now grown but still enjoy this easy-to-make treat.
—Verdi Wilson, Visalia, California

- **1 package (8 ounces) cream cheese, softened**
- **1 can (15 ounces) chili without beans**
- **1/4 cup finely chopped green onions**
- **4 to 8 garlic cloves, minced**
- **1 can (4 ounces) chopped green chilies**
- **1 can (16 ounces) refried beans**
- **1 cup (4 ounces) shredded Mexican cheese blend**
- **Breadsticks**

In a small mixing bowl, beat cream cheese until smooth. Spread into a greased microwave-safe 1-1/2-qt. dish. Layer with chili, onions, garlic, green chilies and refried beans. Sprinkle with cheese.

Microwave, uncovered, on high for 6-8 minutes until cheese is melted and edges are bubbly. Serve warm with breadsticks. **Yield:** 5 cups.

Editor's Note: This recipe was tested in a 1,100-watt microwave.

Veggie Checkerboard Sandwiches

Our home economists use purchased eggplant hummus to hold together these mini sandwiches. Feel free to use your family's favorite veggies.

- **1 package (3 ounces) cream cheese, softened**
- **1 carton (7 ounces) roasted eggplant hummus**
- **10 slices white bread, crusts removed**
- **10 slices whole wheat bread, crusts removed**
- **20 cucumber slices**
- **20 spinach leaves**
- **1 large sweet red pepper, cut into 2-inch strips**
- **10 slices red onion, halved**
- **8 pimiento-stuffed olives, drained and patted dry**
- **8 pitted ripe olives, drained and patted dry**

In a small mixing bowl, beat cream cheese until smooth. Add hummus; beat until combined. Cut each slice of bread in half widthwise. Spread hummus mixture over 10 white bread halves and 10 wheat bread halves. Top each with cucumber, spinach, red pepper and red onion.

Top white bread halves with remaining white bread; top wheat bread halves with remaining wheat bread. Thread toothpicks through olives; insert into 16 sandwiches.

Arrange sandwiches on a platter or covered board to resemble a checkerboard, placing the green olive-topped sandwiches on one side, black olive-topped sandwiches on the other side and the four plain sandwiches in the center. **Yield:** 20 sandwiches.

Breadsticks Jenga®

(Pictured at right)

These breadsticks have little oil, so it's quite nice for anyone keeping an eye on fat intake. A dear friend gave me the recipe.
—Lise Thomson, Magrath, Alberta

1 package (1/4 ounce) active dry yeast
1-1/4 cups warm water (110° to 115°)
1/4 cup olive oil
3-1/4 teaspoons sugar
1 teaspoon salt
3 cups all-purpose flour
1 egg yolk
1 tablespoon water
1 tablespoon sesame seeds

In a large mixing bowl, dissolve yeast in warm water. Add the oil, sugar, salt and 2 cups flour. Beat on medium speed for 3 minutes or until smooth. Stir in enough remaining flour to form a soft dough (dough will be sticky).

Turn onto a floured surface; knead until smooth and elastic, about 6-8 minutes. Place in a greased bowl, turning once to grease top. Cover and let rise in a warm place until doubled, about 1 hour.

Punch dough down. Turn onto a lightly floured surface; divide into fourths. Cut each portion into eight pieces; roll each into a 5-in. rope. Place 2 in. apart on greased baking sheets. Cover and let rise until doubled, about 30 minutes.

Beat egg yolk and water; brush over breadsticks. Sprinkle with sesame seeds. Bake at 350° for 8-10 minutes or until golden brown. Remove to wire racks to cool.

To build game tower, place three breadsticks about 1/2 in. apart and parallel to each other on a serving board. Stack three breadsticks at right angles to the previous layer; repeat layers six times. Serve remaining breadsticks separately. **Yield:** 32 breadsticks.

Bacon Chicken Skewers

Your whole family will fall for these moist, flavorful chicken strips. I serve them every year at my daughter's birthday party because her friends request them!
—Lynn Lackner, Worth, Illinois

1/2 cup ranch salad dressing
1/2 cup barbecue sauce
1 teaspoon chili powder
2 drops hot pepper sauce
1-1/4 pounds boneless skinless chicken breasts, cut into 12 strips
12 bacon strips

In a large resealable plastic bag, combine the ranch dressing, barbecue sauce, chili powder and hot pepper sauce; add chicken. Seal bag and turn to coat; refrigerate for at least 2 hours.

In a large skillet, cook bacon over medium heat until partially cooked but not crisp. Drain on paper towels. Drain and discard marinade. Place a chicken strip on each bacon strip; thread each onto a metal or soaked wooden skewer.

Grill skewers, covered, over medium heat or broil 4-6 in. from the heat for 10-14 minutes or until juices run clear, turning occasionally. **Yield:** 6 servings.

Domino Brownies

Our home economists created these flavorful double-decker bars for folks who have a fondness for brownies!

BLOND LAYER:
6 tablespoons butter, softened
1/2 cup sugar
1/2 cup packed brown sugar
2 eggs
1/2 teaspoon vanilla extract
1-1/2 cups all-purpose flour
1-1/4 teaspoons baking powder

CHOCOLATE LAYER:
10 tablespoons butter, cubed
1-1/3 cups sugar
1-1/2 teaspoons vanilla extract
3 eggs
2/3 cup all-purpose flour
1/2 cup baking cocoa
1/2 teaspoon baking powder
1/2 teaspoon salt
2 tubes white decorating gel
1 cup M&M's miniature baking bits

In a large mixing bowl, cream butter and sugars until light and fluffy. Add eggs, one at a time, beating well after each addition. Beat in vanilla. Combine flour and baking powder; add to creamed mixture just until moistened.

Press into a greased 13-in. x 9-in. x 2-in. baking pan. Bake at 350° for 8-10 minutes or until lightly browned.

Meanwhile, melt the butter in a large saucepan over medium heat. Remove from the heat; stir in the sugar and vanilla. Add eggs, one at a time, stirring well after each addition. Combine the flour, cocoa, baking powder and salt; stir into the butter mixture just until combined. Spread over warm blond layer.

Bake for 20-25 minutes or until a toothpick inserted near the center comes out clean (do not overbake). Cool on a wire rack.

Cut into 36 rectangles (3-1/4 in. x 1 in.). With decorating gel, draw a line dividing each rectangle in half widthwise; attach baking bits with dabs of decorating gel to resemble dominoes. **Yield:** 3 dozen.

Trivial Pursuit® Cheesecake

(Pictured at right)

Wrap up Family Game Night with wedges of this colorful cheesecake from our Test Kitchen.

2-1/2 cups crushed vanilla wafers (about 70 wafers)
1/2 cup butter, melted
1 vanilla bean
2 cups (16 ounces) sour cream
4 packages (8 ounces *each*) cream cheese, softened
1-3/4 cups sugar
4 eggs, lightly beaten
2 tubes *each* blue, red, green, yellow, brown and orange decorating gels

In a small bowl, combine vanilla wafers and butter. Press onto the bottom and up the sides of a greased 9-in. springform pan. Place on a baking sheet. Bake at 325° for 14-16 minutes or until lightly browned. Cool on a wire rack.

Split vanilla bean and scrape seeds into sour cream; stir to combine. Set aside. Discard vanilla bean. In a large mixing bowl, beat cream cheese and sugar until smooth. Beat in sour cream mixture until blended. Beat in eggs on low speed just until combined.

Pour into crust. Place pan on a double thickness of heavy-duty foil (about 18 in. square). Securely wrap foil around pan. Place in a larger baking pan; add 1 in. of hot water to larger pan.

Bake at 325° for 1-1/2 hours or until surface is no longer shiny and center is almost set. Remove pan from water bath. Cool on a wire rack for 10 minutes. Carefully run a knife around edge of pan to loosen; cool 1 hour longer. Refrigerate overnight.

Remove sides of pan; cut cheesecake into six wedges. Squeeze each color of decorating gel onto a different wedge and spread carefully. **Yield:** 12 servings.

Editor's Note: You may substitute 3 teaspoons vanilla extract for the vanilla bean if desired.

Vanilla Bean Basics

VANILLA BEANS can be found at specialty grocery stores. Look for those that are labeled "premium" and that are 6- to 8-inches long. The beans should have a rich, full aroma and should be supple, moist and glossy. Avoid beans that are dry and short and that have no scent.

You can store vanilla beans indefinitely in a cool, dark place in an airtight container. Refrigeration will cause them to harden and crystallize.

Sweet 16 Celebration

SWEET 16 parties are all the rage these days. But you don't have to break the bank to celebrate in style.

A fun-filled Mexican fiesta with friends is all you need to make cherished memories for your soon-to-be grown-up girl.

Welcome guests to a taco bar buffet with refreshing Mock Strawberry Margaritas.

Then have the teens fix their own nachos and hard- and soft-shell tacos with Mexican Beef and Spicy Seasoned Chicken.

Round out the casual get-together with fixings like shredded lettuce, sliced ripe olives, shredded cheese, sour cream, Traditional Salsa and Spicy Refried Beans. (All recipes are shown at right.)

TEEN SCENE

(Clockwise from top left)

Mock Strawberry Margaritas (p. 393)

Traditional Salsa (p. 392)

Spicy Refried Beans (p. 396)

Mexican Beef (p. 394)

Spicy Seasoned Chicken (p. 392)

Spicy Seasoned Chicken

(Pictured on page 390)

Seasoned with a zesty combination of garlic and chili powders and cumin, this specialty from our Test Kitchen can be used as a fabulous filling for tacos, burritos and more.

1 pound boneless skinless chicken breasts, cut into strips
1 teaspoon ground cumin
1 teaspoon garlic powder
1 teaspoon chili powder
1/2 teaspoon salt
1 tablespoon vegetable oil
Tortilla chips, taco shells *or* flour tortillas
Shredded cheddar cheese, sliced ripe olives, shredded lettuce, sour cream and salsa, optional

In a large skillet, saute the chicken, cumin, garlic powder, chili powder and salt in oil until chicken is no longer pink. Serve with tortilla chips, taco shells or flour tortillas. Garnish with optional toppings. **Yield:** 4 servings.

Traditional Salsa

(Pictured on page 391)

Why buy bottled salsa when you can make a more flavorful variety at home without a lot of effort? You may want to double the recipe because it's sure to be a hit!
—Katie Rose, Pewaukee, Wisconsin

5 plum tomatoes, seeded and chopped
1/2 cup chopped onion
1 jalapeno pepper, seeded and chopped
1 tablespoon lime juice
1 garlic clove, minced
1/4 teaspoon salt
1/4 cup minced fresh cilantro
Tortilla chips

In a small bowl, combine the first seven ingredients. Cover and refrigerate until serving. Serve with tortilla chips. **Yield:** 2-1/2 cups.

Surprise Party Invitation

KEEP your favorite teen guessing about her very own Sweet 16 event by making it a surprise party. When you pen the invitations, remember to tell guests not to spill the beans about the bash. For an extra reminder, tuck a few dried beans into the envelope. Don't forget to end your invite with a happy "adios!"

Not-Fried Ice Cream Cake

(Pictured at right)

Our home economists created this ice cream cake to mimic the fabulous flavor of a popular dessert in many Mexican restaurants. It's a no-fuss treat that feeds a crowd. Plus, it's conveniently made ahead.

1 cup cornflake crumbs
1/3 cup sugar
1/3 cup butter, melted
3/4 teaspoon ground cinnamon
1/2 gallon butter pecan ice cream, softened
4 tablespoons honey, *divided*

In a small bowl, combine the cornflake crumbs, sugar, butter and cinnamon; set aside 1/2 cup. Press remaining crumb mixture into a greased 9-in. springform pan. Spoon half of the ice cream over crust. Sprinkle with reserved crumb mixture; drizzle with 2 tablespoons honey. Cover and freeze for 2 hours.

Top with remaining ice cream. Cover and freeze for 8 hours or overnight.

Remove from the freezer 5 minutes before serving. Remove sides of pan; drizzle with remaining honey. **Yield:** 12-16 servings.

Mock Strawberry Margaritas

(Pictured on page 390)

These refreshing strawberry smoothies from our home economists pair well with spicy Mexican fare. They're a fun addition to any table.

6 lime wedges
3 tablespoons plus 1/3 cup sugar, *divided*
1-1/4 cups water
1 can (6 ounces) frozen limeade concentrate, partially thawed
1 package (16 ounces) frozen unsweetened strawberries
25 ice cubes

Using lime wedges, moisten the rim of six glasses. Set limes aside for garnish. Sprinkle 3 tablespoons sugar on a plate; hold each glass upside down and dip rim into sugar. Set aside. Discard remaining sugar on plate.

In a blender, combine the water, limeade concentrate, strawberries, ice cubes and remaining sugar; cover and blend until smooth. Pour into prepared glasses. Garnish with reserved limes. Serve immediately. **Yield:** 6 servings.

Green Rice

Instead of reaching for a box of Mexican rice, round out the Southwestern menu with this cilantro-spinach dish from our Test Kitchen.

1 medium green pepper
1 jalapeno pepper
2 cups water, *divided*
1 package (10 ounces) fresh baby spinach
2 cups fresh cilantro leaves
2 green onions, chopped
1-1/2 cups uncooked long grain rice
3 tablespoons vegetable oil
1 teaspoon salt

Broil green pepper and jalapeno 4 in. from the heat until skins blister, about 4 minutes. With tongs, rotate peppers a quarter turn. Broil and rotate until all sides are blistered and blackened. Immediately place peppers in a bowl; cover and let stand for 15 minutes. Peel off and discard charred skin. Remove stems and seeds; chop peppers.

Place 1 cup of water in a food processor. Add the peppers, spinach, cilantro and onions; cover and process until smooth.

In a large skillet, saute rice in oil until golden brown. Stir in spinach puree, salt and remaining water. Bring to a boil. Reduce heat; cover and simmer 15 minutes. Remove from heat. Let stand 10 minutes before serving. **Yield:** 5 servings.

Mexican Beef

(Pictured on page 391)

Purchased taco seasoning mixes can't compare to our home economists' flavorful blend.

1 pound ground beef
2 teaspoons chili powder
1-1/2 teaspoons ground cumin
1/4 teaspoon ground coriander
1/2 teaspoon salt
1/2 teaspoon dried oregano
1/2 teaspoon cornstarch
1/3 cup water
Tortilla chips, taco shells *or* flour tortillas
Shredded cheddar cheese, sliced ripe olives, shredded lettuce, sour cream and salsa, optional

In a large skillet, cook beef over medium heat until no longer pink; drain. Stir in the chili powder, cumin, coriander, salt and oregano.

Combine cornstarch and water until smooth. Stir into beef mixture. Bring to a boil; cook and stir for 2 minutes or until thickened. Serve with tortilla chips, taco shells or flour tortillas. Garnish with optional toppings. **Yield:** 4 servings.

Chorizo Cheese Dip

(Pictured at right)

Guests will wipe the bowl clean when you set out this spicy cheese dip from our Test Kitchen. Serve it with tortilla chips or even vegetable dippers.

1/2 pound uncooked chorizo sausage, casings removed
1 small green pepper, chopped
1 small sweet red pepper, chopped
1 small onion, chopped
3 garlic cloves, minced
1 tablespoon vegetable oil
1/2 teaspoon cayenne pepper
2 cartons (12 ounces *each*) white Mexican dipping cheese
Tortilla chips

In a large skillet, cook chorizo over medium heat until no longer pink; drain. Remove and keep warm. In the same skillet, saute the peppers, onion and garlic in oil until tender. Stir in cayenne and chorizo; heat through.

Heat cheese according to package directions; stir into meat mixture. Serve warm with tortilla chips. Refrigerate leftovers. **Yield:** 4 cups.

Baked Jalapenos

(Pictured above)

This baked version of jalapeno poppers was developed by our home economists. The crunchy topping nicely complements the creamy filling.

1 package (3 ounces) cream cheese, softened
1/4 teaspoon ground cumin
2/3 cup shredded Monterey Jack cheese
1 teaspoon minced fresh cilantro
8 jalapeno peppers, halved lengthwise and seeded
1 egg, beaten
3/4 cup cornflake crumbs

In a small mixing bowl, beat cream cheese and cumin until smooth. Beat in Monterey Jack cheese and cilantro. Spoon into jalapeno halves.

Place egg and cornflake crumbs in separate shallow bowls. Dip filling side of jalapenos in egg, then coat with crumbs. Place on a greased baking sheet with crumb side up. Bake at 350° for 25-30 minutes or until top is golden brown. Serve immediately. **Yield:** 16 appetizers.

Mexican Macaroni and Cheese

For a classic casserole with a little more grown-up taste, give our Test Kitchen's zesty macaroni and cheese a try.

3 cups uncooked elbow macaroni
3 tablespoons butter
3 tablespoons all-purpose flour
2 cups milk
1 tablespoon lime juice
2 cups (8 ounces) shredded cheddar cheese, *divided*
1-1/2 cups (6 ounces) shredded pepper Jack cheese, *divided*
2 tablespoons chopped jalapeno pepper
1 to 2 teaspoons chili powder
1/2 teaspoon salt
1/4 teaspoon paprika

Cook macaroni according to package directions. Meanwhile, in a large saucepan, melt butter. Stir in flour until smooth. Gradually stir in milk. Bring to a boil; cook and stir for 2 minutes or until thickened. Reduce heat; stir in lime juice. Stir in 1-1/2 cups cheddar cheese and 1 cup pepper Jack cheese until melted.

Remove from the heat. Stir in the jalapeno, chili powder and salt. Drain macaroni; add to cheese sauce and toss to coat.

Transfer to a greased 8-in. square baking dish. Top with remaining cheeses; sprinkle with paprika. Bake, uncovered, at 350° for 15-20 minutes or until cheese is melted. **Yield:** 6 servings.

Spicy Refried Beans

(Pictured on page 391)

Our home economists jazz up a can of refried beans with jalapeno pepper, seasonings and cheese. Serve with tortilla chips on the side for scooping.

1 small onion, chopped
1 jalapeno pepper, seeded and chopped
1 garlic clove, minced
2 teaspoons vegetable oil
1 can (16 ounces) refried beans
2 tablespoons water
1 teaspoon hot pepper sauce
1/4 teaspoon ground cumin
1/4 teaspoon chili powder
1/8 teaspoon cayenne pepper
1/2 cup shredded Monterey Jack cheese

In a large skillet, saute the onion, jalapeno and garlic in oil for 2-3 minutes or until tender. Stir in the beans, water, hot pepper sauce, cumin, chili powder and cayenne. Cook and stir over medium-low heat until heated through. Transfer to a serving bowl; sprinkle with cheese. **Yield:** 2 cups.

Jalapeno Pepper Pointer

WHEN cutting or seeding hot peppers, use rubber or plastic gloves to protect your hands. Avoid touching your face.

Picture-Perfect Party Favors

(Pictured above)

THE fun times at the Sweet 16 party will go by in a flash. So be sure to capture the special moments forever.

During the party, use your digital camera to snap a photo of the birthday girl with each guest. Then print off the pictures on your home computer.

Place the pictures in cute and quirky photo stands that the guests can take home with them as unforgettable party favors.

You can find these individual photo stands at a variety of discount and department stores. Buy all of the same style or mix and match them for colorful table-toppers.

Elegant Afternoon Tea

IRON your finest linens, dust off the china and polish your silver. Then invite a few girlfriends over for a tasteful tea...it's a fun-filled way to spend an afternoon!

Have hot Sunburst Spiced Tea ready as guests arrive. This delicious drink is fabulously flavored with orange and lemon zest and a blend of spices.

Finger sandwiches are synonymous with tea parties. So offer an appealing assortment, including Tuna Tea Sandwiches, Savory Cucumber Sandwiches and Nutty Chicken Sandwiches. (All recipes shown at right.)

A selection of sweets—like Blueberry Pecan Scones, Green Tea Citrus Sorbet, Pecan Sandies and Almond Petits Fours—round out the mid-afternoon menu.

Ladies' Luncheon

(Clockwise from top left)

Tuna Tea Sandwiches (p. 400)

Savory Cucumber Sandwiches (p. 403)

Nutty Chicken Sandwiches (p. 400)

Sunburst Spiced Tea (p. 404)

Tuna Tea Sandwiches

(Pictured on page 398)

A friend brought tuna sandwiches to a picnic years ago. I never got the recipe from her, but these are close and just as delicious.
—Lisa Sneed, Bayfield, Colorado

1 can (6 ounces) light water-packed tuna, drained and flaked
1 to 2 tablespoons mayonnaise
1/4 teaspoon lemon-pepper seasoning
4 tablespoons soft goat cheese
4 slices multigrain bread, crusts removed
4 large fresh basil leaves

In a small bowl, combine the tuna, mayonnaise and lemon-pepper. Spread 1 tablespoon of goat cheese on each slice of bread. Spread two slices with tuna mixture; top with basil leaves and remaining bread. Cut in half or into desired shapes. **Yield:** 8 tea sandwiches.

Nutty Chicken Sandwiches

(Pictured on page 399)

Pineapple gives these chicken salad sandwiches a bit of sweetness, while pecans add a bit of crunch.
—Nancy Johnson, Laverne, Oklahoma

1 cup shredded cooked chicken breast
1 hard-cooked egg, chopped
1/2 cup unsweetened crushed pineapple, drained
1/3 cup mayonnaise
1/2 teaspoon salt
1/8 teaspoon pepper
1/4 cup chopped pecans, toasted
1/2 cup fresh baby spinach
8 slices white bread, crusts removed

In a small bowl, combine chicken, egg, pineapple, mayonnaise, salt and pepper. Cover and refrigerate at least 1 hour.

Just before serving, stir in pecans. Place spinach on four slices of bread; top with chicken salad and remaining bread. Cut each sandwich into quarters. **Yield:** 16 tea sandwiches.

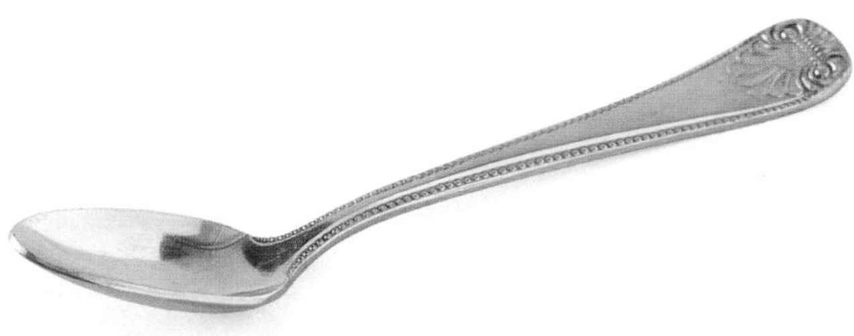

Almond Petits Fours

(Pictured at right)

Dainty, bite-sized cakes are often the highlight of a ladies' luncheon. Our home economists share their mouth-watering version here.

1 can (8 ounces) almond paste
3/4 cup butter, softened
3/4 cup sugar
4 eggs
1 cup cake flour
1/4 cup seedless raspberry spreadable fruit
GLAZE:
4-1/2 cups sugar
2-1/4 cups water
1/4 teaspoon cream of tartar
1-1/2 teaspoons clear vanilla extract
1/4 teaspoon almond extract
6 cups confectioners' sugar
Assorted food coloring

Line a 15-in. x 10-in. x 1-in. baking pan with parchment paper; coat the paper with nonstick cooking spray and set aside.

In a large mixing bowl, cream the almond paste, butter and sugar until light and fluffy. Add eggs, one at a time, beating well after each addition. Beat in flour. Spread evenly into prepared pan.

Bake at 325° for 12-15 minutes or until a toothpick inserted near the center comes out clean. Cool for 10 minutes before removing from pan to a wire rack to cool completely.

Cut cake in half widthwise. Spread jam over one half; top with remaining half. Cut into assorted 1-1/2-in. shapes.

In a large saucepan, combine the sugar, water and cream of tartar. Cook over medium-high heat, without stirring, until a candy thermometer reads 226°. Remove from the heat; cool at room temperature to 100°. Stir in extracts. Using a portable mixer, beat in confectioners' sugar until smooth. Tint some of glaze with food coloring.

Gently dip petits fours, one at a time, into warm glaze. Remove with a fork; allow excess glaze to drip off. (If glaze becomes too thick, stir in 1 teaspoon hot water at a time to thin.) Place petits fours on wire racks over waxed paper; let dry completely. **Yield:** 2-1/2 dozen.

Editor's Note: We recommend that you test your candy thermometer before each use by bringing water to a boil; the thermometer should read 212°. Adjust your recipe temperature up or down based on your test.

Blueberry Pecan Scones

(Pictured at far right, bottom)

These scones are great any time of year using fresh or frozen blueberries. I serve them alone as a snack or as part of a meal.
—Priscilla Gilbert, Indian Harbour Beach, Florida

2 cups all-purpose flour
1/4 cup plus 1 tablespoon sugar, *divided*
3 teaspoons baking powder
3/4 teaspoon salt
1/4 cup cold butter
1 egg
1/2 cup milk
1-1/2 teaspoons vanilla extract
1 cup fresh *or* frozen blueberries
1/3 cup chopped pecans, toasted
2 teaspoons grated lemon peel
1 egg white, lightly beaten

In a large bowl, combine the flour, 1/4 cup sugar, baking powder and salt. Cut in butter until mixture resembles coarse crumbs. In a bowl, whisk the egg, milk and vanilla; add to crumb mixture. Stir in the blueberries, pecans and lemon peel just until moistened.

Turn dough onto a floured surface. With lightly floured hands, knead 6-8 times. Pat into an 8-in. circle; cut into eight wedges. Separate wedges and place 2 in. apart on a greased baking sheet.

Brush with egg white and sprinkle with remaining sugar. Bake at 375° for 18-22 minutes or until lightly browned. Serve warm. **Yield:** 8 scones.

Editor's Note: If using frozen blueberries, do not thaw before adding to batter.

Shaping Scones

WHEN preparing homemade scones, shape the dough into a circle on a floured surface. Cut it into wedges with a sharp knife.

Vanilla-Scented Tea

This mildly flavored tea from our Test Kitchen complements both sweet and savory items.

4 cups water
1 vanilla bean
4 teaspoons English breakfast tea leaves *or* other black tea leaves

Place water in a large saucepan. Split vanilla bean and scrape seeds into water; add bean. Bring just to a boil.

Place tea leaves in a teapot. Pour vanilla water over tea leaves; cover and steep for 3 minutes. Strain tea, discarding leaves and bean. Serve immediately. **Yield:** 4 servings.

For one serving: Bring 1 cup water and 1-1/2 in. of seeded split vanilla bean just to a boil. Pour over 1 teaspoon tea leaves. Steep and strain as directed.

Lavender Mint Tea

(Pictured at right, top)

With wonderful mint, lavender, rosemary and honey, you won't miss the tea leaves in this hot beverage from our home economists.

1/4 cup thinly sliced fresh mint leaves
4 teaspoons dried lavender flowers
1/2 teaspoon minced fresh rosemary
4 cups boiling water
2 teaspoons honey, optional

In a large bowl, combine the mint, lavender and rosemary. Add boiling water. Cover and steep for 4 minutes. Strain tea, discarding mint mixture. Stir in honey if desired. Serve immediately. **Yield:** 4 servings.

Editor's Note: Dried lavender flowers are available from Penzeys Spices. Call 1-800/741-7787 or visit www.penzeys.com.

For one serving: Combine 1 tablespoon mint leaves, 1 teaspoon lavender and 1/8 teaspoon rosemary. Add 1 cup boiling water. Steep and strain as directed. Add honey as desired.

Savory Cucumber Sandwiches

(Pictured on page 399)

Italian salad dressing easily flavors this simple spread. Serve it as a dip with crackers and veggies or use it as a sandwich filling.
—Carol Henderson, Chagrin Falls, Ohio

1 package (8 ounces) cream cheese, softened
1/2 cup mayonnaise
1 envelope Italian salad dressing mix
36 slices snack rye bread
1 medium cucumber, sliced

In a small mixing bowl, combine the cream cheese, mayonnaise and salad dressing mix until blended. Refrigerate for 1 hour.

Just before serving, spread over rye bread; top each with a cucumber slice. **Yield:** 3 dozen.

Pecan Sandies

These rich, nutty cookies pair well with tea, coffee and milk. One batch never lasts long around our house!
—Leah Stewart, Lewisville, Arkansas

2/3 cup butter-flavored shortening
1/2 cup sugar
1/2 cup confectioners' sugar
1 egg
1 teaspoon vanilla extract
1-1/2 cups all-purpose flour
1/2 teaspoon cream of tartar
1/2 teaspoon baking soda
1/4 teaspoon salt
1/2 cup chopped pecans

In a small mixing bowl, cream shortening and sugars until light and fluffy. Beat in egg and vanilla. Combine the flour, cream of tartar, baking soda and salt; gradually add to creamed mixture. Stir in pecans.

Roll into 1-in. balls. Place 2 in. apart on ungreased baking sheets. Coat the bottom of a glass with nonstick cooking spray; flatten cookies with glass. Bake at 350° for 18-20 minutes or until edges are lightly browned. Cool for 1-2 minutes before removing to wire racks. **Yield:** 2 dozen.

Sunburst Spiced Tea

(Pictured on page 398)

Our home economists use oranges and lemon to lend a lovely citrus flavor to ordinary black tea.

2 medium oranges
1 medium lemon
4 cardamom seeds
4 whole cloves
4 teaspoons English breakfast tea leaves *or* other black tea leaves
4 cups boiling water

Using a citrus zester, remove peel from oranges and lemon in long narrow strips. (Save fruit for another use.) Place the peel strips, cardamom and cloves in a large bowl. With the end of a wooden spoon handle, crush mixture until aromas are released.

Add tea leaves and boiling water. Cover and steep for 6 minutes. Strain tea, discarding peel mixture. Serve immediately. **Yield:** 4 servings.

For one serving: Combine the zest of 1/2 orange, 1/4 lemon, 1 cardamom seed and 1 clove; crush as directed. Add 1 teaspoon tea leaves and 1 cup boiling water. Steep and strain as directed.

Apple and Goat Cheese Salad

(Pictured at right and on front cover)

This makes a light and delicious side dish for almost any meal. The sweetness of the apples, raisins and grapes combines well with the tart goat cheese and dressing.

—Radelle Knappenberger
Oviedo, Florida

6 cups torn mixed salad greens
2 medium apples, chopped
1/2 cup raisins
1/2 cup green grapes, halved
2 tablespoons olive oil
4-1/2 teaspoons balsamic vinegar
1 tablespoon honey
1-1/2 teaspoons lemon juice
1 garlic clove, minced
3 tablespoons chopped walnuts, toasted
2 tablespoons crumbled goat cheese

In a large bowl, combine the greens, apples, raisins and grapes. In a jar with a tight-fitting lid, combine the oil, vinegar, honey, lemon juice and garlic; shake well. Pour over salad and toss to coat. Sprinkle with walnuts and goat cheese. Serve immediately. **Yield:** 8 servings.

Green Tea Citrus Sorbet

Who says tea is only meant for sipping? Green tea cleverly stars in this sorbet from our Test Kitchen.

4 cups water, *divided*
8 individual green tea bags
1-1/2 cups sugar
2 tablespoons lemon juice
2 tablespoons lime juice

In a small saucepan, bring 2 cups water to a boil. Remove from the heat; add tea bags. Cover and steep for 5 minutes. Discard tea bags.

In a large saucepan, bring sugar and remaining water to a boil. Cook and stir until sugar is dissolved. Remove from the heat; stir in the juices and green tea.

Fill cylinder of ice cream freezer; freeze according to manufacturer's directions. Transfer sorbet to a freezer container; cover and freeze for 4 hours or until firm. **Yield:** 1-1/2 quarts.

Reference Index

Use this index as a guide to the many helpful hints, food facts, decorating ideas and step-by-step instructions throughout the book.

General Recipe Index

This handy index lists every recipe by food category, major ingredient and/or cooking method.

Alphabetical Index

Refer to this index for a complete alphabetical listing of all recipes in this book.